informational

ST. TERESA OF AVILA
CATHOLIC COMMUNITY
3000 N. Lompa Lane
Carson City, NV 89706

261.097
HUN
WIL

THE CHURCH BETWEEN GOSPEL AND CULTURE

St. Teresa of Avila
Catholic Community
Parish Library

The Church between Gospel and Culture

The Emerging Mission in North America

Edited by

George R. Hunsberger

Craig Van Gelder

William B. Eerdmans Publishing Company
Grand Rapids, Michigan / Cambridge, U.K.

© 1996 Wm. B. Eerdmans Publishing Co.
255 Jefferson Ave. S.E., Grand Rapids, Michigan 49503 /
P.O. Box 163, Cambridge CB3 9PU U.K.
All rights reserved

Printed in the United States of America

01 00 99 98 97 96 7 6 5 4 3 2 1

Library of Congress Cataloging-in-Publication Data

The church between Gospel and culture : the emerging mission in North America / edited by George R. Hunsberger, Craig Van Gelder.
p. cm.
Includes bibliographical references.
ISBN 0-8028-4109-0 (pbk. : alk. paper)
1. Missions — North America. 2. Christianity and culture.
3. Missions — Theory. 4. Evangelistic work — North America.
5. North America — Religion — 20th century.
I. Hunsberger, George R. II. Van Gelder, Craig.
BV2760.C48 1996

261′.097 — dc20 95-49662
CIP

Contents

Contributors

James V. Brownson is James and Jean Cook Professor of New Testament at Western Theological Seminary, Holland, Michigan.

Inagrace Dietterich is Director of Theological Research at the Center for Parish Development, Chicago, Illinois.

William A. Dyrness is Dean of the School of Theology and Professor of Theology and Culture at Fuller Theological Seminary, Pasadena, California.

Douglas John Hall is Professor of Christian Theology at McGill University, Montreal, Quebec.

John R. "Pete" Hendrick is Lancaster Professor of Mission and Evangelism Emeritus at Austin Presbyterian Theological Seminary, Austin, Texas.

Paul G. Hiebert is Professor of Anthropology and South Asian Studies at Trinity Evangelical Divinity School, Deerfield, Illinois.

George R. Hunsberger is Professor of Missiology at Western Theological Seminary, Holland, Michigan.

E. Dixon Junkin is Dean of the Institute for Christian Formation of the Presbyterian Church (U.S.A.), Stony Point, New York.

Christopher B. Kaiser is Professor of Historical and Systematic Theology at Western Theological Seminary, Holland, Michigan.

Alan J. Roxburgh is Pastor of West Vancouver Baptist Church, West Vancouver, British Columbia.

Paul Russ Satari is Lay Ministry Staff (missions and evangelism) at the Wesley Methodist Church, Singapore.

David Scotchmer was Associate Professor of Mission and Evangelism at the University of Dubuque Theological Seminary, Dubuque, Iowa, until his death.

Wilbert R. Shenk is Professor of Mission History and Contemporary Culture in the School of World Mission at Fuller Theological Seminary, Pasadena, California.

Craig Van Gelder is Professor of Domestic Missiology at Calvin Theological Seminary, Grand Rapids, Michigan.

David Lowes Watson is Professor of Theology and Congregational Life at Wesley Theological Seminary, Washington, D.C.

Charles C. West is Stephen Colwell Professor of Christian Ethics Emeritus at Princeton Theological Seminary, Princeton, New Jersey.

Acknowledgments

The following essays (which have undergone minor revision) were previously published in the journals and sources noted below. Permission has been granted for their reprinting in this book.

George R. Hunsberger, "The Newbigin Gauntlet: Developing a Domestic Missiology for North America," published in *Missiology: An International Review* 19, no. 4 (October 1991): 391-408.

Craig Van Gelder, "Defining the Center — Finding the Boundaries: The Challenge of Re-Visioning the Church in North America for the Twenty-First Century," published in *Missiology: An International Review* 22, no. 3 (July 1994): 317-37.

Craig Van Gelder, "A Great New Fact of Our Day: America as Mission Field," published in *Missiology: An International Review* 19, no. 4 (October 1991): 409-18.

Wilbert R. Shenk, "The Culture of Modernity as a Missionary Challenge," published in *The Good News of the Kingdom,* ed. Charles Van Engen et al. (Maryknoll, N.Y.: Orbis Books, 1993), 192-99.

Christopher B. Kaiser, "From Biblical Secularity to Modern Secularism: Historical Aspects and Stages," published in *Secularism versus Biblical Secularity,* ed. S. Marianne Postiglione, RSM, and Robert Brungs, SJ (St. Louis, Mo.: ITEST Faith/Science Press, 1994), 1-43.

David Lowes Watson, "Christ All in All: The Recovery of the Gospel for North American Evangelism," published in *Missiology: An International Review* 19, no. 4 (October 1991): 443-59.

Douglas John Hall, "Ecclesia Crucis: The Theologic of Christian Awkwardness," published in *Dialog* 32, No. 4 (Spring 1993): 113-21.

Charles C. West, "Gospel for American Culture: Variations on a Theme by Newbigin," published in *Missiology: An International Review* 19, no. 4 (October 1991): 431-41.

James V. Brownson, "Speaking the Truth in Love: Elements of a Missional Hermeneutic," published in *International Review of Mission* 83, no. 330 (July 1994): 479-504.

George R. Hunsberger, "Acquiring the Posture of a Missionary Church," published in *Insights* 108 (Fall 1993): 19-26.

John R. "Pete" Hendrick, "Congregations with Missions vs. Missionary Congregations," published in *Insights* 108 (Fall 1993): 59-68.

E. Dixon Junkin, "Up from the Grassroots: The Church in Transition," published in *Interpretation* (July 1992): 271-80.

George R. Hunsberger, "Sizing Up the Shape of the Church," published in *Reformed Review* 47, no. 2 (Winter 1993-94): 133-44.

Inagrace T. Dietterich, "A Particular People: Toward a Faithful and Effective Ecclesiology," published in *Modern Theology* 9, vol. 4 (October 1993): 349-68. Copyright © Blackwell Publishers Ltd.

Introduction: The Church between Gospel and Culture

There is a crisis in the life of the churches of North America. The crisis, most simply put, is that the social function the churches once fulfilled in American life is gone. We are speaking particularly about "mainline" Protestant and "mainstream" evangelical churches. The crisis is most pronounced there, among the churches that see their heritage as reaching back to the earliest days of evangelical-Protestant dominance on the American religious landscape.

The crisis, however, touches as well the experience of other churches. The Roman Catholic and Orthodox churches, various ethnic and minority churches that have functioned within distinct subcultures, and churches in the pentecostal and charismatic streams all show signs of the same crisis. The experience of it may be somewhat different in these cases, and each of these churches possesses unique foundations from which to respond to it. But even these churches will not be insulated from factors now causing deep uncertainty, malaise, and despair in churches "disestablished" from places of previous cultural importance.

The distress caused by this radical change in social role and cultural value manifests itself in various ways: a lack of focus in the midst of a proliferation of church programs, a loss of meaning in the work of clergy and laity alike, and an uneasiness that our faith does not really fit in the world where we live. All these contribute to a certain dis-ease in our congregations. When a pastor is discharged and after all the reasons are given, we still are not sure we know what is really behind it all; when capable and committed clergy or laity experience burnout, and when all of us sit together in worship week by week feeling a hunger and readiness for something more, something beyond what we have thought and done before regarding ourselves and our programs — then the signs are telling us to look again and see what has shifted to cause such strain.[1]

What we are experiencing in the church may be illustrated by an observation one of the editors of this volume made during a recent visit to his optometrist.

> At one stage in the examination, as I was looking through the lens of that big contraption fitted over my face, the doctor said, "Do you see the red dot on the wall?" I said I did. It was actually a tiny red circle. "Tell me when it becomes two dots," he said. At first nothing happened, but all of a sudden there were two dots. I told him so. Then he went through the same routine several more times. I finally realized what he was trying to do. Even before I "saw" the dotlike circle split into two images, the dots at which each of my eyes were looking were already moving apart. My eyes were adjusting and following the dots in such a way as to continue to see them as one.
>
> I began to notice that each time I went through the routine there was a point at which I felt a strain in my eyes, and then the single dot divided and became two dots. The dot was dividing before it appeared to do so, but for a time my eyes refused to see it that way. The doctor was obviously trying to determine how far my eyes would go before they would yield to the strain and admit that there were two dots, not one.

The church in North America is straining in a similar way. We cling to a vision of culture and church as one, but they have separated. The break point is here and now. We are faced with the choice between straining to hold on to what can be maintained only as an illusion and admitting that things have changed, willingly following God into new, uncharted waters.

There is another side to our dilemma. At the same time that the church is being discharged from its formerly privileged role in society, it

1. On the subject of burnout, see William H. Willimon, *Clergy and Laity Burnout* (Nashville: Abingdon Press, 1989). Willimon attributes burnout not to exhaustion but to the loss of meaning. What he says about clergy and laity "burning out" holds true as well for congregations.

discovers how accommodated it has become to the assumptions of the culture it has so long supported. If on the one hand we are jarred and shaken by the shift in the social landscape that changes our role and our position, then on the other hand we are faced with a rude awakening to the fact that we are very much like the culture we inhabit. Donald Posterski has put it well. He notes that instead of being "in the world but not of the world," we have done the seemingly impossible, inverting Jesus' dictum to become "of the world but not in the world."[2]

Even in the processes leading to our loss of social function, our accommodation is evident. Bishop Lesslie Newbigin has forcefully alerted us to the way in which we have been co-opted into the perspectives of modern Western culture, the fruit of what is commonly labeled "the Enlightenment."[3] He shows how, under the pervasive influence of the "modern scientific worldview," a dichotomy has arisen between so-called facts — those things that can be determined to be true by the methods of science and according to laws of cause and effect — and so-called values — which are held to be the private opinions or beliefs of individuals. The former are accepted in the realm of public discourse, while the latter are strictly relegated to the private realm, in which pluralism reigns. To this dichotomy the church has capitulated, becoming a mere voluntary enclave for the cultivation of private morals and values. It has tended to embrace uncritically the assumptions of the Enlightenment and the culture's ways of knowing as determined by the reigning "plausibility structure," that is, the dominant system for determining what things are plausible to believe. Its witness is intimidated so that it adopts the language of personal preference (as in, "I have found this to be true for me"), and its gospel is stripped of its claim to be the clue to the meaning and purpose of the world's life and history (becoming instead something more like, "Jesus can give peace and fulfillment to your personal life").

Stanley Hauerwas and William Willimon put it even more directly. They note that the world has shifted for the church. But the more important

2. Donald C. Posterski, *Reinventing Evangelism: New Strategies for Presenting Christ in Today's World* (Downers Grove, IL: InterVarsity Press, 1989), 28.

3. Newbigin develops this thesis most completely in his *Foolishness to the Greeks* (Grand Rapids: Eerdmans, 1986). A later volume, *The Gospel in a Pluralist Society* (Grand Rapids: Eerdmans, 1989), extends his thesis in an effort to develop a more comprehensive missiological approach for Western churches.

fact for them is how far we have embraced the Constantinianism that "holds the conviction that with an adapted and domesticated gospel, we could fit American values into a loosely Christian framework, and we could thereby be culturally significant." In this we are all implicated: "Both the conservative and liberal churches, the so-called private (conversionist) and public (activist) churches, are basically accommodationist (Constantinian) in their social ethic. Both assume that the American church's social task is to underwrite American democracy."[4]

Such an accommodationist church, "so intent on running errands for the world, is giving the world less and less in which to disbelieve."[5] Whatever is true about the shifted world of Western culture and about changes in the church's position in it, none of this can be addressed adequately without taking into account the serious ways in which the churches have become vague and indistinct because of our accommodation.

Every church everywhere will embody a local, particular expression of the gospel. God intends this to be so to give variegated witness to the salvation given in Christ. But each local expression is valid as an incarnation of the gospel only as it is faithful to the gospel's version of what is good, true, and beautiful. If there is too little identification with the culture, the church becomes a subcultural ghetto. If it assumes too much of the culture's perspectives and values, it domesticates and tames the gospel. The latter has become the major problem for the churches of North America.

Newbigin thus emphasizes that for the churches of Western, post-Christendom culture to be genuinely missionary, we must learn again to indwell the "plausibility structure" of the Bible so deeply that our churches actually foster a dialogue between the gospel and our culture. How does the gospel address our North American cultural assumptions, perspectives, preferences, and practices, even those that are so ingrained and pervasive that we assume them without question? How does the gospel wish to redraft the assumptions of our life together as Christian communities? How can we be a distinctly American church that does not merely mimic the cultural designs of the society but embodies a powerful version of what it is like to be a community shaped by the gospel and its alternative way of seeing and doing things?

4. Stanley Hauerwas and William H. Willimon, *Resident Aliens: Life in the Christian Colony* (Nashville: Abingdon Press, 1989), 17, 32.

5. Ibid., 94.

According to such an analysis, the present crisis for the churches is not a matter of regaining lost ground or turf. It is not about asserting the claim that we should again hold the privileged position for America's moral and spiritual guidance. Rather, it has to do with our need to encourage the encounter of the gospel with our culture. It will mean learning how to be a church that by its nature lives always *between gospel and culture,* recognizing, on the one hand, the cultural dynamics that shape us as well as everyone else in this society and, on the other hand, hearing the gospel that calls us to know and value and intend things in a very different way.

These are the issues this volume addresses. To do that, it gathers a collection of essays written in recent years by people eager to live on the frontiers of the challenges facing the churches. Many of these essays have previously appeared in journals and periodicals, some have not. Most of them have arisen in the context of the activities of the Gospel and Our Culture Network. That network has become a significant place of collaboration between pastors and scholars, denominational executives and parachurch consultants, women and men, persons of a variety of ethnicity and persons of a broadly ecumenical range of churches. Their work in larger consultations, smaller working groups, and a variety of publications has taken up what Newbigin has called "the missionary encounter of the gospel with our Western culture." That challenge is pursued in the network with particular focus on the culture (and cultures) of North America. It is done out of a conviction that assessing our culture and giving fresh theological response is, and must always be, at heart a missiological task.

The grouping of essays is significant. Following two initial chapters setting the missional frame of the whole project, three groups of essays address in turn culture, gospel, and church. The work of the Gospel and Our Culture Network has been organized around these three poles. But it has always been true of its conversations that the three cohere as aspects of one agenda. They are three orbits of concern that represent a single interlocking quest. They can be pursued separately, and in fact many people are engaged in one or the other of these three tasks. But it is the affirmation of this volume, and the network out of which it grows, that none of the three tasks can be done adequately or faithfully in isolation from the others. To assess our culture begs the question of discernment as we hear again the gospel. To be led to new visions by the gospel implicates change in the way we live as church. Finding new forms for the church's life and witness can never happen apart from cultural assessment and gospel discernment because it is in the missionary encounter between gospel and culture that the Spirit creates us and forms us to be the genuinely missionary communities of Christ.

There are a variety of ways to read this book. Different readers will choose different entry points. For some, the point of greatest concern is the shape and future of the church, and thus their reading may well start in the last part. From there, the issues surrounding the form and mission of the church will raise questions requiring a greater understanding of the culture and a deeper hearing of the gospel, which sets the context for readings in the earlier parts.

For another group of readers, the primary interest is how to understand what is going on in our culture, to gain self-understanding as well as an understanding of people around us. But starting with an assessment of culture never leaves us at ease. It begs the question whether the gospel welcomes the dynamics of our culture's ways of seeing things or whether it contends against them. Invariably it does some of both, but the answer takes sorting out and requires the church to be deeply theological in its way of life. Cultural assessment shapes the questions we bring to a rehearing of the gospel, which in turn changes how we define ourselves as the church.

Still others may come with a sharp sense that at the root of our current crisis lies the need to hear, with newly opening ears, how the gospel addresses us in this modern and increasingly postmodern culture that shapes our thinking and behaving. They may be inclined to begin in part 3. Discerning the gospel's voice as a first step will inevitably change the way we come to the assessment of the culture. It gives us new lenses through which we will view it and by which we will test it. As well, new theological rumblings become the ground out of which we are forced to explore in new ways what it will mean to be the church.

Introductions at the beginning of each part are offered as road maps for the materials there. They help guide the reader to set the most helpful course through the essays by indicating the different strokes with which each author paints. Some paint with the broad, sweeping strokes of the scholar's summary of vast movements of history and thought. Some paint with more detail the way the issues at hand bear upon the routines of daily life or the patterns of a congregation's witness. Some give frames of reference and teach how to approach these issues; others share the fruit of their own work and the implications they are following out in their own contexts. Some cast images that bring to light the problematic we face, while others show gems of vision that shed light on the paths in front of us. All invite the reader to a quest for the new ways the Spirit calls the churches of North America to fulfill, genuinely and faithfully, our missionary nature.

PART I

FOCUSING THE MISSION QUESTION

As noted in the Introduction, the churches of North America are experiencing a new social location. They face a changed context in which former conceptions of their identity and purpose are being challenged. This new situation is requiring churches to approach their context as a missionary encounter. This in turn requires that we develop a contextualized missiology for the North American context.

In recent years, a number of persons working in the Gospel and Our Culture Network (GOCN) have attempted to identify the issues that must be addressed. Two articles in particular have provided a helpful introduction, both of which appear in this part. The first is by George R. Hunsberger, who serves as the coordinator of the entire GOCN. The second is by Craig Van Gelder, coordinator of the Culture Work Group in the GOCN.

Hunsberger's essay "The Newbigin Gauntlet: Developing a Domestic Missiology for North America" presents the basic challenge facing churches in North America today. Hunsberger's thesis is that churches have become domesticated by contemporary Western culture rather than working with a domestic missiology that can challenge this culture. This basic problem, Hunsberger suggests, lies in a lack of theological depth regarding how churches think about their identity and how they relate to the cultural context. He draws heavily on the work of Lesslie Newbigin to develop this thesis. It was Newbigin who framed the general missiological challenge regarding the way the gospel needs once again to confront the churches and nations of the West.

Applying Newbigin's thesis to North America, Hunsberger frames the missiological challenge for the church as a tripartite dialogue between the gospel, the church, and our culture. On the basis of such a dialogue, he identifies three questions for the North American missiological agenda: How must we grasp our identity? How must we seek the common good? and How must we tell the gospel?

Complementing the overview of the missiological task facing the churches of North American presented by Hunsberger is the essay by Van Gelder. His work, entitled "Defining the Center — Finding the Boundaries: The Challenge of Re-Visioning the Church in North America for the Twenty-First Century," attempts to identify the variety of issues that the church must address within its new missionary setting, a setting marked by the general shift taking place today in worldviews. We are in transition from an Enlightenment-based, modern worldview built on Newtonian science to a twentieth-century worldview built on Einsteinian science.

Van Gelder develops his presentation by looking at the areas of context, gospel, and church and identifying fundamental shifts that are occurring within each of these areas of inquiry. He goes on to identify specific issues related to these various shifts that must be addressed if we are to develop a domestic missiology for North America. All of these shifts and issues are framed within an extensive review of representative literature associated with each topic.

In regard to *context,* he identifies as significant shifts an increased globalization of intermingling cultures, the rise of the postmodern condition, and the increased impact of radicalized modernity. In regard to *gospel,* he identifies shifts evident in theological/biblical studies, in the increased influence of narrative theology, and in the refocusing of the wider rationality of the gospel. In the area of *church,* he demonstrates shifts occurring in the emerging post-Christian context, the changing face of denominations in this new setting, and the challenge confronting churches to reposition themselves.

Taken together, these two treatments provide the reader with an extensive introduction into the working agenda of the Gospel and Our Culture Network. Because each presents an overview of the larger missiological challenge facing the churches in North America, these articles are of necessity summary in nature. The essays in the three parts that follow relate to the framework presented in these two pieces while providing a more detailed discussion of many of the issues identified.

The Newbigin Gauntlet: Developing a Domestic Missiology for North America

GEORGE R. HUNSBERGER

At Lausanne II, the 1989 gathering of evangelical missionary forces in Manila, time was reserved in the schedule for national gatherings. In those meetings, people from — or working in — each country met to pray, evaluate, share, and strategize regarding the evangelizing task facing the church in that place. In every gathering, that is, except one. The meetings of the U.S. delegates were noteworthy because their focus was not on evangelizing their country but on continuing to mobilize churches in the United States for evangelizing the other countries of the world. The U.S. participants did not see their country as a field for mission, but only as a launching pad for missionizing the "elsewheres" of the world.[1]

The situation is not much better within ecumenical mainline Protestant denominations. For all the talk about "reciprocal mission" or "mission in reverse," the typical North American Protestant church would simply laugh if it were suggested that an African or Asian be called to be the founding pastor/evangelist for a project to plant a new church in an area inhabited by white middle-class folks. We still send white missionaries to plant churches among nonwhite peoples elsewhere in the world, but we cannot conceive of the need for missionaries from other places and cultures to do that here. We fail to see the need for anyone else to help us, not even

1. See Craig Van Gelder, "Evangelicals and Lausanne II: What Happened to a 'Contextual' Gospel?" *The Gospel and Our Culture Newsletter* 2, no. 1 (1990): 5–6.

with the very aspects of the work of the churches that have become most vexing for us (e.g., evangelism). We welcome colleagues from elsewhere as informants on their part of the world. Perhaps we will allow them to give a measure of critique from the perspective of their culture. Almost by definition, however, we Americans are "not in need" of missionaries to come help us.

These dynamics betray a mind-set that lies at the root of what must be called a glaring gap in American missiology. We have failed to give clear-cut attention to the development of a domestic, contextual missiology for our own North American setting. In its place has grown an implicit, functional missiology suffering from a lack of scrutiny. In most of our churches, ask what people think about "mission," and immediately you get responses about "people over there" in faraway places across the globe, people who have "little or no knowledge" about Christ, among whom our missionaries are working to bring the light of the gospel. Shift the focus by saying, "No, I mean local mission right here." Now what you hear about are benevolent projects for helping the poor and disadvantaged. Again you say, "But what about evangelizing your own community?" Then the conversation shifts to the ways the church is seeking to attract, gain, and retain new members.

"Over there, helping the poor, recruiting members" — these have become the operational missiologies of our churches. And they are not just uninformed notions of laypeople. They are fueled and undergirded by the guidance implicit in the language of missiological institutions and movements. The fund-raising dimensions of denominational and independent global mission agencies transmute what should be occasions for mission education in our churches into mere mission promotion designed to sustain extensive logistic superstructures. The tendency toward social-ethical preaching in our pulpits (whether emphasizing public justice or private moralities) combines with the basic (if fading) American value that every person has a right to material well-being to produce a posture of benevolence toward the poor. The American mystique of growthism makes growing the church larger an end more important than representing the gospel of the reign of God.

Each of these phrases has a measure of validity. But even when taken all together, global mission support (i.e., a large missionary budget), benevolence toward the poor (building houses and supplying food), and church growth efforts (parking lots and visitation programs) form an inadequate notion of a congregation's mission. Its inadequacy shows up in several ways. In the first place, all three facets of the complex enjoy a strong dependence upon root American values (the same values by which we design our economy, gauge national progress, wage war, etc.). We have the attitude that if we *can* do something, we *should* do it. Personal freedom is the greatest good. Material well-being belongs to free people. Growth and success prove that these essential values are right.

While this analysis might suggest that what we have here is, in fact, a very contextualized, domestic missiology — which I have said we lack — I contend that it is not so domestic as it is domesticated. It has arisen comfortably from a set of cultural values that have uncritically been allowed to shape the scope of mission for us.

A second inadequacy follows on the heels of that one. Inherent in the American mythology is a sense that individual freedom — the fundamental myth — is substantiated as a proper foundation for the social order by a supporting myth, material success. The pragmatism, benevolence, and success dimensions of the functional missiology I have been describing function in our congregations in a way similar to their operation in the larger culture, as confirmation and therefore as gauge. If our church grows, the rightness of our faith is somehow verified. We help the poor, but of course we expect to see the proper result, namely, that the poor will then get themselves back on their feet. We support global efforts as long as we see the payoff. The consequence is that these three dynamics of mission function more to serve the self-assurance and self-confidence of the congregation than they serve the world in which the congregation lives or the reign of God that it represents. We feel better when we do these things, and especially when they are done successfully. At bottom, we feel better because we are able to feel OK about ourselves.

The greatest sign of the inadequacy of this reigning missiology is its lack of theological depth, or even theological character. Biblical rationales can always be marshaled, of course. But the fruit of global missiological reflection has scarcely been brought to bear on the need for an operative congregational missiology larger than the present truncated versions. These versions touch so superficially upon the missionary calling of the church that the church in America has become increasingly anemic. As a result, our congregations flounder under the influence of false myths and ultimately unmissionary thinking.

It is to such issues as these that the most recent writings of Lesslie

Newbigin have spoken. In effect, he has thrown down the gauntlet, challenging the churches of the West to look to our own contexts as missionary settings and to be as rigorous about what that must mean for our own missionary life as we have been about mission done elsewhere. He was not the first to see the crisis, nor was he the first to ask about the nature of "the missionary encounter of the gospel with Western culture." But in many ways he has become a potent catalyst for focusing our attention on what must become a primary agenda for Western churches. Newbigin's return in the mid-1970s to England, his native land, provided the occasion for him to draw upon the wealth of missionary perspective and statesmanship that had been his contribution within global missiological conversations for several decades. The fruit of that worldwide dialogue fueled his challenge to the churches of the United Kingdom in *The Other Side of 1984* (1983). His way of putting the agenda was sharpened as it was brought more directly to American attention with the publication of *Foolishness to the Greeks* (1986). In *The Gospel in a Pluralist Society* (1989), the essential agenda called for in the earlier books has been further explored along a number of fronts, including especially the development of what might be called a postmodern apologetic to undergird believing and testifying, and the recovery of what it means to be a missionary congregation that serves as the hermeneutic of the gospel.[2]

If Newbigin has thrown down the gauntlet (in the medieval-glove sense of that word), he has accompanied that challenge with an indication of the nature of the gauntlet (in its other meaning) that we are forced to run. His description (particularly in *Foolishness to the Greeks*) of what he sees to be a rudimentary facet of Western culture — namely, the dichotomy that has come to exist between appropriately public "facts" and essentially private "values" — provides clues for understanding a kind of daily gauntlet each of us navigates, believers in Christ no less than other people in the culture. For the church, the effect of the dichotomy strikes at the heart of our self-understandings. The church's former privileged position in Western societies under a Christendom model is now gone, and it will not be regained. The church, as a faith community, is relegated

2. Lesslie Newbigin, *The Other Side of 1984: Questions for the Churches* (Geneva: World Council of Churches, 1983); *Foolishness to the Greeks: The Gospel and Western Culture* (Grand Rapids: Eerdmans, 1986); *The Gospel in a Pluralist Society* (Grand Rapids: Eerdmans, 1989).

by the culture's frame of understanding to the private world of personal values, beliefs, and opinions. By and large, the church has willingly (if sometimes unknowingly) accommodated itself to that relegation and become a privatized, voluntary association for perpetuating its set of faith opinions. But for a church that believes that the gospel it embraces was God-given and intended as news for the whole world, for its public as well as its private life, there is a deep dilemma. We run the gauntlet between a failed Christendom and a false privatization, in pursuit of new ways of running it.

We run the gauntlet in another way as well. When we recognize that what we are engaging is a cross-cultural missionary situation made more complicated by the fact that the culture in view is our own, we are thrown into serious difficulty. How can we critique our culture, and seek the gospel's critique of it, while our way of judging the culture and our way of reading the Bible are themselves shaped by our own culture? We are forced to develop approaches that navigate between the Scylla of culture bashing on the one side and the Charybdis of absorption into the culture on the other, attempting to avoid both dashing ourselves on the rocks and getting swallowed into the sea.

As much as Newbigin provides many helpful insights for taking up his challenge and running the gauntlet, probably his most important contribution is to have stimulated and framed the agenda. But it is important to recognize the ground from which that framing arises within the broader sweep of his missiological orientation. That will provide help along several lines: for interpreting his essential thesis, for recognizing its missiological character, and for identifying some of the contours for our engagement of the agenda within our own North American context.

Missiological Orientations

A Missiology of Culture

Foolishness to the Greeks is a book in two parts: the first ten pages, and then the remainder of the book. Those reading Newbigin who quickly judge that he holds a "Christ-against-culture" position and engages only in culture bashing have failed to recognize these two parts. The first contains in very distilled form a summary of his orientation toward the culturalness of human life, an orientation that has become standard for missiological reflections regarding places outside the West.[3] While his summary is remarkably unsophisticated in terms of cultural anthropology, it bears with great force the major insights of the global missionary experience and suggests that now we must do business the same way within our Western cultures. Perhaps more than anyone, Newbigin has grappled theologically with the issues of gospel and culture, not just from practical or strategic standpoints. Essential for understanding his proposal is an appreciation of the theology of cultural plurality that implicitly permeates these and others of his writings.[4]

At the heart of Newbigin's theology of cultural plurality lies his sense of a "three-cornered relationship" between the gospel, a particular culture, and the church.[5] Of special importance are the dynamics that emerge around each of the three axes formed: the conversion encounter axis, the reciprocal relationship axis, and the missionary dialogue axis (fig. 1).

Along the first axis, the gospel and its communication present to every culture a "challenging relevance." It is relevant insofar as it is embodied in the terms by which people of the culture have learned to understand their world. It is challenging in that in every culture, Jesus is introduced as one who bursts open the culture's models with the power

3. H. Richard Niebuhr's classic text *Christ and Culture* (New York: Harper & Row, 1951) is not really an exception to that non-Western focus. His treatment has more to do with Christian attitudes and postures along the way in the journey of Western civilization and hardly raises the issues that arise with a contemporary anthropological understanding of "culture." The plurality of cultures in the world does not bear on his treatment. Increasingly, the categories of his paradigm fail to account for the complexities involved in Christian relationships to cultures and for the evolving configurations of Western culture. For these and many other reasons, the need for a new paradigm is one of the most pressing challenges we face.

4. I explored this feature of Newbigin's missiology in "The Missionary Significance of the Biblical Doctrine of Election as a Foundation for a Theology of Cultural Plurality in the Missiology of J. E. Lesslie Newbigin" (Ph.D. diss., Princeton Theological Seminary, 1987). Understanding the biblical doctrine of election as the inherent logic of mission (see Newbigin, *Foolishness to the Greeks*, 53, 98–99, 127; *Gospel in a Pluralist Society*, 80ff.), Newbigin develops a theology of cultural plurality that provides theological grounding for discussions of cross-cultural mission, ecumenical relationship, and interfaith dialogue.

5. Lesslie Newbigin, *The Open Secret: Sketches for a Missionary Theology* (Grand Rapids: Eerdmans, 1978), 165–72.

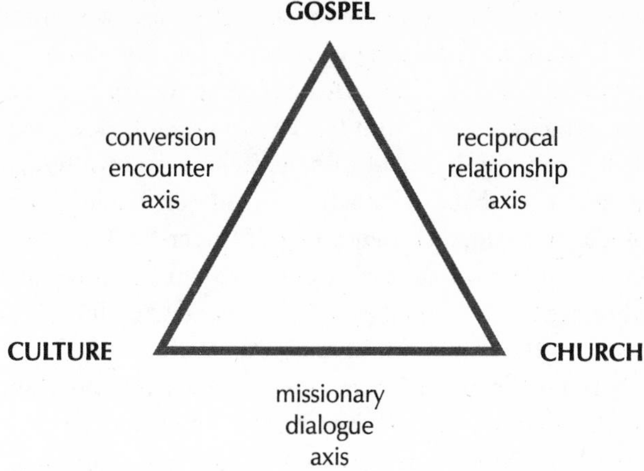

GOSPEL: "challenging relevance" in the culture
"hermeneutical circle" with the church

CULTURE: radical discontinuity regarding the gospel
radical independence regarding the church

CHURCH: adherence to the given tradition
dialogue with the varied cultures

FIGURE 1. A Triangular Model of Gospel-Culture Relationships

of a wholly new fact.[6] Embodiment without challenge would lead to syncretism; challenge without embodiment would be irrelevant. This encounter between the gospel and a culture is a conversion encounter in that it precipitates a fundamental paradigm shift that brings about a new ultimate commitment at the center. It entails, in that sense, a "radical discontinuity," a break into new directions, for the one embracing the gospel. Never is this a total discontinuity, because the gospel and a person's response to it of necessity remain embodied in a particular culture's way of seeing, feeling, and acting.

6. Lesslie Newbigin, "Christ and the Cultures," *Scottish Journal of Theology* 31 (1978): 11–12.

The second axis, the reciprocal relationship between gospel and church, is the fruit of conversion. A community is established for whom "the Bible is the determinative clue to the character and activity of the one whose purpose is the final meaning of history."[7] But this community that is a "people of the book" is also the community that bears the Bible as its own testimony. The community's tradition shapes its reading of its book, while its reading and rereading of the book further shape its self-understanding. The church's commitment to the Bible's authority, embodied in an active discipleship, enables the hermeneutical circle between Bible and church itself to become the hermeneutic of the gospel among the cultures of the world.

The third axis is that between the missionary church and a local culture, regardless of how similar the two are culturally. The church's style of life becomes a missionary dialogue, which implies a multiplex church in full ecumenical dialogue among its own members in the variety of human cultures. Furthermore, it suggests that witness is always given with the recognition that when heard and embraced, it is not the form of embodiment already achieved in the missionary church that will dictate the way conversion and discipleship will emerge in the new culture. Newbigin calls for a sense of the radical independence of the new convert (and newly converted church) vis-à-vis the missionary church through which the message has come. That complements the radical discontinuity of conversion itself, vis-à-vis one's own culture, and thus affirms the proper enculturedness of the forms that that conversion will take. Again, this radical independence cannot remain a total one, in that the new church takes its place alongside the other churches of the world in the necessary ecumenical conversation between the various inculturations of discipleship.

It is important to grasp these features of Newbigin's missionary approach that are briefly stated here. The authority of the Bible, its affirmation and critique of every culture, and the church's attitude toward both of these elements are essential for a serious missiological encountering of the Western culture that is for us in North American churches both our assumed reality and our missionary assignment. Newbigin's model helps us become more discriminating in our concern to avoid both syncretism and irrelevance, more focused upon inhabiting the biblical vision as part of a multicultural Christian community, and more open to the ongoing dialogue with our own culture, which is as much an inner dialogue as an outer one.

7. Newbigin, *Foolishness to the Greeks,* 62.

A Theology of Conversion

The second feature of Newbigin's missiological orientation that governs his approach to Western culture is his way of understanding conversion. He sees it as threefold. Conversion means "being turned round in order to recognize and participate in the dawning reality of God's reign. But this inward turning immediately and intrinsically involves both a pattern of conduct and a visible companionship. It involves membership in a community and a decision to act in certain ways."[8] For Newbigin, conversion has mental, ethical, and communal dimensions.

It is not accidental that the outline of *Foolishness to the Greeks* reflects this pattern.[9] After establishing his central thesis in the earlier chapters and showing how the missionary encounter he describes is born by a community that inhabits a different plausibility structure than that shared by the surrounding society, Newbigin takes up in turn these three dimensions of conversion. In chapter 4, entitled "Dialogue with Science," he demonstrates the "wider rationality" that can be claimed for Christian faith, which, unlike the predominant modern scientific worldview, does not exclude the category of purpose in regard to knowing (90). Chapter 5, "Dialogue with Politics," follows with the ethical dimension of conversion. There Newbigin portrays the calling of the church to be "resident aliens," embodying in its life "a witness to the kingship of Christ over all life — its political and economic no less than its personal and domestic morals" (102–3). In the final chapter, he gives a preliminary description of the resultant call to the church to recover "its proper distinction from, and its proper responsibility for, this secular culture that we have shared so comfortably and so long" (135). He asks the church to consider the forms of its life appropriate to a community governed by the vision of the coming reign of God (127–29, 134–37). In other words, the second half of this book is given over to an account of the shape of the radical paradigm shift to which the gospel calls the church in the midst of contemporary Western culture, a shift that leads to a new vision of how things are and, not all at once but gradually, to the development of a new plausibility structure in which the most real of all realities is the living God, whose character is rendered for us in the pages of Scripture (64).

8. Lesslie Newbigin, *The Finality of Christ* (Richmond, VA: John Knox Press, 1969), 96.

9. Page numbers in the text are from *Foolishness to the Greeks.*

This framework is important to recognize when one is tempted to see in Newbigin's proposals an accommodationism either to a residual Christendom model or to a ghettoized sectarianism.[10] He is attempting to avoid both and, as with all of us, runs the risk of falling prey to either. But whether or not his own specific visions for renewal and recovery achieve the goal, his pursuit is indeed governed by a fundamental conviction that whatever form the church's witness takes, it must represent a genuine and essential conversion of mind, behavior, and communal commitment.

A Postmodern Apologetic

It is perhaps Newbigin's richest contribution to Western Christian persons plagued by the nagging failure of nerve in regard to overt and explicit witness to a faith in Jesus Christ that he has supplied what I believe can be properly called a postmodern apologetic.[11] In a way that gives deep and empathetic response to the culture's intimidation that repels us into silence in all but our most formal opportunities to speak the gospel, Newbigin draws upon Michael Polanyi's sense of the ways of knowing in order to affirm the legitimate "rationality" of believing the gospel to be true, and true for all.[12] In so doing, he addresses not only the failure of nerve but its twin, the internal crisis of faith that it finally entails.

The most comprehensive development of this apologetic appears in *The Gospel in a Pluralist Society.* There, in the first five chapters, Newbigin seeks to provide a way of believing and knowing that shows how both scientists attempting to know physical objects and persons attempting to know God engage in the knowing in distinct but comparable ways. The

10. M. M. Thomas has taken the former position ("Mission and Modern Culture," *Ecumenical Review* 36, no. 3 [1984]: 316–22), Christopher B. Kaiser the latter ("The Foolishness of the 'Greeks,'" *Perspectives* 2, no. 4 [1987]: 7–9).

11. By introducing the term "postmodern" in reference to Newbigin's apologetic approach, I do not intend to make any particular claim regarding whether postmodernism is a newly emerging cultural paradigm, merely another extension and expression of modernity, or something more like the sense of a coming fin de siècle similar to that which expressed itself at the end of the nineteenth century (see Stjepan G. Mestrovic, *The Coming Fin de Siècle* [London: Routledge, 1991]).

12. See Michael Polanyi, *Personal Knowledge: Towards a Post-Critical Philosophy* (Chicago: University of Chicago Press, 1958).

supposed objective factuality of scientific knowing is broadly assumed in our culture to lie in contrast to religious conviction. But as Polanyi has observed, all knowing — scientific no less than religious — is subjective in that it is an act of personal commitment. Along with a focal dimension, it includes a tacit dimension of frames of reference and tools for knowing (including language) that are relied upon, at least for the moment, as investigation proceeds. Even doubt, as a knowing tool, rests upon beliefs held without doubting. In addition, all reasoning depends upon and is embodied within some rational tradition maintained within a particular community. In these ways, scientific knowing is not fundamentally different from religious knowing.

Religious knowing, which is likewise subjective, nevertheless bears features similar to those our culture has more readily assigned to scientific knowing. Personal knowing has an objective referent, and it is offered with universal intent. What is claimed to be known by "scientist" or "believer" is offered not as private opinion but as public fact and begs to be published and shared so that it can be questioned and checked in the public forum. In science as in religion, innovation is not so much by reason of new facts as by paradigm shift, and such shifts result from acts of imagination or intuition. It is the imagined "clue" that gives rise to advances in knowing. In the case of Christian faith, the gospel, the sense "that in the ministry, death, and resurrection of Jesus God has acted decisively to reveal and effect his purpose of redemption for the whole world,"[13] provides the clue to the meaning and purpose of the world's life.

Seen in the light of these observations about "personal knowing," religious knowing is no less credible than scientific knowing when both are rightly understood. In obvious ways, the apologetic Newbigin offers gives encouragement to move beyond intimidation, secure in the sense that the alternate "rational tradition" borne by the Christian community can be understood to be a credible "wider rationality" than that offered by the reigning plausibility structure of the culture. A sense of the ways we know gives rise to new ways of believing and witnessing.

13. Newbigin, *Gospel in a Pluralist Society,* 5.

The Missionary Congregation

A recurrent and forceful theme in Newbigin's missiology has been his challenge to the church to embody its true missionary character. Invariably, he focuses that challenge upon the fabric of the local congregation, emphasizing the necessity for visible unity among "all in each place" who believe the gospel and the implications of the catholicity of such truly united local bodies. Indeed, he has played a critical role in the definitions of unity and catholicity within World Council of Churches deliberations. Unity and catholicity are always crucial for Newbigin owing to their connection to the church's missionary character. A local church bears in itself all the marks of the catholic church and fully represents its fellowship to neighbors close at hand. That local church's unity is evidence that God has in fact sent Jesus into the world to be its savior. In that and a myriad of ways, the local congregation is the essential "hermeneutic of the gospel," the lens through which it may become known and by which it can rightly be interpreted.

The glaring absence of missionary character in the churches of the West has most alarmed Newbigin and has spurred his engagement of "the missionary encounter of the gospel with Western culture." That encounter, after all, is one that belongs to the heart and birthright of the church. So when he wrote *The Other Side of 1984,* it was in order to raise, as its subtitle states, "Questions for the Churches." *Foolishness to the Greeks* concludes with "Call to the Churches," focused on the question "What must we be?"[14] The concluding chapters of *The Gospel in a Pluralist Society* attempt to sketch the congregations' hermeneutical importance and the form of ministerial leadership required for such a missionary recovery. There, in a telling observation, he touches the raw nerve most illumining of the central missiological problem for the Western churches: the need for recovering a practical missionary ecclesiology, a self-understanding of and by the churches that envisions our missionary character and guides us in faithful living. Newbigin observes:

> We have lived for so many centuries in the "Christendom" situation that ministerial training is almost entirely conceived in terms of the pastoral care of existing congregations. In a situation of declining numbers, the policy has been to abandon areas (such as inner cities) where active

14. Newbigin, *Foolishness to the Greeks,* 124ff.

> Christians are few and to concentrate ministerial resources by merging congregations and deploying ministers in the places where there are enough Christians to support them. Needless to say, this simply accelerates the decline. It is the opposite of a missionary strategy, which would proceed in the opposite direction — deploying ministers in the areas where the Christian presence is weakest. The large-scale abandonment of the inner cities by the "mainline" churches is the most obvious evidence of the policy that has been pursued.[15]

The implications for a domestic missiology for North America are important. There is a crisis touching the character of evangelism in a pluralist, secularist setting. But that crisis is first one of the identity of the church itself that renders its witness in such a setting. There is a crisis regarding the nature of the church's responsibility in and for the public order of the larger society. But that responsibility cries out for a new, post-Christendom definition of the church itself. The priority of questions surrounding the re-imaging of the church corresponds to Newbigin's longstanding convictions about the essential ecclesiological rootedness of the church's engagement in mission:

> The basic reality is the creation of a new being through the presence of the Holy Spirit. This new being is the common life (koinonia) in the Church. It is out of this new creation that both service and evangelism spring, and from it they receive their value. . . . These different acts have their relation to one another not in any logical scheme, but in the fact that they spring out of the one new reality.[16]

A North American Missiological Agenda

Most simply and directly put, it is the church's mission to represent the reign of God. It is the characteristic language of Newbigin to speak of the church as the "sign, instrument, and foretaste" of that reign,[17] language that has come to be shared broadly in ecumenical and Roman Catholic ecclesi-

15. Newbigin, *Gospel in a Pluralist Society,* 235–36.

16. Lesslie Newbigin, *One Body, One Gospel, One World: The Christian Mission Today* (London: International Missionary Council, 1958), 20.

17. Newbigin, *Open Secret,* 163; cf. *Foolishness to the Greeks,* 117.

ology. It emphasizes that the church dare not equate itself with God's reign, which it only serves, but also it must avoid divorcing itself from that reign. As Newbigin has put it:

> The . . . danger to be avoided is the separation of the Kingdom from the church. It is clear that they cannot and must not be confused, certainly not identified. But they must also not be separated. From the beginning the announcement of the Kingdom led to a summons to follow and so to the formation of a community. It is the community that has begun to taste (even only in foretaste) the reality of the Kingdom which can alone provide the hermeneutic of the message.[18]

In its mission under the reign of God, the church represents it as its community (koinonia), its servant (diakonia), and its messenger (kerygma). In its very life, as well as in its deeds and words, the church provides the locus and occasion for the Holy Spirit's manifestation of God's reign.[19] This basic understanding of what is properly the church's mission anywhere and anytime becomes suggestive regarding the mission of the moment for the churches in North America. The agenda before us gathers around three questions cast in light of the new circumstances: Christendom is gone, the church has been relegated to the private realm, and God is viewed by our contemporaries as neither necessary nor effective. With utmost seriousness, the churches of North America are faced with three matters of immediacy that are crucial for recovering our missionary character.

How Must We Grasp Our Identity?

In the latter half of the twentieth century the North American churches have experienced a great sea change in their social location and function. No sooner had the Protestant-Catholic-Jew consensus of mid-century provided a place for the more formal elements of what Robert Bellah described as America's civil religion (e.g., inserting the phrase "under God" in the Pledge of Allegiance and adding "In God we trust" to our coinage) than we found ourselves experiencing a "restructuring of American religion." Robert Wuthnow documents the factors that have contributed first to a cleavage

18. Lesslie Newbigin, *Sign of the Kingdom* (Grand Rapids: Eerdmans, 1980), 19.
19. Ibid., 41.

between two competing versions of civil religion and then to its collapse altogether.[20] As a result of these and other trends, we have come to a place in which the fundamental "legitimating myths" underlying the American social order have shifted. In place of "inalienable rights" with which we have been "endowed" by our Creator, the first principles have now come to be (1) freedom; (2) material success, as confirmation of the rightness of the freedom myth; and (3) technology, as the infrastructure supporting the other two. What was once "freedom in the interests of religious faith" has become "faith under the protective cover of freedom." Freedom has become the "guiding principle that needs no further justification or definition." Religion is seen merely as a story that illustrates the value of freedom.[21]

Such a shift means a change in social location for the churches. As Kennon Callahan has put it in more popular fashion, "The day of the churched culture is over."[22] The day has gone when the church was generally valued by the society as important to the social and moral order and when, for that reason, people tended to seek out a church for themselves. We sail today in a different kind of sea.

If our caretaker days are over and the church is no longer looked to for legitimation or moral underpinning, we have scarcely begun to live as though that were true, which explains why we experience these changes as a crisis. The Christendom experiment has run its course and is over, but our images and instincts are still formed by its memory. We play out the church's routine as though the concerns of the church and the quests of the culture go hand-in-glove. We are never quite sure which is the hand and which the glove, but we are certain they form common cause. The rude awakening breaking in on us is that whatever such connection there may have been in the past, it is vanishing.

We are caught between a Constantinian Christendom that has ended and to which we cannot return and the culture's relegation of the church to the private realm, which is untenable if we have understood rightly that the gospel is news that has relevance to the public life of the whole world.[23] Repeatedly, the image of exile has best seemed to capture who we have

20. Robert Wuthnow, *The Restructuring of American Religion: Society and Faith since World War II* (Princeton: Princeton University Press, 1988), chap. 10.

21. Ibid., chap. 11.

22. Kennon L. Callahan, *Effective Church Leadership* (San Francisco: Harper & Row, 1990), 13.

23. Newbigin, *Foolishness to the Greeks*, 101–2.

become and how we might live in hope in the place of our planting.[24] Perhaps the image is especially pertinent because in its dislocation an exile community feels most keenly the loss — or simply the absence — of a clear sense of its identity or a focused center for its life. To know itself as exile is the beginning of recovery.

Israel's experience of exile in Babylon elicits a rich tapestry of identity for the church in a new exile. Exiles hold the ultimate power to name themselves (Dan. 1; cf. John 1:12). Or, more accurately, they have the freedom to use the names given them by the empire while boldly retaining names that assert its limits! They are possessed with promises that this is not the way things will end, while carrying instructions to seek the welfare of the city in the meantime (Jer. 29:1-14). They are full of danger for the empire, driven by dangerous memories and promises, expressing themselves with dangerous songs and criticism, eating dangerous bread, and making dangerous departures.[25] They are at once both a "chosen out" people of distinct character and a "scattered abroad" (diaspora) people of common similarity (1 Pet. 1–2).

Stanley Hauerwas and William Willimon propose a "confessing church" model as a "radical alternative" to the "activist" (Constantinian) or "conversionist" (privatized) models that are current. What they envision is the church as "an alternative *polis,* a countercultural social structure called church." Such a church has as its overriding political task "to be the community of the cross." They wish to see a church "that again asserts that God, not nations, rules the world, that the boundaries of God's kingdom transcend those of Caesar, and that the main political task of the church is the formation of people who see clearly the cost of discipleship and are willing to pay the price." They invite us to see ourselves with exilic eyes as "resident aliens, an adventurous colony in a society of unbelief."[26]

24. The most complete depiction of an exilic model comes from Stanley Hauerwas and William H. Willimon, *Resident Aliens: Life in the Christian Colony* (Nashville: Abingdon Press, 1989). Others who move in this direction include Ephraim Radner, in his article "From 'Liberation' to 'Exile': A New Image for Church Mission," *Christian Century,* October 18, 1989, pp. 931–34; Walter Brueggemann, in *Disciplines of Readiness* (Louisville: Theology and Worship Unit, Presbyterian Church [U.S.A.], 1988); and Jeremiah Wright, in an unpublished address given in 1988 at the presidential inauguration at Tougaloo College, Jackson, Mississippi.

25. Brueggemann, *Disciplines of Readiness;* cf. Isa. 40–55.

26. Hauerwas and Willimon, *Resident Aliens,* 44–49.

The inevitable charge that these proposals constitute a new sectarianism warns of a danger that a sharper sense of being an alternative community will make the church aloof from the culture's need for its healing presence. But being "of" the world (culture) has never been a better guarantee that the church is "in" the world.[27] In fact, only by adopting alternative principles can the church free itself from the social segregation it experiences at the hand of the culture's principles. Already in the early 1970s, George Lindbeck predicted what he termed "the sectarian future of the church." He noted that "to the degree generalized social support disappears, it becomes necessary for Christians or members of any other deviant minority to gather together in small, cohesive, mutually supportive groups. They must become, sociologically speaking, sectarian." This is different from an ecclesiastical or theological sectarianism that splinters into competing groups. The early church, a "strongly deviant minority, unsupported by cultural convention and prestige," remained "catholic" and "ecumenical" for all its diversity.[28] It was the merging of that sociological sectarianism with the divisive and schismatic theological variety that has plagued the church subsequently. A recovery of the sociological form without its attachment to the ecclesiastical form is Lindbeck's proposal for a responsible sectarianism for our age.

The practical agenda that emerges in light of our present circumstances includes four basic tasks for congregations and their leaders. Two relate to the healing of the church's identity and its intimidation: (1) forming an alternate, communal "world"; and (2) casting a "wider rationality." The other two concern the church's inner and outer dialogue with the culture: (3) healing our fragmentary "worlds" (work, home, leisure, commerce, education, politics, church, etc.); and (4) igniting a subversive witness.[29]

27. See Donald C. Posterski, *Reinventing Evangelism: New Strategies for Presenting Christ in Today's World* (Downers Grove, IL: InterVarsity Press, 1989), 28.

28. George A. Lindbeck, "The Sectarian Future of the Church," in *The God Experience,* ed. Joseph P. Whelan, S.J. (New York: Newman Press, 1971), 227, 230.

29. George R. Hunsberger, "The Changing Face of Ministry: Christian Leadership for the Twenty-First Century," *Reformed Review* 44, no. 3 (Spring 1991): 224–45.

How Must We Seek the "Common Good"?

An exilic image helps, rather than hurts, the church's inclination toward seeking the common good, if properly understood. But if Jeremiah's letter to the exiles in Babylon provides any guidance at all in that regard, it is to be found in the absence of Constantinian language (Jer. 29:1-14). The exiles were to seek the welfare of the city, but not from any impulse that they must somehow seize control of its policies and dictate its ideology. Nor was their welfare-seeking to be done in order to justify themselves as pragmatically useful in the eyes of the ruling ethos, as the church has been pressed to do in modern American society. The impetus to seek the city's welfare was not even to be borne along by expectations of success in refashioning the shape of Babylon, but only by the recognition that their service announced greater realities than those upon which the Babylonian society was based (see Dan. 3:16-18).

If the Christendom image of our fit in the social scheme of things has played out and our prior sense of social responsibility was largely attached to it (in the espousal of both liberal and conservative agendas), what new sense must we gain of our God-given call to seek the common good? In a religiously and ideologically plural setting, what is the place of Christian visions for what makes the common order "good"? How must they be sought or offered amid the alternate visions? If we seek the good not from a hope of success, then from what hope can we find motivation for representing the justice, peace, and joy of the reign of God? A new cast to the very way we ask the questions is called for.

While the carving of new paths for our thinking and action will not be easy and cannot be quickly achieved, at least several contours would appear to be important features for the way ahead. First, we must be self-conscious that *we offer our action for the common good within a pluralist setting and according to pluralist rules.* While the church seeks and finds its own identity beyond the definitions given by the culture, we cannot expect our participation in the social struggles to follow our rules. In this respect we will need to learn from the churches of the world that live out responsibility for the common good from their positions as minorities. The dynamics of mission in weakness and persistence at the margins will need to characterize our work.

Second, *our pursuit of the common good must be marked by a more rigorous holism.* The polarization between Christian action for social justice and Christian action for personal morality is problematic because both too easily represent an accommodation to the culture's individualist rights and interests. If the church only mimics the culture's loosening grip on the question about that which serves the *common* good and reflects the same tendency toward single-issue politics and constituency satisfaction, there will be little contribution that will distinguish the character of the coming reign of God the church represents.

Third, *our action for the common good requires more complete communal integrity within the church.* Whatever we espouse for the good of the society must be demonstrated by a living community that believes the vision enough to form its life around it. Ephraim Radner describes the shift implied as a movement from our tendency to think in terms of totalistic, theocratic transformation (a liberationist model) toward the recovery of a sense that it is "the growth and expansion of religious communities, separate but within the larger society, that will engender vehicles for noncoercive deliverance."[30] The church that pronounces concern for the homeless on the White House lawn, based on a set of values at odds with the culture, will welcome the homeless themselves into the shelter of their homes and houses of worship. For that integrity, Radner suggests, the image of exile serves better than one of liberation. In that image, the church becomes "a vessel of deliverance" rather than its agent.

Fourth, *our care for the common good must grow from a care-filled eschatology.* To say it that way is to distinguish such an eschatology from an overly "careful" (in the sense of reticent) eschatology that holds back from risk taking and vulnerability. It also distinguishes it from a "careless" (in the sense of reckless) eschatology that blusters on triumphalistically. We must learn a pursuit of the common good that sets aside both our hand-wringing and our utopianisms, both our hand-washing self-justifications and our demanding impositions. It is the reign *of God,* after all, that is coming, our assurance of which creates confident and humble action.

How Must We Tell the Gospel?

The third critical issue facing churches wishing to recover their missionary character is evangelism. From one perspective, the issue concerns telling

30. Radner, "From 'Liberation' to 'Exile,'" 933.

the gospel in terms appropriate to an audience of people who live with post-Christian, secular convictions. As George Hunter has pointed out, the genius of such diverse people as Samuel Shoemaker, Robert Schuller, and Bill Hybels lies in the seriousness with which they saw and pursued the matter of communicating with secular people.[31] Such a nuancing of our gospel-telling, lacking for the most part in the dominant programs of evangelism, is a long overdue development.[32]

But something more crucial is needed. The very way in which we conceive evangelism needs an overhaul. We cannot expect that in our new circumstances its shape as a Christian practice will not be remade. At least four features are implicated in that renewal.

1. We have already hinted that it is important to the vitality of today's churches to show that the Christian faith provides a "wider rationality" than that of a culture for which the reigning paradigm explains things in terms of cause and effect without any recourse to questions of purpose. The silenced witness of the church grows out of the intense intimidation that the culture breeds. Here is where Newbigin's postmodern apologetics helps. Unless North American Christians are helped to find confidence in *ways of knowing* that are demonstrably rational but liberated from false cultural shackles, there is hardly a way to expect witness to emerge. Our guilt-ridden motivational strategies and church growth technologies will never provide adequate substitutes.

2. A tandem requirement is that evangelism be grounded in a *credible demonstration* that life lived by the pattern of commitment to Jesus is imaginable, possible, and relevant in the modern and postmodern age. This requires more than what we meant previously when we called for verbal witness to rest on consistent Christian living. That tended to mean living exemplary, moral lives as upstanding citizens. The requirements of moral faithfulness are no less now; more important, though, the current need is for a demonstration that a faith in the gospel of God can be the genuine organizing center integrating the fragmented pieces of modern living. Only when that is seen lived out by someone who believes that way will the message about the reign of God have credibility. "The gospel will be per-

31. George G. Hunter III, "Communicating Christianity to Secular People" (church growth lectures, Fuller Theological Seminary, 1989).

32. See George G. Hunter III, *How to Reach Secular People* (Nashville: Abingdon Press, 1992), which explores important features of this issue.

ceived as a feasible alternative when those who do not know God have some positive, personal experiences with people who do."[33]

3. A reshaped evangelism will include a new *willingness to influence.* It is, perhaps, Donald Posterski's most important contribution to the "re-inventing" of evangelism that he seizes the horns of the pluralism dilemma and offers a way to witness by going into and through the culture's pluralist assumptions rather than an evangelistic stance formed out of resistance and opposition to those dynamics. He encourages a style that moves alongside "the principles that govern a pluralistist society: acceptance of diversity . . . , appreciation of options . . . , and interaction with alternatives." He judges that the tolerance factor in pluralism is an open opportunity for evangelism, not a barrier that stymies it. "When people sense they are accepted and appreciated for who they are, they are ready to interact without being defensive."[34] An evangelistic style, therefore, that begins with acceptance and appreciation will have gained the opportunity and freedom to influence.

4. All of this implies a deepening *humility of witness.* New images commend themselves. Newbigin suggests the image of a witness giving testimony "in a trial where it is contested" and where the verdict "will only be given at the end." It is the function of such a witness "not to develop conclusions out of already known data, but simply to point to, report, affirm that which cannot come into the argument at all except simply as a new datum, a reality which is attested by a witness."[35] David Lowes Watson has suggested a shift from a sales model to a journalist model, keying on the recognition that evangelism is a global announcement that the reign of God is at hand.[36] Another model that commends itself in an age requiring that evangelists become meaning-makers is that of docent, in the sense of its use in museums and the Atlanta Zoo.[37] At the latter, docents are volunteers trained to mix among the crowds and be available to explain the various

33. Posterski, *Reinventing Evangelism,* 32.

34. Ibid., 168, 169.

35. Newbigin, *Foolishness to the Greeks,* 64; idem, *The Light Has Come: An Exposition of the Fourth Gospel* (Grand Rapids: Eerdmans, 1982), 14.

36. David Lowes Watson, "The Church as Journalist: Evangelism in the Context of the Local Church in the United States," *International Review of Mission* 72 (1983): 57–74.

37. See Posterski, *Reinventing Evangelism,* 31–48.

animal behaviors and habitats, providing interpretations of the worlds represented in the exhibits. Evangelism implies casting the "wider rationality" of a world seen as the location of the saving purposes of God.

Paying Attention

Such an agenda will require us to be more attentive in several areas. If our practical missiology points us toward developing patterns of life, deed, and word, the wider missiological task includes the attention we give in three other directions.

First, we must *pay attention to the culture.* For us to assume we know it has cost too much. It has led too easily to accommodation. Only an insightful analysis of the cultural and social systems shaping, and being shaped by, life in North America can enable us to keep our missiology contextual. Current studies in these areas are plentiful. The special need is for missiologically sensitive readings of America's cultural history, of the new sociological histories of the role and fate of the churches, and of the depictions of current cultural trends and future scenarios.

Second, we must *pay attention to the gospel.* A theological agenda here must correspond to the phenomenological one. The central question of theology — What is the gospel? — must be asked in more culturally particular ways. And the more particular the question, the more will be our sense that the answer will emerge in unexpected ways. It will come more out of Christian communities that increasingly learn the habit of "indwelling" the gospel story so deeply that it shapes their life of common discipleship.[38] The meaning of work and vocation, the integrating of our pluralistic experience, and a declericalized relocation of theology to the province of the laity are all implicated as elements of a missiologically sensitive theological agenda.

Third, we must *pay attention to each other.* It will require of us a new range of "ecumenical" partnership if we are to hear the gospel as it takes form in the variety of cultures, subcultures, denominational cultures, and ethnic cultures of North America. There is no substitute for that breadth of listening if the forms of our common mission are to be seriously directed toward the dominant undercurrents of the culture as a whole. At this point,

38. See Newbigin, *Gospel in a Pluralist Society,* 232.

the agenda takes on global dimensions because the growing pervasiveness of Western culture, carrying with it its pattern of resistance to the gospel, has made the agenda Newbigin has fostered a world-encircling one. Our openness to help from the world church and its own missionary encounter with our culture can no longer be avoided. We are one church in our common mission to represent the reign of God in a modern, secular, pluralist world.

Defining the Center — Finding the Boundaries

The Challenge of Re-Visioning the Church in North America for the Twenty-First Century

CRAIG VAN GELDER

There are occasions in history when it becomes increasingly evident that a familiar framework of interpretation is shifting to a dramatically new perspective. I believe we are living in such a period of time in North America as we prepare to enter the twenty-first century. Both secular and religious voices are now observing that the modern worldview that has guided our interpretation for several hundred years is being overturned. New ways of understanding reality are being tested. With this shift, the church is being challenged to rethink its fundamental identity and reshape its organizational life.

From a mission perspective, this period of transition affects the entire West and is beginning to be discussed in terms of the relationship of the gospel and Western culture. The missiological question was perhaps best shaped by Lesslie Newbigin as, Can the West be converted? which he posed in his widely read book *Foolishness to the Greeks.* Various networks of missiologists and church professionals have come together on the European continent, in England, and in North America, with each attempting to give direction to the discussion of this question. While this is an important question to address throughout the West, this essay will focus specifically on the issues related to the North American context.

One of the more popular ways today of carrying on the discussion about this crisis of interpretation is through the concept of paradigms. Ever since the work of Thomas Kuhn in his *Structure of Scientific Revolutions,* paradigm debates have provided a helpful framework for understanding different plausibility structures. It is becoming increasingly clear in North American culture that we are experiencing a crisis of paradigms. As suggested by Anderson in *Reality Isn't What It Used to Be,* we are beginning to recognize the socially constructed nature of our various paradigms, along with a multiplication of competing paradigms. With this recognition, there is a growing perception that it may no longer be possible to find the center of metanarrative that can explain the whole, or the essence of the world that we encounter.

For the first several hundred years, North American culture was shaped largely by the ideas and institutions that flowed out of the sixteenth-century Protestant Reformation and the Enlightenment of the seventeenth and eighteenth centuries. These two streams created two parallel story lines of explanation in the shaping of our national identities. These were the sometimes complementary and sometimes conflicting story lines of God's providential destiny and humankind's noble experiment. In this century, both of these story lines have become problematic as the Christian-shaped culture in North America has begun to collapse and as the Enlightenment-shaped modern project has begun to lose its sense of optimism.

These changes are making it necessary to reshape the paradigm for mission to North America. While little has been done historically to develop a specific missiology for North American mission, there have been a series of what might be called operational missiologies at work within this context. These operational missiologies include the following: (1) denomination building, which was carried on for most of the nineteenth century; (2) the alternatives of culture caretaking and privatized faith developed by different streams of these churches at the turn of the century; (3) the church renewal and church growth efforts designed to refocus the mission of many of these churches in the past several decades; and (4) the recent church-effectiveness approach, which seeks to help the church adjust to a rapidly changing environment.

These operational missiologies, however, are less and less helpful in providing adequate approaches for defining the relationship of the gospel to contemporary North American culture. There are two problems in this regard. One is that the shadow of Christendom thinking still tends to cast its image over these missiologies. The other is that the modernist assumptions of social progress and institutional success are woven into their core beliefs. It is now being recognized that fundamental shifts in our cultural context are creating the need for a new way to shape the missiological relationship of gospel and culture.

Interestingly, the church in North America appears to be still predominantly modern in its worldview. But the foundations of our culture are now shifting, and in the emerging context we are finding that our operational missiologies no longer provide adequate answers to the questions we face. In this regard, much of our church life is becoming marginalized, and many of our gospel presentations are becoming trivialized. A missiological approach needs to be developed in North America that can address the fundamental issues associated with the magnitude of this shift that is taking place.

This chapter will address three different perspectives that have a bearing on this task of re-visioning the ministry of the church for the twenty-first century. We look first at our context, asking what kind of world we now live in. Second, we look at the gospel. What is good news about the gospel in the contemporary world? Third, we look at the church, asking how we can be the body of Christ in this kind of world with this kind of message? Our approach will be to offer a brief critique in each area and then discuss some issues and implications for developing a more relevant missiology for the church in North America as we prepare to enter the twenty-first century.

Context — What Kind of World Do We Live In?

It seems that just about the time we figure out how to relate to the world as it is, the world changes to new expressions of life that challenge us to adapt once again. Applying the thesis that we are experiencing a fundamental shift in contemporary culture, we find three primary images that give shape to an emerging paradigm for mission — globalization, postmodernism, and radicalized modernity — each of which has its own particular consequences for relating the gospel and the church to the changing culture.

Globalization

One of the more familiar themes of social analysis in the past twenty years is the concept of globalization. In a spatial sense we have become a global village, where everyone must function within an emerging world culture and a globalized world economy. In a cognitive sense, we are made aware of this emerging global culture through modern communications media, which are able to take us around the world in a matter of minutes. As Max Stackhouse suggests in his work *Apologia,* globalization means that every local context must now be interpreted from a global perspective.

While globalization makes us aware that we are part of one world, it also introduces us to a diverse world of alternative cultural traditions. Globalization in this sense means that we are aware of pluralism. With pluralism, we lose the capacity for any one cultural tradition to claim that its perspective offers a superior tradition or viewpoint over others. The effects of globalized pluralism are noted well by Drucker in his book *The New Realities,* in which he describes how we have passed over a threshold into a world culture where we no longer have the rules to govern the political and economic realities we now face. In our globalized world, we are seeing the end of the world-conquering, cultural elitism that characterized Western nations during the past two hundred years. At the same time, we are experiencing the balkanization of cultural-ethnic traditions with the collapse of ideology as the binding force of the modern nation-state. This has been illustrated so poignantly in the past several years with the unraveling of the Communist bloc of nations.

We may be experiencing a new world order, but it is an order that has yet to find an adequate way to assign meaning to the pluralism we are encountering. A good illustration of this defect can be seen in Canada, with its 1982 charter that called for the acceptance of multiple cultural traditions in shaping the Canadian story. As Reginald Bibby points out in his book *Mosaic Madness,* the great experiment has institutionalized relativism, individualism, and pluralism, but it has notably failed to create any center to adjudicate differences. There is no longer a common story shared by Canadians. Canada's noble experiment may just be an early version of twenty-first-century Western history. The equivalent of Canada's experiment is being functionally experienced by almost every other Western country.

We are seeing in our day the end of cultural elitism. Globalization has brought to us a new awareness of our common humanity, but it has also introduced us to the reality of pluralism. The emerging paradigm of mission to North America must be able to respond to the realities of globalization and its accompanying pluralism. To do so, the following two issues will need to be addressed.

> 1.1. *De-ideologizing the gospel.* We will need to differentiate our Christian story from the national ideologies that have shaped our countries. For too long we have used "Christian" as a descriptive adjective to define our national identity. Cultural elitism and national ideology are obsolete as frameworks for interpreting the church's mission. In a globalized and pluralized culture, the gospel as good news needs to be good news in spite of any particular national ideology, not because of it. This has far-reaching implications for both our mission to North America and our participation in mission in the broader world.

> 1.2. *Developing a theology of unified diversity.* We will need to develop a theological and missiological perspective that can understand diversity as God's gift rather than as a problem to be solved. As we participate in a culturally diverse context, we need to let diversity serve as a doorway into a deeper and broader understanding of the nature and character of God. In a globalized world, no particular expression of the church has the privilege of locking the gospel into one cultural expression and calling it *the* biblical mission.

Postmodernism

Another theme of social analysis being brought to our attention is postmodernism. As Steven Connor points out in his book *Postmodernist Culture,* this concept grows out of the work of authors such as Lyotard, Derrida, Foucault, Habermas, Baudrillard, and Jameson, who in the 1970s and early 1980s began calling for a shift in our understanding of modern life. Building on early expressions of postmodern styles in art and architecture, these voices broadened the application of the deconstruction of metanarratives to every area of life. Their thesis is that any particular expression or narrative is relative, and that it is preferable to experience life in terms of eclecticism or as a collage of narratives.

This view toward the deconstruction of metanarratives and the decentering of absolutistic models is a direct challenge to the assumptions undergirding the modern project that grew out of the Enlightenment. The Enlightenment philosophers stressed rationalism, individualism, and progress and sought to remove the necessity of the God equation from the human story (note Francis Schaeffer's discussion in *Escape from Reason*). God's order and law were replaced by natural order and law, and the emerging modern paradigm turned to the scientific method as an epistemological substitute for revelation as the basis for understanding life.

As Paul Johnson masterfully develops in his work *The Birth of the Modern*, the Enlightenment assumptions gained institutional expression in shaping modern Western culture during the nineteenth century in the forms of the modern nation-state, market capitalism, and bureaucracy. The shaping power of these new forms was undergirded by the ever-expanding science-based technologies. The modern project carried with it the expectations of the capability of finding rational solutions to the core problems of life. For a time toward the end of the nineteenth century, it appeared that the modern project was achieving its aims. The realities of twentieth-century world wars and totalitarian regimes, however, ended this illusion on the European continent and in England. As David Harvey notes in his book *The Condition of Postmodernity*, the unraveling of Keynesian economics and capitalistic Fordism in the midst of the radical cultural shifts of the 1960s and 1970s has accomplished the equivalent collapsing of this illusion in North America.

The modern project has begun to unravel. The underlying assumptions of the Newtonian worldview and the Enlightenment are now being challenged by almost everyone. It is no longer defensible to hold a view that we can bring rational management to improving the quality of life through technological developments. The confident claim of objectivity in both reason and method, which undergirded the project for so many decades, has been shown to be but yet another paradigm of social construction subject to the same relativity of all social constructions. The insights of sociologist Peter Berger and Thomas Luckmann in their 1963 work *The Social Construction of Reality* have now become common knowledge as the character of our modern dilemma.

While the impact of globalization is pluralism, the impact of postmodernism is relativity of viewpoint. Some authors, however, have tried to resurrect an essential center for our culture, such as Daniel Bell in his work *The Coming of the Post-Industrial Society;* E. D. Hirsch, Jr., in his *Cultural*

Literacy; and Allan Bloom in *The Closing of the American Mind.* Bloom, for example, wants to reestablish a center around the classics in the Western tradition in the face of the now-pervasive relativism. In light of this relativism, however, he shares the same pessimism and nihilism discussed in the nineteenth century by Nietzsche, who first demonstrated our inability to construct a unified meaning by starting with the individual and reason.

Most postmodernists, however, fail to feel this nihilism. In its place, many enjoy the parody and playfulness inherent in their use of eclectic themes. Rather than feeling the despair of something lost in our inability to construct the rational whole or find the essential center, they celebrate the relativity of all viewpoints and the freedom this brings to individualized choices. The emerging paradigm of mission to North America must be able to respond to postmodernism and its accompanying relativity. To do so, the following two issues will need to be addressed.

2.1. *Building communities of faith.* The building of living communities that practice wholeness and healing will constitute one of the greatest missiological challenges for the church in the twenty-first century. The individualization of our lives in a postmodern world means that the task must begin with converting North American Christians to establish these types of Christian communities. Part of the difficulty of the challenge involves finding new expressions of such communities beyond the geographic-social and program-participation models we have relied on so heavily until now.

2.2. *Addressing fragmentation and brokenness.* Within the living communities of faith, we will need to concentrate on developing a message of wholeness and healing to a postmodern world characterized by fragmentation and brokenness. This message will need to be directed to both the church and the world. Our church practices can no longer assume that Christian people have their lives together. In our ministries we will need to develop more capacity to allow people to engage in a process of experiencing healing and living lives of holistic discipleship.

Radicalized Modernity

A third theme of contemporary Western culture is what might be labeled radicalized modernity, a term British sociologist Anthony Giddens uses in his book *The Consequences of Modernity.* Giddens argues that we are not so much living in a postmodern world as we are experiencing a fundamentally changed condition of modernity. He draws attention to the scope and pace of change that we are now experiencing in the third phase of late capitalism. The changing forms of technology now work at an increasing pace in shaping and reshaping our cultural forms.

Others have called attention to this aspect of modernity as well. It is the theme of Alvin Toffler in his three works *Future Shock* (1970), *The Third Wave* (1980), and *Power Shift* (1990). What is relevant is the compression of time required for one technology to displace another. Also significant is the impact of computer technology in shifting our work from developing more efficient machines to expanding our capacity to process information. We are now living in the information age. The literature on futurology and cultural trends by authors such as John Naisbitt in his books *Megatrends* (1983) and *Megatrends 2000* (1990) develops this theme of radicalized modernity. The focus is on the changing shape of culture stemming from technological developments.

Several processes at work within radicalized modernity are important for us to understand. These are discussed by authors such as those noted above, as well as by many postmodernist authors. First, there is the attention given to the multiplication of choices and fragmentation of meaning stimulated by our expanding and changing technology. Not only are individuals now free to create their own constructed meanings of life, but they also have available to them an endless array of choices for every aspect of life from which to select a particular collage of meaning.

Second, there is the attention given to surfaces and images as the primary conveyors of meaning in contemporary culture. Space and location both collapse in the rapidly changing context, and the need for depth and meaning is displaced. In addition, the electronic forms of communication maximize the use of images as substitutes for the actual realities. Depthless images now frame our impressions of reality rather than rational discourse, as pointed out by Neil Postman in *Amusing Ourselves to Death.*

Third, there is attention given to the nowness of life, the present tense as the only reality that exists. In the climate of radicalized modernity, time and history have collapsed in terms of shaping and controlling our interpretations. Both contingency and consequence have been lost in this new way of experiencing reality. With radicalized modernity we live in a constant process of change. The emerging paradigm of mission to North America must be able to respond to the consequences of radicalized modernity with its incessant change. To do so, the following two issues will need to be addressed.

3.1. *Constructing communities with a historical consciousness.* In a society shaped by radicalized modernity, we will need to develop an ability to help people reconstruct a conception of both time and place. The communities we create will need to have built into their very character an understanding that these particular persons in this particular place are part of an ongoing history being shaped by the God who was, who is, and who will be forever.

3.2. *Creating relevant forms.* We will need to develop a capacity to respond to the increasing pace of change, not by clinging to outdated forms as the substance of our faith, but by working to express the essential nature of God's truth in relevant terms. This will require the church to become much more proactive in processing change, moving beyond simply responding to the latest fad.

Gospel — How Do We Make Sense of the Good News Message in This Kind of World?

The second area we examine in this study concerns the gospel. How are we to understand God's special communication to us that we have contained in the Bible, and how are we to offer the message of this communication as good news to a pluralized, relativized, and ever-changing North American context? This part will consider three themes: the post-ness of theological studies, the rise of narrative theology, and the wider rationality of the biblical story.

The Post-ness of Theological Studies

One of the more dramatic developments in recent years in biblical and theology studies is the growing recognition of the obsolescence of the historical-critical method as an adequate paradigm for understanding the Bible. There is an increased awareness that the whole modern project's approach to the Bible was built on a faulty assumption of treating the text as object. Consistent with the assumptions of the modern project, the quest of biblical studies focused on understanding the true historical context that gave birth to the final form of the text, and on clarifying the one univocal meaning that the text conveyed in this final form.

As Sandra Schneiders points out in her article entitled "Does the Bible Have a Postmodern Message?" one problem with this approach was that the more we seemed to come to an understanding of what the text really meant, the further the text came to be removed from the people by being locked in the exclusive domain of the scholars. Building on the work of Brevard Childs, who sought to understand the shape of the canon, and James Sanders, who sought to understand the process of the canon, numerous biblical scholars such as Walter Wink, James Smart, and Walter Brueggemann have all issued the same declaration that the focus of the critical apparatus was misdirected. They call instead for a serious treatment of the Bible on its own terms, which translates into a rediscovery of its essential narrative character.

It is important to point out the epistemological revisions that are required in dealing with a narrative approach to the Bible. This has been especially emphasized in the work of Lesslie Newbigin, who builds on the work of sociologist Michael Polanyi. In order to approach the Bible in this manner, one has to understand three essential things: (1) it is a product of a believing community who shared a common language, (2) there is a shared tradition into which new adherents are incorporated, and (3) certain faith commitments are necessary to understand its meaning. Enlightenment assumptions moved in the opposite direction on all three of these points, but it is becoming increasingly clear that such epistemological requirements shape the character of all human knowledge. This is true whether one is dealing with scientific knowledge or religious knowledge.

Accompanying the biblical scholars in signaling the end of the hegemony of historical criticism in shaping our understanding of the Bible are a growing number of theologians. The foundation was laid by Hans Frei in his seminal work *The Eclipse of Biblical Narrative,* which critiqued the inadequacy of eighteenth- and nineteenth-century hermeneutics. Building on this work, others like George Lindbeck, Alasdair MacIntyre, Stanley Hauerwas, and Gregory Jones have published similar expressions of the thesis that we need to take the Bible on its own terms in shaping our theological understandings.

The issue of theological interpretation has been further extended by

Thomas Oden in his three-volume systematic theology, which makes the point that the universally accepted early church fathers and ecumenical creeds need to set the framework for our understanding and the shaping of theology in our day. All of these interpretive streams share the point that in the face of the collapse of the Enlightenment-shaped epistemology, we need to take the Bible seriously on its own terms. What is intriguing in our day is that just about the time some evangelicals, such as Clark Pinnock in his book *Tracking the Maze,* are getting a little more comfortable with the use of historical criticism as an interpretative scheme, those who represent streams that pioneered its development are calling for a postcritical approach to the Bible.

In another sense, however, there is a need for a post-ness to theological studies besides the postcritical development in the past few decades. This is the need to develop a post-ness to the rational-literal approach employed by many fundamentalists and conservatives. The whole enterprise of trying to develop a rational-literal defense for the Bible, such that it can stand on its own as an objective referent in the face of all challenges, fails on the same basis as historical criticism. It buys into the same Enlightenment assumptions of rationality and objectivity, with the radical division between subject and object. It tries to beat the opponents on their own turf but fails to recognize that the opponents control the rules of the game. This whole enterprise is an interpretive cul-de-sac.

If we are going to move forward in biblical and theological studies, we need to take a fresh look at the Bible. We will need to free ourselves of the residual effects of the Enlightenment assumptions and learn to reenter the Bible on its own terms. The emerging paradigm of mission to North America must be able to respond to the post-ness of biblical and theological studies and find renewed perspectives within the biblical narrative. To do so, the following two issues will need to be addressed.

> 4.1. *Renegotiating historic models of interpretation.* We must face up to the inadequate or faulty epistemologies that stand behind so many of our models of interpretation, which we have accepted as normative. We must have the courage to reenter the biblical story on its own terms and let it once more reshape our story. This will require us to risk losing some of the sureness of our interpretations if we are to experience the fullness of God's message for us. Reformation paradigms, scholastic-styled confessions, and modernist theological schemes will all need to be placed on the table for renegotiation, both in categories and in method.

4.2. *Developing a theological method of process.* The character of human knowledge is emergent. We continue to grow in our understanding of what God has revealed to us. In this regard, we will need to develop a method of approaching our understanding of the Bible as an emergent process. This development of a theological method of process will need to be carefully distinguished, however, from the approach of process theology; which tends to eclipse biblical categories in favor of contemporary ones.

The Rediscovery of Narrative

One of the more substantive developments in human studies the past several decades has been the shift away from the radical individualism rooted in Enlightenment thinking, toward a social understanding of life in context and text. This movement gained direction earlier in this century from the work of cultural anthropologists who sought to identify common characteristics to be found in all cultures. It was further developed by mid-century by the work of the structural-functional sociologists who sought to clarify the essential principles operating within every social system. This approach of studying the social system as a whole decentered the individual from a privileged position. It shifted attention away from individual rationality as the basis of choice, toward socially constructed reality as the primary influence that shapes the formation of individuals within society.

This socially constructed aspect of our social systems has come to be discussed in terms of narrative. Narratives represent the basic belief systems or legitimizing myths that we adopt or construct to give meaning and direction to our lives. Almost everyone today speaks to the human condition from the perspective of narrative, although the poststructuralists have used critical theory to posit conflict as the essential character of social life in contrast to the harmony implied in the structural-functional model, and the postmodernists have deconstructed both of these positions as illegitimate efforts to impose metanarratives on a pluralistic social order. But all agree that life is narrative in character. As such, we participate in the shaping of our own narrative story as we live within a social context, and this context in turn is guided by various narratives that give it meaning and direction.

The challenge of trying to let the Bible speak on its own terms has renewed our focus on the essential narrative character of the biblical materials. The task before us is to let the biblical story shape and reshape our own story. In this regard, the approach of biblical studies and theological interpretation is to provide a representative and meaningful understanding of the biblical narrative. This approach, as noted in the previous section, represents a fundamental shift away from treating the text in an objective and rational manner through the use of critical studies.

The natural use of Scripture, as Lindbeck suggests, is imaginative and behavioral as well as cognitive. The purpose of a narrative approach to the Bible and theological understanding means that we must move from ideology to engagement, from objective principles to reflective participation, and from cultural Christianity to alternative Christian community, as Schneiders has pointed out. In carrying out a narrative approach, our task is threefold: (1) to reenter the biblical story on its own terms, (2) to listen to this story through the historic interpretation of the Christian tradition, and (3) to let this story and reinterpretation shape or reshape our own story.

The third aspect is what often causes the rub, for every story by its nature is culturally bound, and every story affects the reading of the biblical story. As David Bosch makes clear in his chapter "The Emergence of a Postmodern Paradigm" in his *Transforming Mission,* this means that there is a relative aspect to understanding the true truth of God's self-communication to us. While we may properly profess that we understand the truth of the biblical story in our theological expressions of it, we must forgo our arrogance of saying that we have understood or expressed this truth in all of its fullness or intent. All reality is interpreted reality. In this regard, it is also time for us to reckon with the fact that there are limits in getting to the meaning of the narrative text by reading it through the lens of our constructed confessions. This relative nature of our formulations of truth requires us to leave the process open for our further understanding of the meaning and intent of the biblical story as we let it reshape our own story.

In moving from absolute, objective categories of understanding and expressing truth in both our biblical studies and our theology, the alternatives available to us are not just emergent process or empty relativism, as so many fear. What we have is a true understanding of God's eternal truth in which we are still growing in our comprehension and expression of its intent and meaning. While losing the pride of being absolute, we gain the privilege of fresh insight into both the text and our context. The emerging paradigm of mission to North America must be able to help the church develop a narrative approach both to the Bible and to its own story. To do so, the following two issues will need to be addressed.

> 5.1. *Dealing with a multitude of stories.* We must address the problem of trying to develop a renewed focus on a Christian story in North America by incorporating multiple Christian stories within the growing diversity of cultural traditions. We will need to develop more capacity for hearing the truths of the text through the stories of others. This will help us both better understand the text and also grow in unity with others in shaping a renewed Christian story.
>
> 5.2. *Rediscovering God's narrative.* We will have to develop fresh and creative methods for helping a present-tense generation come to appreciate the historical character of life as presented to us in God's narrative. While the created soul may hunger for a sense of context, place, and meaning, the cultural dynamics of radicalized individualism with its endless succession of "nows" works against our presentation of the good news of God's narrative as a text rooted in time/space history.

The Wider Rationality

The third aspect of our analysis of the gospel concerns the convincing character of the biblical narrative. In *Foolishness to the Greeks,* Newbigin speaks of this as the wider rationality of the Bible. He suggests that this wider rationality includes both a creation design and a purposeful direction to history. The world is God's creation, and the Bible tells us about the order and purpose God intends for that creation. At first blush this approach sounds like some type of reaffirmation of the various natural-theology arguments for God as postulated by Aquinas. But Newbigin takes the analysis a different direction. His purpose is not to try to prove the existence of God but to let God prove himself to contemporary persons through letting the biblical story speak on its own terms. The key is for this demonstration of God's reality to be lodged in a living community of his believers.

In his book *Christian Belief in a Postmodern World,* Diogenes Allen takes this approach a step further. Allen, like Newbigin, argues that the Bible offers a wider rationality to persons shaped by the postmodern culture, but he goes on to suggest that persons coming from this culture who are rational will be seekers. For Allen, it is rational to be a seeker in the face of the pervasive fragmentation and relativism of contemporary culture. But the problem for the church is that it has failed to shift adequately from a Newtonian worldview. It is still being intimidated by modernity and is timid in the face of the secular. It is time to recognize that many contemporary secular persons accept the reality of the spiritual within their secular worldview. This offers a new opportunity for the church to let the message of the Bible address persons shaped by contemporary culture. George Hunter's book *How to Reach Secular People* moves in this direction, although more work needs to be done in addressing the spiritual dimension of postmodern secularity.

As noted above, the wider rationality must function as an expression of the living community of God's people. It is in the community context of listening again to the biblical story that the wider rationality takes on meaning, both for the believer and for the seeker. The truths of the wider rationality must be present within the story of the community, if they are to be self-evident within the biblical story. These are dynamically interrelated aspects of coming to understand and articulate the self-communication of God for the entire human family.

This approach calls for the church to be a community that shares several characteristics. It must be a community that is shaped by the gospel story. It must be a community that can tell its own story in light of the gospel story. And it must be a community that proactively allows for its understanding of God's self-communication to grow in both its meaning and intent. The emerging paradigm of mission to North America must be able to develop a community context that can offer the wholeness of the gospel to rational seekers and as well as broken persons. To do so, the following two issues will need to be addressed.

> 6.1. *Developing confidence in the wider rationality.* We will need to help the church rediscover the power of the Bible in shaping the life of the community and individuals within the community. As we work toward helping the church become a living community of God's people that takes the Bible on its own terms, we need to be aware of the transforming power the wider rationality has under the influence of the Holy Spirit in changing lifestyle commitments.

> 6.2. *Developing skills in the wider rationality.* We will need to help the church develop skills in letting the Bible speak on its own terms in

relating to unchurched persons shaped by contemporary culture. This must include helping church members develop both relationship styles and ministry structures that can place the Bible meaningfully in front of secular persons. The present models of relationship-based and seeker-service evangelism are just an initial foray into the task of transforming congregations from local churches to mission outposts.

Church — How Do We Live as God's People in This Kind of World?

The third issue that we need to address deals with the church. How are we to be the church in a pluralized and relativized culture that has marginalized many of our institutions, ghettoized much of our congregational life, and privatized the meaning of our gospel? This section will be developed along the following three lines of discussion: the reality of the post-Christian context, the changing face of denominationalism, and the necessity of repositioning the church in the contemporary context.

The Post-Christian Context

Just as the culture can be described in one sense as postmodern, and our approach to the Bible as postcritical, so also the relationship of the church to contemporary North American culture can be described as post-Christian. As noted in an earlier section, we are experiencing the end of our particular version of Christendom. The post-Christian reality of contemporary culture means that the church no longer has a privileged position and can no longer expect to receive preferential treatment. It is becoming just one more truth claim in the midst of a plurality of alternative truth claims, all of which are seen as relative.

While the history of the entire West can be discussed in terms of the end of Christendom and the collapse of Christian culture, there are different expressions of this development within the West. Secularity has presented a different face in confronting the church's effort to shape a Christian culture. A thesis developed by Martin Marty in *The Modern Schism* suggests that in continental Europe the approach of modernity was to introduce an "utter secularity" that sought to collapse the Christian paradigm head-on. In England the approach was a "mere secularity" that sought to domesticate the church with a legitimate but only partial role in society. In the United States the approach was a "controlled secularity" that sought to draw a line between the secular state and the work of the church. In Canada we find a hybrid mixture between English mere secularity and American controlled secularity.

The great constitutional compromise of the separation of church and state in America left the church free to offer a set of Christian values as a normative guide for the secular state. As Martin Marty notes in *Righteous Empire*, most churches in the nineteenth century accepted it as their responsibility to join the crusade of trying to impregnate culture with Christian values. This project was originally the competitive enterprise of the expanding Protestant denominations. The voluntaristic principle of organization, a culture-shaped gospel of individual morality, and a biblical theism in public discourse all worked to create an emerging Christian culture in the United States throughout the 1800s. According to Webster Grant's *Church in the Canadian Era*, a similar story emerged in Canada after confederation in 1867. A public morality of shoulds and oughts, based on the Bible's teachings, came to express the success of the Protestant project in both the United States and in Canada by the end of the century.

By the end of the nineteenth century, however, this project broadened in the United States to include the participation of Catholics and Jews. From that time down to the 1960s, one had to speak of the Judeo-Christian heritage, which shaped the basic values of our society. The Canadian story unfolded mostly as a Protestant story for all the provinces except Quebec. During the 1960s and 1970s, however, North American culture went through a transition of staggering dimensions, impacting the Christian culture that had been shaped by the churches for over 150 years. As Wade Roof and William McKinney note in their work *American Mainline Religion*, the counterculture collapsed the public version of the shoulds and oughts of the historic Christian culture and of its stepchild, civil religion. Robert Wuthnow, in *The Restructuring of American Religion*, notes that this collapse led to a substantial restructuring of both denominational systems and parachurch organizations. The Canadian equivalent of the story is told by Reginald Bibby in *Fragmented Gods* and by Arnell Motz in *Reclaiming a Nation*, which describe the nominalization of Canadian Christians, the rise of a consumer approach for the purchasing of the rites of passage, and the minority status of the evangelical churches.

The message that we are now living in post-Christian culture was well stated by Kennon Callahan in his book *Effective Church Leadership*, where he poignantly makes three observations: "The day of the professional minister is over. The day of the missionary pastor has come. . . . The day of the churched culture is over. The day of the mission field has come. . . . The day of the local church is over. The day of the mission outpost has come" (3, 13, 22). Rapidly declining are the days of privileged position and preferential treatment. The church now finds itself increasingly two steps removed from persons shaped by the contemporary culture. The church no longer shares a common language with these persons, and it finds itself living with forms that for the most part have been either marginalized or privatized in meaning. The emerging paradigm of mission to North America must be able to address the issue of helping the church develop a new self-understanding of its identity and role. To do so, the following two issues will need to be addressed.

> 7.1. *Accepting a changed status.* The church in North America for the most part has developed expectations of success and cultural status, either directly through participation in our culture or through standing in the shadow of those who led the way. We need to adjust this self-concept of the church to one that is able to accept a minority status and face cultural indifference. We will need to shake off the remaining vestiges of a Christendom perspective that expects the world to take the church seriously, refocusing our attention to how we should now seek out the world.

> 7.2. *Developing a public theology.* As we learn once more to seek out the world, we will need to help the church redevelop a public theology that can relate the truths of the Bible and the wider rationality to the social order. The gospel, as both Newbigin and Hauerwas remind us, is public by nature. But this task must be done without falling subject to the old Christendom expectations of culture conversion. This will be a difficult task for those churches that practiced the trade of culture caretaking, as well as for those churches that practiced a personal and privatized version of the gospel. Neither model is viable any longer in the face of the collapse of Christian culture.

The Changing Face of Denominationalism

As Martin Marty has pointed out in his *Righteous Empire*, denominationalism is the one great contribution that North America has made to the ecclesiastical development of the church. After immigrating to North America, members of the state churches and sectarian movements of Europe adopted an entirely new structure in the milieu of the American colonies. The denominational principle rooted in democratic individualism was institutionalized in America following the Revolutionary War, and in Canada following confederation in 1867. This new form of church proved to be a growth industry on the American frontier, expanding from an original 36 denominations in 1800 to over 400 today. In Canada there has been a somewhat different history, with various mergers and fewer new denominations, although the denominational principle has been the basic form of church life there as well, with 125 groups reported in Jacquet's 1990 *Yearbook of American and Canadian Churches.*

One key to understanding denominations is that a particular denomination tends to define itself in terms of differences over against other denominations. While many were shaped by the social, cultural, or ethnic expressions of a specific tradition, others grew out of efforts to keep the church pure through separating from a church body perceived to be going astray. The expansion of the whole enterprise has been an inwardly focused activity that accepted the denominational context as normative. The defining character was over against one another rather than over against the world.

During the past two hundred years, it was unnecessary for the church to use the world as the basis of defining denominational identity. This was because the North American context accepted and promoted the legitimacy of the Christian enterprise. The denominational churches did not have to wrestle with their core identity over against a hostile or indifferent world. As Richard Neuhaus notes in *The Believable Futures of American Protestantism* and as Donald Posterski clarifies in *Reinventing Evangelism,* this situation has changed dramatically in the past few decades in both the United States and Canada. Churches now find themselves increasingly in foreign territory. Complicating the problem of denominational identity is the loss of denominational loyalty over the past three decades. Members no longer feel attached primarily to a denomination as an institution of personal meaning. They are increasingly identifying with local congregations that meet their needs or with charismatic leaders who can hold their attention.

On the one hand, the denominational scheme is coming apart. Declining levels of identity and loyalty at the grassroots level are forcing changes at the denominational level as membership and income both decline. Although the denominational, institutional form of the church will continue to exist for decades to come, its structures and essential logic will undergo significant restructuring. On the other hand, the continued drift toward the development of large, independent community churches, with their focus on user-friendly, needs-oriented, market-driven models described by George Barna in *User Friendly Churches,* is in need of careful critique. While celebrating their contextual relevance, we need to be careful that we are committed in using these approaches to maintaining the integrity of both the gospel and the Christian community. These churches may just be the last version of the Christian success story within the collapsing paradigm of modernity and Christian-shaped culture.

We need to do some serious thinking about ecclesiology. The mission theology developed in the past few decades, which understands the local church in its place as the locus of mission, needs to be augmented by an understanding of the visible unity of the church in its place. Both of these issues have yet to be seriously addressed in the North American context. Denominations will remain as a feature in the twenty-first century, but the forms as we know them today will undergo dramatic changes. The emerging paradigm of mission to North America must be able to address the issues of denominational fragmentation and institutional obsolescence. To do so, the following two issues will need to be addressed.

8.1. *Rethinking the principle of denominationalism.* As we learn to reenter the biblical story in reshaping our story, we will need to place the denomination principle on the table for discussion in light of the biblical requirements for ecclesiology. In this type of discussion, the concept of diverse forms does not need to be an issue so much as our historic practice of defining our identity over against each other, rather than over against the world. We will need to develop an understanding of the purpose of our church structures from this changed perspective.

8.2. *Practicing the principle of unity.* We will also need to find ways to help churches experience and express the principle of unity in mission in our place. This does not necessarily require the merging of structures, but it will require that we learn to celebrate what we share in common over those things that divide us. Learning to present a united front to a fragmented world will be essential if the wider rationality of the gospel is to have its maximum impact.

Repositioning the Church

In light of the changes that have taken place in the broader culture, and in light of the collapse of Christian culture, the church is in need of a fundamental repositioning of its life and ministry in the North American context. Part of this repositioning involves addressing the marginalizing of those churches that saw their primarily role as shaping culture. This includes the ethnic-based churches that accepted a view of culture transformation but practiced this only within their own subculture. Another part of this repositioning involves addressing the trivializing of the gospel by those churches that adopted the modern view that faith is only a personal and private matter.

A number of different images have been suggested in the past few years by different authors to address this task of repositioning the church. Stanley Hauerwas and William Willimon, coming from the United Methodist tradition, suggest in a popular book that the image of "resident alien" provides a viable way for the church to disengage from the fading illusions of Christendom. In his *Disciplines of Readiness,* Walter Brueggeman suggests the image of exile in his discussion of the work of the Presbyterian Church, noting that this denomination now finds itself like a stranger in a foreign land. Both of these images are working from the premise that the church has been too involved in trying to shape a cultural Christianity and now must disengage in order to rediscover its own identity and mission.

Other denominations, however, have taken a different approach to the broader culture. While being able to stand in the shadow of mainline denominations that sought to shape Christian culture, they maintained a fairly separatistic attitude toward the broader culture. Some operated by focusing only on trying to shape a Christian subculture, while others adopted an individualistic view of salvation and spirituality as the center of God's work in the world. Callahan's image of the church as mission outpost, or Hunsberger's view of the church as town meeting, is probably more appropriate for churches in this stream. They need to develop both a self-conscious commitment to engage the world and a self-conscious commitment to a gospel that has a public theology to address the issues of life.

Whatever direction a church is moving, whether from the center to being marginalized, or from the shadow to being privatized, the challenge for repositioning remains the same. The missiological challenge is to develop an identity for the church that looks first to God and his kingdom, and second to the world and its present condition. Howard Snyder's book *Models of the Kingdom* is a helpful tool for furthering this reflection. Only through focusing on the broader redemptive work of God in the world can we hope to move past our denominational tribalism and the present marginalizing and privatizing of the faith taking place. The emerging paradigm of mission to North America must be able to address the issue of the repositioning of the church in a dramatically changed context. To do so, the following two issues will need to be addressed.

9.1. *Developing a kingdom-oriented ecclesiology.* The purpose and structure of the typical North American church was developed around a church-centered focus rather than a mission-centered theology. We will need to rethink our North American ecclesiology and the role of the church in the world from the perspective of the *missio Dei.* We need to develop a mission-shaped ecclesiology that takes seriously the kingdom of God and God's work in the world.

9.2. *Developing alternative church styles.* The diverse contexts and the multiple stories of North American churches mean that a wide variety of repositioning styles will be required in the post-Christian culture. We will need to develop a missiological approach that can appreciate this diversity both within and between the various denominations. These alternative forms will also require churches to develop adaptive approaches to church governance in the twenty-first century with flexible church orders.

Conclusion

This survey has attempted to cover a broad landscape in trying to identify the missiological issues facing the church in North America as we reach the end of the twentieth century. We began this survey with the important question that Lesslie Newbigin raised in his book *Foolishness to the Greeks:* Can the West be converted? The answer suggested was that if we were to take this task seriously, it would require that we develop a paradigm of mission to North America that is fundamentally different from the operational missiologies of denomination building, culture caretaking, privatized faith, church renewal, church growth, and church effectiveness that have been or are now at work. We noted that such a missiology would have to incorporate into its formulation a response to the changes taking place in the North American context, in our understanding of the gospel, and in our practice of the church.

In shaping such a missiology, this essay has suggested some eighteen issues that a twenty-first-century missiology to North America would need to address within the areas of context, the gospel, and the church This list of issues is intended as a basis for further reflection and discussion. Much work remains to be done in developing our analysis and sharpening the focus of issues such as these as we seek to re-vision the church in North America for the twenty-first century. Because of the complex and interrelated nature of many of these issues, it is likely that such work will require us to use a wide variety of disciplines and multiple levels of analysis as we pursue the task. In this regard, it is likely that it will also require us to function in a much more collaborative manner by working together in various networks. What these networks will look like remains to be seen, but it does appear that they are now beginning to emerge.

Bibliography

Allen, Diogenes. *Christian Belief in a Postmodern World.* Louisville: Westminster/John Knox Press, 1989.

Anderson, Walter T. *Reality Isn't What It Used to Be.* San Francisco: Harper & Row, 1990.

Barbour, Ian. *Religion in an Age of Science.* San Francisco: Harper & Row, 1990.

Barna, George. *User Friendly Churches.* Ventura, CA: Regal Books, 1991.

Bell, Daniel. *The Coming of the Post-Industrial Society.* New York: Basic Books, 1973.

Berger, Peter, and Thomas Luckmann. *The Social Construction of Reality.* New York: Doubleday, 1963.

Bibby, Reginald W. *Fragmented Gods.* Toronto: Irwin Publishing, 1987.

———. *Mosaic Madness: Pluralism without a Cause.* Toronto: Stoddart Publishing, 1990.

Bloom, Allan. *The Closing of the American Mind.* New York: Simon & Schuster, 1987.

Bosch, David J. *Transforming Mission: Paradigm Shifts in Theology of Mission.* Maryknoll, NY: Orbis Books, 1991.

Brueggemann, Walter. *The Creative Word: Canon as a Model for Biblical Education.* Philadelphia: Fortress Press, 1982.

———. *Disciplines of Readiness.* Occasional Paper no. 1. Louisville: Theology and Worship Unit, Presbyterian Church (U.S.A.).

Burnham, Frederic B., ed. *Postmodern Theology: Christian Faith in a Pluralist World.* San Francisco: Harper & Row, 1989.

Callahan, Kennon L. *Effective Church Leadership: Building on the Twelve Keys.* San Francisco: Harper & Row, 1990.

Childs, Brevard S. *Introduction to the Old Testament as Scripture.* Philadelphia: Fortress Press, 1979.

Connor, Steven. *Postmodern Culture.* Cambridge, MA: Basil Blackwell, 1989.

Drucker, Peter. *The New Realities.* New York: Harper & Row, 1989.

Frei, Hans W. *The Eclipse of Biblical Narrative.* New Haven: Yale University Press, 1974.

Giddens, Anthony. *The Consequences of Modernity.* Stanford, CA: Stanford University Press, 1990.

Grant, John Webster. *The Church in the Canadian Era.* Toronto: McGraw-Hill Ryerson, 1972.

Harvey, David. *The Condition of Postmodernity.* Cambridge, MA: Basil Blackwell, 1989.

Hauerwas, Stanley. *After Christendom?* Nashville: Abingdon Press, 1991.

Hauerwas, Stanley, and Gregory L. Jones, eds. *Why Narrative?* Grand Rapids: Eerdmans, 1989.

Hauerwas, Stanley, and William H. Willimon. *Resident Aliens: Life in the Christian Colony.* Nashville: Abingdon Press, 1989.

Hawking, Stephen W. *A Brief History of Time.* New York: Bantam Books, 1988.

Hirsch, E. D., Jr. *Cultural Literacy.* Boston: Houghton Mifflin, 1987.

Hunsberger, George R. "The Newbigin Gauntlet: Developing a Missiology for North America." *Missiology* 19, no. 4 (October 1991): 391–408.

Hunter, George G., III. *How to Reach Secular People.* Nashville: Abingdon Press, 1992.

Jacquet, Constant H., Jr. *Yearbook of American and Canadian Churches.* Nashville: Abingdon Press, 1990.

Johnson, Paul. *The Birth of the Modern.* New York: Harper Collins Publishers, 1991.

Kuhn, Thomas R. *The Structure of Scientific Revolutions.* 2d rev. ed. Chicago: University of Chicago Press, 1970.

Lindbeck, George. *The Nature of Doctrine.* Philadelphia: Westminster Press, 1984.

MacIntyre, Alasdair. "The Virtues, the Unity of a Human Life, and the Concept of Tradition." In *Why Narrative?* edited by Stanley Hauerwas and Gregory L. Jones. Grand Rapids: Eerdmans, 1989.

Marty, Martin E. *The Modern Schism.* New York: Harper & Row, 1969.

———. *Righteous Empire: The Protestant Experience in America.* New York: Harper & Row, 1970.

Motz, Arnell, ed. *Reclaiming a Nation.* Richmond, B.C.: Church Leadership Library, 1990.

Naisbett, John, and Patricia Aburdene. *Megatrends.* New York: Warner Books, 1982.

———. *Megatrends 2000.* New York: Wm. Morran, 1990.

Neuhaus, Richard John, ed. *The Believable Futures of American Protestantism.* Grand Rapids: Eerdmans, 1988.

Newbigin, Lesslie. *Foolishness to the Greeks: The Gospel and Western Culture.* Grand Rapids: Eerdmans, 1986.

———. *The Gospel in a Pluralist Society.* Grand Rapids: Eerdmans, 1989.

Oden, Thomas C. *Systematic Theology.* 3 vols. San Francisco: Harper & Row, 1987–91.

Pinnock, Clark H. *Tracking the Maze.* San Francisco: Harper & Row, 1990.

Polanyi, Michael. *Personal Knowledge: Towards a Post-Critical Philosophy.* Chicago: University of Chicago Press, 1958.

Posterski, Donald C. *Reinventing Evangelism: New Strategies for Presenting Christ in Today's World.* Downers Grove, IL: InterVarsity Press, 1989.

Postman, Neil. *Amusing Ourselves to Death.* New York: Penguin Books, 1985.

Roof, Wade Clark, and William McKinney. *American Mainline Religion: Its Changing Shape and Future.* New Brunswick, NJ: Rutgers University Press, 1987.

Sanders, James A. *Torah and Canon.* Philadelphia: Fortress Press, 1972.

Schaeffer, Francis A. *Escape from Reason.* Downers Grove, IL: Inter-Varsity Press, 1968.

Schneiders, Sandra M. "Does the Bible Have a Postmodern Message?" In *Postmodern Theology,* edited by Frederic B. Burnham. San Francisco: Harper & Row, 1989.

Smart, James D. *The Strange Silence of the Bible in the Church.* Philadelphia: Westminster Press, 1970.

Snyder, Howard A. *Models of the Kingdom.* Nashville: Abingdon Press, 1991.

Stackhouse, Max L. *Apologia.* Grand Rapids: Eerdmans, 1988.

Toffler, Alvin. *Future Shock.* New York: Bantam Books, 1970.

———. *Power Shift.* New York: Bantam Books, 1990.

———. *The Third Wave.* New York: Bantam Books, 1980.

Wink, Walter. *The Bible in Human Transformation.* Philadelphia: Fortress Press, 1972.

Wuthnow, Robert. *The Restructuring of American Religion.* Princeton: Princeton University Press, 1988.

PART II

ASSESSING OUR CULTURE

Culture consists of the integrated systems of beliefs, values, and behaviors held by a people. Culture frames our human existence. We cannot know ourselves apart from possessing a particular perspective. It is important to note that God takes culture seriously. This is clear through the creation of the world and the instructions God gave to human persons created to live in it, instructions regarding how to develop a social order and build their physical environment. This interaction between human society and the physical world represents the creation of what we think of as culture.

God takes seriously not only culture in general but also each particular culture. This reality is most clearly demonstrated in the incarnation of Jesus Christ as he entered time/space history within a particular culture for the purpose of accomplishing a universally applicable redemption.

The people of God live within particular cultural contexts and have a dual responsibility in carrying out their participation in God's redemptive work in the world. First, they must try to understand God's self-communication that is mediated through the Bible. This is a dynamic task because of the diversity in the cultural character of the Bible's record and the influence of one's own culture in understanding the culturally mediated message of the Bible. (The next part of this book addresses issues associated with this task.)

Second, God's people must communicate the truthful reality of God's message to persons living within particular cultural contexts. This task makes it imperative that God's people understand the culture within which they live and minister. There is a critical need at the present time for the churches of North America to do so, gaining a careful reading of the culture in which we are located and by which our world is shaped. For too long, churches in this context have either ignored the shaping influence of culture or have tried to develop a mutually supportive relationship between the church and the culture. Many are now beginning to realize the importance of rethinking the relationship of the church to its own cultural setting. This task requires the use of a missiological way of reading and understanding the context. While such an approach has been common in world mission for many years, it is now being increasingly used to address the North American context.

The six essays in this part introduce the reader to this discussion. Although written as separate articles, they are complementary in their approach and analysis. A general overview of the new situation facing the church in North American culture is provided by Craig Van Gelder in "A Great New Fact of Our Day: America as Mission Field." His basic thesis is that the modern project developed through decades of Enlightenment-based culture has become uncentered in the midst of the emergence of a postmodern culture. In addition, the churched culture that accompanied the development of the modern project is rapidly eroding. This is forcing the church to rethink its identity and purpose within a new landscape. He draws the conclusion that America must now be seen as a mission field.

Wilbert Shenk, in "The Culture of Modernity as a Missionary Challenge," builds on the thesis introduced by Van Gelder by noting how the church was itself shaped by the emerging character of modernity. He points out the way that many of the basic assumptions of the modern mission movement bought into key premises of Enlightenment-based culture. Using some historical examples from earlier in this century, Shenk points out the importance of bringing a missiological critique to our present understanding of the church and our culture. Such a critique must be rooted in a biblical understanding both of the reign of God within the world and of the foundation of God's redemptive work within the incarnation of Jesus Christ.

To give a full critique to the shaping character of modernity on the church, one needs to understand something of the historical development of this particular culture. The flow of this development and something of its complexity are summarized in an essay by Christopher Kaiser entitled "From Biblical Secularity to Modern Secularism: Historical Aspects and

Stages." He notes with keen insight the difference between a biblical understanding of secular life that allows for God to intervene within the created world and modernity's development of a secularism that cancels out the god-hypothesis. Kaiser's basic purpose is to provide the reader with a working model to understand the development of this difference over the past four hundred years. His model examines six different sociocultural aspects of life within five different stages that have led to the formation of modern secularism.

Kaiser's analysis brings into focus the importance of grasping the shaping influence of modernity in regard to our understanding of the place and work of the church within our culture. However, it is increasingly being noted by a variety of authors that yet another shift is taking place today toward what is being labeled the postmodern condition. Craig Van Gelder, in "Mission in the Emerging Postmodern Condition," offers an introduction to help understand this shift. His essay identifies some of the cultural changes that have led to the postmodern condition, discusses some of the characteristics that are often associated with it, and offers suggestions regarding how the gospel and church must function if they are to address this new cultural context.

It is one thing to say that the church must critique its cultural context and quite another to actually conduct such a critique. Both modern and postmodern contexts are critiqued in an article by Paul Hiebert entitled "The Gospel in Our Culture: Methods of Social and Cultural Analysis." What is most helpful about his approach is the incorporation of tools and perspectives from the social sciences, especially the discipline of anthropology, for use in his analyses. This article brings together both a general approach for conducting a critique of one's culture and a suggestive interpretation of modernity and the postmodern condition.

Sound missiological critique of a cultural context requires the careful use of analytic tools. In its development of an approach for understanding culture, the field of missiology has drawn heavily from the methodological tools of the social sciences while attempting to avoid the incorporation of unbiblical assumptions sometimes imbedded in them. Complementing the work of Hiebert, but going further to identify a working model for conducting a specific cultural analysis, is an essay by the late David Scotchmer entitled "Symbols Become Us: Toward a Missional Encounter with Our Culture through Symbolic Analysis." Using the work of anthropologists Geertz and Ortner to construct his overall framework, Scotchmer provides a working model for exegeting a particular cultural context. Central to his model is the importance of understanding the function and meaning of symbols.

These six essays, taken together, provide the reader with a helpful introduction to the missiological task of assessing our present North American culture in both its modern and postmodern expressions. Of central concern to the authors of all of these articles is the need to critique more carefully the shaping influence that our culture has had and is having in our understanding of the gospel and our definition of the purpose and work of the church. If the churches of North America are to engage in a missionary encounter with our culture, it will require them to learn skills enabling them to engage in the task of carefully exegeting the cultural context.

A Great New Fact of Our Day: America as Mission Field

CRAIG VAN GELDER

It comes to us in different images and names, but the expressions are describing a common reality. One expression comes from a variety of secular authors. Allan Bloom refers to it as a pervasive relativism that has leveled the social order and collapsed the role of a mediating history. Peter Drucker refers to it as "new realities," a condition where modern Western nations now lack the rules to govern the emerging economic and political order. Alvin Toffler, who introduced the metaphors of future shock and the third wave, builds on these ideas with the concept that a major "power shift" is now under way in the world order. David Harvey identifies it as a shift to a postmodern world with the demise of the Enlightenment-based modern project. Steven Connor builds on this concept of postmodernity, noting that deconstruction has collapsed the grand narrative for our society.[1]

These secular writers are not alone, however, in noting that something fundamental has shifted within our American culture in the past several decades. They are joined by a variety of religious authors. Wade Clark Roof and William McKinney note that the role of mainline denominations has

1. Allan Bloom, *The Closing of the American Mind* (New York: Simon & Schuster, 1987); Peter F. Drucker, *The New Realities* (New York: Harper & Row, 1989); Alvin Toffler, *Power Shift* (New York: Bantam Books, 1990); David Harvey, *The Condition of Postmodernity* (Cambridge, MA: Basil Blackwell, 1989); Steven Connor, *Postmodernist Culture* (Cambridge, MA: Basil Blackwell, 1989).

shifted in our country with the "collapse of the middle," pointing out that these groups now find themselves on the sideline. Robert Wuthnow follows this same line of analysis in noting that many denominations now find themselves as fragmented and divided as the world they try to address. In the midst of these changes, Stanley Hauerwas and William Willimon have called for Christians and the church to reposition themselves as "resident aliens in a colony" in the midst of the collapse of Christian culture. Kennon Callahan builds on this thesis by noting that the day of the professional minister is over and that the day of the "missionary pastor" has begun.[2]

These are but a few of the numerous authors, both secular and religious, who have been writing that we now find ourselves in a new landscape. The dominant culture, influenced for decades by both the rationalistic strains of the Enlightenment and the moral influences of Christianity, has now become globalized and pluralized. Many denominational churches, dependent for many decades on the symbiotic relationship between church and culture, have become marginalized and fragmented. In this context, the new landscape is often referred to as both postmodern and post-Christian. It is critical that we understand something about how we arrived at this point and what influences are presently working to shape this new reality if we hope to be responsive in ministry in the 1990s and beyond. This article will attempt to provide a historical and cultural context for understanding this new reality Christians face today.

The Development of the Modern Project and Its Subsequent Demise

A cursory reading of history indicates that the modern societies that grew out of the medieval world experienced a transformation to a fundamentally different worldview. This transition gave birth to the "modern project" —

2. Wade Clark Roof and William McKinney, *American Mainline Religion: Its Changing Shape and Future* (New Brunswick, NJ: Rutgers University Press, 1987); Robert Wuthnow, *The Restructuring of American Religion* (Princeton: Princeton University Press, 1988); Stanley Hauerwas and William H. Willimon, *Resident Aliens: Life in the Christian Colony* (Nashville: Abingdon Press, 1989); Kennon L. Callahan, *Effective Church Leadership* (San Francisco: Harper & Row, 1990).

the effort to construct a rational social order that was capable of human improvement and social progress. Today we are becoming aware of yet another shift in worldview, to a postmodern reality, as we observe the uncentering of this modern project. Some differences between these three worldviews are listed in table 1.

Both the Renaissance and the Protestant Reformation played major roles in helping what became modern Western nation-states emerge from the medieval period into the modern world. But the most formative influence came during the period from 1700 to 1850, which is known as the Enlightenment, or the age of reason. The critical contribution of this era was the fundamental shift away from the concept of truth coming to persons and society from the outside to the idea that truth that could be discovered within the social order through reason and science. In this context, the role of God was dethroned as a valid claim to authority.

This role was replaced by an emphasis on objective facts. The driving force behind this movement was the scientific method, which studied the relationships between cause and effect. This orientation, growing out of the work by Isaac Newton in physics, soon spread to the other natural sciences, and eventually it began to shape the emerging social sciences in the 1800s. The core concepts of rational order, historical progress, and the management of social life became the framework of the modern project. The physical and social sciences were joined by the human arts in an artistic expression of these core values. In time, the modern project was brought to its most complete form in Western countries through the development of (1) a capitalist-based economy, (2) bureaucratic organizational structures, and (3) the ideology of the nation-state as the primary focus of citizen allegiance.

For many decades the modern project gave evidence that this system of thinking and organization was working. The quality of life improved for large segments of the population in Western countries. People began to live longer, travel faster, communicate more easily, work more productively, and enjoy more leisure time. But there was always a darker side to the modern project, which began to make itself felt by the mid-1800s. The breakdown of traditional social patterns, the loss of one's sense of community-based identity, the negative effects of industrial hardships and pollutions, the devastation of modern warfare, and a consumer-based economy that required an endless supply of resources all gave evidence that modernity came with a high price tag.

TABLE 1 Changing Views of the World

Medieval	Newtonian	Twentieth-Century
Fixed order	Change as rearrangement	Evolutionary, emergent
Teleological	Deterministic	Law and chance
Substantive	Atomistic	Relational and interdependent
Hierarchical	Reductionistic	Systems, organic
Dualistic (spirit/matter)	Dualistic (mind/body)	Multidimensional
Kingdom	Machine	Community

Note: This table is a modified form of one appearing in Ian Barbour, *Religion in an Age of Science* (San Francisco: Harper & Row, 1990).

The Collapse of the Modern Project — A Postmodern World

After 1890, dramatic transitions occurred both on the technical level in the fields of the arts and sciences and on the popular level within the broader culture. On the technical level, for example, philosophy witnessed the gradual collapse of foundationalism as a basis for constructing a rational order. In painting, there was a gradual transition from classical forms to those labeled impressionism, expressionism, and abstract art. Parallel transitions occurred in music, theater, and literature. All of these fields shared the gradual shift from objective reason to subjective experience as the basis for knowing and sharing human meaning, and each recognized the role of a special avant-garde in leading this change process.

In the physical sciences, the development of quantum physics, the clarification of the theory of relativity by Einstein, and the discovery by Heisenberg of the uncertainty principle challenged many of the core assumptions of the Newtonian worldview that undergirded the modern project. The world came to be understood as operating with both law and chance, both order and chaos. The social sciences went through similar effects of becoming relativized with the new disciples of Freudian psychology, Weberian sociology, and Boasian anthropology. With the emergence in the 1960s of the framework of general systems theory and the interdependency of all of life, all hope of preserving a rational, predictable social order rooted in the assumptions of logical positivism was dead.

In the areas of economics and politics, the shift to relative systems took longer to be felt but has now begun to come of age. Capitalism, undergirded by the twentieth-century developments of Keynesian economics and Henry Ford's assembly line production, has begun to unravel as a viable economic system in a globalized economy, with its reliance on the expansion of debt as the basis of its viability. Nation-state politics, with its primary allegiance of the citizen to the state, has also begun to unravel with the collapse of specific political ideologies as a basis for shaping the social and economic order.

In the broader culture, the shift to a relativistic worldview has begun to be felt by the masses, especially since the threshold of social change that occurred in the 1960s. A variety of movements introduced elements of this change. The civil rights movement challenged the society to be consistent in balancing equality with freedom. The counterculture dethroned the shoulds and oughts of Christian culture as the basis of guiding social behavior. The Vietnam War and the antiwar movement reshaped our notions of the reliability of technology to render final solutions to social and moral complexities. And the Watergate scandal worked to demythologize the intrinsic authority of institutions over our lives. Changes such as these in the broader culture led irreversibly toward fragmentation and relativism. We see this trend expressed even within missiology with the current plethora of writing on religious pluralism[3] and the heated debate over the centrality of Christ and Christology in Christian mission.[4]

3. E.g., Eugene Hillman, *Many Paths: A Catholic Approach to Religious Pluralism* (Maryknoll, NY: Orbis Books, 1989); Paul F. Knitter, *No Other Name?* (Maryknoll, NY: Orbis Books, 1985); David J. Kreiger, *The New Universalism: Foundations for a Global Theology* (Maryknoll, NY: Orbis Books, 1991); Leonard Swidler, ed., *Toward a Universal Theology of Religion* (Maryknoll, NY: Orbis Books, 1987).

4. E.g., Gavin D'Costa, *Christian Uniqueness Reconsidered: The Myth of a Pluralistic Theology of Religions* (Maryknoll, NY: Orbis Books, 1990); John Hick, *God and the*

The assumptions of the Enlightenment-based modern project of rational order, historical progress, and the management of human life have all been found to be insufficient to provide meaning and direction for modern life. These assumptions have now been exposed as both inadequate and faulty. With this awareness has come the recognition that we are now living in a postmodern world. We have lost the grand narrative, the story line that gave direction and meaning to our lives as a society. We have begun to experience the implications of a pluralistic society, where multiple perspectives now offer us conflicting truth claims, all of which are viewed as relative in value.

The shape of this emerging postmodern worldview is characterized by a collapse of the importance of history, with attention being given to an endless succession of "nows." There is a focus on surfaces and images, rather than on depth and substance. The endless expansion and multiplication of choices now challenge our capacity to process information and make decisions. Patterns of relationships continue to expand around rootless associations, rather than around context and place. Change and flux are seen as normative and endless. And there is a recognition that all meaning systems are, in the end, only social constructions that have been shown to be inadequate for establishing the possibility of a grand narrative. The overarching story line has been lost and cannot be reinvented.[5]

The implications of this shift can be visualized quite simply by contrasting the worldviews of the various generations of present-day adults. The differences between generations and the core values that shape their identity are quite significant. People may still speak some of the same words, but they no longer share the same meanings. We are in a fundamentally different landscape, both within the secular culture and within the church, as illustrated in table 2.

These worldviews stand in distinct conflict with one another. The traditional generation is looking for stability and rational order in a world that no longer offers such a viewpoint. The early boomers, oriented toward

---

Universe of Faiths (New York: St. Martin's Press, 1974); John Hick and Paul F. Knitter, eds., *The Myth of Christian Uniqueness: Toward a Pluralistic Theology of Religions* (Maryknoll, NY: Orbis Books, 1987); Stanley J. Samartha, *One Christ — Many Religions: Toward a Revised Christology* (Maryknoll, NY: Orbis Books, 1991).

5. See Walter Truett Anderson, *Reality Isn't What It Used to Be* (San Francisco: Harper & Row, 1990).

TABLE 2 Multiple Worldviews of Contemporary Generations

Area	Traditional	Early Boomers	Late Boomers	Emerging
Born	Pre-1946	1946–55	1956–65	1966–75
Age today	50–older	40s	30s	20s
Worldview	Progress	Competing	Fragmentation	Pluralism
View of church	Preserve heritage	Instrument for change	Pragmatic; meets needs	Place for acceptance
Key values	Tradition Family Community Stability	Relationships Relevance Equality Justice	Me Now How Wow	Relational Compassion Accepting Entitled

trying to change the social order, now find their social ideologies somewhat sidelined and out of touch, compared with the more conservative and materialistic late boomers. These late boomers turned inward toward their own pragmatic welfare in the midst of the fragmentation of worldviews in the 1970s. And the emerging generation, also known as vidiots, is giving evidence of being the first generation raised with a pluralistic worldview, tending to be nonjudgmental toward ideological differences in the midst of their own personal search for relational acceptance.

The Development of an American Churched Culture and Its Demise

The story of the church in America can be written from the perspective of the twin themes of disestablishment and pluralism. It is a story that is filled with significant shifts as the broader society transitioned from its rural roots in the 1800s, to an urban-based society in the early 1890s, and to a globalized society by the 1980s.

The initial phase of pluralism and disestablishment came after the Revolutionary War, when the various church groups were forced to form national associations. The decision by the founding fathers to separate churches from the state led to the first disestablishment. The diversity of Protestant denominations that emerged in this context gave birth to the first form of pluralism. Following the pattern in the Middle Colonies, it was a pluralism of differences between Protestant denominations within a shared vision of creating a Christian society.

The roots of this Protestant establishment came primarily from Calvinist groups such as the Presbyterians and Congregationalists before 1800. By the mid-1800s, however, the upstart denominations — Methodists, Baptists, and Disciples — had displaced these earlier groups in both number and prominence. Regardless of denominational affiliation in mid-century America, all of these groups shared a common vision for making America a Protestant nation on the basis of a biblical theism that promoted revivalism, individual conversion, and personal morality.

The transition to the second phase of disestablishment and pluralism came around 1890 and was fairly well completed by the 1920s. Its effects and the system it produced lasted until the 1960s. By the late 1800s, changes were taking place in the patterns of immigration, industrialization, and urbanization that led to a challenge to the Protestant establishment to reshape their churches and reposition their role in the broader society. It was in the cities that the massive influx of settlers from southern and eastern Europe entered the American story, with most of these immigrants being Catholic, Jewish, or Orthodox in religious affiliation. This flood of foreign immigrants into the cities was accompanied by a Protestant migration to urban areas.

These population changes led to two major changes for the churches. The first was a tremendous growth in the number of churches, which increased from 63,000 in 1890 to 213,000 in 1914. The second was the breakup of the older Protestant alliance as the guardian of the social order. By the 1920s, this role of the general responsibility to shape society had to be shared with both the Catholic and the Jewish populations. The focus shifted from an individualist Protestant America to a socially focused Judeo-Christian pluralism. This was the second disestablishment of the Protestant churches as they began to share the cultural agenda with Catholics and Jews.

The third disestablishment of the churches took place in the transition noted earlier in this article — the period of the 1960s and 1970s. The various social movements during this period collapsed the Christian culture that had been built up over a 150-year period. With this collapse, the mainline denominations that had served at the center of legitimizing culture found themselves on the sideline. The evangelical churches, which had come to mistrust many mainline churches, found themselves with little or no ability to speak to the new secularity that was emerging in the postmodern world.

The reality of pluralism, as we have come to understand it in the 1990s, is the multiplication of worldviews and paradigms of truth claims all working within the same context of an accepted relativism. This situation has led to the third disestablishment for the churches, as they now find their role reduced to providing a minimal influence for individuals who are making decisions from the new epistemology of self and situation.

Changes and Challenges for the Church in Keeping Pace with Change

Local churches have always tended to reflect the particular context and time period in which they were begun. In this regard, the development of local churches in the story of American Christianity can be understood as having passed through a number of phases. A typology of these changes is displayed in table 3.

The geographic practice of local church life, where there was a natural fit between the church and its community, lasted through the period of time when the suburban neighborhoods expanded our cities after World War II. By the 1960s, this type of church was becoming increasingly obsolete as a viable approach to reaching and serving people. Both the mobility offered by modern forms of transportation and the shift to people grouping by affinities rather than geography shifted the patterns of local church life to a new model of lifestyle churches.

These lifestyle churches tend to follow the pattern noted earlier regarding the differences between generations. The early boomers were the ones who started the alternative churches in seeking to deal with racial reconciliation and community development. The late boomers were attracted to the ministry centers of the 1970s and 1980s to have their needs met. It is the secularized version of the late boomers that the seeker centers are attempting to reach in the 1980s and 1990s. It will be interesting to watch the style of church that will develop in the 1990s and following to serve the emerging generation that is looking for relational acceptance.

TABLE 3 Typology of Local Churches in the Development of American Church Life

Type of Church	Model	Shaping Influence
Geographic churches	Village church (1800s)	Family networks
	Old first (1890ff.)	Institutionalism
	City neighborhood (1900ff.)	Urbanization
	Family suburban (1940ff.)	Suburbanization
Lifestyle churches	Alternative (1960s/1970s)	Changing society
	Ministry centers (1970s/1980s)	Meeting needs
	Seeker centers (1980s/1990s)	Reaching the lost; consumers

A Church Seeking to Reposition with a Search for New Rules

In light of the shifts that have taken place in the broader culture and the specific patterns of change within churches, it is becoming evident that many local churches are struggling to reposition themselves within their contexts. This repositioning is somewhat complicated at the present time by two different strains at work in the church. On the one hand, many churches are aggressively trying to become needs-oriented, market-driven, and user-friendly groups by relying on all of the latest technologies and methods available to reach their target populations. The question this approach raises is whether these churches have themselves become a reflection of a set of postmodern processes. On the other hand, some churches are having to examine seriously the core relationship between gospel and culture and are working to disengage from the dominant culture. The question this strategy raises is whether these churches will be able to reposition adequately without retreating from an effective engagement of the broader culture(s).

While churches are in the process of trying either to adapt to the new context or to reposition themselves within it, many pastors are having to focus on retooling in order to stay relevant in ministry. There are a series of new rules that are emerging within this retooling process.

Rule 1: From "denominational loyalty" to "shared vision." The primary glue that used to bond a local church together in the form of institutional, denominational loyalty has shifted and is being replaced by a commitment to a shared vision. This vision concept is at the core today of almost all new church development starts, as well as the majority of renewal efforts.

Rule 2: From "professional minister" to "missionary pastor." As Callahan has noted, there has been a clear shift from the days of a churched culture, when the world was seeking out the church, to the reality today that the church must seek out the world. This has significant implications for the role of the minister. It is no longer adequate for the minister to function primarily within the professional role of being the preacher, administrator, and counselor. Pastors must now lead local churches in significant ministry to engage the world and seek out the unchurched.

Rule 3: From "administrative decision making" to "participation planning." In light of the decline of institutional loyalty and the continued fragmentation in worldviews and social meanings, local churches are finding that they are having to shift their patterns in making decisions. It is no longer possible for a church council or board to make decisions, announce them, and expect compliance. Members today must be involved in helping to shape the strategic decisions that influence the direction of the church if they are to have a sense of ownership in its ministry.

Rule 4: From "single cells" to "multiform" congregations. The local church that seeks to serve its members and reach the unchurched today has to develop a multiform program model to accomplish this. The practice of offering the same program on the same schedule to all the members worked well within a churched culture. Today, people expect and need choices if they are to become involved in the life of the local church.

Rule 5: From "cultural uniformity" to "unified diversity." It is clear that both the broader culture and local churches are becoming increasingly diverse. Different people hold multiple viewpoints, many of which are not easily harmonized within one expression of faith. One major challenge facing many local churches in the postmodern world is that of trying to find an adequate basis for creating a unified diversity without having to insist upon uniformity.

Summary

We are living in a new day in America. The shifts in the cultural context have presented a new challenge for the churches to address America as a mission field. The awareness of this need is growing rapidly within many denominations that are now attempting to retool in order to respond to this shift. This awareness is also growing among many who are seeking to start new forms of the church outside of the historic denominations with community-based models. It is not yet clear what will happen to the churches involved in these two trends, but it is certain that Christianity as we have known it in America is undergoing a systemic shift.

In this article we have attempted to identify some of the contours and dimensions of this shift both for the general culture and for the churches that work within this culture. Our conclusion regarding the general culture is that we are clearly living in a postmodern world where we have seen the loss of the grand narrative and the collapse of shared meanings within a relativized pluralism. Our conclusion regarding the churches working in this context is that they are having to reposition themselves significantly in order to respond to these changes, as they seek to find new patterns and forms of ministry to respond to the needs of their members and those they seek to reach.

The Culture of Modernity as a Missionary Challenge

WILBERT R. SHENK

Although the culture of modernity has yet to be taken seriously as a subject of sustained missionary concern, my argument will be that this represents one of the most urgent frontiers facing the church in the twenty-first century. As always, "the past is prologue." Both church and culture today are products of a long historical process. The church of Christendom has been deeply implicated in the culture of modernity. Today we are hearing appeals for a fresh engagement by the church with modern culture. This calls for careful preparation. We need to sort through and get fresh perspective on the past as the first step into the future.

Over the past century there has been an undercurrent of uneasiness about the status of the church in the West. Survey after survey tells the same doleful story: the church of technocratic culture is in deep difficulty.[1] The church's travail coincides with the deepening crisis of modernity as it phases into postmodernity. Here we shall use "modern culture" as the comprehensive term for modernity and postmodernity.

Modernity is the result of intellectual developments in European culture over a period of several centuries on the basis of the influence of thinkers such as Bacon, Newton, Kepler, Galileo, and Descartes, who established the "scientific method" and laid the foundations in mathematics and

1. E.g., *"Christian" England: What the English Census Revealed,* ed. Peter Brierly (London: MARC Europe, 1991).

physics for modern science. In the seventeenth and eighteenth centuries philosophers like Locke and Kant forged a new intellectual framework. The Enlightenment emphasized the potential of rational human reason to solve problems, unaided by the supernatural, and radical skepticism as the hallmark of all authentic intellectual pursuits.

Enlightenment culture put a premium on "facts," defined as that which can be tested in the laboratory — what is rational, objective, and verifiable. Public discourse was to be conducted on the basis of objective fact, what we can know with certainty. Values and religious beliefs were regarded as the realm of the superstitious and the subjective — that is, the unprovable — and thus necessarily relegated to the private sphere. Faith and knowledge were held to be irreconcilable. This schism in modern culture has yet to be healed. The Enlightenment, which did so much to raise the dignity of the individual through a vision of human freedom and responsibility, has also produced profound alienation and anomie in the modern individual.[2]

Modern culture has been characterized by the triumph of science and technology. Scientific experimentation and technological innovation constituted the engine driving industrial development. By the nineteenth century the industrial revolution was well along. The scale and pace of industrialization forced rapid restructuring of Western societies as workers were drawn from the rural areas into factory towns. Urbanization brought new pressures to bear on civic and family life, raising new questions about the meaning of human existence as the worker was perceived to be only a cog in the industrial machine.

Christendom was the dominant religious influence in the West for fifteen hundred years.[3] It arose in the fourth century when Christianity was

2. For a historical analysis, see Martin Marty, *The Modern Schism: Three Paths to the Secular* (New York: Harper & Row, 1969). For a sociological interpretation, see Peter Berger, Brigitte Berger, and Hansfried Kellner, *The Homeless Mind: Modernization and Consciousness* (New York: Vintage Books, 1974). For a theological probe, see Colin Gunton, *Enlightenment and Alienation* (Grand Rapids: William B. Eerdmans, 1985).

3. "West" refers to the geographic-historical reality associated with Europe at least since Leo IX excommunicated the Eastern church in 1052. North America and Australasia, by virtue of being settled by Europeans and having similar economic and political systems, are included in the West. Latin America occupies a different position. Culturally it owes much to Europe, although economically it has never achieved parity with the West. Japan is a different sort of hybrid. It has preserved much of its cultural

first officially recognized by the emperor and gradually became the religion of state throughout Europe. The church viewed itself as the religious institution for society as a whole. At times this meant the church was actually the dominant power in society. Always the church had an unquestioned role alongside the social, political, economic, and military institutions. By the time of the Protestant Reformation in the sixteenth century, there were signs that Christendom was beginning to crumble, but the breakdown was protracted, continuing into the twentieth century. Today vestiges of the old tradition remain in private, public, and religious spheres; overall, however, Christendom is a spent cultural force.

Nonetheless, the legacy of Christendom is crucial for understanding the missionary challenge of modern and postmodern culture because of the way the modern church is an extension of Christendom.

The church of Christendom was a church without mission.

Christendom politicized mission by making it an instrument of state policy. Once the tribes of Europe had been pacified and brought under control by church and state, there was no further need for even this politicized mission. The notion of mission within the territory of Christendom contradicted the meaning of this new society.

Scholars have long debated whether the leading Protestant Reformers of the sixteenth century were advocates for missions.[4] It is a largely irrelevant exercise of forcing twentieth-century questions on the sixteenth century. Missions within Christendom were unthinkable, and Protestant Europe had not yet embarked on colonial expansion in the manner of the Catholic Portuguese and Spanish.

By the twentieth century, fundamental questions were being raised about the reality of Christendom because of its disturbing inertia in the face of dehumanizing spiritual and social conditions of the masses and its intellectual defensiveness. Two examples must suffice.

---

heritage but borrowed freely from the West as a part of its modernization starting in the late nineteenth century.

4. For an overview of these debates, see John H. Yoder, "Reformation and Mission: A Bibliographic Survey," in *Anabaptism and Mission,* ed. Wilbert R. Schenk (Scottdale, PA: Herald Press, 1984), 40–50.

In the 1909 Bampton Lectures, Canon Walter Hobhouse canvassed the whole history of Christendom to develop his argument that the church had been domesticated to fit political and cultural realities. Consequently, it was a church without a mission to its world. Hobhouse urged that the church reclaim its apostolic character as "a missionary Church, not only in heathen lands and among races which we are pleased to call 'inferior,' but in every country."[5]

Another example is Cardinal Suhard, who served as archbishop, first of Rheims (1930–40) and then of Paris (1940–49). He was preoccupied with finding new answers to the social and spiritual conditions of modern society.[6] He called for reevangelization, and he encouraged the worker-priest movement.[7] But the Vatican was negative toward Mission de France, founded by Cardinal Suhard. Pius XII granted only provisional approval on Suhard's deathbed in 1949.

Hobhouse and Suhard were voices crying in the wilderness. Hobhouse sent up a trial balloon that apparently attracted no attention. Suhard challenged the old assumptions that defined Christendom and promoted a missionary ecclesiology. With imagination he created new institutions and programs, only to meet resistance at the highest levels of the hierarchy. Christendom was deeply entrenched.

The Christendom mentality inhibited the church from interacting critically, constructively, and pastorally in the modern period, when society was undergoing fundamental change.

Throughout the nineteenth century, the church was on the defensive in a culture dominated by science. Antagonists of the Christian faith played science off against religion in a successful effort to discredit the church in the popular mind. The church was also compromised by its reputation of being for the classes rather than the masses.[8]

5. Walter Hobhouse, *The Church and World in Idea and History,* 2d ed. (London: Macmillan, 1911), 320.

6. Pierre Renard, "Cardinal Suhard and the New Evangelization: A Review Essay," *Lumen Vitae* 41, no. 3 (1986): 350.

7. The story of Abbe Godin, inspirer of the worker-priest movement, is told in Maisie Ward, *France Pagan? The Mission of Abbe Godin* (London: Sheed & Ward, 1949).

8. The story of religion in Europe is complex and the literature vast. Two accessible accounts of the recent period are Alan D. Gilbert, *Religion and Society in Industrial*

Arthur Winnington-Ingram, who became Anglican bishop of London in 1901, observed that "it is not that the Church of God has lost the great towns: it never had them." Pius XI reportedly said, "The greatest scandal of the Church in the nineteenth century was that it lost the working class."[9] Although bishop and pope differed in emphasis, they were agreed that by the twentieth century the church had little credibility with the working masses.

By 1900 working-class consciousness was fully formed and entrenched, including a distinctive attitude toward religion. The working class might continue to celebrate the rites of passage in the church, but otherwise they seldom attended services, and "many of them regarded the church and clergy with hostility."[10] Whether Protestant or Catholic, workers had a negative attitude toward church.

Throughout the modern period another process was at work that had important implications for the church. Dietrich Bonhoeffer spoke of humankind "coming of age." In the years following World War II, Europe was called a post-Christian society. The triumph of secularization was said to be inevitable and irreversible. In the 1960s theologians reinterpreted the Christian message in light of secularization. Harvey Cox caught the mood of the times in his bestseller *The Secular City*, in which he said, "Secularization rolls on, and if we are to understand and communicate with our present age we must learn to love it in its unremitting secularity."[11] The message was clear: any peace settlement between church and culture would be on terms set by secular culture.

Other careful observers, however, found evidence of religious activity on all sides, including the places where there was supposed to be none, such as rapidly modernizing Japan. Secularization had to be redefined. Secularization was real, but a more nuanced understanding was required.

Because the church must live within the plausibility structure of its

England (London: Longman, 1976); and Hugh McLeod, *Religion and the People of Western Europe, 1789–1980* (London: Oxford University Press, 1931).

9. Hugh McLeod, "The Dechristianisation of the Working Class in Western Europe (1850–1900)," *Social Compass* 27, nos. 2–3 (1980): 191. Note also the remark by Archbishop Lang that people "have never fallen from the church, for they were never within it" (cited in Hobhouse, *Church and World*, 323).

10. McLeod, "Dechristianisation," 192.

11. Harvey Cox, *The Secular City* (London: SCM Press, 1965), 4.

culture, it is always vulnerable to the temptation to conform to that structure. The modern plausibility structure sought to exclude religion altogether. Accommodation would assuredly spell trouble for the church, but there were theologians who advocated such a strategy. By contrast, a missionary stance vis-à-vis culture could have offered a constructively critical position from which to interact with modern culture. The Christendom inheritance militated against such a stance.

Missiologists have reinforced the Christendom viewpoint with regard to mission.

In no small measure because of the heroic exertions of Gustav Warneck, pioneer German missiologist, mission studies finally were admitted to the university late in the nineteenth century. Warneck insisted on a distinction between "missions" and "evangelization."[12] Missions were efforts outside historic Christendom to establish the church. Evangelization was the action by which nominal Christians were called to actualize their latent faith. This formulation remained influential in mission studies until after 1945. No missiologist addressed the question of mission to the West; mission studies remained the servant of cross-cultural missions.

A conceptual shift was signaled by the slogan coming out of the meeting of the Commission on World Mission and Evangelism (CWME) of the World Council of Churches in Mexico City in 1963: "Mission from six continents to six continents." The CWME followed up with a study in Europe and North America of "the missionary structure of the congregation," an initiative that never fulfilled its promise. At the same time the Second Vatican Council was forging a new position for Roman Catholics that emphasized the missionary responsibility of the whole people of God. This conceptual shift, however, was not translated into reforms — whether ecclesial, missiological, or in theological education.

12. In his address to the Centenary Missions Conference in London in 1888 on the need for comity agreements, Warneck included this appeal: "Dear brethren in England and America, I believe that I speak in the name of all my German fellow-believers, if I urge upon you to cease from looking upon Germany, the land of Luther and Melanchthon, Arndt and Spener, Francke and Zinzendorf, Tholuck, Fliedner and Wichern, as a half heathen and rationalistic country" (Warneck, "The Mutual Relations of Evangelical Missionary Societies," in *Report of the Missionary Conference on Protestant Missions of the World*, ed. James Johnson [London: James Nisbet & Co., 1888]).

The problematic had various dimensions. Two centuries of worldwide missionary exertions sponsored by Western churches largely failed to effect a fundamental reorientation in their ecclesial consciousness. Christendom remained a self-sufficient and insular reality. Church history and theology continued to be taught in the West as a largely Western affair. What happened "out there" was missions; what happened in the West was church. Owen Chadwick's two-volume *Victorian Church,* which discussed the period when British missions had the largest missionary contingent of any nationality, contained not a single reference to this movement.[13] Few missiologists have challenged this state of affairs. Christendom assumptions and habits of mind furnished the conceptual framework even among those with an experience of global mission.

> *Missionary encounter with modern culture requires that we hold together* basileia *(the reign of God), as the content and goal, and incarnation, as the essential strategy, as we listen carefully, respectfully, and compassionately to the modern world.*

Various calls for missionary witness among the peoples of modernity have been made during the past two decades, including by W. A. Visser 't Hooft, John Paul II, and Lesslie Newbigin. We characterize briefly these three appeals.

W. A. Visser 't Hooft, founding general secretary of the World Council of Churches, having experienced Nazism firsthand, was deeply aware of the fundamental contradictions and demonic tendencies within modernity. In 1974 he addressed the new religiosity that was arising in reaction to secularization — which he diffidently termed "neo-paganism" (Rom. 1:25).[14] Visser 't Hooft called first for a thorough "spring cleaning." Then, he said, we must go to the roots of modern culture as seen through philosophers, poets, and novelists. Also, the church itself must encounter the gospel afresh as the first step in discovering the Word for contemporary life.

13. Cited by Andrew Walls in "Structural Problems in Mission Studies," *International Bulletin of Missionary Research* 15, no. 4 (October 1991): 146-55.

14. Visser 't Hooft, "Evangelism in the Neo-Pagan Situation," *International Review of Mission* 63, no. 49 (January 1974): 81-86. Cf. William Edgar, "New Right — Old Paganism," *Nederlands Theologisch Tidjschrift* 37, no. 4 (1983): 304-13; Marc R. Spindler, "Europe's Neo-Paganism: A Perverse Inculturation," *International Bulletin of Missionary Research* 11, no. 1 (January): 8-11.

In 1985 John Paul II appealed to all Catholics to participate in reevangelization/new evangelization: "I urge you in the name of the Lord Jesus Christ, to make yourselves proclaimers of the Gospel, to spread with all your might the saving Word."[15] The pope's appeal has stirred both positive and negative reactions among Catholics. His critics hear a call to reestablish Christendom.[16] The pope has emphasized the importance of culture for reevangelization and has created a new pontifical commission on culture.

The third voice is that of Lesslie Newbigin, missionary and bishop in India and ecumenical leader who returned to his British homeland to retire. What struck him was an observable lack of hope in British society. For over a decade Newbigin has been preoccupied with the question, Can the West be converted? He has spelled out a program in a number of recent books.[17] Newbigin insists that we must critically examine the fundamental presuppositions, the epistemological foundations on which modern culture rests. Only then will we know how the gospel as truth can heal the divisions and contradictions present in modern culture. The stance from which to understand modern culture is that of the missionary. The West needs to hear the gospel, the life-giving news of God's election of a people who live by the Word of God within this story.

These three leaders have not been alone in their concern. Throughout the twentieth century many initiatives have been taken to evangelize or reevangelize Western societies or bring renewal to the churches. What distinguishes these appeals is their insistence on going back to the roots of Western culture in order to understand it in terms of its origins and subsequent development.

The traditional distinction between mission and evangelism played on the assumption that the church knows its own culture profoundly. What remains is simply to employ certain techniques or methods in recruiting

15. In *Lumen Vitae* 41, no. 3 (1986): 246.

16. One example of critical reaction to John Paul's call is *Le Reve de Compastelle: Vers la Restauration d'une Europe Chretienne?* ed. Rene Luneau and Paul Ladriere (Paris: Centurion, 1989).

17. See *The Other Side of 1984* (Grand Rapids: William B. Eerdmans, 1983); *Foolishness to the Greeks: The Gospel and Western Culture* (Grand Rapids: William B. Eerdmans, 1986); *The Gospel in a Pluralist Society* (Grand Rapids: William B. Eerdmans, 1989); and *Truth to Tell: The Gospel as Public Truth* (Grand Rapids: William B. Eerdmans, 1991).

people back to the church. This stereotyping of evangelism had implications for both message and method, exercising a reductionistic effect on both. In the West these techniques and methods are furnished by technocratic culture, which suggests that evangelism itself has been secularized. The fact that the churches have for so long been defined by social categories indicates that, far from knowing the culture, the churches speak largely to their own segment within it. Secularized modes of evangelism are sources of alienation rather than means of personal and social reconciliation.

It is instructive that when our Lord began his public ministry, he stated his presupposition: "The time is fulfilled, and the kingdom of God is at hand; repent, and believe in the gospel" (Mark 1:15). The ministry of Jesus was set within the culture in which he was born and reared. With rare penetration he grasped the presuppositions on which his own culture was based, as suggested by the illuminating questions he put to people and the parables he told. His ministry was notable for the way he engaged the issues that mattered most to people.

The Palestine of Jesus' time was a culture in turmoil and under great strain, near the breaking point. Jesus modeled for us what it means to be in missionary encounter with one's culture. He was the outsider who became the insider without surrendering his outsider status. He never relaxed this bifocal stance. Jesus was recognizably "their own," but they refused to "own" him. He represented to his people *basileia*, a source of judgment and hope. In his person they knew they were encountering both God and themselves. In his incarnation Jesus held together his full identification with the human situation and his total commitment to *basileia*. This was the force field out of which his extraordinary mission was conducted. But every clue Jesus gave his disciples as to their own missionary vocation suggests that this is the authoritative model for them as well. Jesus left no general guidelines, formulas, or methods for his disciples to follow — only a demanding model.

Basing a missionary encounter with modern culture on *basileia* and incarnation will have several implications. First, this calls us to reject the Christendom notion, whereby we claim a culture as being Christian. Every culture is incomplete without the gospel, but no culture is ever completely evangelized, for no culture is completely submitted to the reign of God. In every culture there are forces that contradict the reign of God. Because the church should know its own culture best, it has a special missionary vocation to that culture.

This leads to the second observation: the church's normal relationship to every culture is that of missionary encounter. The faithful church, living out God's reign, cannot feel completely at home in culture; yet in light of *basileia,* the church is responsible to every human society to witness to God's saving intention. This calls the church to a twofold action in relation to every culture. Incarnation signifies full identification, but it is incarnation in the service of disclosing God's love and will for humankind. This is the way marked by the cross.

Third, there is no biblical or theological basis for the territorial distinction between mission and evangelism. To accede to this dichotomy is to invite the church to "settle in" and be at home. The church is most at risk where it has been present in a culture for a long period so that it no longer conceives its relation to culture in terms of missionary encounter. The church remains socially and salvifically relevant only as long as it is in tension with culture. The ongoing task of the church is to train its members to view culture through the critically constructive lenses of the missionary. This means learning to view a culture through kingdom categories in order to discern and expose the forces that bring death rather than life.

The culture of modernity is an unprecedented missionary frontier. It is the first culture that has had a long encounter with the Christian faith but in which vast numbers of people live post-Christian lives. The nonmissionary church of Christendom remains a dominant form of church in modern culture. This ecclesial reality can be made salvifically and socially relevant only if reshaped by basileia to become the means of incarnating the reign of God in modern culture.

From Biblical Secularity to Modern Secularism: Historical Aspects and Stages

CHRISTOPHER B. KAISER

In this chapter I shall try to outline the historical processes by which our civilization has become secularized, that is, how it moved from being a traditional, religiously motivated culture to being a modern, secular one.[1]

Secularity and Secularism Defined

For the purposes of this chapter, I shall assume basic agreement on the terms "biblical secularity" and "modern secularism." By "biblical secularity" I mean the positive value placed on time, temporal events, and temporal goals in Holy Scripture. God created the world of space and time as a medium of divine self-expression and self-revelation to humanity. God also gives some space and time to each creature as an opportunity for self-fulfillment and service to others. Therefore, the seasonal times of individual life and the historical times of communal history are viewed in Scripture as being filled with theological significance. The stories and the predictions that shape the public life of a people like Israel are filled with supernatural agents, as well as human and natural ones.[2] In Peter

1. This chapter is a preliminary study for a larger program of research on the origin and causes of secularization in the West.

2. Note, for example, the role of divine judgment in the appeal for justice in

Berger's terms, there is a "sacred canopy" embracing time and eternity, God and nature, contingency and order. I take it as agreed that this view characterized the people of Israel and the early church.[3] The writings of Augustine, particularly his *City of God*, and their influence on the early Middle Ages are just one illustration of this initial condition.

The placing of such a positive value on time is certainly a characteristic feature of Judaism and Christianity. In cultures that have been influenced by Judaism and Christianity, secular activities and professions have enjoyed a high degree of theological legitimation. Accordingly, scholars have sometimes pointed to Judaism and Christianity as the ultimate source of modern secularism.[4] I disagree with this attribution for two reasons.

First, our knowledge of world civilizations is not comprehensive enough to allow us to draw such a sweeping conclusion. At this stage of history, we simply do not know whether secularization is a general trend in world development or whether it is peculiar to Western civilization.[5] The fact that Jewish and Christian cultures of eastern Europe, Asia, Africa, and

---

Neh. 5:1-13. The reader will observe that this essay is written from the standpoint of modern secularism in that no appeal is made to supernatural agencies in the history presented. At some point, however, we must recover the *discernment of spirits* if we are to make real progress.

3. It is important that we take ancient Israel and/or the early church as our baseline here. We now know that there was a good deal of diversity of faith and practice in these contexts, in spite of an overarching belief in the rule of God. Studies that take high medieval Christendom as the baseline often assume a (relatively) higher degree of control by a single religious institution (e.g., Jan Swyngedouw, "Secularization in a Japanese Context," *Japanese Journal of Religious Studies* 3 [1976]: 293–96).

4. E.g., Max Weber, *The Protestant Ethic and the Spirit of Capitalism* (New York: Charles Scribner's Sons, 1958; orig. pub., 1904–5), 105 and throughout; Arend T. van Leeuwen, *Christianity in World History: The Meeting of the Faiths of East and West* (New York: Charles Scribner's Sons, 1964), 16 and elsewhere; Peter Berger's earlier work, like *The Sacred Canopy: Elements of a Sociological Theory of Religion* (Garden City, NY: Doubleday, 1967), 110–25. It is fair to say that Berger (a sociologist, not a biblical scholar or historian) here confused biblical secularity with modern secularism and read the Old Testament in light of the latter.

5. "Secularization" is a descriptive term that refers to a process that can be described with historical and sociological tools. "Secularism," however, is a normative term; it affirms the rightness (and possibly the inevitability) of secularization. See, e.g., Peter E. Glasner, *A Sociology of Secularisation: A Critique of a Concept* (London: RKP, 1977), 332–32; David Lyon, *The Steeple's Shadow: On the Myths and Realities of Secularization* (London: SPCK, 1985), 30–31.

Latin America did not develop on their own toward secularism (even though some like the Byzantines, who were also Christian, placed a high value on the secular power) makes the putative connection between biblical religion and secularism seem very tenuous indeed.

Second, even aside from questions of comparative history, there are profound differences between biblical secularity and modern secularism that make any causal connection problematic.

Here is the tricky part. Just how do we define modern secularism? One procedure is to define secularism in strictly substantive terms as the gradual decline of religious belief (the "decline-of-religion thesis"). The decline may be viewed either quantitatively, in terms of declining statistics, or qualitatively, in terms of a decline of personal faith from some premodern standard.[6] In this case, the difference between modern secularism and biblical secularity is clear: the faith upon which traditional secularity was based is simply no longer present in its original strength (quantitatively or qualitatively).

There are, however, at least two problems with this approach to modern secularism. For one thing, the persistent popularity of religious belief in secularized countries like the United States and the recent resurgence of fundamentalism around the world have called this form of the "secularization thesis" into serious question.[7] Another problem is that the decline-of-religion thesis usually implies (or presupposes) some incompatibility between religious belief and science and technology (or some other

6. E.g., Bryan Wilson, *Religion in Sociological Perspective* (Oxford: Oxford University Press, 1982), 42, 46, and elsewhere. As noted below, I agree with Wilson's analyses in other respects.

On the difference between substantive and functionalist approaches to secularization, see Peter Berger, "Some Second Thoughts on Substantive versus Functional Definitions of Religion," *Journal for the Scientific Study of Religion* 13 (June 1974): 126–28; *The International Encyclopedia of Sociology,* ed. Michael Mann (New York: Continuum, 1984), 346. WARNING: The subtleties of sociological debate about the procedure for defining religion and secularization can be unsettling to the uninitiated! As a general rule, functional approaches work well for cross-cultural comparisons, but substantive considerations must be taken into account in diachronic studies.

7. Peter Berger, *A Far Glory: The Quest for Faith in an Age of Credulity* (New York: Free Press, 1992), 28–29, 32–34. Average church attendance in the United States peaked at 49 percent in 1955 and has leveled off at about 43 percent since then. About the same percentage of Americans report that they read the Bible at least once a week (George Gallup, Jr., and Jim Castelli, *The People's Religion: America's Faith in the 90s* [New York: Macmillan, 1989]).

form of rationality).[8] However, recent developments in the history of science indicate that religious belief was one of the primary motivations behind the rise of modern science and technology (and rationality generally).[9] Moreover, various sociologists have shown that religious belief is capable of adapting to the conditions of the modern world.[10]

Personally, I am persuaded by scholars like Thomas Luckmann and Peter Berger, who define secularism not as the decline of religion but as a redefinition of its role in such a way that religious beliefs are dissociated from the secular processes of world-structuring, and secular values are alienated from the sphere of religion (a combination of functional and substantive approaches).[11] In Thomas Luckmann's terms, it is the privatization of the traditional "sacred cosmos."[12] In Peter Berger's terms, it is the dissolution of a "sacred canopy" and the emergence of a radical plurality of spheres of life — public and private, secular and spiritual.[13] Let us look at each of these two points in turn.

8. Wilson, *Religion,* 38–39, 54–55, and elsewhere. Note the echoes here of the old historiographical warfare between science and religion.

9. I have reviewed the case in Kaiser, *Creation and the History of Science* (Grand Rapids: Eerdmans, 1991).

10. E.g., Thomas Luckmann, *The Invisible Religion: The Problem of Religion in Modern Society* (New York: Macmillan, 1967).

11. On the changed role of religion, see, e.g., Luckmann, *Invisible Religion,* 35–39; Berger, *Sacred Canopy,* 107, 132–34 (where a functional approach is utilized, in spite of the protestations to the contrary on pp. 176–78); Peter Berger, Brigitte Berger, and Hansfried Kellner, *The Homeless Mind: Modernization and Consciousness* (New York: Random House, 1973), 79–81, 156–57.

Berger later eliminated the "ambiguity" he found in his earlier work and became more militant in his "opposition to functional definitions" (Berger, "Some Second Thoughts," 127, 132). For an insightful analysis of this shift, see Robert C. Fuller, "Religion and Empiricism in the Works of Peter Berger," *Zygon* 22 (1987): 497–510.

For some helpful criticisms of Luckmann and Berger's treatment of secularization as "segmentation," see Glasner, *Sociology of Secularisation,* 50–56.

12. Thomas Luckmann, "The Structural Conditions of Religious Consciousness in Modern Societies," *Japanese Journal of Religious Studies* 6 (1979): 123, 133; cf. idem, *Invisible Religion,* 116–17.

13. Berger, Berger, and Kellner, *Homeless Mind,* 4–65, 79–80, 156–57. In functional theories, religion continues to give meaning to the everyday, secular aspects of life, even in secularized societies (*International Encyclopedia of Sociology,* 175b, 346b). However, the religious significance of secular activities pertains only to their end results (e.g., providing for one's family, being a good citizen), not to the concrete behaviors or materials involved.

On the one hand, secularization entails the dissociation of religious beliefs from the social mechanisms of world structuring.[14] It is the systematic avoidance of any reference to spiritual agents in the stories that shape the public life of a people.[15] It is the denial of the likelihood of supernatural visitation in the processes of public life, particularly the processes of transportation, manufacture, and commerce. It is the emptying of objective time, space, and matter of spiritual significance and the relegation of the divine to private, inner experience (functional emphasis).

On the other hand, secularization entails the alienation of traditionally secular functions like law and medicine from the reconstituted sphere of religion (substantive emphasis). In other words, the guardians of religion

14. Olivier Tschannen summarizes this aspect of secularization under the heading of differentiation, that is, the separation of religion from other domains of social life ("The Secularization Paradigm: A Systematization," *Journal for the Scientific Study of Religion* 30 [1991]: 400–405). The problem with the term "differentiation" is that it is usually associated with general theories of societal evolution toward greater complexity. Examples of this approach include Talcott Parsons, "Evolutionary Universals in Society," *American Sociological Review* 29 (1964): 339–57; Robert N. Bellah, "Religious Evolution," *American Sociological Review* 29 (1964), reprinted in idem, *Beyond Belief: Essays on Religion in a Post-Traditional World* (New York: Harper & Row, 1970), 20–50; Richard K. Fenn, *Toward a Theory of Secularization* (Storrs, CT: Society for the Scientific Study of Religion, 1978). In this context, the idea of secularization can become a universal myth rather than an empirical category, as Glasner argues in *Sociology of Secularisation*, 26–31.

While differentiation must be regarded as part of the secularization process, it might need to be balanced with the concept of recombination. Functions and values that are differentiated from their religious roots are often combined with other functions and values. In medieval Europe, for example, most mechanical improvements were developed in monastic settings. Commercial enterprise, in contrast, was generally controlled by the state. The secularization process involved the differentiation between the mechanical and the monastic (and between the commercial and the political), but also the recombination of the mechanical with commercial enterprise.

15. In contrast to pure functionalists like J. M. Yinger (*The Scientific Study of Religion* [New York: Macmillan, 1971]), I do not regard modern Western nationalism as a modern form of religion because reference to the active role of spiritual agents is generally absent. References to the acts of God are generally archaic and limited to God's primordial act of creation. Here I agree with Wilson, *Religion*, 54, 169–70.

Much confusion about the role of religion in modern nation-states is caused by the fact that, even in the public sphere, religious beliefs can still be celebrated at important junctures in order to mobilize grassroots popular support (as distinct from establishing public policy). Political conventions are good examples of such quasi-religious mobilization in the American context.

were not just pushed out of secular areas as though they were entirely passive in the process. They actively disengaged from many secular concerns and turned them over to new secular elites (in relation to whom religionists became "laypeople").[16] For most believers today, reason, science, technology, and medicine are entirely secular affairs.[17] Even believing scientists and physicians often regard their professions in secular rather than religious terms. It becomes increasingly difficult to explain to believers that many spiritual giants of the past regarded secular professions as gifts of God and viewed their exercise as expressions of their faith.

Secularization, in the sense adopted here, occurs even in contexts of resurgent fundamentalism. In fact, fundamentalism can be viewed as a concomitant of secularization rather than an exception to it.[18] Though some fundamentalists are involved in politics, their involvement rarely touches on theological issues or values that were prominent in Scripture or the early church.[19]

16. Karel Dobbelaere treats this aspect of secularization under the heading of laicization in his "Secularization: A Multi-Dimensional Concept," *Current Sociology* 29 (1981): 1–153. "Laicization" was originally a French term (*laicisation,* related to *laicité*) meaning "disestablishment," esp. in the founding of nondenominational (in France, non-Catholic) schools (Glasner, *Sociology of Secularisation,* 32–33, 47).

17. Other traditionally religious values like prophecy, dream interpretation, faith healing, and magic were alienated in a different direction, that of folk culture. Phenomenologically, these values embody a unity (or correspondence) of subject and object, whereas the new, secularized versions of science and medicine were experienced as purely objective.

18. On American evangelicalism, see Fenn, *Toward a Theory of Secularization,* 73; Robert Booth Fowler, *Unconventional Partners: Religion and Liberal Culture in the United States* (Grand Rapids: Eerdmans, 1989), 111–28; Bruce B. Lawrence, *Defenders of God: The Fundamentalist Revolt against the Modern Age* (San Francisco: Harper & Row, 1989), ix–x, 1–6, 17–18. See also the debate between Richard C. Martin and Bruce Lawrence in *Religious Studies Review* 19 (October 1993): 293–96.

Whether Islamic (or Hindu) fundamentalism is countermodernizing, as Berger contends (*Far Glory,* 34–36), or merely another form of accommodation to modern secularism remains to be seen. But one hardly expects the military or the oil industry to go back to indigenous Islamic technologies, even in fundamentalist orders like that of Iran (see Berger, Berger, and Kellner, *Homeless Mind,* 164–67). Devout Moslems who perform the hajj already rely on modern systems of transportation, sanitation, and air conditioning, just as do religionists in the West (Jeffrey L. Sheler, "A Pilgrimage in Flux: The Fourteen-Century-Old Muslim Hajj Is Colliding with the Modern World," *U.S. News & World Report,* May 31, 1993, pp. 67–69).

19. The prohibition of abortion in the early church was part of a nurturing

Even with this more nuanced (substantive-functionalist) definition, it is clear that secularism differs drastically from biblical secularity. In fact, it is exactly the opposite! Instead of God revealing Godself in space and time, God is isolated from creation (in practice, if not in formal creed). Instead of God being an agent in history, God is confined to the experience of the individual and (perhaps) the liturgy of the church.

These preliminary observations on the meaning of secularism lead us to the principal question of this chapter: How did our particular (Western) civilization change from an orientation of biblical secularity to one of modern secularism?[20]

The Historical Development Introduced

Personally, I am not adverse to tackling big questions. On this one, however, I must confess extreme apprehension. Secularization has obviously been a long, complex process. It has involved many stages, not just a single decisive event. The best we can ask for is a model of the overall development.

Another problem I anticipate stems from the fact that this inquiry is not a purely objective one for any of us. For those of us who find our hope for this world and the next in the stories of the Bible and the creeds of the early church, any developments that may be said to carry us in a radically different direction will automatically be suspect. Consequently, we feel defensive about the slightest suggestion that a movement we personally cherish may have contributed to secularization. For example, as a scientist, I wince when it is suggested that modern science may have contributed to secularization in some way. As a Protestant, I squirm when it is suggested that the Reformation has undermined the sense of the sacred (although many Protestants have championed the notion!). Roman Catholic readers

---

environment for children that would probably be regarded as socialist by modern fundamentalists. Values of the extended family and the community have been replaced by those of the nuclear family.

20. Among the few available historical studies of secularization, I have been particularly influenced by Martin Marty, *The Modern Schism: Three Paths to the Secular* (New York: Harper & Row, 1969), which compares religion in nineteenth-century France, England, and America. Richard D. Brown, *Modernization: The Transformation of American Life, 1600–1865* (Prospect Heights, IL: Waveland Press, 1988; orig. pub., 1976), is far more comprehensive in treating the American context.

may feel the same way when I discuss the effects of the medieval conflict between the papacy and the secular powers of Europe. In short, the history of secularization is a minefield for historians who also participate in the major professions and institutions.

Difficult and contentious as this sort of history may be, I also feel it is necessary to have some kind of overview. If we are to translate our biblical faith into terms of the contemporary world, we must have at least an approximate idea of how they differ and of how the transition from secularity to secularism took place.

Accordingly, I offer the following model. Chronologically, it comprises five stages, from the eleventh century to the nineteenth.[21] Typologically, it comprises six aspects of modern secularism that emerge in those stages. Each stage and aspect further involves a dialectic between socioeconomic conditions and the world of ideas (substructure and superstructure).

The five stages of secularization I propose to discuss are:

a. the development of the medieval dialectic of natural and supernatural in the context of the power struggle between church and state (late 11th–12th centuries);
b. the construction of uniform space and time in an era of emerging nation-states and market economies (14th–15th centuries);
c. the rise of the mechanical philosophy in the context of the stabilization of nation-states against post-Reformation confessional disruption (17th century);
d. the popularization of the mechanical philosophy and the construction of the modern self along with the rise of the "new men" of long-range commerce (18th century); and

21. The eleventh century serves as a starting point because the "barbarian invasions" ended, stability was restored, and rapid economic growth began in western Europe soon after A.D. 1050. The Norman conquests of 1061–91 were temporarily disruptive but hardly barbarian. In fact, they were foundational to the new sociopolitical order of Europe. The resurgence of western Europe beginning in the eleventh century is described by Lester K. Little, *Religious Poverty and the Profit Economy in Medieval Europe* (Ithaca: Cornell University Press, 1978), 7–18; Alexander Murray, *Reason and Society in the Middle Ages* (Oxford: Clarendon Press, 1978), 25–26, 53–57. Interestingly, Little regards the entire period from the mid-eleventh century to the early nineteenth as a single movement of preindustrial, commercial revolution (*Religious Poverty*, p. x).

e. the restructuring of communities and the privatization of religion during the transportation and industrial revolutions (late 18th–19th centuries).

At the outset, I should differentiate the idea of these five stages of secularization from the use of the idea of stages in a regular process like education or personal growth. I do not wish to suggest a deterministic account of the process — at least not in its early stages. The challenges of medieval dialectic were met by a variety of scholastic syntheses and spiritual visions that inspired leaders of both church and state in the later Middle Ages (thirteenth and fourteenth centuries). And the development of the basic tools of perspective, mechanics, and mercantilism in the fourteenth century was followed by thoroughgoing reformations (Protestant and Catholic) of both church and society.

The secularizing tendencies of the first two stages I have listed thus did not by themselves lead to modern secularism. It was only with the perceived failure of religiously motivated social programs in the seventeenth century (see 1c below) and the alliance of the mechanical philosophy with market forces and industrial processes in the eighteenth century (4d) that secularization accelerated and took on a certain air of inevitability. Even that acceleration, however, depended on factors like the existence of huge reserves of fossil fuels that were entirely fortuitous as far as the contingencies of history are concerned. Before the late eighteenth century (stage e), history might have proceeded in a very different direction from the one that we now take for granted. For all we know, the process may still be contingent, if not reversible.

For our present purposes, it is helpful to differentiate several dimensions or aspects of the secularization process and briefly review their development through the five stages I listed above. I propose to treat six such aspects:

1. Sociopolitical — emergence of the modern nation-state;
2. Spiritual — spirits disengaged from the objective, public world;
3. Sociopsychological — individuals abstracted from social roles;
4. Cosmological — cosmos de-animated and matter commodified;
5. Phenomenological — split between subject and object; and
6. Cultural — life patterns transcending tradition, community, and place.

The aspects labeled sociopolitical, spiritual, and sociopsychological have roots as early as the eleventh century. By my reckoning, the cosmological and phenomenological aspects originated in the seventeenth century. The cultural is the latest development, since it depends on mentalities of the society as a whole, not just on the views of educated elites.[22]

There is obviously a good deal of overlap between these six aspects, particularly in the later stages of their development. They are all theological in that they relate to our understanding of ourselves and the world within which we live.

With five stages (*a* to *e*) and six aspects (1 to 6) of secularization, we may produce a matrix, as in the accompanying diagram.

The elements of the matrix, each represented by an *x*, are stages of history for which I find evidence for the aspect of secularization considered. There are twenty-four elements in all. A dash means that I find no evidence for that particular aspect of secularization at the stage in question.

In order to explore the relationships of the various stages and aspects, I shall discuss each of the twenty-four elements of the matrix in turn.[23]

1. The Sociopolitical Aspect — Emergence of the Modern Nation-state

The first efforts to establish a strong centralized state in the West date back to Charlemagne in the late eighth and early ninth centuries. The Carolingian efforts, however, were anything but secularizing. Their inspiration came from Augustine's *City of God*, from which Charlemagne had passages read to him regularly. The sanction for Carolingian power was both sacral and ecclesiastical, and many of the officials of the state were taken from the clergy. The aggressive Carolingian development of secular power may have had its faults; in itself, however, it was not secularizing.

1a. The motivation for the aggrandizement of the European states was rather different by the time of the Investiture Controversy, 1075–1122. Several heads of state struggled to establish power bases free from papal influence, particularly in France, England, and Norman Sicily and later in

22. I use the term "cultural," not as a higher level than the social and political, but rather as a broader category that includes ancestors, places, and buildings.

23. Detailed documentation for the following is available from the author.

	a Middle Ages	b Renaissance	c 17th century	d 18th century	e 19th century
1. Sociopolitical	X	X	X	X	X
2. Spiritual	X	X	X	X	X
3. Sociopsychological	X	X	X	X	X
4. Cosmological	—	—	X	X	X
5. Phenomenological	—	—	X	X	X
6. Cultural	—	—	X	X	X

The elements of the matrix, each represented by an "x," are stages of history for which I find evidence for the aspect of secularization considered. There are twenty-four elements in all. A "—" means that I find no evidence for that particular aspect of secularization at the stage in question.

Germany. They intentionally developed bureaucracies that were independent of the church and legal codes that were distinct from canon church law.

Still there was no attempt to become secular in the modern sense. All of the European kings still viewed their positions in theological terms and cultivated traditions of sacral kingship. The political struggle for independence from Rome should not be equated with secularism, at least not in its earlier stages. If anything, the secularizing impetus came from the side of the church, particularly from proponents of the Gregorian reform (begun under Pope Gregory VII, 1073–85), who attacked the idea of sacral kingship and made it more difficult for secular rulers to view their positions as divinely sanctioned.

1b. The fourteenth and fifteenth centuries are noted for the emergence of the first modern nation-states and the rise of the commercial bourgeoisie — in a word, mercantilism. What makes the modern nation-state different from traditional states (mostly either city-states or empires) is its definition in terms of legal regulations rather than social relations. The boundaries of a nation-state are defined by lines on a map (the territorial state) and tariffs on trade rather than in terms of natural boundaries, the current distribution of tribes, or the conquests of a particular dynasty. The nation-state is made up of citizens whose loyalty is to the state itself — to its constitution or code of law — rather than to a particular king (or dynasty) or city. These citizens share a national language and an official history, which supersede all local dialects and traditions. In contrast to traditional empires like the ancient Egyptian, Roman, Abbasid, or Chinese, nation-states are more unified internally and more competitive internationally.

It is remarkable how highly developed the ideology of state control was, even in the fourteenth century. In fact, major publications by John of Paris (1302–3), Dante (ca. 1313), Marsilius of Padua and John of Jandun (1324), as well as William of Ockham (ca. 1334–47) legitimated the secular state (French or imperial) in its struggle with the pope.

The means of modern transport and warfare needed to make these ideas workable were only beginning to become available during the late Middle Ages and Renaissance. Gunpowder and cannon, which later broke down the resistance of local feudal lords, were first used in 1326 (Florence); they took precedence over the use of cavalry and bowmen at the conclusion of the Hundred Years' War in 1453. But artillery could also be used in defense of strategic towns. The development of elaborate defensive works like the *trace italienne* gave the advantage to the local defenders.

1c. For many historians the key turning point in the emergence of the nation-state was the long series of wars of religion, particularly the Thirty Years' War (1618–48), that characterized the post-Reformation era. Before this time, Christianity was still viewed as an international order, superior to all states in prestige if not actual power. But by the later phases of the Thirty Years' War, hostilities had become more political than confessional. By the time of the Peace of Westphalia (1648), religion was widely regarded as an internal affair, to be governed by each state, rather than a higher order of reality encompassing all spheres of life.

Already during the early stages of the Thirty Years' War, Hugo Grotius wrote *De jure belli ac pacis* ("On the law of war and peace," 1625), in which he argued that religious beliefs and practices would have to be set aside in the management of affairs between states if European civilization was to survive. The basis for social life must be a strictly rational one, based on immutable natural law, acceptable to all people and independent of their particular beliefs about God.

However secularizing the implications of their writing, Grotius and many other seventeenth-century thinkers were still deeply religious in their outlook. They were not trying to eliminate Christian faith but to make it workable in the real world of confessional differences. Grotius himself believed in an ideal (generic) Christian order that transcended national identities and confessional differences, and he appealed to the Christian conscience of European leaders to uphold this ideal. Others, however, like Herbert of Cherbury (1625) and John Locke (1690), appealed to reason and natural law independently of any confessional stance at all.

1d–e. In the eighteenth and nineteenth centuries, the expansion of commerce became a principal concern of the state, and the first nationwide economies emerged, first in England and later in France and the United States. Wealth and power that could not be derived from the institutional church (now greatly impoverished economically) or directly from the people (most of whom still lived at a subsistence level) was seen to be available through the development of extensive commercial networks at home and abroad. Many of the structural changes that brought about the new social order were legitimated by an appeal to national interests and were legislated, and often subsidized, by national governments.

For the majority of people, commercial networks became the matrix of life rather than just an appendage. Both long-range commerce and the nation-state transcended the particularities of ancient traditions and churches. The ideology of modern democracy, encouraged (in fact, required) people to view themselves as loyal members of the nation rather than members primarily of a particular community or sect. The implications of this shift for social psychology and culture will be considered later (under 3 and 6).

2. The Spiritual Aspect — Spirits Disengaged from the Objective, Public World

Normally, secularization is viewed as a characteristic of the state or of other strictly secular areas of life. But the sacred, too, can be secularized (according to our definition) in the sense of being made peripheral or restricted to the private domain.[24] Even God can be secularized in this sense. That is, the action of God can be relegated to personal experience and stories about ancient biblical times and completely eliminated from the stories and processes that govern public life. What we are concerned with here is not so much the writings of theologians (which could become a commercial

24. Fenn, *Toward a Theory of Secularization,* 64–65.

industry in their own right) as the way in which the action of God was understood by secular people like scientists, physicians, and tradespeople.

2a. Such a secularization of God was already clearly in evidence in some of the natural philosophers of the early twelfth century. Two good examples are Adelard of Bath and William of Conches (both d. ca. 1150). Adelard and William were placed in the awkward position of having to defend their interests in rational science against conservatives who stressed the teaching authority of the institutional church. Unfortunately, this sort of polarization has come to characterize many of the science-theology conflicts of Western history.

In order to protect their interests, naturalists like Adelard and William argued that God created nature in such a way that it could function rationally and autonomously. Therefore, human reason need not appeal to the action of God unless there turned out to be no rational, natural explanation for an event. The God of Adelard and William of Conches was thus more remote and static than that of Scripture. In fact, it approached the modern concept of a God of the gaps.

Adelard and William of Conches were admittedly radicals for their time. Other philosophers like Hugh of St. Victor in the twelfth century and Grosseteste, Bonaventure, Aquinas, and Lull in the thirteenth developed more integrated views of God and nature.

However, the differentiation between the processes of nature and the activity of God was also taking place within the practice of medicine. Already in the eleventh century, Rashi (d. 1105) commented on the tendency of (Jewish?) physicians to disavow reliance on God, a critique that might reflect Rashi's prejudices as much as the actual practice of physicians. But Oswei Temkin has recently argued that, in the Hippocratic tradition of medicine, medieval physicians kept their science and their religion quite separate.[25] At the same time, as a result of the Gregorian reform of the church, canon law attempted to prohibit clergy in major orders from practicing surgery or attending the sick except as spiritual directors. So a separation between the spiritual and the natural was already occurring in practical as well as theoretical terms.

2b. The most significant event of the fourteenth century in this respect was the development of early machinery and the rudiments of the me-

25. Oswei Temkin, *Hippocrates in a World of Pagans and Christians* (Baltimore: Johns Hopkins, 1991), 177, 250, 253–56.

chanical philosophy. Sometime in the late thirteenth century the verge and folio escapement was invented, and the first mechanical clocks were developed. In the mid-fourteenth century Parisian natural philosophers like Jean Buridan and Nicole Oresme began to portray the entire cosmos as a giant clocklike mechanism that continued in motion without God's intervention. People's sense of time undoubtedly became more uniform as town clocks were built in the fourteenth century and portable, spring-driven clocks came into use by elites in the fifteenth.

Before the nineteenth century, however, only urban populations had access to clocks of any sort, and the time discipline of town life was still understood as an enclave within the variable, diurnal cycle of day and night. In fact, the operation (or reading) of clocks was often adjusted to the seasonal duration of the day so that daytime hours were longer in the summer and shorter in the winter. The time of day at any given location was also specific to its meridian or longitude. In other words, time was still fairly elastic and relational.

Another factor that helped to eclipse the objective presence of spirits was the development of geometric perspective in art and architecture. Medieval art had portrayed earthly scenes as open to the heavens. A continuous narrative with several distinct events could be presented within a single composition The sizes of figures could represent spiritual stature as seen from a divine viewpoint (esp. in medieval representations of Christ and Mary). But the Renaissance fascination with viewer-standpoint perspective and lines converging at a vanishing point on the horizontal plane froze events in space and time and made the appearance of the Deity and even the presence of angels seem more alien in a terrestrial scene. According to the new rules, the presence of the divine in humans could no longer be portrayed by the simple expedient of greater relative size. Other means, however, could be employed such as positioning within the composition, atmospheric modeling, and the dramatic use of light and shadow.

2c. In the seventeenth century the mechanical philosophy was fully developed, and by the middle of the eighteenth century it had become the dominant paradigm for the physical sciences. The principal contributors were Galileo, Descartes, Gassendi, Boyle, and Newton, all of whom still possessed a vital religious faith. There was no conflict between science and theology in the later (nineteenth-century) sense. Yet all of these contributors viewed the laws of mechanics as deterministic, and many like Boyle made a sharp distinction between the action of God in creation and miracle and the relatively autonomous processes of inanimate nature.

The mechanical philosophy was a programmatic attempt to differentiate matter from spirit and to eliminate the element of contingency from the realm of nature. In effect, it was a program of cultural exorcism. The idea of strict determinism was present as early as Descartes's *Discourse on Method* (1637), which was published as a sample of his more comprehensive *Treatise on the World* (written 1628–32). The idea of banishing contingency was clearly in evidence in Spinoza's bolder version of Cartesian philosophy and was carried to its logical conclusion by eighteenth-century philosophers like Hume and Laplace.

The de-animation of matter by scientists, however, did not at once eliminate belief in the action of angels and demons in the lives of humans. The witch hysteria in Europe and America testified to widespread belief in spectral evidence in the seventeenth century. An educated minister like Cotton Mather not only believed that witches were demon possessed but encountered angels himself in the late seventeenth century. And an uneducated man like Joseph Smith could encounter angels as late as the early nineteenth. Belief that supernatural agents played a role in history, however, was gradually being relegated to the status of folklore and superstition (see 5d).

Historians of theology have observed that, in seventeenth-century England, the doctrine of the Trinity began to be viewed as a logical puzzle at odds with human reason. The loss of the trinitarian dynamic of the biblical God seems to have contributed to the distancing of God from the ordinary processes of nature in the minds of enlightened deists like Voltaire, Benjamin Franklin, and Thomas Jefferson.

2d. The developments considered so far have primarily involved small groups of intellectuals like natural philosophers. The eighteenth and nineteenth centuries saw the gradual spread of the mechanical outlook among the populace. Such widespread trends are more difficult to document, but partial evidence can be correlated with the emergence of enlightened leadership in eighteenth-century public affairs and the gradual discrediting of popular beliefs in supramechanical forces as being backward and ignorant. In other words, what we moderns have been trained to view as quaint superstition and folklore are really remnants of the sacred canopy that once embraced all of life.

The irony here is that Isaac Newton had consciously tried to preserve a role for supramechanical forces (and hence for God) in his theory of universal gravitation. During the eighteenth century, however, the idea of mechanism was generalized to include gravitation, and Newton's ideas were reinterpreted as a vindication of the mechanical philosophy. This reinterpretation of Newtonian physics points to a strong underlying tendency to redefine matter and force as being devoid of spirit.

2e. The final stages of the separation of God from public life occurred for most people with the rational organization of work and the commodification of materials in the nineteenth century. Religious experiences and celebrations were confined to holidays (not the same as the traditional holy days), and the plausibility structures of technology and work were redefined in terms of efficiency, reproducibility, and the interchangeability of parts. Elements like light and water that were traditionally thought to mediate a sense of the divine presence in the world were harnessed and marketed as commodities (see 4d below). During the Gothic architectural revival, an attempt was made to recapture the spiritual meaning of space and light, but the plausibility of such associations was now confined to ecclesiastical settings and, for most people, to Sunday services. At the same time, the banks, the media, and the political parties left no doubt about what was real and what was merely optional in public life. Western societies had become fully secular in the sense that spiritual agents were bracketed out from the major part of people's lives.

3. The Sociopsychological Aspect — Individuals Abstracted from Social Roles

One of the principal aspects of modernity is individualism. By "individualism," I do not mean self-reliance or independence of mind and action. Such qualities are as rare (or rarer) in the modern world as in any other.[26] In fact, traditional figures like David, Paul, and Francis of Assisi could be regarded as rugged individualists, but there would clearly be no implications of modern secularism. What it means to be an individual is a matter of social definition — the definition of one's self in relation to others. It is not just a mode of personal decision-making or action.

26. On the paradox of conformity and dependency in an age of supposed individualism, see Luckmann, *Invisible Religion*, 97; Robert N. Bellah et al., *The Good Society* (New York: Alfred A. Knopf, 1991), 59–60, 70–71.

Traditional individuals understood themselves and related to others primarily as members of a group — their family, their ancestors, their guild, their caste. They identified themselves in terms of what we would call their societal roles or functions.[27] But there was no difference between the existential and the functional in traditional anthropology. The very givenness of family and estate involved individuals in stories of foundings and journeys, humiliations and redemptions, which tied them immediately to the natural and supernatural worlds as well as to their social contexts. The story of a person could not be reduced to a series of merely human choices, even though such choices were part of a larger story involving God and the ancestors.

Modern individuals will have none of this. We painstakingly differentiate ourselves from our families, our upbringings, and our jobs. We affirm our freedom, even at the expense of the extreme psychological discomfort occasioned by a sense of homelessness. While belief in God and respect for traditions may still play a role in our personal choices, the social world of institutions and conventions is perceived as something external, and even alien, to us.[28]

3a. How did this shift in social definition come about? According to Colin Morris's classic work, the discovery (I would say the construction) of the individual took place in western Europe between 1050 and 1200.[29] Celebrated twelfth-century figures like Adelard of Bath, William of Conches, and Peter Abelard were well known for their sense of independence of traditional authority in matters of natural philosophy and theology.

In the late eleventh century and after, autobiographical confession became a popular form of self-examination and self-expression. Particularly striking is the confession of Otloh of St. Emmeram (1010–70), the first autobiographer of the new era: "For a long time," he says, "I found myself

27. Patricia Crone, *Pre-Industrial Societies* (Oxford: Basil Blackwell, 1989), 109–16.

28. Luckmann, *Invisible Religion,* 95–99; Berger, Berger, and Kellner, *Homeless Mind,* 33–35, 77, 92–94, 212–14. For some helpful insights into the (very different) development of individualism in Japan, see Robert Lee, "The Individuation of the Self in Japanese History," *Japanese Journal of Religious Studies* 4 (1977): 5–39.

29. Colin Morris, *The Discovery of the Individual, 1050–1200* (London: SPCK, 1972). Alexander Murray discusses the emergence of the "social fact" of social mobility and the "psychological fact" of ambition in the twelfth century (*Reason and Society,* 81–109).

tormented by a compulsion to doubt altogether the reliability of Holy Scripture and even the existence of God himself." Fortunately, Otloh's doubts were dispelled by God's light. But if these are the words of a pious monk in the eleventh century, what may we expect of a skeptic in the seventeenth?

A walk through any gallery of medieval art will show that the portrayal of human forms shifted away from the archetypal display of social status and took on a distinctively personal (if not realistic) character, particularly in the Gothic period (beginning in the late twelfth century). It was becoming increasingly important for leaders to be portrayed as unique personalities. However, the medieval affirmation of the individual was limited to elites (the first and second estates), and it did not weaken the identification of individuals with their social roles.

3b. The Renaissance is known as a time of emerging individualism and a time when critical thought was first developed along modern lines. For example, Lorenzo Valla demonstrated the spuriousness of the *Donation of Constantine* in 1440. The traditions of antiquity and of the early church were henceforth subject to critical assessment, even if they were still valued once they had been deemed authentic and reliable. For Pico della Mirandola in 1486, man was different from all other creatures in that he (gender intentional) had no fixed place or given form or set laws that would determine his nature. Humans were free to choose their own location, form, and laws. At one level, this view was an astute observation of the plastic nature of humanity, already affirmed in Scripture. On another level, however, it was a declaration of independence from natural structures and of separation from the nonhuman creation.

Still the context of Renaissance humanism was a theistic one, based on the biblical teaching of humanity as created in the image of God and the traditional imagery of humanity as the microcosm of God's creation.

Incipient individualism was not limited to elites in the Renaissance era; it also occurred among the peasant class. Through a series of revolts between 1380 and 1480, peasant traders won a measure of freedom from their traditional manorial obligations and gained greater control over their land and the products of their labor. At the same time, arable farming of the medieval manor yielded to a more profit-oriented pastoral economy. The result was an unprecedented degree of competition among peasants and the emergence of a yeoman farmer class that succeeded in accumulating landholdings and monopolizing the means of subsistence. The situation was thus not unlike the emergence of market elites in Third World countries today.

It was also during the Renaissance that the concept of human dignity began to displace the traditional concept of honor. Dignity pertains to the individual as a human being, irrespective of any social or cultural ties, whereas honor was defined in terms of those very ties. By the early seventeenth century, Shakespeare's Falstaff could thumb his nose at the traditional standards of chivalry and recite, "Honour is a mere scutcheon."[30] But the concept of honor was still vital enough to be parodied in the eighteenth century, when Robert Dodsley (1703–64) contrasted it with the law of nature:

> Honour! What's honour? A vain phantom rais'd,
> To fright the weak from tasting those delights,
> Which nature's voice, that law supreme, allows.[31]

There are a few important exceptions to the overall trend toward the obsolescence of honor, however. An archaic sense of honor survives even in modern institutions like the armed forces and the nation-state. When there is a perceived threat to national security, for example, distinctions of race, religion, and regionality (though not sexual preference) dissolve, and one's unquestioned loyalty is to a flag and "to the republic for which it stands." But it is noteworthy that the traditional sense of honor survives only near the periphery of modern everyday life, particularly at times when its stability is threatened.

3c. While individualism had its beginnings in the Middle Ages and Renaissance, it became legitimate only in the modernizing movement of the seventeenth to nineteenth centuries. In philosophy, we naturally think of Descartes's resolve "to study no other science than that which I could find within myself or else in the great book of the world." In religion, we think of Herbert of Cherbury's advice: "Retire into yourself and enter into

30. Shakespeare, *1 Henry IV*, 5.1; cf. Berger, Berger, and Kellner, *The Homeless Mind*, 88, 90.

31. R. Straus, *Robert Dodsley: Poet, Publisher, and Playwright* (London, 1910), 249, cited in Paul Langford, *A Polite and Commercial People* (Oxford: Oxford University Press, 1989), 464. On the vitality of the concept in seventeenth-century English drama, see Charles L. Barber, *The Idea of Honour in the English Drama, 1591–1700* (Gothenburg: Almquist & Wiksell, 1957).

your own faculties; you will find there God, virtue, and the other universal and eternal truths." And, lest we seem to base our case merely on rationalists and deists, consider the counsel of a staunch pietist like Comenius: "Return to the place whence you came, to the home of your heart, and shut the door behind you!" Or the amazingly Schleiermacherian words of John Smith, the Cambridge Platonist: "To seek our Divinity meerly in Books and Writings, is to seek the living among the dead. . . . No; *intra te quaere Deum*, seek for God within thine own soul."[32] Such breathtaking breaks with the identities of the past may be seen as the culmination of the Renaissance development sketched above. In retrospect, we can see in them a foreshadowing of the modern personality type.

During the seventeenth century, narratives of travelers to distant parts of the world became part of the reading of intellectuals. Writers like Descartes and Le Comte concluded from accounts of non-Western cultures that cultural mores and beliefs were merely a matter of social conditioning and therefore were not universally valid. Accordingly, the individual in search of the truth must purge himself (a decidedly male perspective) of all such cultural accretions.

Still the vast majority of people in the seventeenth century identified themselves with the communities and traditions of their birth. As long as early modern individualism was held in check by the natural and communitarian ties of local groupings, the prevailing sense of identity was still defined in terms of social roles rather than by the nature of individuals.

3d. During the eighteenth century, the "new men" of modern commerce emerged (the bourgeoisie), equipped with the rudiments of the new (mechanical) philosophy and granted the freedom to accumulate wealth, provided they could effectively organize workers and harness the forces of nature. A clear differentiation emerged between the privacy of domestic life and the public roles of commerce and society. The scope of early modern individualism was greatly widened. But it was still limited to elites until, toward the end of the eighteenth century, the emergence of power-driven technologies and the exploitation of fossil fuels (along with extensive state support as a catalyst) made possible a transportation revolution that would break down the natural and communitarian ties of local groupings.

3e. From the 1770s to the 1850s, turnpikes and canals were built in

32. John Smith, *Discourse,* vol. 1 (1660), 1–4, quoted in Basil Willey, *Seventeenth Century Background* (New York: Doubleday Anchor, 1953), 144–45.

Britain, France, and America that shifted the economic horizons of the majority of people from their homes and farms to national markets and beyond. As transportation costs dwindled to a mere fraction of overall market costs, neither church nor clan could retain the automatic loyalty of the majority of the people in a community. Those who continued to place such loyalties ahead of market enterprise were quickly marginalized and lost their traditional influence. If necessary, they could be labeled parochial, or even corrupt.

The transportation revolution was accompanied by an industrial revolution in the late eighteenth century and followed by a corporate revolution in the late nineteenth. Mass media and mass marketing redefined people in terms of transcommunal norms. The stories people told about their lives had more to do with forces of mass production and patterns of mass consumption and less to do with face-to-face encounters with other humans.

The latest influence in the development of modern individualism was the rise of the modern corporation. As mechanical manufacture was developed on a massive scale, commensurate structures of organization were developed. By the final decades of the nineteenth century, business firms employed large numbers of people in roles defined without reference to their personal backgrounds or identities. For most people, the estrangement of personal identity from public affairs was complete.

4. The Cosmological Aspect — Cosmos De-animated and Matter Commodified

In retrospect, our view of the material world is a mirror image of our view of God — a living God can be correlated with dynamic matter, and inert matter with a static God. Historically, however, the more modern view of matter seems to have lagged behind that of God by several centuries. While the action of God was being surgically separated from that of nature as early as the twelfth century (2a above), matter was viewed as imbued with form (Aristotelian philosophy), spirit (hermetism), and active principles (Neoplatonism); physical events were viewed as filled with spiritual significance as late as the seventeenth century. Popular belief in alchemistic and magical powers in America seems to have persisted on a wide scale at least until the early nineteenth century.

4c. The principal change in outlook in the seventeenth century was the differentiation of primary and secondary qualities associated with the rise of the mechanical philosophy. Galileo was one of the first to make this distinction. It was further developed by Descartes, Newton, and Locke, among others. All of the features of matter that gave it warmth and beauty were stripped away and relegated to subjective human experience. Matter itself consisted only of location, geometric shape, motion, extension, mass, and inertia. For Galileo and Descartes, even gravitation was an occult quality and therefore could not be regarded as an irreducible force in nature. For Newton, gravitation was a central concept, but it could not be a primary quality of matter itself, since matter was entirely passive.

There is a remarkable contrast here with early seventeenth-century natural philosophers like Gilbert and Kepler, for whom matter was still living and active. Leibniz was one of the last natural philosophers to retain a sense of the vital quality of matter. He articulated it in his concept of *vis viva* (living force), a rudimentary concept of physical energy. But in the eighteenth century, both gravitation and energy were mathematized and absorbed into a mechanical framework. The living quality of matter was thoroughly disguised by inanimate, mechanical concepts.

A corollary of the de-animation of matter was the attempt to empty natural events of all spiritual significance. On the basis of the newly discovered laws of motion, for example, Pierre Bayle argued in 1682 that events like comets and eclipses occurred independently of human affairs and no longer had any meaning for those seeking to know God's will. His polemical comments were directed against the tendency, still widespread in the seventeenth century, to view all unusual events as signs of God's providence.

Concurrent with the de-animation of matter in seventeenth-century science was a parallel development in political economy: the emergence of a mass market for cash crops and the subsequent commodification of land. The population expansion of the late fifteenth and sixteenth centuries led to an increased demand for food and hence for arable land. The growth of the cloth industry also led to an increased demand for wool and hence for land to graze sheep on. In England and America, land began to become a marketable commodity, subject to a logic of investment and speculation that had previously applied only to luxury goods.

In England the demand for land promoted attempts to consolidate holdings and enclose fields to augment their agricultural and/or grazing capacities. Laws passed by Parliament under the Tudors had protected the land against enclosure and depopulation. During the first half of the seventeenth century, these laws were gradually repealed in order to facilitate private agricultural improvement.

For many seventeenth-century colonists in America this new emphasis on land improvement was already an inherited tradition. For Euro-Americans the land was empty, and there were no preexisting (European) communal structures to resist commodification. In fact, the need to build new communities, together with the apparent availability of land for distribution, led to an American version of land enclosure at the expense of Native Americans.

These two major seventeenth-century developments — the new mechanical science and the new market economics — came together in the philosophy of John Locke, who, more than any other writer, influenced the leaders of eighteenth-century England and America.

But there was also a reaction. Contemporary English observers also noticed the shift in the understanding of matter and pointed out its theological significance. As early as 1652, Isaac Barrow criticized the Cartesians for making matter "blocklike and inanimate." Such a view was unworthy of the God who created matter, according to Barrow. It made him appear "like some carpenter or mechanic repeating and displaying ad nauseam his one marionettish feat." A decade later, Richard Baxter objected to the Cartesian emphasis on "meer Matter and Motion," which was like "a Carcas or a Clock" in comparison to the true principles of motion, which are "Spirits, active Natures, and Vital Powers." Henry More led a counterattack (1659 and after) by developing a Neoplatonically inspired science of the spirit world comparable to Galileo's science of mechanics. The more mathematical physics of Newton (also Neoplatonically inspired), however, was to prove more useful to the new social constructors of the eighteenth century.

The reduction of land to a market commodity was also protested. In 1653, John Moore charged the enclosers with not caring for the poor as Christ has commanded; even if enclosers were the legal owners, they were spiritually usurpers. Similar concerns were raised by Americans like John Winthrop and Roger Williams. So the seventeenth-century de-animation of matter is not just an (etic) interpretation by modern historians; it was an observable phenomenon of which people were conscious at the time.

4d. The mechanical philosophy clearly typifies the modern secular attitude toward matter. Yet few people even today are trained enough in modern science to be influenced by it directly. It might still be an esoteric outlook, like the more recent theory of relativity, if eighteenth-century lecturers had not popularized its concepts and ingrained them in a generation of rising entrepreneurs and industrialists.

4e. During the late eighteenth and early nineteenth centuries, Western civilization was completely reconstructed from top to bottom. The reality in which we live today is largely the work of the world-builders of those three or four generations. Like all emerging elites, the entrepreneurs and policy-makers of that time needed an ideology that was both practical and credible. The mechanical philosophy — in a popularized form — was the one that captured their imaginations (much as hermetic and alchemistic philosophies had appealed to princes and generals in the fifteenth and sixteenth centuries).

As a result of the hegemony of the mechanical philosophy among the new elites, the industrial revolution projected a new world in which most forms of matter were inert substances. Matter was no longer of value in its natural state. In order to have value, it needed to be improved or used as the raw material for industrial purposes. The significance of land was redefined strictly in terms of market value. Even the more subtle elements of water and light were harnessed, marketed, and distributed as commodities.

Matter for moderns is a commodity with a brand name. It is reproducible, interchangeable, buyable, and disposable. Even in the form of food and clothing, it is related to athletic stars and shopping malls more than to its sources — plants and animals. The very substance of our lives is divorced from creation, and thereby from God the Creator. There are no intrinsically theological issues involved in the use of matter. As long as the purposes for which it is exploited are justifiable, neither God nor theology enters into questions of its use.

With regard to land, the shift I am describing can be revisited today by anyone who flies westward across the United States. Once the plane moves beyond the Atlantic seaboard states, the irregular fields and curved roads give way to a nearly Euclidean (or Cartesian) grid of plots, which extends all the way to California. In most midwestern states, the checkerboard pattern is only occasionally distorted by the presence of natural features like large lakes and rivers.

To some extent this Euclidean structure is due to the flatter land of the Midwest, but historically the settlement of these areas took place soon after the land surveys of the 1780s. The shift in the patterns of settlement shows how the Enlightenment emphasis on uniformity and the modern understanding of land as a commodity came together in the construction of a new reality, devoid of spirit.

5. The Phenomenological Aspect — Split between Subject and Object

Encounter with God in the world depends on some sort of correspondence between the voice within us and the shades and hues of the world in which we live. The secularity of biblical life and thought presupposes that almost any object can become the medium for an encounter with the supernatural. Donkeys speak like people. People who speak to us turn out to be angels. The words that come from within us (at least from within the holy among us) have power to change the course of nature and to call disciples. The stories of Moses, Elijah, Jesus, and Francis of Assisi would be inconceivable otherwise.

Such correspondences between subject and object were called into question by changes in the views of humanity and matter, which we discussed above. But modern secularism is more than just the abstraction of personality from society and the draining of life from matter. It is the redefinition of both subject and object in opposition to each other. The *object* is deliberately defined in rational terms that eschew all tones of personality; the *subject* is defined in pristine isolation from the environment and even from personal possessions.[33] There are no immediate correspondences or sympathies between the two.

The modern subject may be referred to as a self, or perhaps as a mind. But it is not the same as a spirit. A spirit exists in relation to other spirits, in a world of spirits and the spiritual forces of nature. But such spirits can be known only in some material form — experienced through the senses or in dreams. Since matter is now entirely devoid of spirit, the modern subject exists in splendid isolation, much as the modern God does.

33. I do not claim that it is possible to make this distinction consistently, only that the distinction is essential to modern secular consciousness. Daniel Bell describes the "contradictions" involved in the separation of the social and the cultural spheres — the "social" including the technological and economic, which are ideally impersonal and objective, and the "cultural" including the family, leisure, and religious, which are personal, self-expressive, and subjective (*The Cultural Contradictions of Capitalism* [New York: Basic Books, 1978], xvi–xvii, 10–15).

5c. The emergence of the subject-object split seems to have occurred first in response to the theoretical de-animation of matter in the seventeenth century. For many intellectuals, the rise of the mechanical philosophy resulted in the estrangement of the inner person from the world of matter and motion.

I find the first awareness of this estrangement in passages of the *Pensées* of Pascal, which were written in the late 1650s in reaction to the mechanical philosophy of Descartes:

> When I see the blind and wretched state of man, when I survey the whole universe in its dumbness and man left to himself with no light, as though lost in this corner of the universe, without knowing who put him here, what he has come to do, what will become of him when he dies, incapable of knowing anything, I am moved to terror, like a man transported in his sleep to some terrifying desert island, who wakes up quite lost and with no means of escape.[34]

Pascal found personal faith and at least some comfort in God and in Christ (so his *Memorial*). But his God was now a strictly personal God, not the God of the philosophers or the Logos of mathematics, which Pascal had himself studied so assiduously in his earlier days. *L'esprit géometrique* was of no use in ethics or theology; for that, one had to develop the quite different *esprit de finesse.*

The popularity of Pascal among evangelical Protestants and Catholics today stems from the fact that he experienced God and described his experience so vividly in terms of the modern, secular reality in which we also live. Faith in the modern world is not weaker than it was in the traditional world of biblical secularity. If anything, it is more intense precisely because it is defined over against the world of science, technology, and commerce. Whatever the gain in intensity, there is a loss of the subject-object unity that characterized biblical secularity.

Other examples of a widening chasm between the realms of subject and object could be cited. A series of theologians from John Smith to Friedrich Schleiermacher made theology a matter of inner consciousness rather than objective knowledge. A complementary series of philosophers from John Locke to John Stuart Mill made all reliable knowledge a matter

34. Blaise Pascal, *Pensées* 198, trans. A J. Krailsheim (Baltimore: Penguin Books, 1966), 88.

of rational judgments based on verifiable sense experience and differentiated it from imagination and enthusiasm. This leads us to consider a further stage of development.

5d. The eighteenth century made two principal contributions to the subject-object split: the discrediting of all subject-object correspondences, and the Romantic reaction to mechanical science and neoclassic art.

At first, claims to subject-object immediacy were disparagingly portrayed as the result of fraud and fanaticism. Then, toward the end of the eighteenth century, they were rationalized in terms of quasi-scientific constructs like animal magnetism. At the same time, many popular beliefs and practices were collected by elites and marketed under the heading of folklore.

"Folklore" is the modern term used to refer to regional traditions inherited from a premodern world. In earlier times, these traditions were highly credible. Institutionally supported elites might try to systematize or reform or even repress the ideas of magic and astrology, but they accepted the underlying premises. But as the mechanical philosophy became more influential, a gap was opened between the new ideas of the educated elite and traditional folk beliefs and practices. Any suggestion of real, immediate relations between inner consciousness and external events became a sign of ignorance or even fraud.

The Romantics were one class of elites who developed a genuine sympathy with folk traditions. The English longed for chivalry and the intimacy of Chinese gardens; the Scots celebrated Highland traditions, and the Germans collected myths and fairy tales. There was quite a market for books, poems, and songs on these subjects. In fact, Romanticism itself rapidly became a commodity, a marketable form of self-discovery and rejuvenation that compensated for the rigors of busy schedules. Whether we are Anglicans singing Blake's "And Did Those Feet in Ancient Time" or New Englanders reading Thoreau's *Walden* (to name two of my own favorites), we are stirred in our hearts and enabled to reexert ourselves in a world of objects and schedules. Far from being an exception, a commodified Romanticism is essential to the modern secular world in which subject and object must be kept apart, lest the spirits are heard to speak again and the real business of life be slowed down.

5e. Again, however, modern secularism is not just a matter of philosophers like Pascal and Mill or Romantics like Blake and Thoreau. None of these developments would count for much if there had not been a systematic separation of work from community as a result of the discipline of the factory.

As Peter Berger and his associates have shown us, we are doubly socialized. Passing through the portals of our workplaces, we enter the objective world of mechanical production and mathematical time. Upon reentering our homes and churches, we are reconstructed in terms of personal relations and religious beliefs. (There is also an intermediate state called commuting, but to my knowledge its sociology has not yet been worked out.) I use the term "intrapersonal pluralism" to refer to this subdivision of the individual's life-world.

It is no longer a question of consciously thinking about mechanics (Descartes) or locating the self (Pascal). The separate reality of each is a fact of modern life. In everyday life, we hardly notice the discrepancies; we therefore need sociologists and philosophers to point them out to us.

6. The Cultural Aspect — Life Patterns Transcending Tradition, Community, and Place

The cultural aspects of secularization described here have been alluded to earlier in our discussion of sociopsychology (individual-society split) and phenomenology (subject-object split), particularly in the later phases (eighteenth to nineteenth centuries) of those aspects. The thoroughgoing character of secularization may be missed, however, if it is not seen in terms of supraindividual aspects of our lives like tradition, community, and place — our life-world *(Lebenswelt)* in the temporal, social, and spatial senses.

Such changes of environment are the most concrete aspects of secularization. They are truly social constructions depending on the views and outlooks of entire populations, not just the ideas of educated elites. Accordingly, they are also the most recent aspects of secularism to have developed.

Here I describe the process of secularization as the transcending (rather than simply the losing) of tradition, community, and place. The term "transcending" is used in its basic meaning of exceeding prior limits. We all still follow traditions, live in communities, and exist in places. Nothing will ever change that. But our relationship to tradition, community, and place has changed radically. In traditional cultures, people experienced their traditions, communities, and places as matrices within which they existed and upon which they depended. Most people married within their communities and rarely traveled more than a few miles beyond. From a modern, secular viewpoint there was an absence of liberty and a certain parochialism.

People were literally embedded within, or embraced by, their temporal, social, and spatial environments.

One of the striking features of the Hebrew Bible was that God was described not just in personal attributes but also in terms of the nation of Israel, events like the Exodus, and even places like Bethel (Gen. 31:13; 35:7). Every year I point out this feature of God's attributes to my theology students, and I encourage them to write about God in terms of the events and places of their own lives. In nineteen years of teaching I have yet to get a paper back in which this recommendation has been followed. The radically relational character of God is apparently lost on us. Undoubtedly this loss reflects our individualism. But it also reflects our tendency to see traditions and places as somewhat arbitrary and unbecoming to God. The real for us is the uniform and the standardized, not the local or the particular.

In comparison with traditional, biblical secularity, modern secularism is more limited in temporal terms. In spite of the discovery of the deep past of cosmogony, earth history, and evolution, modern consciousness is experientially oriented to the present and the short-term future more than to the generations of the past or the ages to come.[35] In contrast, modernity is more cosmopolitan in its social and spatial horizons than traditional cultures. Moderns are attuned to events in distant markets and exchanges, more than they are to the soil under their feet or the people who live next door.[36]

How did this change come about?

35. Openness to the future is sometimes cited as a distinguishing feature of modernity (e.g., Brown, *Modernization,* 13). However, traditional restorationist movements generally based aspirations for the future on models from the deep past. See, e.g., Theodore Dwight Bozeman, *To Live Ancient Lives: The Primitivist Dimension in Puritanism* (Chapel Hill: University of North Carolina Press, 1988), 340, 347–48.

36. Patricia Crone describes the shift from local communities to large-scale associations as "cultural integration," in contrast to economic and sociopolitical integration (*Pre-Industrial Societies,* 178–80). She also notes the paradox of limitation across time and breadth over space (196–97).

Bryan Wilson describes the shift as "societalization" (*Religion,* 45–46, 153–65, 171–74). See Lyon, *Steeple's Shadow,* 47–52, for a critical evaluation of this idea, which Lyon calls the "community-lost" thesis. Our definition of secularization as a dissociation, rather than decline, of religion avoids the brunt of Lyon's critique; cf. Lyon's own point about "boundary definition" (141). It is also important to avoid Wilson's simplistic equations of community with affective language, and society with technological rationality, as pointed out by Luckmann in "A Critical Rejoinder," *Japanese Journal of Religious Studies* 3 (1976): 277–78.

6c. First, it seems that traditional community life was weakened by the emergence of the yeoman farmer class in the Renaissance and the land enclosures of the seventeenth (and eighteenth) century. Villagers who were used to working in cooperation for mutual survival now found themselves subject to the improvement schemes of a single landowner. Enclosure disentangled each person from the web of community obligations, including celebration and ceremony as well as labor.

The positive transcendence of the traditional, local environment began with the criticism of the ancients begun by early moderns like Francis Bacon and René Descartes. In his programmatic *Refutation of the Philosophers* (1608), Bacon praised his own age for its knowledge of two-thirds of the globe and disparaged the ancients as belonging to an age of fables. His sense of transcendence of tradition was matched by an incipient transcendence of place.

Nowhere is this transcendence more dramatically illustrated than on the title page of Bacon's *Instauratio magna* (1620), where three European ships (presumably Columbus's) are seen passing through the ancient Pillars of Hercules to cross the ocean beyond. The Latin caption cites the words of the prophet Daniel, "Many shall runne to and fro, & knowledge shall be increased" (Dan. 12:4b, Geneva Bible). The shift in European mentality, here portrayed by Bacon, was an event even more important than the actual crossing of the Atlantic. No longer did Europeans view themselves as encompassed by a great unknown. The unknown had become an enclave within the known.

In his *Discourse on Method* (1637), Descartes explained how he could no longer accept the classical arts education of the Jesuit school of La Flèche as the framework for his thinking. For him the test of truth was a certain invariance with respect to local traditions. Therefore Descartes had to travel as widely as possible (in Europe) and forsake any attachments to the received traditions of his youth. He thus typified the modern in being broad geographically and, at the same time, narrow historically.

6d. The influence of Bacon and Descartes was immense in the centers of the early Enlightenment. During the crisis of European thought at the turn of the seventeenth century, the new style of radical doubt and independence from tradition became quite fashionable among intellectuals. The founding fathers of Georgian England, Enlightenment Scotland, and early republican America were schooled in this style of thought. The rhetoric used by elites to legitimize economic development and national unity ridiculed traditional attachments to local interests and associated the broadening of horizons with the lure of profits for the more competitive.

6e. The market revolution of the early nineteenth century redirected people's sense of dependence from their local communities and unseen ancestors to more distant legislatures and invisible market forces.

The major impetus to transcendence of community came from the invention of the steam engine (1695–1781) and the subsequent growth in factory employment in the late eighteenth century. Thanks to the newly developed systems of transportation, factories could be built in locations that suited the logistics of commerce. Laborers then had to seek their employment where it could be found; less and less was available in their home villages. Managers struggled to reeducate their labor forces in the new values of mechanical production, work discipline, and time management. The ideas of seventeenth-century philosophers gradually became the objective reality of ordinary people.

As often noted by historians and sociologists, the relative homogeneity of local communities was replaced in the nineteenth century by a pluralism of worldviews and lifestyles, particularly in larger towns and cities. This interpersonal pluralism matches the intrapersonal pluralism noted under 5e above.

Pluralism, however, is not unique to modern secularism. While there may be more diversity within communities (interpersonally) and even within individual life-worlds (intrapersonally), there is far more homogeneity as one moves from one community to another (and even from one country to another) than there was in the premodern world. In Holland, Michigan, we now have Kentucky Fried Chicken as well as Dutch-American food, but the fried chicken is the same as that found in franchises around the world. In other words, we have the paradox of greater diversity at the local level but greater homogeneity on larger scales.[37]

A clear indication of this shift in the nineteenth century was the gradual weaning of communities from their local frames of time. At the beginning of the nineteenth century, most communities still oriented their daily life in accordance with the local diurnal cycles of sunrise, noon, and sunset. During the early decades of the century, the uniform time of most clocks established a public sense of equal hours of night and day, regardless

37. The paradox of differentiation and integration is well described by Richard Bendix, "Tradition and Modernity Reconsidered," *Comparative Studies in Society and History* 9 (1967): 319–20.

of the time of year. With the advent of railway schedules in the middle decades of the century, the local noon was adjusted to the standards of major cities with which communication and commerce were becoming more important than an orientation to the sun, moon, and stars. For instance, in the early 1870s Pittsburgh adopted the local time of Philadelphia. The solar standard of local time became a fiction, a mere relic of antiquity. Finally, in 1883 the United States adopted the wide-band time zones, which we accept as normal today.

The rhythms of our lives are now governed by standards oriented to no particular location, just as the behavioral norms by which we live (publicly) are oriented to no particular tradition. People who live in St. Louis are fortunate in being very near the ninetieth meridian, which is the base meridian for Central Standard Time. In the winter months, their clocks strike noon when the sun is directly overhead in towns like Belleville and Collinsville, just across the Illinois state line. But the clocks in Holland, Michigan, strike noon when the sun is overhead in Mohawk, New York, in winter and when it is overhead in Goose Bay, Labrador, in the summer!

Conclusion

I have constructed a model of the historical process of secularization in western Europe and America. The model is presented in the form of a grid: six aspects of modern secularism are traced through as many as five stages of historical development. Each aspect and each stage allow for interactions between philosophical ideas and social structures. Although the details are subject to amendment and revision, the model as a whole will be useful in locating historical figures in the overall process and in assessing our present situation in historical perspective.

Modern secularism is at the same time massive and contingent. Its massiveness is demonstrated by the complex web of secularizing features we have discussed. Secularism is not simply a matter of the separation of church and state or of a particular style of theology (or science). It involves all of these, but also it is embedded in everyday features of life like our sense of self and our experience of time and place — features we normally take for granted. We see this massiveness whenever we observe the development of children. The strange world of clothes and media they grow up in is very real to them, and it is very effective in communicating the basic messages of secularism. Sermons and sacraments are not likely to avail against them (humanly speaking).

Yet modern secularism is also highly contingent. After all, it is a human construction, and archaeology shows that even the firmest of human constructions can be sidelined by history. The very massiveness of the edifice of secularism means that there are many contingencies, such as the relatively low cost of energy and transportation. The near hysteria of the quest for efficient nuclear energy in our time is an indication of how sensitive our system is on this particular issue.

The contingency of modern secularism can be seen even more directly by cross-cultural experiences. People from other cultures and other times often present us with life-worlds totally different from our secular reality. Ironically, their worlds are often much closer to the one we read about in Scripture than the supposedly Christian culture we live in.

There are, then, at least three witnesses that testify against the permanence of secularism: historical (and economic) contingencies, people from other cultures, and Scripture. And these three agree: the days of secularism as we know it are numbered (1 John 5:6-7; Dan. 5:26).

Mission in the Emerging Postmodern Condition

Craig Van Gelder

The air we now breathe has changed. According to Steven Best and Douglas Kellner, we are living in a new epoch.[1] David Harvey points out that there has been a shift in the way we experience and relate to our world.[2] Walter Truett Anderson claims that we are awash today in a sea of symbols and an ocean of words with no objective criteria to guide or shape our choices.[3] And Steven Connor says that the old distinction between knowing and experiencing has collapsed, leaving us with the challenge of capturing moments of meaning from a constant pattern of flux.[4]

These various authors are all describing a common reality: the cultural landscape we occupy in the West in the latter part of the twentieth century has fundamentally shifted. The emerging landscape, of which there has as yet been no unified definition or description, is being referred to as the postmodern condition. In simple terms, the postmodern condition is that which replaces what came to be known as modernity over the past

1. See Best and Kellner, *Postmodern Theory: Critical Interrogations* (New York: Guilford Press, 1991), p. 2.

2. Harvey, *The Condition of Postmodernity* (Cambridge: Basil Blackwell, 1989), p. 38.

3. Anderson, *Reality Isn't What It Used to Be* (New York: Harper & Row, 1990), p. ix.

4. Connor, *Postmodernist Culture: An Introduction to Theories of the Contemporary* (Cambridge: Basil Blackwell, 1989), p. 4.

several centuries. But it should be noted that the use of the prefix *post-* points to the fact that we are not fully clear about the direction in which this cultural shift is moving or what its future shape will be. Even the use of words like *direction* and *shape* tends to reflect the biases of the perspective of modernity. It is coming to be recognized that reframing or collapsing categories such as these may be part of the very shift that is taking place in the postmodern condition.

Describing the postmodern condition and attempting to theorize about it are producing a new vocabulary that can sound strange at first. Concepts such as *indeterminacy, deconstruction, diversity, decentering,* and *the aestheticization of all of life* challenge the vocabulary of modernity, which emphasized prediction, certainty, absolutes, centers, and the privileging of a particular style as a preferred culture. When some people first encounter this language and the new perspective it is seeking to describe, they react negatively; to them it seems that all is now lost in a sea of relativism and nihilism.

This darker side of the emerging postmodern condition is certainly present within a number of the perspectives that are being developed. But there is more to the emerging postmodern condition than this. The negative reaction, in itself, usually reflects basic values and assumptions that were woven into the belief system of modernity. Many recent authors working within postmodern perspectives are taking a more positive view toward the world.[5] While they assume the reality of a relativity in perspective, they do not feel they have to capitulate to relativism as such.

Mapping the Task

However one chooses to describe what is taking place, it is becoming increasingly clear that the worldview shaped by the Enlightenment is changing. Indeed, this view, developed over the past several centuries and now indicated by the phrase "modern Western culture," is undergoing a fundamental shift. The purpose of this essay is to identify the basic character of this shift and to lay out some of the emerging features commonly associated

5. See Best and Kellner, *Postmodern Theory;* and *After Postmodernism: Reconstructing Ideological Critique,* ed. Herbert W. Simons and Michael Billig (Thousand Oaks, CA: Sage Publications, 1994).

with what is being called the postmodern condition. I will pursue this task in four steps.

First, I will clarify the historical developments and intellectual contributions that gave shape to what we refer to as modernity, the particular culture of Western nations that emerged between the eighteenth and twentieth centuries. I will also identify some of the core beliefs and values of this culture, along with a number of the social and institutional developments that gave concrete, historical shape to these beliefs and values.

Second, I will identify a number of key transitional steps that began to call into question some of the core assumptions of modernity and worked to reframe our perspective. Identifying some of these diverse perspectives that began to critique and challenge modernity is important for our understanding of the various streams that exist in the emerging postmodern condition.

Third, I will present the basic themes and viewpoints of those who are attempting to provide some theoretical understanding of the postmodern condition. I will introduce these various perspectives by reviewing briefly the contributions of a number of authors who have worked in this area. While certain elements are common to many of these authors, they are also advancing a number of distinct theoretical perspectives in their reflections on the postmodern condition.

Fourth, I will identify some of the challenges and some of the opportunities that confront the church as it engages in the mission of the gospel among people shaped by the emerging postmodern condition. The challenges arise principally out of discontinuities between the emerging postmodern condition and our understandings of the gospel as delivered to us within the historic Christian faith. But not all that is taking place within the emerging postmodern condition is problematic relative to making a clear presentation of the gospel. Opportunities are afforded by bridges of continuity between these alternative ways of viewing reality.

Over the centuries, the gospel has proved remarkably adaptable to translation.[6] It has been able to enter into a variety of particular worldviews in diverse cultures, to be shaped to some extent by these worldviews and yet bring new direction and expression to them. While on the one hand we are always susceptible to the cultural captivity of the gospel, on the other hand we encounter fresh ways to express the truths of the faith.

6. On this, see in this volume Paul Russ Satari's essay "'Translatability' in the Missional Approach of Lamin Sanneh," pp. 270–83.

As the church in the West approaches the end of the twentieth century, it needs to be careful that it does not judge the emerging postmodern condition too quickly or too harshly. It must first ask some fundamental questions about what the gospel brings to this worldview and what the gospel might draw from it. All the old struggles to make the gospel relevant to a modern worldview and all the old battles to resist the corrosive influence of modernity are being reframed as similar struggles within the emerging postmodern condition. The church needs to be careful that it does not hang on to obsolete categories or fight enemies that no longer exist. We stand, in the West, at an exciting and challenging threshold of human history. How will the church respond?

The Enlightenment Worldview and the Culture of Modernity

When considering the shift we are encountering from the world of modernity into the emerging postmodern condition, it is helpful to recall the profound shifts that took place as the condition we now know as modernity emerged out of the medieval worldview. A number of profound changes in perspective occurred between the thirteenth and sixteenth centuries. These changes worked to reshape the medieval worldview of the European peoples who were religiously and organizationally bound together by Christendom, both Roman Catholic and Protestant versions. The Renaissance in the 1300s gave new life to intellectual pursuits and artistic expressions. The focus of life substantially shifted from divine concerns to human interests and from the spiritual world to the world of nature. These emphases were given direction and discipline by the Protestant Reformation, which focused on the abilities and responsibilities of persons to shape their individual and corporate lives. The discovery of a broader world geographically, along with newly expanding economies, helped lay the groundwork for what would become modern nation-states and a system of colonialism. Developments in math and physics served to frame the concept of natural laws. The application of these laws by astronomers reframed our understanding of the physical universe. These developments highlighted the importance of reason and observation as tools for discovering truth and made the created world the arena within which such truth was to be discovered.

Developments such as these gave birth to a fundamentally different way of conceiving the human condition. A number of persons were instrumental in this regard. Francis Bacon (1561-1626) developed the idea that a rational knowledge of life — what came to be known as scientific knowledge — could (and should) be used as a tool for mastering the natural world. Rational knowledge gave humans the ability to control and predict. Reason came to function instrumentally, giving human beings power over nature and allowing them to use it for whatever ends they felt to be desirable.[7] Complementing this perspective was the work of René Descartes (1596-1650). Rather than starting with revelation and the God-hypothesis to understand life, he constructed a different epistemological method for discovering truth by starting within himself as an autonomous individual. By employing reason and assuming objectivity, he developed a type of knowledge different from that derived from revelation and tradition. Knowing now became a rational process, and knowledge became a rationally constructed view of reality.[8] The logic of this mastery over the physical world and a rationally constructed worldview was extended to the construction of a preferred human society by Thomas Hobbes (1588-1679) and John Locke (1632-1704). Hobbes stressed the importance of each individual using reason to maximize his or her self-interest. Locke added the concept of constructing a common order through a social contract that spelled out everyone's rational rights, responsibilities, and privileges.[9] All of these ideas were grounded in the assumption that a rational understanding of the world and human life reflected natural laws.

This rational construction of reality gave rise to a very distinct cultural perspective known as the Enlightenment worldview. Its distinct beliefs and values were foundational for the emergence of what we have come to know as modern Western culture. The autonomous, rational human being was taken to be the starting point for understanding and constructing meaning. Objective science, with its practice of disciplined observation and the logical use of reason, was accepted as the preferred method for developing knowledge, and in this knowledge a dichotomy was established between facts and values. Facts were identified as true and reliable knowledge produced by rational, scientific thought; values were relegated to the arena of personal and private choice. This sort of thinking was based on a pair of assumptions:

7. See Robert Hollinger, *Postmodernism and the Social Sciences: A Thematic Approach* (Thousand Oaks, CA: Sage Publications, 1994), pp. 21-22.

8. Hollinger, *Postmodernism and the Social Sciences,* pp. 22-23.

9. Hollinger, *Postmodernism and the Social Sciences,* p. 22.

(1) that the natural order of the physical world could be discovered and manipulated to our individual and corporate benefit, and (2) that human life had a natural social order and a universal moral structure that could be directed toward social progress. History was viewed as developmental, and it was taken for granted that this new phase of human knowledge was superior to what had preceded it. The new enemies to be overcome were any reliance on the God-hypothesis as the basis for knowing truth and any use of historical tradition as the basis for constructing a social order.

This "enlightened" worldview gained quick ascendancy throughout Europe and was soon given new strength and direction through a number of institutional developments. The work of Adam Smith (1723-1790) tied the worldview to a new economic form that became known as capitalism. Economies were restructured around the invisible hand of the market, which operated as the collective effect of individual self-interest.[10] New applications of science-based technologies led to the Industrial Revolution, introducing processes of mass production, which led to patterns of mass consumption and an endless search by capital for new markets. These economic developments coalesced with political developments in the seventeenth and eighteenth centuries and helped give birth to modern nation-states that were based on social-contract theories of natural rights. Parallel with and to a large extent the result of these developments were the rise of massive urban populations and accompanying forms of modern urban life. The increased differentiation of life produced by economic specialization in the growing cities was given order and coherence through the rational structure of bureaucratic organization.

This entire set of developments, both intellectually and institutionally, has come to be known as modernity, or the modern project. By the nineteenth century, the shape and character of modernity was clearly in place. During that century, its forms were rapidly developed within every Western nation and spread throughout the rest of the world through an aggressive colonial system of governance and economic domination. The superiority of Western culture was assumed, and by the late nineteenth century the adjective *Western* was consistently being used to modify *civilization.*[11]

10. Hollinger, *Postmodernism and the Social Sciences,* pp. 22-23.

11. See Silvia Federici, *Enduring Western Civilization: The Construction of the Concept of Western Culture and Its "Others"* (Westport, CN: Praeger, 1995).

This ideology of modern Western civilization as a preferred social, political, and economic order was not left unchallenged, however. In the nineteenth century, a counterforce emerged that began to push back on the rational, objective, and instrumental character of the modern project: modernism.

Immanuel Kant (1724-1804) divided modern life into three spheres — science, politics, and art — which he saw as discrete enterprises and fields of knowledge, and this division helped foster the division between what we now think of as modernity and modernism.[12] For many, the rise of modernity as a distinct stage in the history of Western civilization began to have a stifling effect because of its reliance on science-based technology, a capitalist economy, and the employment of liberal-democratic political ideals. The spheres of science and politics that coalesced into modern nation-states came increasingly to be seen as restricting human freedom. This reaction, which came to be known as modernism, was significant and far-reaching. While modernism was clearly a product of modernity, it expressed a different spirit and sought to incorporate a different set of values into the cultural mix. It emphasized the subjective, emotional, and creative dimensions of the human condition. While usually associated with the sphere of the aesthetic, modernism also flirted from time to time with the spheres of politics and science to challenge both the validity of their assumptions and the adequacy of their reliance on instrumental rationality.

The themes developed within modernism emphasized the transitory, the dynamic of change, and the fleeting character of life. The stress on human emotion and subjectivity within modernism unleashed great creativity, but it did so within a world that was in constant flux. These views clashed with the culture of modernity, which sought to establish the rational, objective, predictable, and manageable character of life. An avant-garde developed within the arts to express the challenge being mounted by modernism against the limits and controlling character of modernity. A succession of movements within the arts (e.g., impressionism, expressionism, abstract expressionism) arose from the middle of the nineteenth century well into the twentieth. These were efforts to express the aesthetic spirit in contrast to the limits and/or inherent contradictions of modernity and the modern project. But despite these efforts, the aesthetic was never successful

12. See Hollinger, *Postmodernism and the Social Sciences,* pp. 9-11.

in fully politicizing or rationalizing its role in the attempt to critique and express the human condition.

The two movements of modernity and modernism were played out most directly in the construction of the modern self. Modernity placed the modern self as an autonomous individual at the center of life and contended that it functioned by making enlightened rational choices based upon the use of an objective scientific methodology. Modernism likewise placed the autonomous individual at the center of life but contended that it functioned on the basis of emotion and experience as much as reason.

By the early twentieth century, several major changes began to challenge and reshape our understanding of both modernity and modernism and their respective visions of the modern self. Karl Marx challenged the notion of enlightened self-interest as the best way to achieve social progress. He unmasked capitalism as an economic substructure of the liberal-democratic ideals that served to privilege those who owned the means of production or those who were in political power. Max Weber demonstrated the iron-cage effect of modernity that often functioned to limit human freedom. He noted how instrumental rationality served the forces of institutionalized bureaucracy and the modern nation-state by bringing control to human life. Friedrich Nietzsche attacked the God-hypothesis when he declared that God is dead, and he dismissed the notion that human beings are able to construct any rational meaning for life beyond the will to power. Emile Durkheim illustrated the darker side of the effects of mass urbanization in the midst of the Industrial Revolution with his studies on anomie and suicide rates within urban populations. Sigmund Freud uncovered the substructure of human rationality and consciousness, giving new impetus to many of the notions that modernism had been expressing for decades. The thousands of young men killed on the battlefields of Europe during World War I shook the faith of many in the superiority of Western culture. Albert Einstein discovered that the ostensible absolutes of natural laws based on Newtonian physics were in fact relative within the context of time and space. With this discovery he set in motion the still-unfolding realization that all truth is known only from a given perspective.

By the early twentieth century, modern Western culture, with its contrasting themes of modernity and modernism and their contrasting views of the modern self, was beginning to experience significant erosion. Increasingly it inspired less rational confidence and seemed less socially viable. Within a few more decades, the Nazi Holocaust, the dropping of the atomic bomb, and the radicalized presentations of Dadaism in the arts put the lie to the optimistic assumptions that had once undergirded the political, scientific, and aesthetic spheres of modernity. But even though it suffered life-threatening wounds, modern Western culture did not die. Many of its noble aspirations and technological achievements continued to challenge new generations to try to shape meaning and structure life within the modern project. And yet, by the middle of the twentieth century, it was becoming increasingly clear that these efforts to lead modernity and modernism in new directions were in fact journeys into a different landscape, the landscape of an emerging postmodern condition.

Transitions from Modern to Postmodern

As noted above, there were a number of developments occurring both intellectually and institutionally at the turn of the twentieth century that began to reshape the modern project. In this section, I will discuss in a bit more detail several developments that served as forerunners of the emergence of the postmodern condition. These include changing views within sociology and the philosophy of language, along with the rise of critical theory.

Following the line of thinking introduced by Durkheim, sociology developed a view of society as being structured around the interactive, specialized functions of modern life. It conceptualized society as a complex, interrelated set of relationships that tended toward a functional balance in the midst of the dynamic character of life. This structural-functional view of society effectively deemphasized the modern self. The autonomous individual who made rational choices out of enlightened self-interest was no longer the key variable in the social equation. The whole came to be viewed as greater than the sum of the parts.

Parallel to these developments in sociology were developments in the philosophy of language spearheaded by the Swiss linguist Ferdinand de Saussure. Language, said Saussure, is a system of arbitrary rules in which specific words are arbitrarily assigned to external phenomena. He contended that there are no "natural connections" between language and the world.[13] Individuals participate in a language system, but this system was

13. Hollinger, *Postmodernism and the Social Sciences,* p. 86.

historically constructed within an ever-changing social context. This view, which became known as structuralism, had a distinct antihuman bias built into it. Claude Lévi-Strauss further developed this view by stressing the scientific nature of the task of understanding language systems. His work implied that the notions of historical progress and the superiority of Western civilization were myths. The emergence of structural-functional sociology along with structuralism in language studies contributed to a growing awareness that we were now encountering the "decentering of the subject" and the "death of (modern) man" within the modern project.[14]

Coming at modernity from a related but somewhat different angle, another group of theorists reshaped Marxist analysis into what came to be known as "critical theory." The genesis of this viewpoint is usually attributed to the Frankfurt school, which was active in Germany between the two world wars. Two of the most prominent theorists of this school were Theodor Adorno and Max Horkheimer, who described the limits of modernity and demonstrated the inherent contradictions within it. While avoiding Marx's naive optimism regarding the creation of a new society and his dream of a proletariat revolution to bring this about, the Frankfurt school shared Marx's convictions about the repressive aspects of modernity. In particular, the critical theorists delineated the limits of capitalism with its reliance on technological rationality.[15] Critical theory became a powerful tool in the hands of a new generation of thinkers. In the 1960s they used it to define the inherent limits of classical sociology and linguistic structuralism.

A number of French theorists who led the way in this critique became known as post-structuralists. One of the better-known of this group was Jacques Derrida, who provided us with the concept and practice of deconstruction. He claimed that the structuralists were naive and optimistic in their attempts to discover some origin or meaning within the text of social systems. Following in the intellectual tradition of Nietzsche, Derrida proposed that the basic meaning that an individual finds in a text is the one that he or she brings to the text. Deconstruction has become a method for approaching the reading of social discourse, and it has shifted attention away from history to the essence of being, away from intrinsic meaning to

14. Hollinger, *Postmodernism and the Social Sciences,* p. 86.

15. Best and Kellner, *Postmodern Theory,* pp. 217-25. Much of the material for this section was drawn from the first chapter of this volume.

the reality of "playfulness."[16] When applied to life, deconstruction demonstrated that everything is to be understood as arbitrary and constructed. It assumes that no inherent value can be found in either the broader social order or the autonomous self of modernity and modernism. In this way, deconstruction implicitly shifted attention away from critiquing modernity and toward theorizing about an emerging postmodern condition.

In many ways, there is a remarkable parallel between the transition now under way from a modern to a postmodern worldview and the earlier transition from a traditional to a modern worldview during the sixteenth and seventeenth centuries. As noted above, a wide variety of sources and historical developments over the past hundred years have contributed to the formulation of the concept of the postmodern. Two streams of viewpoints are evident in the present transition. One stream interprets the transition primarily in negative terms from the perspective of something being lost, or in terms of foundations that are eroding. The other stream offers a more positive interpretation of events, noting that new opportunities are inherent within the changes now taking place.

The term *postmodern* did not appear as such until the late 1800s, and it was not much developed as a concept until after World War II. The earliest use of the term to connote something of its current meaning has been attributed to the English painter John Watkins Chapman, who used the term "postmodern painting" to describe a style that appeared to be moving beyond the work of the French impressionists.[17] Taking a slightly different approach, Rudolf Pannwitz used the term *postmodern* in 1917 in a book describing the collapse of values within European culture after the turn of the century. His negative critique of the shift that he saw taking place reflected the more pessimistic view of Nietzsche, who at the end of the nineteenth century wrote a stinging critique of the naive optimism that he felt had dominated Enlightenment philosophy.[18]

After World War II, there was a growing recognition among social historians that some fundamental changes were taking place in the structures of society and the role of nations in the modern world. One of the more

16. Best and Kellner, *Postmodern Theory,* p. 229.

17. Dick Higgins, *A Dialectic of Centuries* (New York: Printed Editions, 1978), p. 7.

18. Wolfgang Welsch, *Unsere Postmoderne Moderne* (Weinheim: VCH, 1988), pp. 12-13.

interesting of these historians was Arnold Toynbee, who used the term in the 1960s in his massive treatment of the history of Western civilization. He divided Western history into four periods: the Dark Ages (675-1075), the Middle Ages (1075-1475), the Modern age (1475-1875), and the the "post-modern age" (1875-present). Toynbee contended that the postmodern age was characterized by an erosion of the rational order and social progress achieved through the influence of the Enlightenment expressed most notably in an endless cycles of wars, revolutions, and social disruptions. Although he never developed a theory of the postmodern, his perspective was dominated by the pessimistic view that somehow Western society was regressing.[19]

The work of social historians was paralleled by that of contemporary social commentators in the 1950s, many of whom wrote of the postmodern from a more balanced perspective of both the problems and the opportunities it presented. Their reflections focused mainly on changes in modern society associated with developments in the economic order. Bernard Rosenberg and David White discussed the basic changes taking place within the urban and industrial environment, where the extensive increase in available commodities made the "postmodern man . . . an interchangeable part of the whole cultural process."[20] While this new level of affluence was associated with a certain standardization of life, it created many new opportunities for individuals to shape lifestyles of their own choosing. Peter Drucker offered a similar assessment in a volume entitled *The Landmarks of Tomorrow: A Report on the New Post-Modern World.* He assessed the shift to the postmodern chiefly in terms of a transition from a world tightly managed by rational bureaucracies to a world that was more open and dynamic as a result of developments in technology and education.[21]

Not satisfied with the tendency of these social commentators to accept many social structures as normative, some scholars pressed a more basic critique of Western culture in the late 1950s and 1960s. Representative of this school of thought in North America was C. Wright Mills, who argued that a postmodern period was replacing the modern age through fundamental changes in the structures of society.[22] He pointed

19. See Toynbee, *A Study of History* (New York: Oxford University Press, 1963).

20. Rosenberg and White, *Mass Culture* (Glencoe, IL: The Free Press, 1957), p. 4.

21. Drucker, *The Landmarks of Tomorrow* (New York: Harper & Row, 1957), p. ix.

22. See Mills, *The Sociological Imagination* (New York: Oxford University Press, 1959), pp. 165-66.

out that the Enlightenment belief that an increased use of reason would lead naturally to increased freedom was now breaking down. In both the rationalized totalitarian states and the rationalized and managed democratic states of the modern world, people had less freedom than their ancestors, not more. Contrary to modern dogma, increased rationality often led to diminished freedom. Geoffrey Barraclough joined Mills in asserting that a fundamental shift was taking place within society, but he also stressed the importance of finding elements of continuity amidst the growing discontinuities that were increasingly being identified. He used the concept of the postmodern to note the emergence of a new scientific worldview, technological developments, new cultural forms, and the shift from individual to mass society.[23]

Paralleling this movement toward a definition of the postmodern among social historians, social commentators, and critical sociologists was a movement in the arts during the 1960s and 1970s. Artists broke loose in a host of new directions, challenging basic assumptions about the ways in which art/performance/manuscript provides a message for an audience. While some offered a negative critique of these new developments, the majority embraced them as fresh opportunities to break with the oppressive character of the modern style that had privileged the concepts of rational order and inherent meaning. Authors such as Susan Sontag, Leslie Fiedler, and Ihab Hassan stressed the positive side of the new movement. Sontag celebrated breaking with the need to privilege the hermeneutics of meaning. She demanded the freedom to enjoy style and form without having to link these of necessity with purpose and meaning. That one experienced something was as important as, or replaced in importance, the notion that there was some message to be understood.[24] Fieldler celebrated the demise of the distinction between high and low culture and rejected the necessity of conforming to "modernist elitism."[25] This signaled a shift away from the shaping influence of the avant-garde that had influenced the development of the arts for over a century. But probably the most influential of this series of authors

23. See Barraclough, *An Introduction to Contemporary History* (Baltimore: Penguin, 1964), pp. 9, 23.

24. See Sontag, *Against Interpretation* (New York: Dell, 1972).

25. See Fiedler, *The Collected Essays of Leslie Fiedler* (New York: Stein & Day, 1971), pp. 461-85.

was Hassan, who didn't just describe a postmodern perspective but began to actually write in a postmodern style. He incorporated into his work the techniques that we now associated with the postmodern style — playfulness, the use of irony, and the assemblage of a collage of sources without clear purpose or logic. His work has become known as an "anti-literature" or "literature of silence."[26]

One of the expressions of the postmodern most familiar to the general public emerged in the field of architecture. During the 1970s, architectural style went through a major transformation as reliance on modernity's emphasis of form being circumscribed by function was replaced by an emphasis on eclecticism and popular local tastes. Charles Jencks was one of the first to describe this shift, in his book *The Language of Post-Modern Architecture* (1977). The urban skyline, long dominated by functional glass-and-steel skyscrapers is increasingly being broken up by buildings incorporating collage, irony, and playfulness in their designs.

During the 1970s, an increasing debate began to develop between those who viewed the emergence of the postmodern (in its variety of expressions) as a loss of the Western tradition and those who celebrated the break from rational order, purpose, and functionality. The most common criticism raised by the former group was that the postmodern represented a break with rationality and could only end up in relativism and nihilism. George Steiner, for example, characterized the postmodern as a break with Enlightenment reason and its accompanying trust in science and art to improve society and make it more humane. He called for a return to the tenets of classical humanism in shaping our social order.[27] Daniel Bell issued a call similar in intent, though different in content, when he charged that postmodernism promoted irrationality, hedonism, and rebellion against authority, and proposed a return to traditional religious values to combat its corrosive effects.[28]

Although not clearly recognized during the 1960s and early 1970s, much of the change and many of the shifts that were being discussed grew out of fundamental economic changes — among them increased af-

26. Hassan, *The Dismemberment of Orpheus: Toward a Postmodern Literature* (Madison: University of Wisconsin Press, 1971), p. 5.

27. See Steiner, *In Bluebeard's Castle* (New Haven: Yale University Press, 1971).

28. Bell, *The Cultural Contradictions of Capitalism* (New York: Basic Books, 1976), p. 51.

fluence, the ready availability of credit, a tremendous expansion of available goods and services, and a globalization of the world economy. It was in this milieu of change that the debate over whether the emerging postmodern condition was to be celebrated or cursed began to take place. As this debate intensified, many scholars worked to develop a more thoroughgoing theory of what is actually giving birth to and/or constituting the postmodern condition.

Transition Period

Most postmodernist theorists identify the student revolution of the 1960s, and especially the Paris riots in 1968, as the key transition point. It was in the midst of this tumult that a number of the leading post-structuralists turned their attention in another direction. The catalyst for this shift was the unmasking of the naive assumption on the part of the student movement that somehow the institutional systems would change to reflect the values of a new social order. The resistance from what came to be labeled the "knowledge industry" (i.e., the university system) led post-structural analysts to theorize about an emerging postmodern condition. Different people took the analysis in different directions. It is to this part of the unfolding story that we now turn.

Theorists and Themes regarding the Emerging Postmodern Condition

One of the chief characteristics of the postmodern condition is its uncertainty. We are in the midst of a period of transition, and it is not yet clear exactly what we are emerging from or where we are going. Various authors have begun to theorize about what is emerging in order to sketch the shape the postmodern condition is taking. In this section, we will take a look at some of the more important of these postmodern theorists. I will try to identify the basic perspective each offers and describe some of the basic lines of analysis within each perspective. It should be stressed at this point that there is no one postmodern theory — and that the postmodern condition itself suggests that no one theoretical perspective can or should be achieved.

Difference and Intensities by Jean-Francois Lyotard

One of the earliest and most prominent of the postmodern theorists was Jean-Francois Lyotard. He was working on an advanced degree in the French university system during the turbulent years of the student revolution. Profoundly affected by the events of this period, Lyotard abandoned all hope of realizing a social revolution. He shifted his focus to the issue of difference, asserting that there are multiple forms of knowledge and that these multiple forms cannot be compressed into or subsumed under any kind of grand theory or metanarrative.

He popularized this perspective in his 1979 publication *The Postmodern Condition,* which was translated into English for publication in 1984. Lyotard's theory about the postmodern rested on the notion that life needs to be understood in terms of narrative. He held that every narrative, or discourse, has its own internal set of rules and self-understanding. He believed that Enlightenment thinkers made a great mistake when they set one particular kind of knowledge — scientific knowledge — above all others and insisted that all experience be interpreted in terms of it. He challenged the premise that it was possible or desirable to construct a grand narrative, especially one that focused all reality through the narrow lens of instrumental reason.

Lyotard related the concept of difference to human desire. He appealed for a kind of living that would allow for the full potential of human desire, the full intensities of life, to be expressed within the diverse discourses of human existence. He maintained that sense and experience were more valuable than abstractions and concepts, and he endorsed the value of a patchwork of minority discourses.[29] Lyotard's work remains influential in postmodern discussions, although it has not escaped criticism. The primary charge leveled against his argument that difference and intensities make up the essence of the postmodern condition is that it denies the possibility of making normative judgments.

Desire and Micropolitics by Gilles Deleuze and Felix Guattari

Two French theorists, philosopher Gilles Deleuze and practicing psychoanalyst Felix Guattari, brought their respective disciplines together into a

29. See Best and Kellner, *Postmodern Theory,* pp. 153, 159.

single theoretical perspective in a 1972 publication entitled *Anti-Oedipus*, published in English in 1983. While they rejected the notion that the postmodern is some new phase of Western thought, their work is characterized by many of the themes associated with theories of the postmodern. The primary focus of their work was on critiquing and dismantling assumptions associated with modernity. They undertook a relentless attack on the concepts of "unity, hierarchy, identity, foundations, subjectivity and representation" and turned their attention instead on the principles of "difference and multiplicity in theory, politics, and everyday life."[30]

In many ways, their work is a contemporary extension of Nietzsche's devastating critique of the concept of "being" in an ideal sense. Deleuze and Guattari stress that all of life is a process of becoming and that this becoming is rooted in human desire. The expression of desire, they say, produces an endless multiplication of human possibilities. They add a revolutionary twist to their theorizing by challenging the idea that there is any preferred expression for human existence. They advocate the liberation of human passion and desire from any control or direction by a priori assumptions or claims to essential truths about life. This collapses any possibility for a generalized order, for any type of total perspective or hierarchy of value.[31]

The term often associated with their work is "schizoanalysis." They see life shaped by desire as schizophrenic but do not consider this to be an illness. They view human beings as desiring-machines that can overcome repressive hierarchies, destroy all group identities, and dissolve any notion of the individual. It is their insistence on the mechanistic character of desire that has incurred the most criticism of their approach to understanding the postmodern. Many have questioned whether all notions of identity, rationality, and human solidarity are in fact inherently repressive. Critics maintain that if we are not able to construct any level of human meaning beyond desire, it is improbable that we will be able to sustain any form of human community.

30. Best and Kellner, *Postmodern Theory*, p. 76.
31. Best and Kellner, *Postmodern Theory*, p. 82.

Power/Knowledge and Discontinuity by Michel Foucault

Working within the post-structuralist perspective, Michel Foucault has become one of the most important theorists identified with the attempt to understand the postmodern. While he rejects the postmodern label as a description of his work, his contributions interact extensively with postmodern themes. The basic premise that Foucault developed was the inherent connection between human knowledge and human power. Following in the tradition of Nietzsche, he challenged the assumptions that instrumental reason and scientific knowledge are either objective or necessarily rational. He described at length the limiting character of Enlightenment ideology, which placed emphasis on historical progress and universal truths. He viewed this perspective as reductionistic and charged that it obscures the diverse and plural character of human existence.[32]

Foucault worked from the premise of discontinuity within human existence and sought to establish the multiplicity of different forms of knowing and knowledge. He was particularly concerned with unmasking the repressive character of Enlightenment thinking, which sought to establish a center, an essence, or an essential purpose. On the basis of historical studies into madness, punishment, and human sexuality, he argued for the existence of an important connection between knowledge and power. His thesis that all knowledge is inherently political in character has been hailed as a profound insight in the postmodern discussion and has helped decenter notions of the objectivity and neutrality of scientific knowledge.

Foucault extended his analysis to the concept of the modern self. He rejected the view of the self as engaged in an endless search to discover its own essence and purpose as a product of Enlightenment ideology and proceeded to declare the death of modern man. In its place he proposed a notion of a self that is always producing itself through a full expression of desire. This view, he maintained, implies the obligation of learning to master creatively one's own body and desires in an effort to overcome socially imposed constraints. Foucault has been criticized for failing to describe in any substantive way what this "producing self" would look like and also for failing to propose any ways to achieve human alliances in the context of a continuous individualized self-creation.

32. Best and Kellner, *Postmodern Theory,* p. 38.

Signs and Simulation by Jean Baudrillard

One person who openly identified with the postmodern in attempting to theorize about it was Jean Baudrillard. Working from the perspective of neo-Marxism in the 1960s, Baudrillard gradually shifted his focus away from a critique of the political economy in Marxist terms toward a fundamental redefinition of reality in light of consumer capitalism. The Marxist framework for analyzing the market gave him a useful jumping off point for postmodern theorizing. Marxist analysis held that the use-value of products within feudal economies was replaced by exchange-value within industrial economies, in which all production was turned into commodities. Baudrillard argued that Marx anticipated a third market shift, from exchange-value to sign-value, but failed to appreciate how radical and far-reaching the shift would be; postmodern life is defined, he says, by "the political economy of the sign."[33]

According to Baudrillard, our current marketplace culture, shaped by the mass media and driven by the technologies of production, has separated the sign from any concrete referent. Consumer life has become an open marketplace of simulations, of signs, codes, and symbols that blur the distinction between the real and the unreal. We now live in a type of hyperreality in which the model is more real than the real, in which we encounter movies that reconstruct in our consciousness the texts of history, slogans and infomercials that replace political discourse, and technologies of virtual reality that reconstruct a choice of time and place upon demand. This hyperreality has rendered unnecessary the historic connection between a sign and what it signifies.

Over time Baudrillard moved to a more radical position and abandoned any hope for constructing any meaning for the individual or the social order. His work in the 1980s displayed strong nihilistic themes, a cynical attitude toward life and an apolitical view of theoretical discussion; in clarifying his position on the postmodern condition, he intentionally adopted the most "hyper-avant-gardist position" possible.[34] Critics have charged that in developing his concept of the simulation of signs Baudrillard engaged in a high level of abstraction that failed to take into account the complexity of life as it is encountered and lived by most people in the

33. Connor, *Postmodernist Culture,* p. 51.

34. Best and Kellner, *Postmodern Theory,* p. 122.

midst of the increased production of signs without referents. Others note that, despite the fact that he collapses the categories of history and the social, he consistently references his critique in terms of these concepts.

Late Capitalism and Consumer Society by Fredric Jameson

Like Baudrillard, Fredric Jameson draws on Marxist analysis in developing a theory of the postmodern, linking cultural expressions with the economic realities of capitalist society. He developed his thesis at length in "Post-modernism, or the Cultural Logic of Late Capitalism," published in 1984. In this work he distinguishes three epochs of capitalist expansion: (1) market capitalism (1700-1850), in which large national markets were established; (2) monopoly capitalism (1850-1950), an exploitive period that developed in concert with the colonial empires; and (3) late capitalism (1950-present), in which multinational corporations function within an international marketplace that exceeds national boundaries and political controls.[35]

This third stage of capitalism, says Jameson, has introduced accelerating of cycles of fashion and been pervasively influenced by consumer-driven advertising, and it has produced endless consumer choices. Late capitalistic culture is characterized by a loss of a sense of history, a fondness for what James calls "the pastiche," and a fascination with surfaces and images. It has produced a self devoid of intrinsic value and without a social reference for significance. The postmodern individual, a consumer of endless products marketed primarily on the basis of image and style, has aestheticized all of life, rendering it flat in texture and undifferentiated in meaning.[36]

Jameson contends that we do not have the option of viewing the postmodern as an alternative perspective: for better or worse, all of us are now living within the postmodern condition brought on by the third stage of capitalism. Every day, the expansion of information systems further decenters available perspectives in the context of the global network of multinational capitalism. We have to gain our bearings in the midst of the constant flux of this situation, and Jameson acknowledges it no mean task. How does one describe in a meaningful way that which has lost a sense of

35. Connor, *Postmodernist Culture,* p. 45.

36. Connor, *Postmodernist Culture,* pp. 46-47.

meaning? We find evidence of his Marxist roots in his own efforts to secure meaning: he utilizes a dialectic approach of trying to identify both the positive and negative aspects of the postmodern condition.

The Unfinished Enlightenment Project by Jürgen Habermas

While working out of a perspective substantially different from those of the theorists discussed above, Jürgen Habermas needs to be included in our survey of theorists because he explicitly challenges the postmodern perspective that collapses Enlightenment-based culture into difference, personal experience, desire, or sign systems. Habermas believes that the cultural crisis we are facing is actually the challenge of the Enlightenment's modern project, which was never completed. While noting the limits of instrumental rationality and rationalized scientific knowledge, he wants to build on the basic values established in the Enlightenment, including the essential meaning of the individual and our rational capacity to make moral choices in the context of social community.

What is unique in Habermas's approach is the way he supplements the use of instrumental reason in the natural sciences with a communicative rationality in the public and moral realm. He proposes a kind of community-in-dialogue, using a discourse of consensus-building to make ethical choices. Such a discourse would make use of "democratic practices that can provide rational methods for resisting colonization and legitimize a rationally restructured world."[37] He contends that this approach would accommodate diverse perspectives while ensuring a basic commitment to rational discourse and ethical choices.

Habermas has had a profound influence on the postmodern discussion. Almost everyone theorizing about the postmodern condition has interacted with the basic premises of his argument. While most do not agree with his conclusions, they nevertheless have been obligated to broaden their discussion and critique of Enlightenment culture and the modern project in light of his views. Most of them contend that Habermas is too idealistic regarding the potential of communicative reason to construct social community. Many argue further that his view of dialogue is too apolitical and that he fails adequately to appreciate the disruptive nature of difference.

37. Hollinger, *Postmodernism and the Social Sciences,* p. 157.

Positive Postmodernism

As I suggested earlier, several recent authors have expressed a more positive view of the emerging postmodern condition.[38] They accept many of the tenets of the early postmodern theorists but contend that they do not necessarily lead to relativism and nihilism. They approach an understanding of our culture in much the same manner that Einstein approached an understanding of the physical world — on the basis of an assumption that all knowledge is relative to one's perspective.

It is their belief that the fact that truth is relative does not rob it of all meaning. The worlds in which we live, both physical and social, are real, and we can come know meaningful things about them. They simply caution that we can't possess knowledge about them in an absolute sense. We have to use adjectives such as *contextual, perspectival,* and *interpreted* to define both the process by which we come to know and the content that we learn. In this way they have worked to shift much of the discussion from modernity's focus on epistemology (the nature and grounds of knowledge) to hermeneutics (the principles of interpretation). In large part this shift defines the ground common to positive postmodernists and those attempting to extend the Christian mission within the emerging postmodern condition.[39]

A Christian Response to the Emerging Postmodern Condition

One of the most significant developments in thinking about Christian mission the past several decades is the emerging belief that the gospel is inherently contextual. There is no gospel except that which is mediated through history and clothed in human culture. It is assumed that this gospel is inherently translatable — that the truths of the gospel that have been clothed in the assumptions of a given culture can be brought to fresh expression in terms of the assumptions of another culture. There is evidence supporting this view in the four Gospel narratives of the New Testament, which reflect different contextual perspectives on the part of both the authors and the intended audiences and yet all manage to bear

38. E.g., Hollinger, Best and Kellner, and Simons and Billig.

39. For more on this, see essay by James V. Brownson in this volume (pp. 228–59).

witness to the truths of the one gospel of Jesus Christ. No one narrative expresses the full truth of that gospel in an absolute sense, yet all bear witness truthfully to the gospel. The witness they bear is contextual, perspectival, and interpreted.

In this regard, doing mission in the emerging postmodern condition involves finding both bridges of continuity between the gospel and a postmodern worldview and also challenges deriving from their discontinuity. A few examples of each will provide suggestions for further engagement in the mission of God within the emerging postmodern condition. These ideas do not exhaust such bridges and challenges, but they do illustrate the type of missiological thinking needed as we continue to encounter the transition from modernity to postmodernity.

Bridges of Continuity

There are several clear connections between perspectives inherent within the emerging postmodern condition and the worldview of the gospel set forth in the Bible. First, there is a shared awareness that what is primarily at stake is an interpretation of the human condition and that no one possesses a secure position on the basis of which to define this reality objectively. In this sense, there is agreement that no single understanding of the human condition is true in an absolute sense. We all work out of the position of hermeneutics, of principles of interpretation that shape various plausibility structures for understanding reality. From the perspective of Christian mission, what we are attempting to understand and set forth is the wider rationality of the plausibility structure of the biblical worldview. Lesslie Newbigin makes this point in his important work *The Gospel in a Pluralist Society* (1989), arguing that the church living in faithfulness to the biblical worldview becomes the compelling evidence to the world of the "truthfulness" of this position.

Second, there is continuity in perspective between the postmodern and biblical perspectives regarding the holistic character of human existence. Both perspectives deny modernity's privileging of the cognitive and seek instead a wholeness that incorporates the rational, volitional, and emotive aspects of human existence. In a real sense, both perspectives seek to weave Kant's trichotomy of scientific, political, and aesthetic realms back into a unified whole. While many positive postmodern theorists struggle to find an operative perspective to express this wholeness, it is implicit in the conviction of the biblical worldview that humankind is created in the image of God. It is crucial that those seeking to extend the Christian mission in the emerging postmodern context make sure that both the process and content of this mission expresses the holistic character of the human condition.

Third, there is a similarity of perspective between positive postmodernists and a biblical view of Christian mission on the point of legitimizing particular viewpoints. There are natural connections between the postmodern assertion that difference is inherent in the human condition and the theme of contextualization in Christian mission. The key to making these connections lies in realizing that being particular and/or contextual does not prevent us from expressing a truthful interpretation of the gospel. The incarnation of Jesus Christ as the God-man makes it eternally clear that the universal truthfulness of God's good news can be expressed within the particularity of history — what Newbigin refers to as "the scandal of particularity."[40] The fact that we live within the reality of difference does not mean that we do not have access to God's truthfulness. It is especially important that the church comprehend this as it seeks to engage in mission within a multicultural world.

These examples make it clear that not everything within the perspective of the emerging postmodern condition is necessarily a threat to the gospel. There are some clear points of continuity that can serve as bridges for shaping a more faithful and true understanding of the biblical worldview and conveying this to the world. But it is also clear that there are a number of aspects of the postmodern perspective that directly challenge a biblical worldview.

Challenges to Confront

Among the challenges to the Christian faith inherent in the perspective of the emerging postmodern condition are three that I would like to consider as illustrative of the point. First, the perspectival character of the postmodern perspective tends to focus attention on the "now" of life as

40. Newbigin, *The Gospel in a Pluralist Society* (Grand Rapids: William B. Eerdmans, 1989), p. 72.

the only important reality. There is bias against *being* in favor of *becoming.* This results in a loss of historical perspective and awareness of the contingent character of all human existence. The biblical perspective clearly connects the relevance of human existence with the reality of its historical character by affirming that there is both a past that has shaped who we are and a future that we will have a part in shaping. As Newbigin notes, it is critical for the presentation of the gospel in the postmodern context to reassert the teleological element inherent in the human condition. God is a God of human history, which means that there is a purpose to human existence beyond the now, a purpose rooted in our past and defining our future.

Second, the emerging postmodern condition tends to emphasize surface and image over substance. It attributes a kind of depthlessness and transitory character to life that are related to its ahistorical character. This depthlessness tends to make human existence subject to the manipulative power of technique. The biblical worldview sets forth an understanding of life that not only connects us to the past and future but also integrates us into the full substance of human existence. There is a design to life that connects our thoughts to our experiences and that connects both of these to the physical place and historical context in which we find ourselves. The meaning of life cannot be collapsed into self and situation without destroying the essence of what it means to be human. The postmodern tendency to think in terms of surface and image manipulated by technique needs to be confronted and challenged by the gospel perspective of depth and substance mediated through an integrated understanding of thought, experience, and place.

Third, the emerging postmodern condition with its emphasis on difference and its focus on the now tends to lead to a fragmentation and plurality that can easily drift into relativism and pluralism. This often results in a cut-and-paste sort of existence in which collage and playfulness express the constructed character of human existence. In contrast to a diversity that becomes relativistic in perspective, the biblical worldview conveys an understanding of life that is holistic and integrated. Although our perspectives and choices have a relative character, they are not without meaning and connectedness. The challenge facing the church that is seeking to live out of and into the truthfulness of the gospel is to define these meanings and make these connections. This requires active theological reflection, which the church has not always been diligent in undertaking.

Summary

Although the emerging postmodern condition is a complex phenomenon, the reality of its existence is becoming clearer. Doing mission in this context is hard work and will require thoughtful reflection on the part of the church. It must establish a dynamic conversation between the gospel and the postmodern context. I have tried to show that while such a conversation may in some respects be difficult to establish, there are certain points of contact and common vision and concern that can facilitate the gospel mission among persons shaped by the postmodern condition. In seeking to translate the gospel within the emerging postmodern condition, we stand in the long tradition of the historic Christian church working to speak the gospel in relevant terms to a new generation. The process of translation holds the promise not only that this new generation will come to understand the gospel and therefore experience profound transformation in their thinking but also that the church will grow in its understanding of the gospel it is seeking to proclaim.

The Gospel in Our Culture: Methods of Social and Cultural Analysis

PAUL G. HIEBERT

> For our struggle is not against enemies of blood and flesh, but against the rulers, against the authorities, against the cosmic powers of this present darkness, against the spiritual forces of evil in the heavenly places. (Eph. 6:12)

In recent years there has been considerable discussion regarding the nature of the "rulers," "authorities," "cosmic powers," and "spiritual forces" to which Paul and the other New Testament writers refer. Many believe it applies to demonic hierarchies that rule the earth. Others believe it refers to human systems of power and authority. Wink notes that in the New Testament there is no sharp distinction between spiritual and human powers. On the one hand, human systems of rule are divinely appointed (Rom. 13:1-3); on the other, the demonic can gain control of them, causing them to oppose God and those who commit themselves to his rule.[1]

1. Works that view "rulers" as demonic include C. Peter Wagner, "Territorial Spirits and World Missions," *Evangelical Missions Quarterly* 25:3 (July 1989): 278–88; Peter Wagner and Douglas Pennoyer, eds., *Wrestling with Dark Angels* (Ventura, CA: Regal Books, 1990); and Frank E. Peretti, *Piercing the Darkness* (Westchester, IL: Crossway, 1989). Focusing instead on human authorities are Hendrikus Berkhof, *Christ and*

What are some of these human systems in North America for which and with which we must contend? What is the message of the gospel *in* and *to* our culture? Before examining these questions specifically, we need to lay the theoretical groundwork for our analysis.

Theoretical Considerations

In 1952, Talcott Parsons, Edward Shils, Clyde Kluckhohn, Gordon Allport, and other leading social scientists developed a comprehensive view of human organization.[2] They concluded that it is helpful to speak of a system of systems in which three systems — society, culture, and the individual person — interact (see fig. 1). Since we are interested here not in individuals but in corporate systems, we will confine our discussion to the first two of these.

Society

By "society," we mean the systems of relationship in which people live. These systems define our identity in the society and shape our lives. They include microsystems such as the family, clubs, and communities; mid-level systems such as clans, institutions, and cities; and macrosystems such as tribes and nations.

Social systems have several dimensions to them. The *social dimension* has to do with the way a social system defines, allocates, and uses social relationships. For example, in our culture, one person is recognized as a "doctor," which permits him or her to act in certain ways toward "patients." We organize clubs and corporations, and we construct a democratic, capitalistic society. The *economic dimension* involves the definition, allocation, and use of resources. These may be material, such as money, land, and possessions, or they may be immaterial, such as time, copyrights, and

---

the Powers (Scottdale, PA: Herald Press, 1962); and John Howard Yoder, *The Politics of Jesus* (Grand Rapids: Eerdmans, 1972). See Walter Wink, *Naming the Powers: The Language of Power in the New Testament* (Philadelphia: Fortress Press, 1984).

2. See Talcott Parsons and Edward Shils, eds., *Toward a General Theory of Action* (Cambridge: Harvard University Press, 1952).

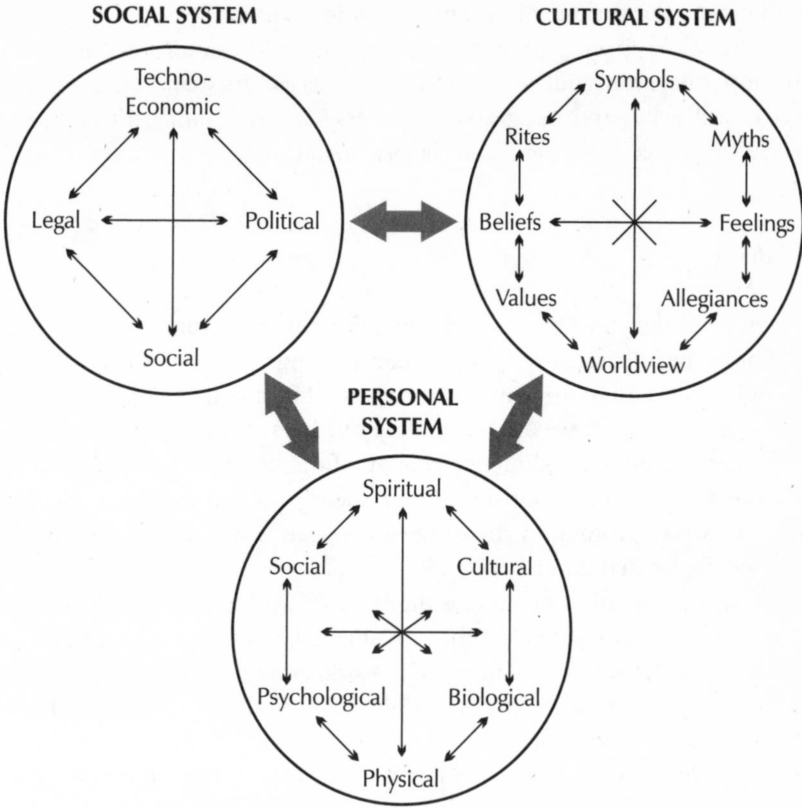

FIGURE 1. The Systemic Nature of Human Organization

reputation. The *political dimension* has to do with the definition, allocation, and use of power. Power includes social pressures, persuasion, and engendering fear, as well as physical coercion. The *legal dimension* deals with the definition, allocation, and use of legitimacy. A person or group may exercise power, but if they lack the socially recognized right to do so, it is rebellion. It is important to recognize that the legal and political dimensions are closely entwined in discussions of the principalities and powers, for these are often involved in one or another form of rule.

All these dimensions are present in every human social system, whether at the level of the family and club, or at that of the corporation and city or the nation and multinational institution. These social systems are one of the "principalities and powers" we must examine in our society because they profoundly shape and control us as Christians. They are both good and evil: good because they are essential for human life, and evil because as sinners we bend and distort them to our own purposes.

Culture

Another of the "powers" that we must examine is culture, which we may define as the integrated systems of beliefs, feelings, and values characteristic of our society. These systems are our mental maps of the world that define reality for us, which we use for guiding our lives.

On the surface, culture is made up of the dominant systems of symbols and beliefs characteristic of our society. In our case this includes English, which profoundly shapes the way we see reality. It also encompasses the ideologies that govern our lives.

At the core of our culture is the Western worldview — or, to be more precise, worldviews. These are the fundamental, unquestioned assumptions we make about the nature of things. Our worldviews give us both a synchronic and a diachronic understanding of reality. *Synchronically,* they define for us the structure of that reality. They give us the categories with which we think and declare which of these are real and important, and which are not. They provide us the logic we use to explain reality, and they define the fundamental values and allegiances that demand our worship and our lives. Our worldviews are what we think with, not what we think about.

For the most part, worldviews are implicit in the culture and therefore are hard to detect. Their power over us exists, in part, in that we are not aware of them or the ways they shape our lives. Because they are foundational, however, they are at the heart of the Western "principalities and powers."

Diachronically, our worldview provides us with the big story of "what is really going on here." This cosmic myth provides meaning to all our corporate and personal stories.[3] For example, the Exodus, as a historical

3. I use the term "myth" here in its technical sense, as a paradigmatic story taken to be true. It does not mean fictional cases or fantasies of the mind. See Mircea Eliade, *Myth and Reality* (New York: Harper & Row, 1963); and Rollo May, *The Cry for Myth* (New York: Dell, 1991).

event, was for the Israelites the paradigm by which they interpreted all their experiences. Western cultures and worldviews also belong to the "principalities and powers" with which we must contend.

A Theoretical Model

In our analysis of our Western world, we will examine our social and cultural systems and the relationship between them. The two act as semi-autonomous systems that reinforce each other. Changes in one often, but not always, produce comparable changes in the other. Frequently there is a tension between our cultural ideals and our social realities. The result is cognitive dissonance in our lives.

This interlocking nature of social and cultural systems makes it most difficult to introduce change. We may change people's beliefs and worldviews, but this does not guarantee change in society. Furthermore, the unreformed social order, in time, can subvert even the most fundamental cultural changes. The opposite is also true. Social change does not guarantee culture change.

Because we live in a time of sociocultural flux, we cannot speak, even in the broadest sense, of a single North American culture or a single North American society. Many have noted that our dominant systems of modernity are being challenged by postmodern ones.[4] It is not yet clear whether in fact modernity will be replaced by postmodernity as they and others such as Barry Smart and Alvin Toffler think, or whether, as Peter Berger and Ernest Gellner argue, postmodernity is another rearguard revolt that will fail in the face of the triumph of science, technology, consumerism, and business.[5] For our purposes, we will examine both

4. E.g., see Pauline M. Roseneau, *Post-Modernism and the Social Sciences: Insights, Inroads, and Intrusions* (Princeton: Princeton University Press, 1992); and Margaret A. Rose, *The Post-Modern and the Post-Industrial: A Critical Analysis* (New York: Cambridge University Press, 1991).

5. Barry Smart, *Postmodernity* (London: Routledge, 1993); Alvin Toffler, *The Third Wave* (New York: William Morrow, 1980); Peter Berger, Brigitte Berger, and Hansfried Kellner, *The Homeless Mind: Modernization and Consciousness* (New York: Vintage Books, 1974); Peter Berger et al., *Pyramids of Sacrifice: Political Ethics and Social Change* (New York: Basic Books, 1974); Ernest Gellner, *Postmodernism, Reason, and Religion* (London: Routledge, 1992).

modernity and postmodernity, as well as their challenge to the church and God's rule.

Modernity

What are the "powers" of modernity, and how should the church in North America respond to them? We can only sketch a few illustrative themes characteristic of modernity. A full listing and analysis of modernity and what should be the church's response is the larger task to which we have committed ourselves.

The Social Systems of Modernity

Modern social systems have several common attributes, including their size and complexity.

Scale

Traditional societies are generally small. Modern societies are large, being linked together in global networks. As they grow in complexity, more levels of social organization are added, and on each level new social structures emerge that encompass the social systems below them. These upper-level systems are not just large in size; they are also different in character from the systems below. They are based not on ties of kinship but on power and economics. The result is macroinstitutions such as government, banking systems, factories, and schools. Modernity is being spread around the world through these systems. Traditional ways are discredited, and modern Enlightenment knowledge (science, free capitalistic markets, global laws) is taught as unquestioned truth and good. Reliance on hierarchy and bureaucratic organization is seen as the most efficient way of maintaining order.

Churches in the West have bought deeply into this model of progress and have identified themselves uncritically with modern styles of organization. Institutionalization and bureaucratic structures are widespread in most of them, and hierarchy is common in their organizational patterns.

A Technological Approach to Organization

Jacques Ellul has commented on the role in our society of what he calls technique.

> No social, human, or spiritual fact is so important as the fact of technique in the modern world. . . . Technique certainly began with the machine. . . . [But] technique has now become almost completely independent of the machine, which has lagged far behind its offspring. . . . Technique has enough of the mechanical in its nature to cope with the machine, but it surpasses and transcends the machine because it remains in close touch with the human order.[6]

In *The Homeless Mind*, Peter Berger and his associates have pointed out that central features of the modern social order are the factory, in which we control nature, and bureaucracies, by which we reduce humans to machines.

In this mechanical mode of organization, the focus is on tasks, production, efficiency, control, profit, and success. Management is by objective. Means, separated from ends, become ends in themselves. People must conform to the impersonal roles because an intrinsic requirement of technological production is to define each other as anonymous functionaries. People must manage their emotions because free expression of emotions destroys the impersonal, rational, ordered nature of the factory and bureaucracy.

This management style has shaped many of the Western churches. Pastors are increasingly seen as administrators who must manage by objective, and church growth is thought to be the result of human engineering. We even measure our spirituality by the work we do. This "spirit of human management" is one of the "powers" that we must challenge if we are to recapture a biblical vision of the church and of society.

Complexity and Specialization

A second characteristic of modern societies is specialization. This springs out of the growing complexity in the technological areas of society, and it spreads to other institutionalized areas of life, including religion and education.

On one level, specialization leads to the emergence of professional roles

6. Jacques Ellul, *The Technological Society* (New York: Vintage Books, 1964), 3–5.

— experts who "know" what needs to be done. Common folk increasingly rely on these technocrats for answers. On a higher level, specialization leads to specialized institutions. Banks, schools, governments, factories, and the entertainment industry are specialized bureaucracies controlled by a few. Even the church tends to be a special-interest group, a place where people worship God and share in spiritual fellowship. All other parts of their lives are controlled by other institutions. Most Western churches operate more like clubs or corporations than covenant communities that minister to whole lives.

The Cultural Systems of Modernity

What are the cultural systems of modernity? We will focus here primarily on the North American worldview, which shapes how we see both the structure and the story of reality. As Morris Opler points out, our view of the structure of things is shaped by a few "worldview themes," or, as others commonly call them, "root metaphors."[7] What are some of the "cultural themes" or "root metaphors" of modernity?

Dualism: The Split between Spirit and Matter

One root metaphor is the split in Western culture between spirit and matter, between subject and object, and therefore between subjective faith and objective truth. This distinction came from Greek thought, which came to the West through the Crusades. In theology this found expression in Thomas Aquinas. In society it appears in the Cartesian split of the world into *res cogitans* (mind) and *res extensa* (matter).

One consequence of this split has been the division of life into the public and private sectors described so well by Lesslie Newbigin.[8] The public sector involves the world of work and public discourse, where reason, hard facts, and universal truths rule. The private sector involves the arts and religion, where feelings, values, personal beliefs, and diversity are in charge.

Another consequence was to divide the world into natural and su-

7. Morris Opler, "Themes as Dynamic Forces in Culture," *American Journal of Sociology* 51 (1945): 198–206.

8. Lesslie Newbigin, *Foolishness to the Greeks: The Gospel and Western Culture* (Grand Rapids: Eerdmans, 1986); idem, *Truth to Tell* (Grand Rapids: Eerdmans, 1991).

pernatural realms. The former is the domain of science and deals with material realities as if they are mechanistically determined. The latter is the domain of religion and deals with spirits, miracles, feelings, and values.

The effect of this metaphor on Christianity in the West has been devastating. Christianity has been privatized, relegated to personal piety, while science controls public truth and life. Within Christianity, it has led to a division between evangelism and social concern.

Mechanistic Worldview

A second theme of the modern public American worldview is mechanism.[9] Alwyn Jones discusses the Cartesian paradigm, which has divided the world between mind and matter, pointing out that it

> allows scientists to treat matter as dead and completely separate from themselves, and to see the material world as a multitude of different objects assembled into a huge machine. . . . Priority is . . . given to the parts over the whole, the presumption being that a knowledge of the whole can gradually be built up from a detailed understanding of the relationship between the parts. The model of reality that emerges from this is a vast machine whose fundamental characteristics can be understood by an analysis of its parts and the laws that govern their working. . . . This has led to the "searchlight" effect — of high specialization but not seeing the whole.[10]

The authors of *The Homeless Mind* trace the consequences of this view of reality. Orderliness, organizability, predictability, and rationality are the underlying means; control, production, and profit are the ends.

As we have seen, this bureaucratic worldview is invading Western Christianity. Order, organization, planning, control, and production are common values in many North American churches and mission agencies. Prayer, waiting upon God, and seeking his leading are used only to introduce our planning meetings or are relegated to the aged and marginalized.

9. See E. J. Dijnksterhuis, *The Mechanization of the World Picture: Pythagoras to Newton,* trans. C. Dikshoorn (Princeton: Princeton University Press, 1986; orig. pub., 1950).

10. Alwyn Jones, ed., *Logic and Knowledge Representation: An Introduction for Systems Analysts* (Aulander, NC: Pitman Publishers, 1987), 236–40.

Order and Hierarchy

One consequence of a mechanistic view of reality is a strong stress on order. We see this factor in such things as our obsession with clearly defined, discrete categories in time and space and our rejection of fuzzy relational ones.[11] It leads to an emphasis on "cleanliness" and "law," defined as high order.

Order in modernity is largely created through a hierarchical view of life and of society. Biological sciences create hierarchical taxonomies of life that hark back to the Greek belief in the great chain of being.[12] This hierarchy is also reflected in the modern view of social organization that is based on hierarchy and clearly defined roles.

Individualism and Freedom

As Robert Bellah and others have shown so well in *Habits of the Heart*, a fourth theme of North American culture is individualism. The concept of the individual as an autonomous person is a product of modernity. Allan Bloom traces the linguistic shift from "soul," which connotes dependence on God, to "self," which carries the idea of an autonomous being.[13] This latter term, coined by Locke, gave rise to the concept of the "self-made" person, then to self-achievement and self-fulfillment, and now to self-realization in the transcendental and New Age sense.

The impact of this individualism on Christians and the church is far reaching. As Lamin Sanneh notes, "Our modern tendency to see the Church in terms of individual healthy-mindedness, as a selfhood that is vulnerable to bouts of low self-esteem, is light years removed from the Church as a fellowship of faithfulness to God's promises."[14]

The erosion of the church from being a covenant community, along

11. See Paul G. Hiebert, *Anthropological Reflections on Missiological Issues* (Grand Rapids: Baker, 1994).

12. Arthur Lovejoy, *The Great Chain of Being: A Study of the History of an Idea* (Cambridge: Harvard University Press, 1936).

13. Robert Bellah et al., *Habits of the Heart: Individualism and Commitment in American Life* (Berkeley: University of California Press, 1985); Allan Bloom, *The Closing of the American Mind* (New York: Simon & Schuster, 1987).

14. Lamin Sanneh, *Encountering the West: Christianity and the Global Cultural Process* (Maryknoll, NY: Orbis Books, 1993), 221.

with its transformation into a crowd, club, or corporation, has made Christianity largely a spectator sport or a business activity.[15]

Materialism, Work, and Consumerism

A fifth theme in the Western worldview is materialism. As Max Weber pointed out, the Renaissance marked a shift from an otherworldly emphasis to a this-worldly one.[16] Protestantism incorporated this shift in the Reformation. At first the asceticism of the Middle Ages continued, and hard work and saving became dominant values. Prosperity and the good life — defined in material terms — was evidence that one was among God's chosen people predestined to eternal life in heaven.

Richard Fox and T. J. Lears have shown that a change took place in the North American worldview between 1890 and 1910, when it moved from asceticism to self-gratification, from the work ethic to consumerism. This shift was closely tied to the spread of technique as a way of organizing society. According to Fox and Lears,

> The new professional-managerial corps appeared with a timely dual message. On the one hand, they proposed a new managerial efficiency, a new regimen of administration by experts for business, government, and other spheres of life. On the other hand, they preached a new morality that subordinated the old goal of transcendency to new ideals of self-fulfillment and immediate gratification. This late nineteenth-century link between individual hedonism and bureaucratic organization — a link that has been strengthened in the twentieth century — marks the point of departure for modern American consumer culture. . . . Consumer culture is more than the "leisure ethic" or the "American standard of living." It is an ethic, a standard of living, and a power structure.[17]

15. Richard Halverson puts it succinctly: When the Greeks got the gospel, they turned it into a philosophy; when the Romans got it, they turned it into a government; when the Europeans got it, they turned it into a culture; and when the Americans got it, they turned it into a business.

16. Max Weber, *The Protestant Ethic and the Spirit of Capitalism* (New York: Charles Scribner's Sons, 1956; orig. pub., 1920).

17. Richard Fox and T. J. Lears, eds., *The Culture of Consumption* (New York: Pantheon Books, 1983), xii.

Meaning was tied to acquiring things, and borrowing replaced saving as the way to fund our lifestyles.

Consumerism is a growing value in most North American churches, not only in those preaching a "health and wealth" gospel. Yet, few Christians in the West have challenged not only our affluence but also the consumer mentality that underlies our thinking.

Welfare State and Civil Religion

A sixth theme we note here is the emergence of the welfare state and, with it, civil religion. In the Middle Ages, the state dealt primarily with matters of defense and trade. The church and other institutions took responsibility for the well-being of humans. They established hospitals, schools, orphanages, and poorhouses.

In the nineteenth century, the state came to be the central institution ultimately responsible for the well-being of its citizens. It took control of education, medicine, and welfare, and it set the limits of religion. It also demanded total allegiance, particularly in times of war. Unfortunately, the church was an all too willing partner in this reorganization of loyalties and responsibilities. Increasingly it saw its primary responsibilities to be in the area of the private sphere, which has primarily to do with feelings, values, family life, entertainment, and the women's world.

Cosmic Warfare

Worldviews not only provide us with the root metaphors that underlie the culture, they also supply us with our root myths. These are the big stories that provide us with the paradigms that help us understand other stories. The central Indo-European myth holds that the cosmos is divided into good and evil and that an eternal battle is being waged between them.[18] In this battle, the good may use wicked means if the evil side does so first, because winning is "the only thing." It enables the victor to gain control and to establish order. If the good party wins, it can institute the rule of righteousness and peace. The battle is never fully won, nor is eternal peace

18. See Walter Wink, *Engaging the Powers: Discernment and Resistance in a World of Domination* (Minneapolis: Fortress Press, 1992); and Hiebert, *Anthropological Reflections.*

established. The good side may win for a time, but the evil side revives, and then the battle is renewed. In fact, the excitement is in the battle. This scenario is played out a thousand times a week in our North American entertainment: by Superman, Underdog, Batman, Lone Ranger, Colombo, Rambo, and Star Wars. It is the fundamental myth underlying detective stories, murder mysteries, Westerns, and science fiction. It is relived in football, baseball, basketball, tennis, and most of our sports.

The fundamental message of this myth is that life is based on competition and battle, that the victors gain control and establish order, and that the result is progress. This message lies at the heart of our theory of evolution, our faith in democracy, and our worship of capitalism.

In contrast to the Indo-European myth with its stress on a battle to gain control, the biblical story is clear. There is no question that God indeed rules and that his methods are love, reconciliation, and peace, not competition and warfare.

The American Dream

Peter Berger points out, "Underlying the major ideological models for social change (including Third World development) are two powerful myths — the myth of growth and the myth of revolution."[19] North America is committed to the first of these. It assumes change through incremental improvement and is based on the Enlightenment assumptions of progress, autonomous individualism, faith in reason, and innate human goodness.

According to Jonathan Bonk, "The West continues to be the standard against which 'development' is measured; and Western aid efforts have, until quite recently, been fueled by the certainty that given enough money, time and Western expertise, the rest of the world can become what the West now is — 'developed.' "[20]

In his *Cry for Myth*, Rollo May analyzes the popular myths of North America such as Horatio Alger and the American Dream, the therapist and deliverance from hell, romance and the chase of love, and the myth of patriarchal power. We need more analyses of these and other myths that give meaning to the life stories of many Americans.

19. Berger et al., *Pyramids of Sacrifice*, xi.

20. Jonathan Bonk, *Missions and Money: Affluence as a Western Missionary Problem* (Maryknoll, NY: Orbis Books, 1991), 20.

Postmodernity

Many argue that a paradigm shift is taking place in North American thought — that modernity is dying and a postmodern era is being born. What are the systemic characteristics of this new era, and what challenges does it offer to the church?

The Social Order of Postmodernity

The social nature of postmodernity is only now emerging. A couple of characteristics now seem predominant.

Pluralism

The social root for postmodernity is the growing pluralism of Western societies. No longer can one group remain dominant and control the social order. A myriad of other voices are being heard. This is particularly true in our North American cities. For example, in Los Angeles, public school classes are now being taught in more than eighty different languages.

But postmodern society is more than the fact of pluralism. It is the acceptance of pluralism as the ideal way to organize society in the long run. No longer do we speak of assimilation into one homogeneous society. Rather, we encourage different communities to maintain their distinct identities.

The implications of pluralism for the church are far-reaching. Should the church bless difference by baptizing homogeneous unit churches, or should it try to return to the emphasis on uniformity of the modern era? Should it speak of theologies, or of Theology? What is the motive for missions if we are to affirm other communities and their religious beliefs?

Networks

In reaction to the monolithic bureaucratic systems of modernity, postmodern people seek loose organizations and more personable relationships. Organizational tasks are often performed through networks of relationships that are flexible and less institutionalized.

The Cultural Order of Postmodernity

Postmodernity is also infiltrating our worldview. We see this development with the recent emergence of several new themes.

Deconstructionism, Relativism, and Pragmatism

One fundamental theme of postmodernity is deconstructionism. Not only does this argue against coherent plots and perspectives in art[21] and distinct styles in architecture, it also argues against any single system of objective truth. All truth, it holds, is perspectival, including science. In this sense it breaks down the public-private dualism of modernity and reduces everything to the private sphere. Anthony Giddens has pointed out that

> post-modernity refers to a shift away from attempts to ground epistemology and from faith in humanly engineered progress. The condition of post-modernity is distinguished by an evaporating of the "grand narrative" — the overarching "story line" by means of which we are placed in history as beings having a definite past and a predictable future. The post-modern outlook sees a plurality of heterogeneous claims to knowledge, in which science does not have a privileged place.[22]

In discussing postmodernism, David Harvey notes the "startling fact" of "its total acceptance of the ephemerality, fragmentation, discontinuity, and the chaotic. . . . Postmodernism . . . does not try to transcend it, contradict it, or even to define the 'eternal and immutable' elements that might lie within it. Postmodernism swims, even wallows, in the fragmentary and the chaotic currents of change as if that is all there is."[23]

Postmodernists such as Linda Hutcheon see pluralism and contradiction as inherently good. She writes, "Willfully contradictory, then, post modern culture uses and abuses the conventions of discourse. It knows it cannot escape the implications of the economic (late capitalist) and ideo-

21. See Giles Gunn, *The Culture of Criticism and the Criticism of Culture* (New York: Oxford University Press, 1987).

22. Anthony Giddens, *The Consequences of Modernity* (Stanford, CA: Stanford University Press, 1990), 2.

23. David Harvey, *The Condition of Post-Modernity: An Enquiry into the Origins of Culture Change* (Cambridge: Basil Blackwell, 1984), 44.

logical (liberal humanist) domains of its time. There is no outside. All it can do is question from within."[24]

Postmodernists openly attack science and its search for a unified theory, as they do Habermas for his idea of "unity of experience." Lyotard writes, "We have paid a high enough price for the nostalgia of the whole and the one, for the reconciliation of the concept and the sensible, of the transparent and the communicable experience. . . . The answer is: Let us wage a war on totality; let us be witnesses to the unpresentable; let us activate the differences and save the honor of the name."[25]

The result of pluralism and deconstructionism is relativism. We can no longer speak of objective truth. All beliefs, including those of science, are subjective and private. The effects of this conclusion are now being seen in our Western response to other religions. A great many authors now affirm that our task is not to convert others to Christianity but to affirm the good in all religions.

Subjectivism, Idealism, and Existentialism

A second theme of postmodernity is that the mind creates the realities we know. Its epistemological foundations are either instrumentalism or idealism.[26] The world we live in is a construction of our minds. Walter Anderson has commented,

> In recent decades we have passed, like Alice slipping through the looking glass, into a new world. This postmodern world looks and feels in many ways like the modern world that preceded it; we still have the belief systems that gave form to the modern world, and indeed we also have remnants of many of the belief systems of premodern societies. If there

24. Linda Hutcheon, *A Poetics of Postmodernism* (New York: Routledge, 1980), xiii.

25. Jean-François Lyotard, *The Postmodern Condition* (Minneapolis: University of Minnesota Press, 1984), 80–81.

26. While instrumentalism is a form of realism, and therefore stands in contrast to idealism, the two act in much the same way. Instrumentalism says that there is a real world outside us but that we cannot know anything about it for certain. Consequently, we must reject notions of truth and accept science and other forms of knowledge as useful constructs that help us live. Pragmatism and utilitarianism are the results. Idealism denies that there is a real world outside and says that we mentally construct the worlds in which we live. In both we are left ultimately with images in the mind.

> is anything we have plenty of, it is belief systems. But we also have something else: a growing suspicion that all belief systems — all ideas about human reality — are social constructions.[27]

The logical consequence of this idealism is self-centeredness. We create the world in which we live. Therefore, we must be gods.

Another consequence is existentialism. We are the center of existence, so we should live for ourselves today. We are no longer interested in history, only in News.

Therapeutic Society

A third theme of postmodernity is a stress on therapy and health. R. Fox and T. J. Lears have observed

> the beginning of a shift from a Protestant ethos of salvation through self-denial toward a therapeutic ethos stressing self-realization in this world — an ethos characterized by an almost obsessive concern with psychic and physical health defined in sweeping terms. . . . In earlier times and other places, the quest for health had occurred within larger communal, ethical or religious frameworks of meaning. By the late nineteenth century those frameworks were eroding. The quest for health has become an entirely secular and self-referential project, rooted in peculiar modern emotional needs — above all the need to renew a sense of selfhood that had grown fragmented, diffuse, and somehow "unreal."[28]

This search for the "self" is a reaction to modernity with its depersonalization of human beings. Lamin Sanneh notes, "Our new orthodoxies are now constructed and validated as psychological uplift, self-esteem and other versions of emotional quick-fix, in the name of all of which we would make sacrifices that we would begrudge Church and fellowship."[29]

The shift to therapy and healing as the root metaphors has led to a decline in concepts such as sin and salvation. People are not rebels against God but victims of society or of evil spirits. They need health, defined

27. Walter Truett Anderson, *Reality Isn't What It Used to Be* (San Francisco: Harper & Row, 1990), 3.

28. Fox and Lears, *Culture of Consumption*, 4.

29. Sanneh, *Encountering the West*, 221.

primarily in terms of feelings, not an objective reconciliation with God. What we need is deliverance and self-realization, not justice and peace. Harry Emerson Fosdick asserted, "Multitudes of people are living not bad but frittered lives — split, scattered, uncoordinated."[30] The problem, in other words, is not morality but morale. Robert Bellah's *Habits of the Heart* traces some of the consequences of this theme in contemporary American life.

The Gospel in Our Culture

What is the gospel in our North American culture? I have not given any answers. I have only tried to lay out an agenda for future study. I am convinced that the solutions lie not in a prophet who will lead us through the land but in a community of committed Christians who are willing not only to hear the gospel together in our countries but also to pay the price that obedience to that gospel will demand.

Our task is twofold. We must address both our social order and our cultural order, particularly our worldview. To challenge one or the other is not enough, for the two systems are interlocked. We thus need teaching and action.

We need to remember that the systems of North America are not all evil.[31] Individualism, mechanism, technique, and the rest are beneficial if they are kept in check by higher values and social systems. Groupism, organicism, and relationalism carried to the extreme are equally destructive. The greatest danger is that we accept our social organization and our culture without being aware of it and thereby become its captive.[32] All human systems need to be brought under the lordship of Christ and his kingdom.

As a minority in the country, we Christians must first experience transformation in ourselves and in our churches.[33] Then we must act as salt in the land, subverting systems when they oppose the kingdom of God. Newbigin puts it well:

30. Fosdick, quoted in Fox and Lears, *Culture of Consumption,* 14.

31. See Wink, *Engaging the Powers.*

32. On this point, see Os Guinness, *Dining with the Devil: The Megachurch Movement Flirts with Modernity* (Grand Rapids: Baker, 1993).

33. See Stanley Hauerwas and William H. Willimon, *Resident Aliens: Life in the Christian Colony* (Nashville: Abingdon Press, 1989).

If I understand the teaching of the New Testament on this matter, I understand the role of the Christian as that of being neither a conservative nor an anarchist, but a subversive agent. When Paul says that Christ has disarmed the powers (not destroyed them), and when he speaks of the powers as being created in Christ and for Christ, and when he says that the Church is to make known the wisdom of God to the powers, I take it that this means that a Christian neither accepts them as some sort of eternal order that cannot be changed, nor seeks to destroy them because of the evil they do, but seeks to subvert them from within and thereby to bring them back under the allegiance of their true Lord.[34]

34. Newbigin, *Truth to Tell,* 82.

Symbols Become Us: Toward a Missional Encounter with Our Culture through Symbolic Analysis

DAVID SCOTCHMER

In this chapter I outline a methodology of symbolic analysis that will help us understand and engage our own culture more effectively with the gospel. While the missionary task of communicating the gospel has been part of our heritage at least since our Lord's Great Commission, only recently have we begun to understand the processes by which meaning is made within, and communicated across, the domains of language and culture. The tools of social and cultural analysis have served some missionaries well and have been ignored by others. The same will no doubt be the case for preachers, pastors, and evangelists as we become more intentional about a missional encounter with our own culture.

I attempt here the explication of but one approach, derived from the work of anthropologists Clifford Geertz and Sherry Ortner, for understanding and interpreting culture. However, the interpretation and application of their theories as these relate to a missional encounter are my own. A treatment of the theoretical origins, variations, and issues at stake with a symbolic analysis of cultural analysis is not provided here. That discussion is important in its own right but would add little at this stage to an appreciation of its power for cultural analysis in the first instance, or to its application to a missional engagement. My objective is to work from the social-scientific side of the missional task in an attempt to see more specifically how symbolic analysis can do justice to the complexity of religious belief and behavior, on the one hand, and, on the other, still challenge missional efforts among natives like ourselves.

After a prolegomena about why this discussion should even take place, I divide my treatment into three sections including the following: (1) a general discussion of Geertz's theoretical perspective, (2) an explanation of a typology of symbols and one research instrument for the symbolic analysis of culture, and (3) the application of this theory and method to context.

Why Doing Our Own Cultural Analysis Is Critical

In his article "Christ Is All in All," printed in this volume, David Lowes Watson states that we must be involved in a trialogue between the church/tradition, the gospel/faith, and our culture/society. Here I attempt to lay the groundwork for the church/society side of the triangle to understand better how and where the gospel needs to take root. If we are serious about a missional agenda, there are at least three reasons why we must examine what we think we know and understand about our own culture and the larger society to which we belong.

The first reason is *cultural proximity.* We are simply too close to our own kind, kith, and kin for a truly missional encounter without developing some critical and analytic distance. One of the failures of the contemporary church is its inability to see its own captivity to the rules and norms of Western society. We all too easily rush to meet religious needs with a consumer-oriented religion or to organize our religious institutions into cost-effective businesses, not realizing that we need the objectivity of social science to reveal to us our hidden and unquestioned assumptions about the world, others, God, and how we are engaged in God's kingdom. No theological retelling of the gospel so that others can hear it in their own idiom and with their own metaphors can take place until we know from what we have been saved, given our own cultural idolatry, and to what we have been called, given God's gifts to the church for the sake of others.

Second, the increased *cultural diversity* we are experiencing as a society demands that we begin to see and wrestle with competing worldviews and loyalties. While some congregations are fortifying themselves against the influx of new and different neighbors, and while others wrestle with what it means to be missional in their own block, the church is woefully unprepared to be missional in any cross-cultural sense. Furthermore, the "safe" isolation of congregations that have ensconced themselves in the suburbs signals not their survival but their perdition as sister congregations literally breathe their last breath in urban areas blighted by crime and hopelessness, and in rural communities devastated by foreclosures and abandonment. The Macedonian call is being sounded, but too often it is heard as an annoyance to those at ease in Zion, rather than as a real gift to be heeded. For example, a caucus of black Presbyterians (PCUSA) has issued a stinging rejection of the white church's business-as-usual attitude while "their people" (our people too) see their children in gangs and being murdered, their men drugged and jailed, and their women abandoned and overburdened. We white Christians do not have a clue how to be missional in ways that build solidarity and offer salvation instead of paternalism and patronage.

Third, if we are to be mission outposts and missioners committed to a theological and methodological paradigm adequate for our post-Christendom status, we desperately need the tools of cross-cultural engagement. This I will call *cultural acuity,* or the ability to think and act critically within and outside the comfortable limits and known expectations of our own world and enter that unknown world of the cultural other. The rampant ideological individualism that promotes self-defined and self-referent persons, all the while disguised as pluralism, leads us into uncharted missional waters. If, as Hans Küng suggests, we live among persons who have abandoned the idea of any preexisting divine order of meaning, then meaning itself has lost any ultimate meaning.[1] In such a world, none of the old categories of authority speaks with any otherworldly or self-authenticating validity. Rather, the missioner must appeal to the inherent logic and to the disguised authority implicit in the unnamed gods of the lost even to be heard, much less believed.

This is not just incarnational mission by which we enter the world of the other. It is nothing less than re-incarnational mission in that we must first leave and abandon our own thinking and attitudes toward being Christian. In turn, we will be more prepared to return and engage our own culture in ways we have never imagined. This "leaving" requires that we shed (or die to) our cultural, ecclesial, and theological baggage long enough to see what we must abandon forever and what we may pick up tentatively once again for the sake of "indwelling the gospel" (i.e., engaging in [revived]

1. Hans Küng, cited in Graham Howes, "Religious Art and Religious Belief," *The Arts in Religious and Theological Studies* 5, vol. 1 (Fall 1992): 12–16.

evangelism and mission). We can never stand outside our own context in a missional sense. But we can look hard-and-fast at our own cultural assumptions and expectations through the mirror of symbolic analysis. It is a challenge that cannot be dismissed, given both the needs of the world and the gifts of God, who both leads and equips us for every good work.

A Closer Look at Symbolic Analysis of Culture

For over forty years, Clifford Geertz (1926–) has challenged the very core of anthropological and critical thought. A full recital of his place in the literature is found elsewhere.[2]

Geertz on Culture

Culture theory has evolved and continues to evolve along a path that is more visible as we look back. At the close of the 1950s, three exhausted paradigms ruled anthropological theory: (1) British structural-functionalism (A. R. Radcliffe-Brown, B. Malinowski), (2) American cultural and psychological approaches (Margaret Mead, Ruth Benedict), and (3) American evolutionists (Leslie White, Julian Steward).[3] One of the new movements that emerged in the 1960s was what has subsequently been called "symbolic anthropology." Geertz was one of its prime representatives.

What Geertz did for anthropology is important because of what his approach does for us — namely, free us to interpret culture from within real life experience and not outside it, as if we ourselves were hermetically sealed from it. Geertz, and with him Victor Turner in the British stream, cut a straight line between the materialists and the mentalists by insisting that culture is neither reducible to measurement nor confined to memory. Culture for Geertz is summed up not so much in theories and precise definitions as it is in the simple recognition of what we humans do uniquely, namely, make meaning. This meaning is observed in the symbols we use for articulating, relating, and communicating. Geertz's approach to culture

2. In particular, see Sherry B. Ortner, "Theory in Anthropology since the Sixties," *Comparative Studies in Society and History* 26 (1984): 126–66.

3. *Ibid.*, 128.

is a semiotic one that focuses on the ways and the kinds of "webs of significance" we ourselves have made. "I take culture to be those webs, and the analysis of it to be therefore not an experimental science in search of law but an interpretive one in search of meaning."[4]

The rendering of the meaning of social behavior arises not simply from careful observation, note taking, guided conversation, and acceptance building. The anthropological task of identifying and understanding the meaning of others' behavior and interaction requires "thick description," according to Geertz. Ethnography must be "thick" because what we need to understand, whether a wink or a sigh, never mind a ritual or an idea, is so critically dependent on the background information or full context that to state otherwise is ethnographic folly.

More vital to the data collector than the observed "facts" themselves must be an analysis of the "structures of significance" within which these facts occur and that give them their social ground and import (9). Anything and all that we can bring to the description (what happened, the way it was done, the language and words used, the reactions, the history of the relationships, those engaged or left out, the roles played and betrayed, the forces at work internally or externally, etc.) add interpretative weight and meaning to the facts of social interaction and behavior.

The accumulated layers of significance read from the text of life gathered by the analyst render the facts both intelligible and interpretable to the outsider. In turn, these constructs are exposed as the guesses of the anthropologist who seeks "to draw large conclusions from small, but very densely textured facts; to support broad assertions about the role of culture in the construction of collective life by engaging them exactly with complex specifics" (28). Furthermore, "A good interpretation of anything — a poem, a person, a history, a ritual, an institution, a society — takes us into the heart of that of which it is the interpretation. . . . Anthropological interpretation consists in tracing the curve of a social discourse, fixing it into an inspectable form" (18–19).

We can say some very specific things about culture and the task of anthropology that are critical for Geertz. Culture is public because meaning, which lies at the core of human interaction, cannot exist without being public. Culture is then interpretable because facts have significance within

4. Clifford Geertz, *The Interpretation of Cultures* (New York: Basic Books, 1973), 5. Subsequent page references in the text are to this work.

real contexts of individual and institutional existence. Accordingly, the goal of symbolic anthropology, like that of a missional encounter with our culture, is not to go native or to imitate, but to converse. In so doing, we effectively enlarge our universe of human discourse, of understanding, of interaction, and of community (14).

Furthermore, a culture is composed of symbols that are publicly created and subscribed to, which act as models of meaning for particular groups of people in a specific time and place. This is unavoidably the popular systematization of the terms, rites, domains, and relationships that reflect a people's values, expectations, and attitudes.

Geertz on Symbols

Geertz's most enduring legacy will probably be his rescuing anthropology from both mentalism and materialism in favor of meaning expressed through symbols. This was accomplished by his recognition that symbols embody the meaning of culture and serve as vehicles and repositories of meaning. Symbols express a worldview and join it to an ethos in ways that make it both meaningful and coherent, given the vagaries and humdrum of human existence.

Following Weber, Geertz places the individual, not the society, at the center of his theory of culture. Ultimately, even within highly ordered institutional life, it is people who make meaning of their worlds in ways that surprise and satisfy. This ordering through the use of symbols that we call culture represents the internal logic of human action and organization. Others like David Schneider focused on the internal logic of symbol systems as these expressed the cultural as opposed to the social. Analysts like Victor Turner developed more thoroughly how it is that symbols act, not just as windows into a worldview, but more tangibly how symbols act as operators and produce social transformation in individuals and societies. We are indebted to Turner for terms like "liminality," "marginality," "antistructure," and "communitas," which express the social dynamic of symbols at work.[5]

For Geertz, then, what are symbols? What do they do, and what do they make possible? A symbol may be anything that serves as a vehicle for meaning, whether a word, an act, an object, a ritual, an event, or even a person. Above all, symbols are "*extrinsic* sources of information" (92).

5. See Ortner, "Theory in Anthropology," 130-31.

Culture coheres and consists not so much in the rules and order that people create but through the symbols they use to unite, express, and summarize the rules and understandings between people, both within and across communities. Thus one is "acculturated," not when one has learned the rules of relations, or even the words of a culture, but when one manages the symbols or tools for making meaning, interpreting "facts," and communicating effectively in context. This is no less true for a new seminarian taking on the symbols of the professional clergy than it is for the missionary seeking to make a home and gain a hearing among strangers. What makes symbols *cultural* with enormous social impact is the fact that there is always a *context* for their use and their misuse, their death and their resurrection.

Whether the community we focus on includes two persons or two hundred million, symbols serve to define the identity of both those who belong and those who do not. Communities that share a particular symbol do so because they have learned how to participate together toward a shared kind of understanding about the essence and meaning of that symbol, whether enthusiastically or reluctantly. One's understanding and experience of community, however defined by its leaders, will be determined by members who orient themselves to those symbols around which the community is organized and out of which it moves. While key or core symbols, like a flag or a baseball team, have long been recognized for their power to coalesce and to produce allegiance, what is significant for symbolic anthropology is the insistence that everything within a community has symbolic potency. In this sense anything on the symbolic playing field is fair game for the anthropologist, and certainly for a missional encounter with our own culture.

The ambiguity or diffuse quality of symbols, as we will see shortly, provides the basis for uniting people of widely divergent interests and values — up to a point. Boundaries, however, are essential, and symbols serve to identify what these boundaries are and when they have been crossed inappropriately. For example, for mainline Protestants the ordination of confessed and practicing homosexuals is creating a crisis in the boundaries of what it means (1) to be a minister; (2) to believe God's Word as authoritative; (3) to understand the divine nature of human sexuality; (4) to define Christian marriage and family; (5) to determine how the church will come to a divinely inspired, informed, and democratically representative decision (i.e., is following a democratic decision the same as obeying God's will?); (6) to define the nature of sin and salvation; and, not the least important, (7) to determine the strength of the law of love provided by

Christ's own example. At stake is nothing less than the very nature of community, that is, who's in and who's out.

Symbols provide powerful models *of* reality, as well as models *for* it, by giving meaning — that is, objective conceptual form — to social and psychological reality both by shaping themselves to it and by shaping that reality to themselves (93). How people spend their time, money, and energy reveals dramatically where their loyalties lie and which symbols they choose to preserve and promote. Whether a cross is a fetish, a decorative ornament, an aid to or confession of faith, the mere juxtaposition of two pieces of wood, a grave marker, the place of death or disappearance, the sign of a holy site for shamanic worship, an attack on one's racial status, the promise of sins forgiven, or the hope for a life to come depends not at all on the cross itself.

What the anthropologist seeks first are those conceptual structures that sustain and inform a subject's thought about the cross and in turn inform that one's actions because of these intellectual structures. Second, one must weigh these concepts and structures of thought along with the actions that sustain them in a way that makes this interpretation stand out against all other possible explanations of belief and action (278). Again, the goal is not the display of cultural rules or laws (i.e., symbols and systems of symbols) for their own sake but the exhibition of meaning created within and out of the "hard surfaces of life," as Geertz puts it. At all costs we must eschew the facile and the faddish and pursue the rough and the real in any representation of the cultural other, the worlds inhabited, and the imaginings created.

Geertz on Sacred Symbols

Geertz treats sacred symbols within his classic study "Religion as a Cultural System" and in "Ethos, World View, and the Analysis of Sacred Symbols" in *The Interpretation of Cultures.* In the latter essay Geertz explains what sacred symbols are, as well as what they do. Sacred symbols

> relate an ontology and a cosmology to an aesthetics and a morality: their peculiar power comes from their presumed ability to identify fact with value at the most fundamental level, to give to what is otherwise merely actual a comprehensive normative import. . . . The tendency to synthesize worldview and ethos at some level, if not logically necessary, is at least empirically coercive; if it is not philosophically justified, it is at least pragmatically universal. (P. 127)

The role that sacred symbols play to link a worldview with a particular ethos is basic for understanding their power in both validating belief and motivating action. A sacred symbol, like a cross for Christians or the circle for Native Americans, summarizes the larger range of meanings understood in one's religion, which are in turn expressed in varied forms in one's life and actions. The ethos "is made intellectually reasonable by being shown to represent a way of life implied by the actual state of affairs that the worldview describes, and the worldview is made emotionally acceptable by being presented as an image of an actual state of which such a way of life is an authentic expression" (127).

Drawing on Geertz's own terms, the following list details what sacred symbols do. They:

- mediate genuine knowledge;
- dramatize positive and negative values;
- formulate a world of which good and bad values are a part;
- ground metaphysical values;
- portray values of a world as given;
- provide strategies for encompassing situations;
- summarize what is known;
- order and organize experience;
- synthesize a people's ethos;
- render the worldview as convincing emotionally;
- define the imposed conditions of life;
- establish moods and motivations;
- formulate an order of existence;
- validate cosmic concepts as facts; and
- reinforce moods and motivations as real.

For Geertz, sacred symbols and the systems of thought and practice to which they belong are synonymous with religion. As such, sacred symbols unite belief about the world and one's relationship to it, producing "a basic congruence between a particular style of life and a specific . . . metaphysic, and in so doing [they] sustain each with the borrowed authority of the other" (90). Religion both projects and reflects, defines and interprets, motivates and mediates one's outlook on the world and one's stance in that world.

The Symbolic Analysis of Culture

In this section I will summarize a typology developed by Sherry Ortner for an analysis of the symbols of a local culture, whether that of an individual, a group, an institution, or a nation. According to Ortner's typology, every culture contains core or key symbols that the analyst must identify and understand. To the question regarding how one knows what is a key or core symbol, Ortner basically says that one will just know because of its prominence in use and reference to a particular reality (e.g., sexual intercourse as the determiner of kinship ties in American culture; or the chrysanthemum and the sword in Japanese culture as expressive of the tension in

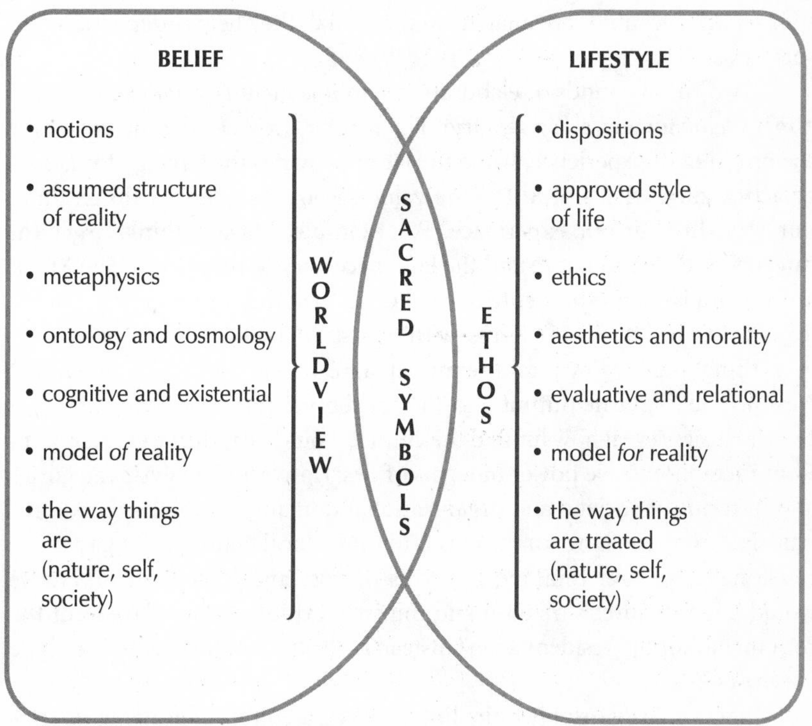

Religion as a Meaningful System of Sacred Symbols

central values). Second, one will be told and will observe the widespread value of certain elements in the culture, especially where they have natural boundaries (e.g., maize to the Guatemala Indian, the automobile to the American).

Key symbols are essentially of two kinds and include "summarizing" and "elaborating" symbols.[6] *Summarizing symbols* are diffuse and serve to crystallize commitment around a central core idea, issue, or reality. They provoke loyalty by speaking to attitudes and emotions in an evocative way. The flag, the cross, and the Bible are examples.

Elaborating symbols work just the opposite in that they help clarify and sort out "complex and undifferentiated feelings and ideas, making them comprehensible to oneself, communicable to others, and translatable into orderly action."[7] Rarely sacred in the sense of eliciting an emotional response, these symbols are analytic and rational; they help order action and sort ideas.

Two specific kinds of elaborating symbols include what can be called a *root metaphor* and a *key scenario.* The former provides the categories for the ordering of experience, while the latter provides the strategy for action or actualizing belief linked to core values. Root metaphors help us think our way through our experience. For example, Mayans think largely in categories related to maize and the land necessary to produce it. The Masai are pastoralists, and their entire social order revolves around cattle. Americans think in "business" terms with a cost analysis linked to practically everything, right down to prenuptial agreements regarding individual wealth. The linguistic output and the conceptual categories dependent on these realities reveal how limited the culture would be if they were removed. Root metaphors have power in terms of descriptive and analytic categories and in terms of societal and organizational domains where they predominate. For example, how common is it to find a local church willing to think missionally without thinking in terms of cost analysis? What difference would a local church's mission and ministry exhibit if they played out the root metaphor of "resident alien" instead of "watchtower of truth" or "lone survivors"?

Key scenarios establish the link between a culture's means-ends rela-

6. Sherry B. Ortner, "On Key Symbols," *American Anthropologist* 75, vol. 5 (October 1973): 1338-46.

7. Ibid., p. 1340.

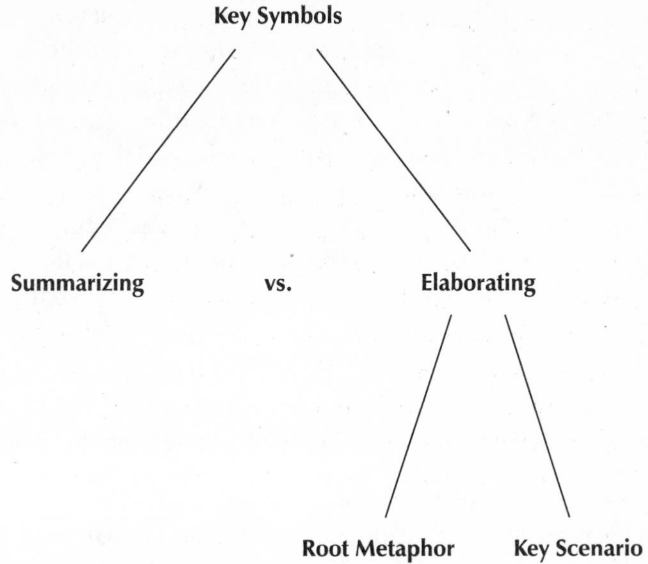

tionships. Culture's essential values are linked to key scenarios and are often preserved in rituals that call for certain kinds of action. They embody a culture's essential notions of success and performance. For example, consider baseball and the hope of a city's team to reach the World Series. Here the importance of the individual to the team effort is a mirror of workers that built American industrial power. Is it any wonder baseball is going through a major redefinition just as America's industrial base continues to shrink in the midst of a global economy?

Another key scenario illustrative of national cultural ideals is the Horatio Alger myth. In this myth, a poor boy makes it rich through hard work, dictates successful social action, and reinforces key values. This perspective underlies a comment such as "The problem with blacks is that they are lazy and unwilling to work. After all, I know Joe Brown, and he's got a good job selling insurance because he works hard." The George Washington cherry tree story is of this latter type, promising greatness if one but tells the truth.

Key scenarios are powerfully operative in local churches but are often unconscious. One particular local church I know about could not select a long-term pastor. Whenever they called a new pastor, he usually lasted only two or three years. At that church, someone faithfully covered the pulpit chair with a shroud every Sunday, year after year. Finally someone asked why this was done, and a longtime member explained. Over twenty years ago a beloved pastor died while in the pulpit one Sunday morning. The death of that pastor had never been discussed, and there was lingering guilt and grief that had never been healed. Each new pastor was compared with the deceased pastor, but no one measured up. The root metaphor was the shroud of the deceased, which could not be buried, and the corresponding key scenario was the "anticipated return" of the beloved pastor to his rightful place (or the arrival of his perfect replacement).

An Instrument for Symbolic Analysis of Context

From my own use of the symbolic method, I have developed an approach that helps reveal the key symbols operative within a particular context. The goal is the unveiling and describing of those larger dominant structures of meaning that are triggered by the use of a culture's key symbols. Because culture is public, it is interpretable. But this interpretation relies on observation of behavior and attention to the words and expressed beliefs (what is meant by what people do, as opposed to the meaning told in what they say they are doing, given the larger context of their symbol system).

Four aspects must be examined in detail and with care as illustrated in the accompanying diagram. Two dimensions must be uppermost in the mind of the researcher. First, the *context* — the real social, economic, political, and psychological realities that prevail for the participants, whether stated or unstated, conscious or unconscious. Second, the *symbols* — the orientations taken by the participants toward their reality that define this reality for them and others in meaningful and socially powerful ways. This I call the horizontal inquiry into meaning.

Equally significant is the vertical inquiry into meaning, which also involves two poles of investigation and clarification. The first is the definition of what person, group of people, or institution is being researched. How is it bounded, and whom does it include? This I call the *unit of analysis.* It is not limited to persons but may include a ritual, an event and all the players, or even a text itself. The second pole is the *problematic,* which encompasses the specific and the larger issue at stake in the context. This reality may not always be recognized for what it is by the participants but

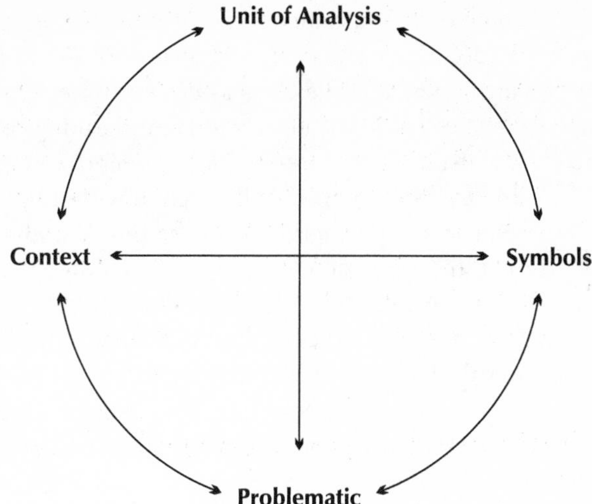

Unit of Analysis — a person, event, text, institution, town, event, or the arena in which the meaning is being made.

Problematic — the particular issue, crisis, or struggle as understood by both the participant and the observer or institution; the point at which change is either hoped for or demanded.

Context — all the factors past and present that contribute to or require an orientation for the making of meaning; the aspects — social, economic, political, and so on — that make up what is real to the observer and the observed.

Symbols — the words, signs, or objects that give or carry meaning for the person or institution; these make the world understandable, communicable, and explainable to the group and to others.

Hermeneutical Instrument for Symbolic Analysis

may be clearer to the observer. One way of thinking about the problematic is to ask, In the minds of the participants and the observer, what do the symbols address?

In our earlier discussion, we noted the diverse meanings that are associated with the use of the cross. To use this as a concrete example of our model, we might observe the following. Consider an evangelistic Bible study for generation X college students who have little or no previous church involvements (unit of analysis). The Bible study uses the Luke 9:18-27 passage, which focuses on the necessity of the sacrificial death of Christ and his calling to others to gain true life by dying to themselves on a cross that is taken up daily. A number of the students present are wearing the cross symbol as decorative jewelry (problematic). The multiple meanings of the cross in the text and the cross as decorative jewelry are set in contrast within a host of broader cultural uses and meanings of the cross that have been part of the experiences of those present (context). Words like death, life, gain, lose, and sacrificial all function within the discussion in an effort to establish some congruence in the minds and attitudes of those participating in the discussion (symbols).

This illustration indicates both the dynamic and the complex character of communication. It also indicates the importance of working within the context of the real-life situation when trying to engage in the process of communication. As the church in North America increasingly encounters a post-Christian context where persons no longer share common meanings, the missioinal task will require of us to become more skillful in conducting symbolic analysis of this context. The purpose of this chapter has been to provide the church with an applied theoretical model for doing so.

PART III

DISCERNING THE GOSPEL

All theological understanding of the Bible must be seen as an interpretation that uses cultural categories and meanings in a particular context to give expression to the gospel of God. To continue to improve our theological understanding, we need to work at letting the Bible's story, which is mediated from within diverse cultural perspectives, speak to us on its own terms, while also taking into account the potentially limiting character of our own cultural perspective. This presents the church of every age with the critical challenge of trying to exegete the Bible faithfully as it seeks to discern the truth of the gospel and apply it faithfully to its life and ministry. This challenge is increasingly emerging as a foundational task for churches in North America if we are to engage in a missionary encounter with our culture.

The six essays in this part provide the reader with an introduction to this foundational task. They offer some key insights into both the content associated with discerning the gospel in our present context and the method we need to use for engaging in the task of doing theology. The first three focus primarily on helping the church think about engaging this task within contemporary North American culture. The last three focus on helping the church become more skillful in doing the work of discerning the gospel from the biblical narrative and understanding it within multiple and varied contexts.

David Lowes Watson, in his essay "Christ All in All: The Recovery of the Gospel for Evangelism in the United States," shows ways the churches have become too enculturated. Focusing specifically on the task of recovering a biblical understanding of the gospel for evangelism, he notes that churches, both in their theological understandings and in their congregational practices, have capitulated to our culture. A radical course correction is required if the gospel is to be reclaimed. This will require the use of a Christocentric emphasis rather than one that is anthropocentric or ecclesiocentric. Watson develops a method for approaching this task by addressing issues that include the nature of the gospel, the character of our present context, and the features of the gospel that make it good news in our context.

Some suggestions for beginning the task of doing theology in our present context are provided by Douglas John Hall in his essay "Ecclesia Crucis: The Theologic of Christian Awkwardness." His basic thesis is that for too long the church has shaped its theological understanding from within the assumptions of the dominant culture. An intentional disengagement from this culture is required if we hope to recover a biblical understanding of God's intent for the church. Following the perspective that the church should be "in" but not "of" the world, Hall asserts that such a disengagement must be seen not as the goal but rather as a necessary first movement in order to position ourselves for a truly missionary engagement with our culture. He suggests that such a disengagement/engagement approach can bear fruit for pursuing four foundational human quests — for moral authenticity, meaningful community, transcendence, and meaning.

Working from a different angle, but in concert with Watson's and Hall's concerns, is the contribution made by Charles C. West in his essay "Gospel for American Culture: Variations on a Theme by Newbigin." Lesslie Newbigin's work offers a general missiological diagnosis of secular, pluralistic Western culture. West is concerned with trying to critique the peculiar character of the American context in light of Newbigin's work in order to lay the foundation for how churches might engage in mission more effectively in the specifically American culture. He develops three important themes that are somewhat unique within our context. These are the covenantal character of our society, the notion of unity in the midst of a growing pluralism, and the role that power plays in validating the national identity.

James V. Brownson, in "Speaking the Truth in Love: Elements of a Missional Hermeneutic," moves the discussion beyond discerning the gospel within the particularities of North American culture toward an exploration of how we understand the Bible in the first place. Noting the failure of the modernist attempt to find the univocal meaning of the text and also the unacceptability of relativizing the text in postmodern interpretation, he suggests the use of a missional hermeneutic that is rooted within the Bible's presentation of its own message. Central to this missional hermeneutic is the reality of diversity. This diversity is rooted within our human condition of being cultural and contextual. Therefore all interpretation of the Bible must of necessity be multicultural. This does not mean, however, that difference reigns supreme, for he also shows how coherence functions within this interpretive approach. Helpful suggestions are offered for using such a missional hermeneutic to discern the message of the gospel and hear it in relation to our particular cultural context. This work is foundational for understanding the gospel in our contemporary pluralistic context.

It is important not only to approach the text on its own terms, as Brownson points out, but also to approach each cultural context on its own terms. This perspective is developed by William Dyrness in "Vernacular Theology." His concern is to highlight the importance of bringing the truth of the gospel into the specific worldview of any particular context, to develop what he calls a vernacular theology. This is best accomplished when it is done within community. Theological reflection must be a communal exercise if it is to engage effectively the full life of people, and it must incorporate a focus on practices as well as beliefs if it is to be balanced. This work helps envision how to assist congregations to engage in doing theology as communities within their particular contexts.

Brownson and Dyrness demonstrate that doing theology must operate from within a multicultural understanding of the text and must be done in community within particular contexts. But the question naturally surfaces, How is the gospel supposed to be understood by those doing theology within diverse cultural settings? Paul Russ Satari, in "'Translatability' in the Missional Approach of Lamin Sanneh," demonstrates how the truthfulness of the gospel functions as persons from diverse cultural contexts come to understand it. He draws on the work of Sanneh, who has researched the translatability of the Christian message from one distinct culture to another throughout the church's history. Satari suggests, following Sanneh, that the gospel has its own inherent power to reshape cultures, while it also possesses the inherent capacity to be given unique expression by each culture. Sanneh indicates the dual effect of the gospel's translatability, the ability of the gospel both to relativize and to revitalize cultures.

Satari offers suggestions regarding how to engage in mission by translation in a way that critiques the colonial character of mission as conducted in the past by the countries of the West.

The essays in this part provide the reader with a helpful introduction to the task of discerning the gospel. If the churches of North America are to engage in a missionary encounter with our culture, it will require that we learn the skill of interpreting the biblical text, doing theology within community, and giving expression to our theology within particular contexts.

Christ All in All: The Recovery of the Gospel for Evangelism in the United States

DAVID LOWES WATSON

The contextual interpretation of the gospel for evangelism in the United States of America is long overdue. Indeed, it is a matter of some urgency. This is not to say that evangelistic studies have neglected the American context.[1] On the contrary, theologians and missiologists alike have given it a great deal of attention.[2] By and large, however, these studies are not being used to provide the average American church member with the means to evangelize. Their analyses remain in the form of evangelistic principles that are conceptually beyond the reach of most American church-goers, or they are applied to evangelistic models and strategies designed primarily to recruit new church members — which is not at all the same thing as evangelism. Accordingly, the evangelistic ministry of the American church has become extremely vulnerable to enculturation; and in a highly churched culture such as the United States of America, albeit increasingly secularized, this has emasculated Christian identity.[3]

1. While the adjective "American" properly applies equally to the cultures of Canada and to those of Central and South America, in this chapter I use it to refer to the United States.

2. See the bibliographic information provided by Craig Van Gelder in *The Gospel and Our Culture (USA) Newsletter.* See also Charles Van Engen, "Evangelism in the North American Context," *Journal of the Academy for Evangelism* 4 (1989): 45–55.

3. The impact of a volume such as *Resident Aliens: Life in the Christian Colony,*

All the more welcome, therefore, is Lesslie Newbigin's concern for a "genuinely missionary encounter with the culture that is shared by the peoples of Europe and North America,"[4] and the renewed attention being focused on this theme by the Gospel and Our Culture Network. It is hoped that such effort will help redirect the ministry of evangelism toward some critical compass headings of recent decades that for the most part have been ignored by the American ecclesial community: for example, the incisive conscientization of *Gospel in Context,* which remains crucial in the field, not least because of the honorable decision of its editor, Charles Taber, to cease publication; the prophetic challenges of Alfred C. Krass, Mortimer Arias, and Orlando E. Costas; and the probing theological agenda of Carl Braaten, Gabriel Fackre, Douglas John Hall, and William J. Abraham.[5]

A Twofold Enculturation

The reluctance of the American church to do the real work of contextualization, as opposed to merely assessing its cultural context in order to maximize predetermined goals and objectives, is at once the cause and the effect of an ecclesiocentric evangelism that "offers a gospel without

---

by Stanley Hauerwas and William H. Willimon (Nashville: Abingdon Press, 1989), is an indication of the hunger in the American church for a clearer identity.

4. Lesslie Newbigin, *Foolishness to the Greeks: The Gospel and Western Culture* (Grand Rapids: Eerdmans, 1986), 1.

5. See Alfred C. Krass, *Five Lanterns at Sundown: Evangelism in a Chastened Mood* (Grand Rapids: Eerdmans, 1978); idem, *Evangelizing Neopagan North America* (Scottdale, PA: Herald Press, 1982); Mortimer Arias, *Announcing the Reign of God: Evangelization and the Subversive Memory of Jesus* (Philadelphia: Fortress Press, 1984); Orlando E. Costas, *Christ outside the Gate: Mission beyond Christendom* (Maryknoll, NY: Orbis Books, 1982); idem, *Liberating News: A Theology of Contextual Evangelization* (Grand Rapids: Eerdmans, 1989); Carl Braaten, *The Flaming Center: A Theology of Christian Mission* (Philadelphia: Fortress Press, 1977); idem, *The Apostolic Imperative: Nature and Aim of the Church's Mission and Ministry* (Minneapolis: Augsburg Publishing House, 1985); Gabriel Fackre, *The Christian Story: A Narrative Interpretation of Basic Christian Doctrine* (Grand Rapids: Eerdmans, 1978); idem, *The Christian Story,* 2 vols. (Grand Rapids: Eerdmans, 1984); Douglas John Hall, *Thinking the Faith: Christian Theology in a North American Context* (Minneapolis: Augsburg Publishing House, 1989); and William J. Abraham, *The Logic of Evangelism* (Grand Rapids: Eerdmans, 1989).

demands and makes demands without the gospel."[6] The resulting enculturation is twofold. On the one hand, the practice of evangelism is often reduced to congregational self-maintenance and aggrandizement; on the other hand, the field of evangelistic studies — the best hope for reforming American evangelism, though still a fledgling discipline — remains a veritable minefield of theological polemics and academic politics.[7]

Congregational Enculturation

The first aspect of this enculturation can best be described as the democratization of the church.[8] This is not a new phenomenon in American religious life, in that the congregation as a voluntaristic association has long been an ecclesial paradigm.[9] Viewed in this role, the church provides, along with other comparable associations, "a locus of public discourse about the collective values of the society . . . an arena in which fundamental values — both political and nonpolitical — can be discussed, experimented with, symbolized, and ritually enacted."[10] It is one thing, however, for the church to fulfill such a cultural role when it is sure of its identity as the servant-messenger of Jesus Christ. It is quite another thing when the culture subsumes its identity to such an extent that the church becomes merely another public institution, providing salutary social influences, or — much more common in the late twentieth century — compensation for social deficiencies. This latter role has reached a point where the soul of the church is being bartered to the state. By allowing community activities that are properly the function of any civilized society to be assumed by congregations, as well as social welfare, which is properly the responsibility of any civilized government, the church profoundly misunderstands its social role. Furthermore, it permits God's justice to be flouted by national leaders in ways that

6. Costas, *Christ outside the Gate,* 79.

7. See Abraham, *Logic of Evangelism,* 2–8.

8. For the historical origins of this development in American culture, see Nathan O. Hatch, *The Democratization of American Christianity* (New Haven: Yale University Press, 1989). Few books in recent years have done more for the self-understanding of American Christians and congregations alike than Hatch's.

9. Avery Dulles, *Models of the Church* (New York: Doubleday, 1974), 190.

10. Robert Wuthnow, *The Struggle for America's Soul: Evangelicals, Liberals, and Secularism* (Grand Rapids: Eerdmans, 1989), 11.

the prophets of Yahweh would have found altogether intolerable, and that contemporary disciples of Jesus Christ should find no less offensive.

We cannot be surprised that the democratized church in the United States is shaped by its cultural context. Little wonder, therefore, that we find narcissism and individualism masquerading as personal salvation and religious experience.[11] The most rudimentary of theological checks exposes these as privatized soteriology and spiritualized discipleship. Both represent a serious mistraditioning of the gospel, and both leave the powers and principalities of the present world order unchallenged.[12]

The scandal of this enculturation is that American church leaders continue to direct a great deal of evangelism toward congregational development without seriously considering, still less questioning, this gross ecclesial slippage. Those who generate models and strategies will often resist theological evaluation on the grounds of dated disagreements.[13] No less frequently, practitioners will disdain it on the grounds that it distracts from the exigencies of the task at hand. Thus the critical challenge of the gospel is muted, and what ought to be creative cooperation between trusted Christian colleagues in preparing the richest nation in the world for the coming reign of God becomes a competitive struggle between consumerist-oriented institutions. Irrespective of theological persuasion or tradition, the evangelistic objectives of American congregations are overwhelmingly shaped by popular demand.

Theological Enculturation

The second aspect of American ecclesial enculturation is no less enervating and in many ways is the reason for the first, in that much of the theology shaping the American understanding of the mission and ministry of the

11. See Christopher Lasch, *The Culture of Narcissism* (New York: W. W. Norton, 1979); and Robert N. Bellah et al., *Habits of the Heart: Individualism and Commitment in American Life* (San Francisco: Harper & Row, 1986).

12. See Walter Wink, *Unmasking the Powers: The Invisible Forces That Determine Human Existence* (Philadelphia: Fortress Press, 1986); Krass, *Evangelizing Neopagan North America,* 135–51; and Lesslie Newbigin, *The Gospel in a Pluralist Society* (Grand Rapids: Eerdmans, 1989), 203–10.

13. See David J. Bosch, "'Ecumenicals' and 'Evangelicals': A Growing Relationship?" *Ecumenical Review* 40 (1988): 471–72; Newbigin, *Gospel in a Pluralist Society,* 135–37; and Wuthnow, *Struggle for America's Soul,* 21–26.

church comes out of a Protestant tradition that has long been predominantly anthropocentric. Wherever one places the onus for this situation — on the nominalist roots of the Reformation,[14] the rational epistemology of the Enlightenment,[15] the bourgeois assimilation of Schleiermacher,[16] the subjective exegesis of Bultmann,[17] or the dereliction of basic catechesis[18] — the particular revelation of divine truth in Jesus Christ has been subjugated by one form or another of the human consciousness. Thus Protestant theology has provided little if any safeguard against the enculturations of a society caught up in a plethora of psychological introspection and sensual self-gratification, and the ministry of evangelism has come to focus on human response to Jesus Christ rather than on Christ himself. Whether one is "born again" or is questing for "authentic existence," the question is the same: What does the gospel do for me and for humanity?[19]

This anthropocentrism has been particularly telling in theological education, where it has engendered a range of pedagogical perspectives that ill serve the church. At one extreme there is a critical pedagogy that inculcates the notion that it is more important to know what the gospel is not, rather than what it is; more important to be clear about what cannot be stated from a pulpit than what should and must be proclaimed; and more important to formulate questions about the Christian tradition than to affirm its essential truths. As one self-styled "reluctant unbeliever" has angrily observed:

> Perhaps no one sins more outrageously in our age, or is more characteristic of the slackness we tolerate, than the priest and the theologian who reduce God to no more than a concept but insist that they believe enough to remain members of their church or temple. They are making it awkward to be an atheist. . . . Why stand outside the doors of the

14. Robert E. Cushman, *Faith Seeking Understanding: Essays Theological and Critical* (Durham, NC: Duke University Press, 1981), xii–xiv.

15. Newbigin, *Gospel in a Pluralist Society,* 18ff.

16. Frederick Herzog, *Justice Church: The New Function of the Church in North American Christianity* (Maryknoll, NY: Orbis Books, 1980), 56ff.

17. Jürgen Moltmann, *Theology of Hope: On the Ground and the Implications of a Christian Eschatology* (New York: Harper & Row, 1967), 182ff.

18. Abraham, *Logic of Evangelism,* 117ff., 174ff.

19. David Lowes Watson, *God Does Not Foreclose: The Universal Promise of Salvation* (Nashville: Abingdon Press, 1990), 99–100.

church as an atheist and think gravely of the falsehoods preached within that one feels compelled to combat, when all the time one could just step inside and in God's own house preach against them in His name?[20]

To some extent this critical pedagogy is due to a lingering reaction against the more blatant bigotries of fundamentalism. But it presupposes something we can no longer take for granted: that theological students will have a grounding in the basics of the Christian faith when they begin their studies. The reality is very different. In many instances, students arrive at seminary with little foundation at all in Christian essentials, and as anyone with classroom experience will readily attest, a course can quickly be dominated by those who question the tradition at the expense of those who affirm it. If, as Newbigin argues, believing is primary and doubting is secondary in the whole enterprise of knowing,[21] then for many theological students today a critical pedagogy operates in what can best be described as a fiduciary smorgasbord. Little wonder that so many pastors quickly succumb to the forces of enculturation and readily resort to secular modes of leadership.

Where such a pedagogy prevails, the ministry of evangelism, which above all requires a clear and concise presentation of the core of the gospel, tends to be minimized or regarded as a political expediency. As a subject, it must be justified repeatedly in curricular discussions, weighting the research and writing of those who teach in such settings toward academic acceptability rather than congregational ministry and mission. Consequently, some of the most important work in the field at present, centered on the recovery of eschatology as the cutting edge of the evangel, remains primarily conceptual. There are countless models and handbooks available on church membership recruitment, but there is little to instruct the average American Christian in how to announce the reign of God.

At the other extreme there is a noncritical and, in some instances, rigid pedagogy that, while affirming the essentials of the evangel, fails to accept the function of theological reflection as an integral component of the evangelistic task. The result is no less anthropocentric, in that response to the gospel becomes stereotyped, and the ministry of evangelism becomes the forging of strategies and methods that will effect such a response. Not

20. Henry Fairlie, *The Seven Deadly Sins Today* (Notre Dame, IN: University of Notre Dame Press, 1979), 5.

21. Newbigin, *Gospel in a Pluralist Society,* 20.

only does this fail to challenge the narcissism and individualism of late twentieth-century North America; it actually fuels a prevailing gnosticism that renders Christian commitment a religious experience, and Christian discipleship a mind-set.[22]

As opposed to the effects of critical pedagogies that distance creative academic research from local congregations, the evangelistic models and strategies engendered by noncritical pedagogies are much more accessible, not least because of the considerable impact of the church growth movement and its prolific publications. Yet these models and strategies are for the most part contingent on unexamined soteriological, eschatological, and ecclesiological principles.[23] In the wide range of seminars and workshops conducted by theorists and practitioners alike in the field of church growth, there is often the implication that the principles and techniques of evangelism transcend such criteria. On the premise that theological reflection is not a priority for evangelism, given the clear commission in Scripture to reach unchurched people, the task becomes primarily that of persuasive communication of a prescribed gospel.[24]

Effective though this approach might be in theory, in practice it is manifestly inadequate for a well-churched culture such as the United States of America. While many students arrive at seminary today with little grounding in the Christian tradition, others arrive with a very good grounding indeed, and with a strong Christian commitment to match it. An uncritical pedagogy operating alongside a fiduciary fortress leaves future pastoral leaders every bit as ill equipped to resist the enculturations of a narcissistic society as a critical pedagogy operating amid a fiduciary smorgasbord.

22. See Philip J. Lee, *Against the Protestant Gnostics* (New York: Oxford University Press, 1987), 192.

23. See William J. Abraham, "Church Growth Theory and the Future of Evangelism," *Journal of the Academy for Evangelism* 2 (1987): 20–30.

24. E.g., see Donald A. McGavran, *Effective Evangelism: A Theological Mandate* (Phillipsburg, NJ: Presbyterian & Reformed Publishing, 1988), 6–7; idem, *Understanding Church Growth*, 3d ed., ed. C. Peter Wagner (Grand Rapids: Eerdmans, 1990), 31–40; and C. Peter Wagner, "The Church Growth Movement after Thirty Years," in *Church Growth: The State of the Art*, ed. Wagner (Wheaton, IL: Tyndale House, 1986), 32–34.

An Acute Pastoral Dilemma

Inasmuch as these are the pedagogies that shape the evangelistic leadership of American congregations, the extent of the enculturation is disturbing. At an early stage in their careers, many American pastors are caught in a professional dilemma: whether to serve Jesus Christ, and truly pastor their people in his teachings; or whether to accept the cultural norms of success, and subject themselves to inappropriate triumphalisms and unnecessary defeatisms. They know one thing for sure: in the final analysis, an enculturated church will measure their pastoral effectiveness by the numerical size and growth of their congregations.

Never mind whether they seek to form faithful Christian disciples, according to the Scriptures and with true ethical freedom;[25] never mind whether they demand Christian service as a condition of church membership or press for social and racial inclusiveness among their membership;[26] in short, never mind what they do to enable their congregations to be the light and salt and leaven and seed of the coming reign of God in the world (Matt. 5:13-16; 13:33, 38). They know they will ultimately be evaluated by two pervasive and all-important questions: How large is your church? and How much has it grown?

Between these two extremes there is a wide range of evangelistic theory and practice, both in schools of theology and in congregations. Moreover, it is encouraging to note that, whereas there once were clearly definable theological "camps" in evangelism, these too have become less distinct in their respective conciliar and evangelical designations. Even so, disagreements continue to be reflected in the arena of world evangelization, which is often a better barometer of American theological concerns than the United States itself, where honoraria can work wonders for collegiality. As recently as 1989, the Commission on World Mission and Evangelism (CWME) of the World Council of Churches (WCC) and the Lausanne Committee on World Evangelization (LCWE) held separate conferences, displaying characteristics that, if not at the

25. See Samuel R. Schulz, "A Goal-Directed Model for Disciple-Making," *Journal of the Academy for Evangelism* 3 (1988): 62–71; Francis E. Ringer, "What Kind of Christian Do We Seek to Make through Evangelism?" *Journal of the Academy for Evangelism* 3 (1988): 33–40.

26. See Jimmy Carter, "The Task of Evangelism," *Journal of the Academy for Evangelism* 3 (1988): 7; William E. Pannell, "Some Reflections on Church Growth," *Journal of the Academy for Evangelism* 2 (1987): 55–57.

two extremes we have just identified, nonetheless projected marked differences of evangelistic method. Notwithstanding many common concerns and some significant convergences, the metaphor of Alan Neely and James A. Scherer is vivid: that while LCWE and CWME do not "pass as ships in the night," they still "pass as ships in the day, occasionally waving at one another."[27] In his excellent assessment of the 1989 CWME San Antonio Conference, Norman E. Thomas notes that in spite of its focus on a theocentric theme, "the pluralism and style of WCC conferences . . . will cause many to continue to doubt its commitment to evangelism."[28] By the same token, Neely and Scherer observe that the more than four hundred seminars and twenty-two plenary sessions of the LCWE gathering "were mostly listening experiences, not dialogues. . . . In fact, the most frequently heard complaint in Manila, not always voiced in private, was resentment about the high degree of control exercised by the Lausanne planners."[29]

Hermeneutical Distinctions

The answer to these problems of enculturation lies in establishing criteria for the ministry of evangelism in the United States that will confront the prevailing anthropocentism of the church and focus instead on a Christocentric message. Evangelism must have a hermeneutic that, while taking human response into account, is not governed by popular response. The first step in this direction is to declare the congregation to be the hermeneutical locus of evangelism. This position concurs with Newbigin's designation of the congregation as the hermeneutic of the gospel for the culture in which it lives and serves: as a community of praise and thanksgiving, a community of truth, a community *for* the world and *of* the world, a community of responsibility for God's new order, and a community of eschatological hope.[30] As an integral

27. Alan Neely and James A. Scherer, "San Antonio and Manila 1989: '. . . like Ships in the Night'?" *Missiology* 18, no. 2 (1990): 140.

28. Norman E. Thomas, "Ecumenical Directions in Evangelism: Melbourne to San Antonio," *Journal of the Academy for Evangelism* 5 (1990): 62; cf. "The San Antonio Conference," *International Review of Mission* 78 (1989): 319, 328.

29. Neely and Scherer, "San Antonio and Manila 1989," 143.

30. Newbigin, *Gospel in a Pluralist Society*, 222–23. The most cogent argument to be made in recent years for the congregation as the locus of evangelism is that of William J. Abraham in his *Logic of Evangelism*. Indeed, the congregation is where he also

feature of the *missio Dei,* evangelism cannot be undertaken apart from such communities. Attempts to do so render the gospel even more vulnerable to enculturation.

Yet herein lies a pitfall. While affirming the congregation as the hermeneutical locus of evangelism, the ministry of evangelism must nonetheless have a distinctive hermeneutic that affirms the world as the locus of God's salvation. Put differently, while the ministry of evangelism must be formed in and through congregations of the church, and must be thoroughly integral to their identity and self-understanding, the purpose of evangelism must still be to proclaim the gospel of Jesus Christ in the world — a proclamation that should in no way be shaped or determined by congregational concerns per se. The gospel of Jesus Christ is for the world, not the church, and congregations must regard themselves solely as Christ's messengers, with all the discretion and self-effacement that such a role implies.

It must quickly be added that drawing this distinction between evangelism and congregational concerns, especially those of membership recruitment, can be done only in the context of a well-churched culture such as the United States of America. Furthermore, it can be done only on the premise that the forming of faithful Christian disciples is an integral component of an inclusive and holistic approach to ministry and mission.[31] But when congregations, called into being as sign communities of the coming reign of God, have come to regard themselves, and not the world, as the locus of God's salvation, and when open houses of grace for the world have become ecclesial safe houses into which people are invited out of the world that Jesus came to save, then radical steps are needed. As with any vessel that requires course correction, the initial rudder to be applied must be extreme. If evangelism is to recover its integrity, there must be a clear break with enculturated habits and attitudes. For at this point in time, any ministry of evangelism in the American church that even remotely shapes its priorities around congrega-

---

focuses the coming reign of God, with evangelism as the necessary initiation. Given the prevailing enculturation of the American church, however, it is not altogether clear how Abraham would safeguard such an approach from appropriation by self-serving congregations. At present, any form of church-oriented evangelism will probably fail to give the necessary degree of course correction.

31. David Lowes Watson, "The Church as Journalist: Evangelism in the Context of the Local Church in the United States," *International Review of Mission* 72 (1983): 71–73.

tional concerns, and especially around membership recruitment and its concomitant needs, risks further enculturation.

Church-forgetfulness is the name of the game if we are to recover the essence of the gospel of Jesus Christ. Paul had to argue the same case before Peter and the Jerusalem church (Acts 15; Gal. 2), and today, in a world on the brink of the mysteries of time and space, we face no less critical a juncture. It is time for an ecclesiocentric church and anthropocentric Christians to abandon their self-indulgences. They must recover a gospel that proclaims Christ as all in all (Col. 3:11) and return center stage to the lead actor in God's drama of salvation. Actually, when the drama reaches its conclusion, they will have to leave the stage altogether. Eschatologically, the church is an anachronism.

A Hermeneutic for Evangelism

How, then, are American congregations to shape such a ministry of evangelism, affirming their responsibility as the hermeneutical locus of the gospel, yet allowing their message to retain its integrity, free of ecclesial impedimenta? It is beyond the scope of this article to offer a comprehensive blueprint. There are whole new areas of research to be explored: for example, the evangelization of God's economic justice, political righteousness, and cosmic splendor. Likewise, new models and strategies must be developed to complement the personal with the prophetic forms of evangelism.[32] But as a beginning — as the initial turn of the rudder, so to speak — we can propose a hermeneutical method to give congregations a means of reliably focusing their evangelism on a Christ-centered gospel — a method that, instead of seeking new ways of faith sharing, makes the starting point of evangelism the gospel itself, thereby releasing much latent power and grace, and more surely avoiding the snares of enculturation.

It should come as no surprise that the groundwork for such an evangelistic method has been laid by a liberated Roman Catholicism in the Two-Thirds world. The importance of this work by Latin American Roman Catholic theologians, and that of some Protestant colleagues, has recently been addressed in a helpful study by Priscilla Pope-Levison, serving to

32. See David Lowes Watson, "Evangelism: A Disciplinary Approach," *International Bulletin of Missionary Research* 7, no. 1 (1983): 6–9.

underscore the potential of these initiatives for the American church.[33] Avoiding the anthropocentrism of the Protestant tradition, and likewise the ecclesiocentrism of the Roman tradition, these theologians have forged a hermeneutical method by which the gospel can be honed as the good news of God's global grace in Jesus Christ, a method that allows particular theological perspectives to be fully acknowledged, and at the same time congregational identity to be fully affirmed.

There is no better exponent of this method than Juan Luis Segundo, whose five-volume study *A Theology for Artisans of a New Humanity* is a classic example of the "hermeneutic circle."[34] In a subsequent volume dealing more directly with hermeneutical method, Segundo defines this circle as "the continuing change in our interpretation of the Bible which is dictated by the continuing changes in our present-day reality, both individual and societal." Drawing on the work of Andrew V. Seumois, Segundo further articulates three hermeneutical principles for evangelism: "1. communicating only the essentials of the Christian message . . . ; 2. communicating it as good news . . . ; and 3. adding nothing further except at a pace that will allow the essential element to remain precisely that."[35]

Adapting both of these methods, a hermeneutic for evangelism can be stated in the form of four questions: What is the gospel? What is our context? What makes the gospel good news in this context? How does contextual response to the gospel further illumine its good news? Applied to the American context, these questions point us in some significant new directions.

33. Priscilla Pope-Levison, *Evangelization from a Liberation Perspective* (New York: Peter Lang, 1991).

34. Juan Luis Segundo, *A Theology for Artisans of a New Humanity*, 5 vols. (Maryknoll, NY: Orbis Books, 1973–74). This project, probably best known for its first volume, *The Community Called Church*, adopts a method of theology "shaped and formed through real-life seminars" (1:169). Each chapter begins with a position paper and is then followed by a series of "clarifications" arising from small-group discussion of the material with laypersons. These discussions represent "a confrontation between what they have heard and what they have learned from their real-life experiences; between that which they accepted uncritically as children and adolescents and that which they have put together into a coherent whole as adults" (1:x).

35. Juan Luis Segundo, *The Liberation of Theology* (Maryknoll, NY: Orbis Books, 1976), 8; idem, *The Hidden Motives of Pastoral Action: Latin American Reflections* (Maryknoll, NY: Orbis Books, 1978), 111, 113, 115–16.

What Is the Gospel?

Interestingly — and significantly — this question is rarely encountered in the vast literature available on evangelistic methods and strategies. Yet when the question is posed and answered, much of American evangelism is shown to be defective in content. Whether one takes the kerygmatic outline of C. H. Dodd, helpfully discussed by Abraham, or the prophetic announcement of Alfred C. Krass, critically expounded by Arias and further addressed by Segundo, or the narrative of the Christian story as portrayed by Lischer and Fackre, there are certain basics to the gospel that our anthropocentric evangelism persistently ignores.[36]

Mortimer Arias expresses this defect most succinctly when he draws attention to the fact that there are two dimensions to the gospel: the gospel *about* Jesus, and the gospel *of* Jesus.[37] The gospel about Jesus is the message that gives our evangelism its personal form and includes the priestly work of Christ and the atoning grace through which we are reconciled to God. The new life we experience through the indwelling power of the Holy Spirit is pivotal to this message, which brings lost, sinful human beings to repentance and forgiveness. It is at the very heart of the gospel.

No less at the heart of the gospel, however, is the prophetic announcement of Jesus in the synagogue at Nazareth: the promise of good news for the poor, release for captives, sight for the blind, and freedom for the oppressed (Luke 4:18-19). If, however, the only aspect of the gospel with which we evangelize is the invitation to personal forgiveness and reconciliation, our message can easily become personalized to the point of gnosticism. When this happens, the prophetic good news of Jesus Christ — his advocacy of God's justice for the poor and abused of the world — is by definition consigned to other ministries of the church, to be addressed as a consequence of evangelism (perhaps), but not as an integral part of the gospel we are commissioned to take into the world. The promises of Jesus announcing God's coming *shalom* are then proclaimed not as good news

36. C. H. Dodd, *The Apostolic Preaching and Its Developments* (New York: Harper & Row, 1936); Abraham, *Logic of Evangelism,* 43–44, 51; Krass, *Five Lanterns at Sundown,* 66–87; Arias, *Announcing the Reign of God;* Juan Luis Segundo, *The Historical Jesus of the Synoptics* (Maryknoll, NY: Orbis Books, 1985), 86–118; Richard Lischer, *Speaking of Jesus: Finding the Words for Witness* (Philadelphia: Fortress Press, 1982); Gabriel Fackre, *Christian Basics: A Primer for Pilgrims* (Grand Rapids: Eerdmans, 1991).

37. Arias, *Announcing the Reign of God,* 8ff.

for the world here and now but as projections for the hereafter, thereby setting the tone for a discipleship that minimizes Christ's directive to join him at work in the world, ministering to the little ones who still suffer and starve.

This bifurcation of the gospel is at the heart of the age-old divide between evangelism and social ethics, a divide that remains theologically unbridged, albeit heavily veneered at present with collegialities of common social concern.[38] Until the issue is addressed hermeneutically, however, these collegialities will have little impact on the average American congregation, the hermeneutical locus of evangelism. The question is not how to link evangelism with social ethics, but rather how to incorporate the social and systemic hope of the gospel into our evangelism at the outset. The evangel must be the cutting edge of social and systemic, no less than personal, transformation. If not, the prophetic tradition of the Scriptures is severed, and the social and systemic dimensions of the gospel cease to be good news from God. They focus instead on what is wrong with the world, rather than on what God is doing to put it right. Much more detrimental to the coming *basileia tou theou,* Jesus of Nazareth becomes a gnostic Christ, available only to the privileged — who are by no means always the poor, the blind, the captives, or the oppressed.

What Is Our Context?

Placing this question second in a hermeneutic for evangelism points to an interesting and significant feature of Segundo's method. On the one hand, context is his point of entry for the hermeneutic circle, a "way of experiencing reality" that leads to an "ideological suspicion." Indeed, he makes it a precondition of this circle that we should have "profound and enriching questions about our real situation," a suspicion that is then applied to the "whole ideological superstructure in general and to theology in particular." This attitude in turn engenders a "new way of experiencing theological reality that leads us to exegetical suspicion," and finally to a "new hermeneutic, that is, a new way of interpreting the fountainhead of our faith." On the other hand, when he adopts the threefold evangelistic principle of

38. See Ronald J. Sider, *One-Sided Christianity? Uniting the Church to Heal a Lost and Broken World* (Grand Rapids: Zondervan, 1993).

Seumois, he begins with the communication of the essentials of the Christian message.[39]

The point could not be made more clearly. The ministry of evangelism must start at a very different place from that of theological reflection on evangelism. The ministry of evangelism must begin with the gospel that has been traditioned for us. Paul stated this very well for the Corinthians: "Now I would remind you, brothers and sisters, of the good news that I proclaimed to you, which you in turn received, in which also you stand, through which also you are being saved, if you hold firmly to the message that I proclaimed to you — unless you have come to believe in vain. For I handed on to you as of first importance what I in turn had received . . ." (1 Cor. 15:1-3a).

This hermeneutical sequence is an important point of clarification for evangelistic studies, and it must be made unequivocally: Theological reflection on evangelism is not the same as the practice of evangelism. For theological reflection, it can well be argued that context is the place to begin. Indeed, it is a maxim of contextual hermeneutics that *all* theology is necessarily governed by its context; as many theologians are now agreed, it has been a blind spot of Western theology not to have taken this point sufficiently into account. In evangelism, however, context comes second, not first, and the starting point of a hermeneutical method for this ministry must be to identify the essential Christian message so that it can be handed on as it has been received. What is done with that message, within the community of faith and beyond, and what its implications are for faithful discipleship and for witness in the world require careful and continued theological reflection. But while such reflections rightly inform the ministry of evangelism, they cannot and must not substitute for evangelistic activity — actually proclaiming, communicating, sharing the gospel message with the world.

This said, the hermeneutical method for evangelism must indeed proceed to a realistic assessment of the context in which the gospel is to be proclaimed. In the contemporary United States, the relevant contextual factors are not nearly so much those of pluralism and diversity as those of a thoroughly homogenous idolatry. Charles Taber has made this analysis devastatingly clear, naming the idols in our midst: unrestrained sexual

39. Segundo, *Liberation of Theology*, 9; idem, *Hidden Motives of Pastoral Action*, 111.

expression, self-indulgence and excess, greed and wealth, autonomous human achievement, and race, land, and nation.[40] Belief in God is not a contextual problem for the American evangelist — not with 94 percent of the population believing in God, and 84 percent acknowledging the divinity of Christ.[41] The contextual challenge lies rather in exposing these cultural idols and proclaiming in their place the one true God, incarnate in Jesus of Nazareth, crucified, dead, buried, raised from the dead, and soon to come again in power and glory.

These contextual factors have been well analyzed, sociologically and spiritually.[42] But for the most part they are winked at by pastoral leaders of the American church, who, rather than proclaim a Christ-centered gospel that condemns these idols for what they are, seek to accommodate them under the guise of meeting people's needs. By contrast, evangelizing with a Christ-centered message requires that we proclaim a jealous God who refuses to share divine status and whose justice favors the widow and the orphan.

What Makes the Gospel Good News in This Context?

In a cultural context rife with such idolatry, a gospel that promises enriched personhood and divine favor is readily accepted as good news, albeit in direct competition with alternative forms of personal fulfillment. To place personal salvation at the cutting edge of the gospel in such a setting is therefore a clear miscontextualization. Anyone even vaguely familiar with American congregational life knows only too well the effects of such spiritual amphetamines.[43] And anyone with a modicum of knowledge about planet earth, its peoples, its poverties, its cruelties, and its ecological habits, knows that a gospel offering only personal salvation is a grave mistraditioning of the Incarnate One. It is also a mistraditioning

40. Charles R. Taber, "God vs. Idols: A Model of Conversion," *Journal of the Academy for Evangelism* 3 (1988): 27–28.

41. George H. Gallup, Jr., *Religion in America, 1990* (Princeton: Princeton Religion Research Center, 1990), 21, 23.

42. See George G. Hunter III, *To Spread the Power: Church Growth in the Wesleyan Spirit* (Nashville: Abingdon Press, 1987); idem, *How to Reach Secular People* (Nashville: Abingdon Press, 1992).

43. See Watson, *God Does Not Foreclose*, 30–31.

of pristine Protestantism, in which *sola fide* and *sola Scriptura* were clarion calls of freedom at a time when personal forgiveness and reconciliation with God were indeed being denied to ordinary people by secular and ecclesial powers.

But this is hardly the plight of the United States in the late twentieth century. In the context of a nation with such wealth and global clout, what truly makes the gospel good news is its eschatological imperative. This is the consensus of a number of key authors across several decades,[44] and it is the dimension of the gospel that must be restored to the forefront of American evangelism. It is the good news *of* Jesus Christ: the assurance that one day there will be neither Jew nor Greek, neither slave nor free, neither male nor female (Gal. 3:28); when the wolf shall live with the lamb, the leopard shall lie down with the kid, the lion shall eat straw like the ox, and the earth shall be as full of the knowledge of God as the waters cover the sea (Isa. 11:6-9); when everyone will know God, from the least to the greatest (Jer. 31:34); when justice will roll down like waters, and righteousness like an ever-flowing stream (Amos 5:24); when there will be no more sound of weeping or cries of distress; when all children shall live beyond infancy, and all old people shall live out their days; when those who build houses shall live in them, and not have others possess them; when those who plant vineyards shall eat of them, and not have others take them away (Isa. 65:19-22).

The watchword for this evangelism is not "Be saved!" but "Be ready!"[45] For the day is coming when time and eternity will be fused into a glorious new creation (Rev. 21:1-4), when the whole of humanity, indeed the whole of planet earth, will be reordered into a new age *(palingenesia),* in which the poor will be cared for, in which those with great wealth will distribute it to the needy, and where the first will be last and the last first — willingly (Matt. 19:16-30). This new age will come not only in heaven but also on earth, as Jesus himself taught us to pray (Matt. 6:10). Its fulfillment consists not in the final gathering of those who cry "Lord, Lord" but in the actual-

44. See Hans Jochen Margull, *Hope in Action: The Church's Task in the World* (Philadelphia: Muhlenberg Press, 1962); Braaten, *Flaming Center;* idem, "The Meaning of Evangelism in the Context of God's Universal Grace," *Journal of the Academy for Evangelism* 3 (1988): 9–19; Krass, *Five Lanterns at Sundown;* Costas, *Christ outside the Gate;* Arias, *Announcing the Reign of God;* Abraham, *Logic of Evangelism;* Raymond Fung, *The Isaiah Vision: An Ecumenical Strategy for Congregational Evangelism* (Geneva: WCC Publications, 1992).

45. See Krass, *Five Lanterns at Sundown.*

ization of Christ's teachings among *all* people (Matt. 7:21-23; Luke 6:46; John 13:13-15).[46]

Contrary to the enculturated evangelism that pampers the comfortable to the neglect of the afflicted, this Christ-centered gospel is a call to spiritual warfare, for God's reordering of planet earth will not come without a struggle. Christ has identified the ruler of a rival kingdom, Beelzebul (Matt. 12:25; Mark 3:24; Luke 11:17-18), and has warned us that the *basileia tou theou* would be in direct confrontation with present worldly powers. But the good news is that final victory is assured. There will be a purging of all that is evil (Matt. 13:41), with nothing less than a total transformation, a different order altogether (John 18:36).[47] The rulers of this world hold transitory power at best. Jesus will reign forever and ever (Rev. 11:15).

If this message were to be proclaimed with the vigor, persistence, and conviction that countless congregations give to sharing their personal faith or to their multifarious programs, the impact on American culture would be tremendous. It is most assuredly good news, for sinners and for those sinned against. The problem lies in getting pastoral leaders to put this message at the forefront of their congregational life and work. Therein also lies the challenge for those of us who make the study of evangelism a professional contribution to the church.

How Does Contextual Response to the Gospel Further Illumine Its Good News?

With this question, our method incorporates its most radical step, in that the world's response to the gospel is made an integral component of evangelism. In taking this step, we break with Newbigin, who, in his assessment of the hermeneutical circle, rejects it as "not adequate to account for what is involved in the relationship between the gospel and this or any culture." Rather, he argues, there are two worlds, "defined in terms of death and rebirth. And those on this side of the boundary are not those who have been able to make a sort of gigantic hermeneutical leap, but those who have

46. See Newbigin, *Gospel in a Pluralist Society,* 85–87; Watson, *God Does Not Foreclose,* 62.

47. On this point, see M. Douglas Meeks, *God the Economist: The Doctrine of God and Political Economy* (Minneapolis: Fortress Press, 1989), 120.

been chosen and called — not of their own will — to be the witnesses of Jesus to the world." Thus, for Newbigin, the hermeneutical circle is one that operates within the believing community. "Every Christian reader comes to the Bible with the spectacles provided by the tradition that is alive in the community to which he or she belongs, and that tradition is being constantly modified as each new generation of believers endeavors to be faithful in understanding and living out Scripture."[48]

While this hermeneutical stance may well be appropriate and necessary on the European side of the Atlantic, it is fraught with risk for American evangelism. Indeed, it could well revert to precisely the evangelism that so badly needs correction, namely, a message structured for a preconceived response. It is important in addressing this final hermeneutical question, therefore, to be clear about how contextual response from the world can further illumine the good news of the gospel, and how it cannot.

For clarification we must return to the first hermeneutical question, which involves the distinction between the gospel *about* Jesus and the gospel *of* Jesus. The gospel about Jesus is not the issue in this fourth question. The nature, the person, and the atoning work of Jesus Christ are, as Newbigin rightly declares, matters for hermeneutical interpretation within the believing community, a "tradition that is being constantly modified as each new generation of believers endeavors to be faithful in understanding and living out Scripture." Moreover, while the *actus tradendi* is continuously interpretative, we can also agree with Newbigin's critique of Hick, Knitter, and others, particularly when he insists that the tradition is established in certain historical happenings that for the Christian are nonnegotiable. "To affirm the unique decisiveness of God's action in Jesus Christ is not arrogance; it is the enduring bulwark against the arrogance of every culture to be itself the criterion by which others are judged."[49] To which can be added that it is a signal breach of Christian collegiality to accept the tradition from our spiritual forebears and then proceed to mistrust their mental faculties.[50]

The gospel *of* Jesus, in contrast, is a message that is open to constant change and illumination. It has been unfolding for millennia, and it

48. Newbigin, *Foolishness to the Greeks,* 53, 56.

49. Newbigin, *Gospel in a Pluralist Society,* 56, 155ff., 166. See also Carl E. Braaten, "Who Do We Say That He Is? On the Uniqueness and Universality of Jesus Christ," *Occasional Bulletin of Missionary Research* 4, no. 1 (1980): 2–7.

50. See Richard R. Niebuhr, *Resurrection and Historical Reason* (New York: Charles Scribner's Sons, 1957), 29.

continues to unfold. The coming *basileia tou theou* has been promised to us, and it has been given a definitive shape by its progenitor and sovereign-to-be, the risen Jew of Nazareth. But its final form and the manner and time of its fulfillment have us all in the dark. It will come "like a thief in the night" (1 Thess. 5:2) and with the suddenness of birth after labor (Rom. 8:18-25). Most important of all, it will happen to "the whole creation" (v. 22).

In other words, the world is custodian of the coming reign of God no less than the church — not through Beelzebul, but through the universal power and presence of God's Spirit, who is preveniently at work in the world preparing for this eschatological event (Rev. 21:5).[51] The church must therefore constantly seek illumination of the gospel of Jesus Christ by the worldliness of the Holy Spirit, lest its evangelism become myopic. Not without good reason did Jesus admonish the chief priests and the elders of the people that "the tax collectors and the prostitutes are going into the kingdom of God ahead of you" (Matt. 21:31). Not without clear insight have Guillermo Cook and others explained to us that the gospel comes to the church from the poor, among whom the grace of God is to be found in abundance.[52] It is this dimension of the gospel that requires worldly attunement so that our announcements might be thoroughly up-to-date — the good news not only of what Christ has done but also of what the Holy Spirit is doing today and tomorrow to bring Christ's work to fulfillment.

For this evangelistic task we need all the interpretative insights we can get: from those who receive our message gladly and from those who do not, from those who share our hope for the world and from those who do not, from those who are working for the *basileia tou theou* in the name of Jesus Christ and from those who are working for the same kingdom but do not yet know its sovereign. There will even be gracious illumination from those who

51. See Jürgen Moltmann, *God in Creation: A New Theology of Creation and the Spirit of God* (San Francisco: Harper & Row, 1985), 206–14.

52. Guillermo Cook, *The Expectation of the Poor: Latin American Basic Ecclesial Communities in Protestant Perspective* (Maryknoll, NY: Orbis Books, 1985), 77ff.; Alvaro Barreiro, *Basic Ecclesial Communities: The Evangelization of the Poor* (Maryknoll, NY: Orbis Books, 1982), 34ff.; Leonardo Boff, *When Theology Listens to the Poor* (San Francisco: Harper & Row, 1988), 30–31; cf. Alan Neely, "Liberation Theology and the Poor: A Second Look," *Missiology* 17, no. 4 (1989): 387–404.

reject the gospel, for there is no one beyond God's grace, and no one whom God cannot use in the awesome plan of salvation (Rom. 10–11).[53]

Some years ago, I suggested that American evangelism needed a new root metaphor: journalism, as opposed to salesmanship.[54] The key to that argument was the issue whether the gospel is a commodity or a message of good news, and if a message of good news, whether the news is still unfolding. A Christ-centered evangel leaves no doubt at all about the answer. For the risen Christ is at work in the world in the person of the Holy Spirit, preparing for the ultimate family reunion promised by God, the ultimate parent. Our evangelism must therefore begin with the headlines of this tremendous good news; it must be informed about the world in which it is to be announced and about the persons with whom it is to be shared; it must be edited so that it is indeed good news; and it must report new happenings as God's salvation unfolds. For too long Christ's editors have filled their columns with in-house gossip and have made personnel their priority rather than news coverage. It is time indeed for a radical change.

53. See Newbigin, *Gospel in a Pluralist Society,* 83.
54. Watson, "The Church as Journalist."

Ecclesia Crucis: The Theologic of Christian Awkwardness

DOUGLAS JOHN HALL

In this chapter, I would like to show that intentional *disengagement* from the dominant culture, with which the older Protestant denominations of this continent have been bound up in the past, is the necessary precondition for a meaningful *engagement* of that same dominant culture. The demonstration of this thesis involves three steps. First, I must clarify what is entailed in an intentional disengagement from the dominant culture. Second, I must explain in a general way how such a disengagement could facilitate meaningful reengagement of that same culture. And third, I must provide enough concrete examples of such a process to give it contextual credibility.

Disengagement as a Work of Theology

What is entailed in an intentional disengagement from the dominant culture? It is one thing to respond to such a question in societies where Christian establishments are of the legal variety (as has been the case for most European societies). It is something else to do so in our North American context, where what pertains is a cultural establishment. Just because ours is an establishment more of content than of form, and just because our close ties with our dominant culture have existed at the level of fundamental beliefs, lifestyles, and rudimentary moral assumptions, any effective extrication of ourselves from this by now (as it seems to me) severely limiting relationship must occur at the more subtle level of original thought. To put it quite clearly, for North American Christians who are serious about re-forming the church so that it may become a more faithful bearer of divine judgment and mercy in our social context, there is no alternative to engaging in a disciplined, prolonged, and, above all, critical work of theology. Here I do not mean merely academic theology but that sort of passionate reflection which Luther had in mind when he wrote, "Vivendo, immo moriendo et damnando fit theologus, non intelligende, legendo aut speculando" (It is by living — no rather, by dying and being damned — that a theologian is made, not by understanding, reading, or speculating).[1]

Concretely speaking, we must learn how to distinguish the Christian message from the operative assumptions, values, and pursuits of our host society — more particularly, those segments of our society with which, as so-called mainstream churches, we have been identified. Since most of the denominations in question are bound up with the middle-class, Caucasian, liberal element of our society, we shall have to learn that the Christian gospel is not a stained-glass version of the worldview of that same social stratum.

This is easily said and, in these days, is said rather frequently. I am not at all convinced, however, that it has been grasped, except by a few. Moreover, the minorities in our midst who *have* taken seriously the need for us Protestants in North America to distance ourselves from the worldview of our conventional socioeconomic constituency seem to me often to err, in two fundamental ways.

First, some of these voices convey the impression that such distancing is the very goal for which we should strive, and not merely a means to our more authentic reengagement of this same society. They give many indications of disliking this social stratum and everything that it stands for. They often seem to assume that First World, white, middle-class societies are by definition irredeemable; that they are driven by an irreversible logic of oppression and injustice. They tell us, in one way or another, that our only salvation as Christians is to cut ourselves off from our WASPish past and to align ourselves instead with those whom we oppress. One may understand the peculiar vehemence of such persons, especially those among them who know profoundly the plight of the victims of our society; but the abandonment of the oppressor is no very likely way of effecting change.

1. *Weimarer Ausgabe* 5.163.28.

Besides, as Wendy Farley of Emory University has aptly written, for those adopting this approach,

> sensitivity to injustice and suffering often becomes a new dualism that categorizes human beings according to membership in the group of the oppressed or the oppressor. . . .
>
> I am not convinced that this objectification of humanity into victim and executioner does justice to the complexity of the human individual or to the dynamic of evil. . . . The web that unites victim and tyrant in the same person is more complex than the white hat/black hat caricature that seems banal even in its natural habitat, the "grade B" movie.[2]

The second questionable way in which minorities in the once-mainline churches try to re-form the churches is by identifying "true Christianity" with the adoption of what are perceived as radical positions on various contemporary issues of personal and social ethics. They insist that Christianity means advocating economic reforms aimed at greater global justice, or full-scale disarmament, or the preservation of species, or gender equality, or racial integration, and so forth. I am entirely in agreement with such ethical conclusions. But they are conclusions, not starting points. The presentation of a radical ethic of economic justice, for example, perhaps can sometimes be a catalyst for genuine Christian evangelism; on the whole, however, profoundly altered moral attitudes and specific ethical decisions are consequences of the gospel. When we present such consequences of grace and faith as if they were immediately accessible to everyone, we are confusing gospel and law.

In that connection, one of the important insights of the recent publication *Christianity: A Social and Cultural History* is that some of "the difficulties of the older Protestant denominations may stem from their willingness to embrace ideas and trends as defined by the nation's media and educational elites, elites that are remarkably unrepresentative of the religion, politics, and values of the nation's population."[3] It seems to me incontrovertible that the Christian gospel erases all distinctions of worth and status between races and sexes. But it is the gospel that achieves this leveling, and if instead of gospel what is proclaimed in the churches is

2. Wendy Farley, *Tragic Vision and Divine Compassion: A Contemporary Theodicy* (Louisville: Westminster/John Knox Press, 1990), 51–52.

3. Howard Clark Kee et al., *Christianity: A Social and Cultural History* (New York: Macmillan, 1991), 734.

nothing more than the kinds of musts and shoulds and ought-tos that one can hear from many other quarters, along with the ubiquitous language of "rights," then we cannot expect church people to be any more receptive to such exhortations than are their counterparts in society at large.

The point is that the great changes that need to be effected in our churches are not first of all changes of behavior but changes of understanding and will. If the *thinking* of the churches — including congregations of middle-class whites — is altered, then we may expect changes also in the realm of *deeds*. If, however, being Christian continues to mean little more than being predictable middle-class liberals with a tinge of something called spirituality, then the few exceptional things that congregations occasionally manage to perform ethically will lack any foundation in repentance and faith and will show up — as they generally do now — as exceptions: ad hoc ethical non sequiturs kept going by the enthusiasm of the few and the guilt of a somewhat larger cross-section of churchgoers.

In criticizing these two positions, I am seeking to establish the point that there are no shortcuts if we are committed to genuine renewal in the churches that we represent; we must begin with basics. We have two or three generations of people in and around the churches now who are for the most part not only unfamiliar with the fundamental teachings of the Christian tradition but largely ignorant even of the Scriptures. I know that some denominations have been more diligent than others in the area of Christian education, but from what I can see — even where candidates for ministry are concerned — it is rather ludicrous for contemporary Protestants to boast that we insist upon an educated laity and uphold the principle *sola Scriptura*. We must even ask ourselves whether we have a well-educated professional ministry, or at least a ministry whose basic theological education is continuously renewed and supplemented, and then incorporated into preaching and congregational leadership.

Professor Gabriel Fackre and Dorothy Fackre have recently conducted an extensive survey entitled "The State of Theology in Churches." In their Newsletter no. 30, dated Advent 1991, they report: "The vast majority of respondents judged the state of theology in the churches to be 'abysmal,' 'dismal,' 'confused,' 'mushy,' 'sparse,' 'inarticulate,' 'deplorable.' "[4]

4. Privately circulated to "friends and former students" under the title "Theology and Culture Newsletter," no. 30, G. and D. Fackre, Andover Newton Theological School, 210 Herrick Rd., Newton Centre, MA 02159.

Such surveys, especially when they are conducted by working theologians, are susceptible to the charge of professional bias. Yet, even if the adjectives gleaned from the responses to the Fackre survey do not represent every church, they are too descriptive of the overall situation to be ignored by any of us. The question we face is: If there is so little understanding of Christian foundations in our congregations, how can we expect ordinary churchgoers to distinguish what is Christian from the usual amalgam of religious sentimentalism and what Ernst Käsemann called bourgeois transcendence? Until a far greater percentage of churchgoing Americans and Canadians have become more articulate about the faith than they are currently, it is absurd to imagine that North American church folk could stand back from their sociological moorings far enough to detach what Christians profess from the mishmash of modernism, secularism, pietism, and free-enterprise democracy with which Christianity in our context is so fantastically interwoven.

The need for such a "right dividing of the word of truth" is clearly borne out by recent sociological studies as well as theological-ecclesiastical investigations like that of the Fackres. In their 1987 study entitled *American Mainline Religion: Its Changing Shape and Future,* Wade Clark Roof and William McKinney write,

> If a revived public church is indeed on the horizon, moderate Protestantism will play a key role in bringing it into being. This will require forms and qualities of leadership that have seldom been forthcoming from the Protestant middle; a revitalized ecumenicity and new, bold *theological* affirmations are critical . . . , especially a theology that resonates with and gives meaning to the experience of middle Americans.[5]

Not incidentally, by "moderate Protestantism" Roof and McKinney mean in particular the Protestantism historically present in Methodist, Lutheran, and ecumenically minded Baptist denominations. I hope therefore that it will be understood that when I affirm, as my first point, that Christian faithfulness today implies an intentional disengagement of churches from their cultural moorings, I am pleading with Lutherans, among others, to enter more and more wholeheartedly into the ecumenical dialogue and common task of the church in North America today. Because

5. Wade Clark Roof and William McKinney, *American Mainline Religion: Its Changing Shape and Future* (New Brunswick, N.J.: Rutgers University Press, 1987), 243.

Lutherans have had a special and different slant on the Christian message, because they have never been quite at home with "the American Dream," and because they have often been more diligent than the more liberal churches as catechists, they have much to contribute. But this will occur only if the rather dormant *theologia crucis* (theology of the cross) in the Lutheran tradition becomes contextually alive, and if it expresses itself also in an *ecclesia crucis* — that is, in a church that is ready to suffer. The kind of disengagement that I am talking about indeed cannot occur apart from the suffering of the church, not least of all the kind of suffering that is inevitably entailed in the movement from a more private, ethnic ecclesiastical engagement to one that is fully public.

Disengagement from our status of cultural establishment is primarily, then, a work of theology. But whoever thinks that theology is a remote, abstract undertaking has not yet been grasped by the Word of the cross!

An Ancient Dialectic: Not "of," Yet "in"

My thesis is that intentional disengagement from the dominant culture is the necessary prerequisite of Christian engagement of that same culture. My first point has been that this work of detachment is a theological work. The second step toward demonstrating the viability of this thesis involves asking how disengagement can facilitate authentic engagement. Is that not double-talk?

I think not. In fact, the idea of disengaging-in-order-to-engage is by no means either contradictory or novel. Indeed, every meaningful relationship involves something like it, and not as a once-for-all movement but as a continuous process. If you are part of something, simply part of it, you cannot engage it. With what, on what basis, would you do so?

Interestingly, the converse is also true: if you are altogether distinct from a given entity — completely different, of another order altogether — you cannot engage it. You lack the necessary connections, involvement, and reciprocity. Genuine engagement of anything or anyone presupposes a dynamics of difference and sameness, distinction and participation, a dialectic of transcendence and mutuality. Just such a relation is what the New Testament has in mind when it calls the disciple community to distinguish itself from "the world" but at the same time clearly sends it into the world — and expects it to be all the more intensively *in* the world just because it is not *of* the world.

This same dialectic of separation and solidarity may be applied to the situation in which, as North American churches of the classic Protestant traditions, we find ourselves at this juncture in our historical pilgrimage. George Lindbeck, in his seminal little book *The Nature of Doctrine,* has expressed our present ecclesiastical situation vis-à-vis our society in what I consider the clearest possible way. We are, he says, "in the awkwardly intermediate stage of having once been culturally established but . . . not yet clearly disestablished."[6] In terms of the dialectic in question, the North American churches are both part of our culture and yet distinct — outside of it, or on the periphery.

Given the almost unequivocal accord between Protestantism and middle-Americanism that has characterized our past, the present duplicity of this relationship is indeed an awkward position for the churches to occupy; and therefore it is not surprising that our first inclination is to overcome it as soon as possible. Accordingly, Lindbeck recognizes two ways, quite opposed to each other, in which Christians try to surpass their present ambiguous estate, socially and religiously.

One is the basically "liberal" theological inclination to attempt, in whatever ways one can, to present the Christian message in "currently intelligible forms," that is, to bridge the gap between gospel and situation, to engage in an apologetic that will reinforce the ties of trust and cooperation between the church and the sociological segments with which we traditionally have made our bed. Here, in other words, the awkwardness is overcome by accentuating the dimension of participation and involvement. We are part of this dominant culture, and we intend to do all we can to keep our standing with it. To that end, we will sacrifice many things dear to the tradition.

The other way of getting beyond the current awkward stage in the relations between "Christ and Culture" (to use H. Richard Niebuhr's convenient nomenclature) is to accentuate the dimension of distance, difference, and discontinuity between the two. Lindbeck calls this the postliberal approach, though he explains that he intends that term to include the concepts "postmodern," "postrevisionist," and "postneoorthodox." The posture of this postliberal stance is kerygmatic rather than apologetic. According to this position, "Theology should . . . resist the clamor of the religiously

6. George Lindbeck, *The Nature of Doctrine* (Philadelphia: Westminster Press, 1984), 134.

interested public for what is currently fashionable and immediately intelligible. It should instead prepare for a *future* when continuing dechristianization will make greater Christian authenticity communally possible."[7]

By that definition, it will be obvious that there is an element of "postliberalism" in what I am saying here. "Disestablish yourselves!" For I do think that the churches will have nothing to say to our ethos, finally, if we simply take our cue from our society and fill its ever-changing but always similar demands from the great supply house of our traditions, loosely interpreted. We must stand off from the liberal culture with which we have been so consistently identified, rediscover our own distinctive theological foundations, and allow ourselves to become, if necessary, aliens in our own country. In this, I am with Karl Barth, with the late Bill Stringfellow, and perhaps with Stanley Hauerwas.[8]

More broadly, I am also *not* with these people, for I am stuck with the belief that the gospel was made for humanity — and not just for some *future* humanity, to be addressed by some *purer* form of the church, but for human beings, sinners, here and now. And because I cannot find myself at home in either the liberal or the postliberal camp, I question whether these are in fact the only two alternatives that we have — indeed, whether we should even admit the legitimacy of these two alternatives.

Agreeing that we are in the position Lindbeck describes as awkward, we may, rather than trying to escape from that position by resolving it one way or another, seek the positive and beneficial implications of just such a position. Awkwardness may be an embarrassment to the urbane ecclesiastical mentality that wishes always to seem cool, but perhaps it is also part of being fools for Christ.

That is, could we not make the awkward relationship between the church and the dominant culture serve the Christian evangel? Could not our situation indeed become highly provocative, with us being at the same time "in" but no longer quite "of" our world of primary discourse?

Such a situation could serve the mission of the Crucified One only insofar as we do sufficiently disengage ourselves from that world — intentionally, and not as pawns of an impersonal fate. If we are faithful and imaginative enough to disentangle our authentic tradition of belief

7. Ibid.

8. See, e.g., Stanley Hauerwas, *After Christendom: How the Church Is to Behave If Freedom, Justice, and a Christian Nation Are Bad Ideas* (Nashville: Abingdon Press, 1991).

from its cultural wrapping, we shall have something to bring to our world that it does not have: a perspective on itself, a judgment of its pretensions and injustices, an offer of renewal and hope. Only as a community that does not find its source of identity and vocation *within* its cultural milieu can the church acquire any intimations of good news *for* its cultural milieu.

Although this "postliberal" sense of discontinuity with the liberal cultures of the United States and Canada is a necessary stage on the way to church renewal, it is still only a stage. The end in relation to which it is a means is a new and existentially vital engagement of the same society from which it must distinguish itself. Here the liberal insight is right: namely, that because, as "liberal" churches, we have known this particular segment of our society, we have both a responsibility toward it and a genuine opportunity to reengage it. Our belonging to that so-called dominant culture (if indeed it is still dominant) constitutes the dimension of reciprocity and continuity without which it would be very difficult, if not impossible, to achieve such a reengagement. Because most of us continue to be part of that white, middle-class, Protestant milieu, we know — from the inside — its questions, anxieties, and frustrations, as well as its answers, consolations, and dreams. Our former "establishment," which in the foreseeable future will still affect most of us, at least at the personal, psychic level, is thus not a complete loss, something to be regretted and shunned, but a long and deep historical experience from which, if we are sufficiently wise, much insight may be gained for the representation of the divine Word to that same world of expectation and experience. Indeed, if we did not have that knowledge and memory of our establishment, we should probably not be able to engage our world, no matter how stunning might be the message that we have for it.

Four Worldly Quests — and Christian Witness

My third and final task is to illustrate the principle of disengagement and engagement, discontinuity and continuity, which I have just described. I shall single out four human quests that are strongly present in the dominant culture of the United States and Canada today. In each case, I want to show, first, how our society longs for something that its performance denies and its operative values frustrate and, second, how, as those who themselves participate in that longing, Christians may engage their society from the perspective of faith and hope. The four quests I consider here are the quests for (1) moral authenticity, (2) meaningful community, (3) transcendence and mystery, and (4) meaning.

The Quest for Moral Authenticity

The emphasis in the quest for moral authenticity should be placed on the word "authenticity." I think that there is a quest for *authentic* morality strongly present in our society today. The reason for this is bound up with the failure of both the old and the so-called new moralities. People know now, better than they did in the 1960s and 1970s, that the permissiveness of the new morality leads to moral chaos and indeed to life-threatening danger. AIDS has dramatized this fact, but it is visible everywhere — to those who have reason to care.

In his book *The True and Only Heaven,* Christopher Lash considers the world from the perspective of a caring parent.

> To see the modern world from the point of view of a parent is to see it in the worst possible light. This perspective unmistakably reveals the unwholesomeness, not to put it more strongly, of our way of life: our obsession with sex, violence, and the pornography of "making it"; our addictive dependence on drugs, "entertainment," and the evening news; our impatience with anything that limits our sovereign freedom of choice, especially with the constraints of marital and familial ties; our preference for "nonbinding commitments"; our third-rate educational system; our third-rate morality; our refusal to draw a distinction between right and wrong, lest we "impose" our morality on others and thus invite others to "impose" their morality on us; our reluctance to judge or be judged; our indifference to the needs of future generations, as evidenced by our willingness to saddle them with a huge national debt, an overgrown arsenal of destruction, and a deteriorating environment; our unstated assumption, which underlies so much of the propaganda for unlimited abortion, that only those children born for success ought to be allowed to be born at all.[9]

9. Christopher Lash, *The True and Only Heaven: Progress and Its Critics* (New York: W. W. Norton, 1991), 33–34.

The failure of the "new morality" sends some of our contemporaries scurrying back into various and mostly desperate attempts to revive the "old morality." Although old moral codes may serve the private interests of some, they are impotent in the face of the great public moral questions; and those who — like the parents Lash describes — know that private and public morality are inextricably connected find little comfort in the ethical absolutes of the past.

Most of us who are members of the once-mainline churches, whether lay or clerical, are well acquainted with this dilemma personally. We ourselves, as parents or teachers or simply citizens, know from the inside how difficult it is to experience anything approaching moral authenticity today. We hardly dare to examine our own lives, for we sense both their moral contradictions and their deep but largely unfulfilled longing for authenticity.

This, surely, is an integral aspect of our real participation in the world that, as Christians, we are called to engage. We know the moral confusion of this world because it is also our own confusion. We seem not to have noticed that the very fact of our own participation in the anguished quest for moral authenticity constitutes the apologetic necessary for beginning to reach out to others. Instead, therefore, of retreating into theological and ethical systems that only insulate us from the moral dilemmas of our contemporaries, we Christians must learn how to go to our Scriptures and traditions as bearers and representatives of those existential dilemmas. How does "gospel" address those who, in our time and place, "hunger and thirst for righteousness" — for moral integrity? How would Jesus speak to affluent young parents, caught between yuppiedom and genuine concern for their children's future and asking how to be "good"? If we can identify with those parents (and we can), then perhaps we shall also begin to hear what our Lord would say to them. I suspect that what we would hear would be something quite different from what is proffered by the television sitcoms.

The Quest for Meaningful Community

The quest for meaningful community, like the quest for moral authenticity with which it is closely related, is also conspicuous today because of a double failure — the failure of individualism, and the failure of most forms of community.

The pursuit of individual freedom and personal aggrandizement has been the ideological backbone of New World liberal society. It grew out of ancient constricting and oppressive forms of human communality, and it was never all bad. But we North Americans drove it to its absolute limits, and it takes little wisdom to recognize that this cannot continue to be the cornerstone of society. There have always been inherent contradictions here, and now these contradictions have caught up with us. There is no significant problem of either private or public life that can be answered responsibly today by liberal individualism.

At the same time, we have witnessed the failure of most familiar forms of communality — dramatically so in Eastern Europe, but also in our own society, where a deep cynicism informs all public life and institutions. In cities, which have become practically ungovernable, the profound alienation of persons is felt particularly by the elderly, who whatever relative success their active middle years may have brought them, must one way or another now, in their extremity, discover their dependence upon others.

In the churches that we represent, we are familiar with this situation because most of us too, as members and ministers of churches, know about this double failure. Our very congregations, which are supposed to be the Christian answer to the human quest for genuine community, are for many if not most churchgoers not genuine, if not simply artificial. Those who do not "fit" the economic, educational, racial, or sexual mold that the churches still project seem only to accentuate the failure of human community.

We participate, then, as middle-class Christians, in this quest and in its terrible frustrations. But instead of allowing the specifics of both the quest and its frustrations to challenge and inform our understanding and profession of the faith, we retreat into well-rehearsed, rhetorical "answers." Because we do not permit the quest and the questions a significant place in our consciousness, we also fail to discern responses that, from the side of the tradition of Jerusalem, might indeed engage those who ask, including ourselves.

What would it mean to go to the Scriptures — for example, to the Pauline metaphor of the body and its members — with such contemporary experiences and questions fully present and articulated? Not the familiar questions of generations of theological classrooms, but concrete questions, posed by the lives we know and honed into graphic forms by the best of our novelists, filmmakers, and social commentators? And would a congregation whose life and work were informed by such a meeting of text and context be satisfied, then, with the kind of community gathered for worship on Sunday mornings in towns and cities throughout North America — or at coffee hours after the worship?

The Quest for Transcendence and Mystery

Several important theological books in the 1960s celebrated the secular city; finally we could see the world for what it was, without investing it with all sorts of semipantheistic holiness! But secularism, too, has failed. Technology, its most precocious offspring, began a decade or so ago to appear to ordinary people the mixed blessing that some of the wise ones of the Western world already understood much earlier — like the scientist-theologian C. F. von Weizsäcker, who, in the final paragraph of his 1949 book *The History of Nature,* wrote, "The scientific and technical world of modern man is the result of his daring enterprise, *knowledge without love.*"[10] During the past ten years, primarily in the wake of environmental awareness, Western peoples have become newly conscious of the devastations of which humanity is capable when it thinks itself accountable to nothing beyond itself.

This realization, perhaps combined with the aboriginal human restlessness of which Augustine spoke in the first paragraph of his *Confessions,* has engendered in many a new and (even when it is packaged in tinsel) entirely earnest search for some sense of transcendence and mystery. Many can now understand such judgments as that of Loren Eiseley, who spoke of human difference from other creatures, not in the glowing terms of the Enlightenment — how we are "rational," capable of "free will," and so on — but, on the contrary, how this "different" creature, *Homo sapiens,* "without the sense of the holy, without compassion," possesses a brain that can "become a gray stalking horror — the deviser of Belsen."[11]

Yet the quest for transcendence and mystery is constantly inhibited by the haunting awareness of our one-dimensionality. The "death of God" — or was it the death of Humanity? — still dogs our footsteps. We try very hard to create depth, to see ourselves against the backdrop of an eternity

10. C. F. von Weizsäcker, *The History of Nature,* trans. Fred D. Wieck (Chicago: University of Chicago Press, Phoenix Books, 1949), 190.

11. See Richard E. Wentz, "The American Spirituality of Loren Eiseley," *Christian Century,* April 25, 1984, p. 430.

in which time is enfolded. Steven Spielberg and others give us ersatz heavens, in which we find ourselves loved by strange beings from outer space. Everyone has learned the word "spirituality." Yet it is not so easy to overcome the rationalist impact of two centuries of Science. Knowledge without love!

In the churches, too, we know these inhibitions. Try as we may, our services of worship bear about them the aura of the theater (and a mostly very amateur one at that) — as though God were really dead and all that remained were our ritual performances for one another. Too often, I confess, these attempts at divine service put me in mind of King Claudius in Shakespeare's *Hamlet:*

> My words fly up, my thoughts remain below;
> Words without thoughts never to heaven go.[12]

Insofar as we Christians recognize the longing and the dissatisfactions of this contemporary quest for transcendence and mystery, we are also in a position to respond to it out of the riches of the Judeo-Christian tradition, newly revisited. Here and there Christians are discovering how to discern the transcendent *within* the immanent — to see creation itself as mystery. But such discoveries depend upon a greater exposure to the bankruptcy of old familiar forms of "spirituality" than for the most part we have managed in our safe and sedate churches. We have been conditioned to look for God in "the beyond"; we are unaccustomed still to looking for "the beyond *in the midst of life*" (in Bonhoeffer's memorable expression). Perhaps if we were to rethink our own tradition, bearing with us the terrible thirst for transcendence and mystery as it manifests itself in the soul of humanity *post mortem Dei,* we would more consistently discover the means for engaging it from the side of the gospel.

The Quest for Meaning

Paul Tillich insisted that the basic anxiety type by which modern Western humanity is afflicted is the anxiety of meaninglessness and despair.[13] For a

12. Act 3, scene 3.
13. Paul Tillich, *The Courage to Be* (New Haven: Yale University Press, 1952).

time the euphoria of secular humanism temporarily blunted the edge of this anxiety. If, as the existentialists affirmed, we could not count on being heirs to a teleological universe, then we would create our own purpose, our own essence. Many found indeed that they could laugh at the old-fashioned search for "the meaning of life."

But a dimension of the alleged paradigm shift through which we are passing also has to do precisely with the failure of that kind of anthropocentric bravado. All over the Western world there are covert and overt attempts to discover purpose — not a purpose we ourselves invent, but a horizon of meaning toward which we may turn. As Kurt Vonnegut says one way or another in all of his strange and wonderful novels, perhaps cynically or perhaps seriously, purposeless things are abhorrent to the human species; and if the human species suspects that it is itself purposeless, it becomes conspicuously suicidal. Under the now-more-conscious threat of nonbeing, humankind asks openly for the meaning of being. Religion is again interesting. The Faculty of Religious Studies at McGill University, my large, secular university, is the fastest growing faculty of all. This phenomenon is duplicated all over the Western world.

After the breakdown of the modern system of meaning, however, purpose is not easily found. Certainly it is not easily found in traditional religions. The increase in curiosity about religion is accompanied by a marked decrease in those very churches that were formerly the cultic bulwarks of our culture. In those same churches, we who remain also know how hard it is to discover meaning for our lives, individually and corporately. We participate both in the quest for meaning and in its limitations and defeats.

We may therefore be in a position to rethink the basic elements of our tradition in such a way as to discover in them that through which we may address our age with fresh insight and conviction. But this will be possible only if we expose ourselves less guardedly to the cold winds of the late twentieth century and are ready to carry the full burden of its spiritual emptiness and yearning into the presence of the Holy One. The gospel may again speak to us, and make of us ambassadors for Christ, if we appear before that One with empty hands — with the questions of those whom we represent, which are also our questions; and wait for answers . . . or rather, for the Answerer.

Conclusion

I began by asserting that the most urgent message of the divine Spirit to the churches in North America today is that they should disestablish themselves. Until they have learned to distinguish the gospel of the Crucified One from the rhetorical values, pretensions, and pursuits of this society, our churches will fail to detect, beneath the rhetoric of official optimism, the actual humanity that it is our Christian vocation to engage. In the service of the Crucified, who is as present in the largely hidden oppressions of First World peoples as he is in the more conspicuous sufferings of the wretched of the earth, North American Christians must liberate themselves from the conventions of cultural religion.

Christian disengagement from the dominant culture is not to be confused, however, with the abandonment of that society. The end that we are to seek is redemption of our world — the "First" World, which, despite its continuing bravado, has been given intimations of the judgment that the first may turn out to be last. Our role as Christians, as the people of the cross *within* that world, is precisely what Jesus said it was: to be salt, yeast, and light. All of our Lord's metaphors for his community of witness were modest. A little salt, a little yeast, a little light. Christendom tried to be great, large, magnificent. It thought itself to be the object of God's expansive grace, and not the beloved world. Today we are constrained by the divine Spirit to rediscover the possibilities of littleness. We are to decrease, that Christ may increase. We cannot enter this new phase without pain, for truly we have been glorious, in this world's own terms. It seems to us a humiliation that we are made to reconsider our destiny as "*little* flocks," as "merely" salt, yeast, and light. Can such a calling, we ask, be worthy of the servants of the Sovereign of the universe?

Yet, if that Sovereign is the One who reigns from the cross, could any other calling be thought legitimate?

Gospel for American Culture: Variations on a Theme by Newbigin

CHARLES C. WEST

J. E. Lesslie Newbigin's thesis is by now well known. Western civilization was once a single society "in which the whole of public and private life was to be controlled by the Christian revelation." It has, in the past two centuries, broken away completely from the public claim of that faith to become not so much a secular as a pagan society "born out of the rejection of Christianity." It is therefore "far more resistant to the gospel than the pre-Christian paganism with which cross-cultural missions have been familiar." This paganism is characterized by a concept of truth as facts established by scientific methods of experiment and generalization, not relationships and obligations; by an understanding of the world in terms of efficient causes that human beings can master and control, not final causes or purposes that determine and guide human lives; and by a public realm limited to technology and economics that allows for total pluralism in the subjective spheres of value, commitment, and faith. It is a world in which "the structure of the DNA molecule is a fact that every child must learn to understand, but the determination of all proper human purposes by the glory of God is an opinion that anyone is free to accept or reject."[1]

Such a world, says Newbigin, has had its moments of self-confidence — its belief in endless human progress and in the freedom of individually

1. Lesslie Newbigin, *Foolishness to the Greeks: The Gospel and Western Culture* (Grand Rapids: Eerdmans, 1986), 101, 20, 67.

selected goals — and its moments of self-doubt, confronted with the limits of nature and human greed. But these are self-centered reactions. In reality this world is in the hands of Christ its Lord and Savior, and the mission of the church is to bear public witness to this truth. The church is therefore called, with its gospel, not to reestablish the traditional Christendom but to confront the dogmas of secular pluralism with the truth claim of faith, and the secular authorities with their responsibility before God.

Is this a description of the gospel for our culture also in the United States and North America? The answer, I believe, must be yes, but with variations. We are part of the same historical drama. The same Enlightenment rationality, the same humanism, the same division of the objective from the subjective, of fact from value, has affected us too. This is a worldview we share with most of Western Europe, and we have brought it to the rest of the world as well. But there is an American version of this drama. It is filled with more conflict and tension. It presents, I believe, three significant variations on Newbigin's thesis.

The Political Covenant

The United States of America differs from the nations of Europe, even including Britain, in being based not upon the structures and customs of an ethnic heritage but upon the decisions and convictions of those who moved to this country. Most of our earliest settlers, those who set the tone for American culture, were protesters, breaking with the dominant religious and political institutions of their homelands. They set forth upon a historical enterprise that took its meaning from the promise and blessing of God on what they would build.

This meant, first, that the colonists who settled New England, Pennsylvania, and, to some extent, New Jersey and New York were profoundly aware of the discontinuity between themselves and the structures of Christendom from which they had in many cases fled. They were, of course, still English, or in some cases Scottish or German or Dutch. They spoke the language and shared the customs of the countries from which they came. But their enterprise was radical reformation of the faith and the ethos of traditional Europe. Their reading was the literature of that Reformation: the Bible, John Calvin, William Ames, George Fox, or John Bunyan, rather than the prayer book, the medieval saints, or the precepts of the natural law. They differed on the radicality of the reformation God required. Some, like John Winthrop and his Puritans, thought they might establish in New England a society so reformed according to the Word of God that it would inspire anew the failed reformation of the church and society in England. Others, like Bradford and the Pilgrims, or Penn on the shores of the Delaware, were first of all concerned to build a faithful community of Christians in the wilderness toward the day of the Lord's coming. But in every case a break with traditional Christendom, a new exodus inspired by an immediate response to the calling and promise of God, was the basic theme.

This sense of exodus and promise has communicated itself to the whole of American society in the centuries since. One after another, waves of immigrants have come into this country from Europe and, more recently, Asia, bringing with them religious cultures that, under the pressure both of the frontier and of our theological heritage, have been transformed into communities of self-conscious faith and action. One can argue that this break has taken place largely within the context of Christendom, which is why the United States today is a more religious country than most in Europe. But it bears witness to the fundamental discontinuity built into the gospel and the church's witness long before humanist rationalism challenged the faith — the discontinuity between all human structures, religious and secular, and the gracious judgments of God. Furthermore, to underline the point, the most radical experience of all, that of African-Americans torn from their homelands to serve as slaves to European masters who called themselves Christians, has been given comfort, empowerment, and hope by this same discontinuous gospel. America is still striving to define itself as a culture in the confrontation between black and white Christianity, both inspired by the themes of Exodus, resurrection, and the promise of the kingdom.

Second, as in the biblical story, exodus, in the American experience, has been followed by covenant. To put it in philosophical terms, an ontological image of reality has been replaced by a relational one. The sacramentally unified structure of time and eternity has given way to a historical calling and promise. These early settlers imparted to our history a lively sense, informed by biblical analogies, that our security and destiny lie in the quality of the relationships that we develop in response to divine guidance and promise. In the words of H. Richard Niebuhr years ago, their society, like their faith, "must be understood as a movement rather than as an institution or series of institutions. It is gospel rather than law, it is more dynamic than static."[2] Everything depended, as indeed it still depends, not on the structure of a tradition, not on reason however conceived, but on faithful response to the living God in building a new society. The words of John Winthrop, preached on the decks of his flagship the *Arbella* in mid-Atlantic to the company of those going to found the colony of Boston, addressed the matter with unforgettable eloquence.

> Thus stands the cause between God and us: we are entered into covenant with Him for this work; we have taken out a commission, the Lord hath given us leave to draw our own articles. We have professed to enterprise these actions upon these and these ends; we have hereupon besought Him of favor and blessing. Now if the Lord shall please to hear us and bring us in peace to the place we desire, then hath He ratified this covenant and sealed our Commission, [and] will expect a strict performance of the articles contained in it. But if we shall neglect the observation of these articles which are the ends we have propounded, and dissembling with our God, shall fall to embrace this present world and prosecute our carnal intentions, seeking great things for ourselves and our posterity, the Lord will surely break out in wrath against us, be revenged of such a perjured people, and make us know the price of the breach of such a covenant.
>
> Now the only way to avoid this shipwreck and to provide for our posterity is to follow the counsel of Micah: to do justly, to love mercy, to walk humbly with our God. For this end, we must be knit together in this work as one man. We must entertain each other in brotherly affection; we must be willing to abridge ourselves of our superfluities, for the supply of others' necessities; we must uphold a familiar commerce together in all meekness, gentleness, patience and liberality. We must delight in each other, make others' conditions our own, rejoice together, mourn together, labor and suffer together: always having before our eyes our commission and community in the work, our community as members of the same body. So shall we keep the unity of the spirit in the bond of peace, the Lord will be our God and delight to dwell among us, as His own people, and will command a blessing upon us in all our ways, so that we shall see much more of His wisdom, power, goodness, and truth

2. H. Richard Niebuhr, *The Kingdom of God in America* (Hamden, CT: Shoestring Press, 1956), xi–xii.

> than formerly we have been acquainted with. We shall find that the God of Israel is among us, when ten of us shall be able to resist a thousand of our enemies, when He shall make us a praise and glory, that men shall say of succeeding plantations: "The Lord make it like that of New England." For we must consider that we shall be as a city upon a hill, the eyes of all people are upon us.[3]

How can a society keep faith in such a covenant as this? How can even a church do so? The Puritans were realists about human hope and human nature. They did not imagine, as later preachers sometimes did, that they were building the kingdom of God in this country. They knew about the temptations and the corruption of human power, whether ecclesiastical or political. They were concerned, as long as this world continues, to structure the common life in both spheres so that justice and charity might be encouraged, greed and pride restrained, and power be limited and ordered to its proper function; in short, so that the sovereign judgment and saving grace of God over all human actions might be acknowledged and celebrated. The result of this was what H. Richard Niebuhr called "Christian constitutionalism in the church and in society."[4] As Robert Bellah has put it, they followed John Calvin, who,

> working carefully from a basically Augustinian starting point, had argued that a well-ordered, nonmonarchical church could operate symbiotically with a well-ordered polity, namely the city-republic of Geneva, to create an ethical social order. . . . The Calvinist Christian commonwealth could not be the City of God on earth but it could be a worthy harbinger of it. It was this conception that the New England Puritans brought to America.[5]

The children of the Reformation went about this constitutional task with different emphases. The Quakers and the Baptists were more attendant to the immediate guidance of the Spirit, the Puritans more to biblical example and analogy. They agreed, however, on structures of governments both in church and in state that limited human authority and were open

3. Quoted in Perry Miller, *The American Puritans: Their Prose and Poetry* (New York: Doubleday, 1956), 82–83.

4. Niebuhr, *Kingdom of God in America*, 59ff.

5. Robert N. Bellah, *The Broken Covenant* (New York: Seabury Press, 1975), 17.

to the participation of all citizens or believers. They stood together for a separation of authority in the church from political authority, yet were a constant challenge of the former to the latter. They were, above all, experimental in their structuring of these relationships, asking always about their faithfulness to the covenant that governed them.

This was not the only root of American democracy. We hear much more about the doctrine of the free individual propounded by John Locke, born with rights that are limited only by voluntary contract by which society is formed. This doctrine may assume the sovereignty of a benevolent God, as Locke himself did. But this God is of natural law, the creation of a benevolent human reason, not the living Lord who judges and redeems human constitutions. This rational humanist individualism is also at work in the American ethos. The U.S. Constitution is an agreement among the citizens, hammered out by the usual political process of negotiation and compromise, as a contract on the basis of which our common life is to be ordered. But it is also more than this. It is neither a reflection of moral reason in legal terms, nor is it an arbitrary document with no meaning beyond its status as positive law. It is rather an attempt to express in a human covenant some analogy to the covenant of God with his people. As such, it is a living document in constant dialogue with the will and purposes of God as expressed in the witness of the church, and with the welfare, needs, and hopes of the people who are governed by it.

Americans live with both the promise and the danger of this constitutional process. John Winthrop's challenge, in its theological and secular dimensions, defines us as a nation still.

This leads, third, to a deeper question: Who is included in the covenant? This is a question on the level of politics and on the level of faith. Theologically, the covenant community is the company of believers, those who have been called and who practice that denial of self and new life in Christ which confronts the world with its Judge and Redeemer and anticipates the coming kingdom of God. This community, like that of the New Testament, is total in its claims and universal in its scope. The early Puritans in Massachusetts therefore regarded church membership as the basis for participation in civil affairs. At the same time, they reached out in friendship and in mission to the native peoples next to whom they lived.

Both policies ran into difficulties. The colony filled up with immigrants whose commitments to the church were weak but who were nevertheless members of the body politic. Meanwhile conflicts over land

and lifestyle between colonists and Indians led to warfare that overwhelmed the missionary calling. All the while African slaves were becoming a part even of New England society. In the words of Robert Bellah,

> Already in the 17th century, precariousness of the covenant and the blessings flowing from it was sharply experienced. The tendency of the people who walk not in the ways of the Lord but in their own ways, to think not of the general good but of their own private interests, was discerned and condemned by the Puritan ministers. But even more than they were aware, the colonists had failed the covenant almost before it had been made, for they had founded their new commonwealth on a great crime — the bondage and genocide of other races.[6]

Nor was the political covenant of the American Constitution free of these ambiguities. It expressed the agreement of the American people about the form of their government and the nature of their liberties. It structured a balance of political power and provided for orderly and responsible processes of amendment and of social change. But it did not trust democracy overmuch. It assumed slavery and even protected the slave trade for a while. Women had no vote. Native Americans were not even mentioned. And nothing was said about the guidance or control of economic power for the public good or the right of the poor to livelihood, security, and participation in the political community.

All these battles had to be fought later. Some of them are raging today, despite constitutional changes. In each of them the integrity of the American nation has been at risk and has come out of the conflict changed. Henry David Thoreau put it bluntly in the middle of the nineteenth century that "this people must cease to hold slaves and to make war on Mexico, though it cost them their existence as a people."[7] The people took the slavery challenge seriously at the cost of a civil war. Other challenges have been less total but in the long run no less wrenching: that of blacks and other minorities for the rights in society that they have won in law; of organized labor for justice, security, and political influence; of women for a new status, and many more. The American political covenant is continually at risk, continually being redefined.

The church is in the middle of these struggles. This is both its problem

6. Ibid., 62.

7. Quoted in ibid., 57.

and its opportunity. A political covenant holds American society together. The Constitution is its legal expression. Its relative transcendence over the moods and prejudices of the moment gives us pause and refers us to a larger and more permanent common good. But its structure of rights and responsibilities, its empowerments and limitations on power, and its protection of the weak against the strong are all relative and can be distorted. Not even the Supreme Court always develops and defends them, as we have learned again in recent years. What is just, what is human, what is liberating, and the social disciplines appropriate thereto need continually to be rediscovered in response to the Lord, whose covenant reaches out to include all peoples, calling them out of themselves to life in Christ. This is the church's mission on both the theological and political levels. In the United States it contains all the divisions of the world within itself. It is uniquely placed to be a laboratory and a witness to God's reconciling work, which holds the world together.

The Ethos

America is a pluralist society with many of the characteristics that Newbigin describes: the separation of fact from value and of knowledge from faith, the tolerance of many convictions in a free market of ideas, and the implicit relativization of them all.[8] The attitude is underlined in the clause of the First Amendment of the Constitution that "Congress shall make no law respecting an establishment of religion, or prohibiting the free exercise thereof." Through the years, the courts have drawn the healthy implication on the basis of this clause that church and state must be free from the domination of each other. This position in turn has led to the view that religion is private, that its truth claims are relative and should not have a place in the public sphere. On this basis, faith convictions are excluded from public schools along with the practice of forms of worship, and theology plays a minimal role in the academic world.

Nevertheless, there is an American ethos, an underlying awareness of binding values, however hard they are to find. Robert Bellah's term "civil religion" for defining the transcendent dimension and claim of this ethos

8. Lesslie Newbigin, *The Gospel in a Pluralist Society* (Grand Rapids: Eerdmans, 1989), chaps. 1–2.

is not without a certain validity, even though attempts to define its precepts always reflect the bias of one group's perspective or faith.[9] This ethos is so hard to define, I believe, because it is caught in a paradoxical interaction between two sources of authority: human experience and divine revelation. As an example of this problem, I quote the following forthright statement from Max Stackhouse:

> A particular branch of the Christian tradition, the free church tradition, although now expanded beyond specific Christian confession, created a distinct arena for community organization, a social space for participation and membership in voluntary associations, that is prior to and inviolable by public authority. The churches prepared the way, demanding a guaranteed autonomy from exterior control. The autonomy was, at first, to insure the freedom of worship and the congregation's right to govern its own affairs. But as the implications of the message and the policy were translated into habit and public behavior, the patterns inevitably spilled over into the reform of professional, political, economical, and familial institutions. The church in effect produced socially active efforts to transform all of society according to a powerful sense of a moral law and godly purpose which could shape a commonwealth and judge its legitimacy. The social space that this effort secured has been expanded so that all sorts of "non-official" and "non-religious" organizations populate the free social spaces of American life once reserved for the churches. Many feel the kinds of commitment and loyalty to these groups also once reserved for the church.

Stackhouse concludes: "This, I intend to argue, is the decisive root of American civil liberties and civil rights. These group rights reflect the basic understanding of what it means to be human, and thus what human rights should be at their deepest."[10]

Here we have not only a statement but a defense of the paradox and how it developed. The nonconformist church groups that settled America in the seventeenth century did not think of themselves as voluntary associations, nor does Stackhouse claim that they did. It is their practical effect upon American society, opening the way for a flood of groups with various

9. Robert N. Bellah, *Beyond Belief* (New York: Harper & Row, 1970), chap. 9.

10. Max Stackhouse, *Creeds, Society, and Human Rights* (Grand Rapids: Eerdmans, 1984), 51–52.

causes and projects, for which he claims the blessing of God. But these voluntary groups are human organizations, human efforts to pursue various human goals. The common good, on this model, is defined and constructed by the interaction and competition of these groups, with the churches as voluntary associations also participating. The ultimate driving force in the process is the free, deciding individual who associates with others to express his or her conviction, or to achieve his or her purposes.

This is indeed the story of what has happened to the American ethos, expressed also in many of its churches. The emphasis slowly shifted, as H. Richard Niebuhr documented so well, from response to the judging and saving work of God toward human self-help projects in the name of God.[11] The Great Awakening, which in the eighteenth century brought the knowledge and assurance of Christ into human lives, became revivalism, a repeated, standardized human experience that was taken as the test of faith. Threatened conservative churches protected themselves by making a human work of particular dogmas, of verbally inspired Scripture, or of certain moral requirements usually involving personal behavior. In all of this, Christian groups and churches, often without ceasing to claim the authority of God, have defined religion essentially as a human work.

To some extent this pluralism is inevitable and even justified. Waves of immigrants, bringing with them their own religious and cultural traditions, have understandably demanded space for these expressions. Black Christianity has developed its own authentic style and culture. The world mission of the church has raised acutely the question of how far European-American traditions of theology, worship, and Christian life should be authoritative for the church and cultures that do not share this history, and indeed what the Christianity of those cultures might contribute to our way of being Christian. Pluralism is the rich result of increased communications and the intermingling of peoples, of rapidly changing lifestyles in a dynamic society.

Still there is in American society a profound uneasiness about this pluralism of values, religions, and lifestyles. Dietrich Bonhoeffer, in his 1939 essay "Protestantism without Reformation," recognized it already. He wrote,

> American Christianity has experienced the consequences of church division but not the act of division itself. It is therefore no longer itself

11. Niebuhr, *Kingdom of God in America,* chap. 5.

> involved in the struggle for the one church, but stands amazed before the results of this struggle, able only to accept the situation in the deepest humility and to heal the wounds. The unity of the church of Jesus Christ is to American Christianity less something essential, originally given by God, than something required, something which ought to be. It is less origin than goal.[12]

Bonhoeffer did not see this mild ecumenicity developing into a spiritual crisis in America. Years later Robert Bellah, writing in the shadow of the youth revolt in the 1960s, was more urgent.

> America began when the great new mythic ordering of the Protestant Reformation was still vital and alive. That pattern combined with the newer myth of republican liberty sustained and reinvigorated us in our first and second times of trial. But now our cultural crisis is deeper. The single vision that has been on the rise since the eighteenth century is now more than ever the dominant cultural orientation. A profound experience of conversion, of the reordering of the deepest levels of the personality in the light of a transcendent vision, is not absent in America, but it is harder than ever to integrate with the dominant cultural mood. The established structures of economic and political power seem perversely set on maximizing wealth and power, regardless of the cost to the society or the natural environment. Under these circumstances, we should not be surprised if efforts at liberation, revolution, and counter culture seem fragmented and chaotic. Anarchy and antinomianism are always present in the effort to change a social order that has become too constricting.[13]

Bellah yearns for this conversion and this transcendent vision. In that yearning he expresses a profound American mood. Sometimes this mood comes out as thoughtless reaction to the symptoms of diversity and disorder around us. At other times outrage and protest in the name of an ideal of peace or justice become its vehicle. In still others it takes the form of cynicism about all public policies and actions. In any case, the mission of the church is clear: to move beyond human religion and ethics to respond

12. Dietrich Bonhoeffer, *No Rusty Swords: Lectures and Notes from the Collected Works* (London: Collins, 1965), 97.

13. Bellah, *Broken Covenant,* 85.

to the reality of Christ taking form in this world, calling, forgiving, and sanctifying sinners in the church and the world. The ecumenical question of the unity of the church for the reconciliation of the world has become acute. On this point of reference, the healing of our ethos depends.

The Power

Newbigin is right, I believe, in his critique of the scientific rationalism that understands all truth only in terms of efficient causes, which are therefore subject to human manipulation and control. I would like, however, to draw a further consequence from this line of thought. The rational self-confidence of modern science and technology is not due primarily to the belief that they are unveiling the structure of natural reality as it is. That illusion was dispelled by David Hume and Immanuel Kant over two centuries ago. What the human mind can know is phenomena, to which it contributes its own organizing categories. What scientists discover are regularities of behavior in the objects of their experiments, which enable them to predict and control. Such discoveries, not the ultimate structure of reality, is what is important. Truth is what works. It is what produces results that enhance human power over nature. The issue, then, from the perspective of this turbulent country, is power: scientific, technological, and economic. We are heirs to an optimistic philosophy of pragmatism whose exponent, John Dewey, believed that truth is discovered and values are realized in the competitive and cooperative interaction of human beings expanding indefinitely the mutually affirming possibilities of human life. We have assumed that technology in this context can solve any problems it produces and can indefinitely expand the horizons of human activity. We have taken economics to be an optimistic science, producing an indefinite expansion of our standard of living. We listened to Karl Marx only as a reminder to Christians and idealists that the fruits of this prosperity must be more equitably shared, that control of economic power should be democratized, and that working conditions should be more humane.

All of this suffered an irreversible shock in the Great Depression of 1929–34. Through Reinhold Niebuhr's analysis of the dynamics of power in a sinful world, we learned to appreciate the Marxist challenge to humanist self-confidence. We learned about the inevitability of class conflict, the setting of power against power in social conflict in order to achieve a relative social justice. We learned about the ideological distortion of human reason to serve the profit and the interest of the dominant economic group. We learned about the hypocrisy of Christian attempts to judge the conflict by ideal standards instead of taking part in the morally messy struggle for power and justice that was going on.[14]

Niebuhr was a rare Christian theologian whose thought influenced the self-understanding of secular society in his time. He broke through the self-confident rationalism of the secular establishment and the self-confident dialectical materialism of the revolutionaries. From his time on, hard analysis of social power became a method not only for Christian ethics but for democratic politics as well. For a generation in the United States, the task of rendering social power — whether of government, industry, technology, or finance — responsible to public justice, and the task of empowering the poor and the disadvantaged in their struggle for that justice, were the work of both Christian and secular reformers. Analysis of the ways in which scientific and technological reason serve the interests of the powers that pay for them was part of this work.

Today the Niebuhrian analysis is as valid as ever. Its relevance has been enhanced by struggles with scientists and industrialists over the ecological responsibility of the production process. But today the terms of the struggle, and therefore of Christian witness, have changed. First, the Marxist-Leninist social revolution has collapsed. The socialist organization of society as a command economy, rather than a free-market economy, has been discredited. This means that the struggle of the poor, the exploited, and the victims of the production process have been deprived of an admittedly ambiguous power resource. What will replace it? How will the power balance, now so decisively tipped in favor of the rich and the technologically advanced, be redressed? Second, we have been deprived of an economic model that claimed to realize justice and equality in an effective system of production and distribution. The model did not work, but it was for years the only one available. Capitalist economists made no serious effort to deal with the justice question. Now we must create new models that are both moral and practical. What form should they take?

A profound cynicism pervades American society today about the possibility of making economic power socially responsible and of using

14. Reinhold Niebuhr, *Moral Man and Immoral Society* (New York: Scribner's, 1949).

government for the purpose. Where lies the hope that greed may be controlled in the public interest and that technology may be curbed and directed in ways that serve the long-term sustainability of our environment rather than the profit of a few in this generation? How can human power be made to serve the purposes of God?

The Christian church has no pat answer to questions like these. We do have the promise of the New Testament, however, that all things hold together in Christ, who is the head of all principalities and powers. We know that power is not brute force but a relation, that it belongs within a covenant where alone it has its meaning. We know that the Savior who was crucified by the powers of this world is now their risen Lord. Starting from here, we can wade into the human struggle with our gospel of hope, side with the victims, find ways to confront influence, modify and make responsible the powers around us, suggest structures of great justice and human compassion, and, above all, let others know who the Lord of the struggle is. This, too, is a form of mission to our culture.

Speaking the Truth in Love: Elements of a Missional Hermeneutic

JAMES V. BROWNSON

Two realities are readily apparent to Christians as they examine the present situation of Christianity in its North American context. First, the increasing marginalization in North American culture of Christian faith in general and of the Christian church in particular must call forth from Christians a fresh vision of what it means to be a Christian and to be the Christian church in our post-Christian setting. Second, Christians also believe that the Christian faith offers good news and hope for our situation, good news that must be lived out and proclaimed with courage and wisdom.[1]

This broad vision is shared by many Christian groups, but it can be further sharpened by discerning more specifically what is happening in our cultural context, and what our response should be. First, we must recognize that our current crisis is, in many respects, a legacy from the Enlightenment. Here the writings of Lesslie Newbigin have been formative.[2] Newbigin correctly and helpfully points out the ways in which the empiricism of the scientific method has pervaded our worldview. This emphasis on the empirical — what can be measured and quantified — has resulted in an

1. Portions of this chapter appeared in a somewhat different form in the *Reformed Review* 45, no. 2 (1991): 85–106, under the title "What Is 'the Gospel'?"

2. See, e.g., *Foolishness to the Greeks: The Gospel and Western Culture* (Grand Rapids: Eerdmans, 1986) or *The Gospel in a Pluralist Society* (Grand Rapids: Eerdmans; Geneva: WCC Publications, 1989).

unhealthy split between the public and the private realm, between facts and values, between science and religion. Religion in general, and Christian faith in particular, has been relegated to the private realm, where truth claims are immaterial and where disputes are not resolved but simply massaged into docility by psychological and sociological analysis. As a result, the public sphere is increasingly stripped of any moral framework (those are private issues), and society as a whole more and more resembles some giant machine gone amok, driven by rapidly expanding economic and technological powers but devoid of any sense of purpose, or even a clear sense of the common good.

Second, we must also recognize another powerful cultural force affecting our situation: the dynamics of postmodernism. Whereas Enlightenment thinkers hoped for a grand synthesis of all human arts and cultures under the banner of reason and science, a postmodern perspective consciously and explicitly eschews such a goal. Postmodernism recognizes that even reason and science cannot always be relied upon to resolve disputes and settle truth claims. Rather, reason and science are often merely tools in the hands of deeper and more powerful forces such as economic and class conflicts, ethnic and racial hostilities, and gender divisions. The title of Alasdair MacIntyre's book underscores the problem: *Whose Justice? Which Rationality?*[3] The postmodern world is a world in which pluralism constantly threatens to devolve into factionalism, in which anomie becomes a perpetual existential reality, and in which the resolution of disputes becomes increasingly problematic, frequently disintegrating into a clutching after power and its dark counterpart, the proliferation of violence.

The challenge of postmodernism moves the discussion regarding the gospel and our culture to a much deeper level. The question is no longer simply how Christian faith can reenter the public sphere, for the public sphere itself has been fractured into a variety of competing interest groups. Now the questions revolve much more around issues of identity, lifestyle, and political strategy: How are Christians to live and bear witness in such a chaotic situation? How can the gospel's claim that Jesus is the gracious Savior and therefore Lord of the cosmos become intelligible in a context where such claims are suspiciously regarded as yet another bid for power

3. Alasdair MacIntyre, *Whose Justice? Which Rationality?* (Notre Dame, IN: University of Notre Dame Press, 1988).

from yet another interest group? Whereas the Enlightenment threatened to turn all religious truth claims into matters of private opinion and feeling, postmodernism threatens to turn the Christian message of mercy and grace into a mask concealing a political grab for domination and control.

Such is the context in which Christians are called to read and interpret Scripture. Such is the context that Christians are called to interpret in light of Scripture. It is a context that calls us to reconsider, at perhaps a deeper level than before, what it means to "speak the truth in love" (Eph. 4:15). What does it mean to be called to speak of the gospel as *truth* in a world that declares that religious speech can never be true, but only "true-for-you"? How can we speak the truth from a posture of loving servanthood in a world that interprets truth claims as political strategies masking inevitable self-interests? Finally, what is the role of Scripture in leading us to the truth and in teaching us how to speak it?

As soon as we begin to look to Scripture for answers to these questions, however, we confront the problems we have just described in a new way. The fragmentation of postmodernism is nearly as pervasive within the church as it is beyond it. We may agree with other Christians that the Bible is our final witness to truth, yet we often find ourselves disagreeing with each other, often radically, over precisely what that truth is and how it should be understood. Hence it is not enough merely to look to the Bible for answers. We must look to the Bible, to be sure, but we must also examine *how* we look to the Bible. We need a model for biblical interpretation that is able to address the problems and challenges of plurality in interpretation. Not only do we need to observe various differences in interpretation; we need to have some understanding of how to evaluate them. We need to ask: When are differences in interpretation a sign of healthy diversity, and when are they a signal that some people are simply mistaken or deficient in the way that they read the Bible? Is the Bible a kind of Rorschach inkblot in which interpreters will necessarily find whatever it is that they are looking for? Or are there controls, disciplines, and parameters that help to mediate between contrasting or conflicting interpretations? These are hotly debated issues in current hermeneutical discussions, and we need a model for interpretation that will help us answer these questions.

For some, diversity in biblical interpretation is merely the sign of an unfinished task. If we can't agree on what the Bible is saying to our world, we need to keep talking and reading with greater effort and intensity until we do agree. Yet such an approach has often led to one of two unfortunate results. Either Christians have become totally absorbed in endless (and often unproductive) attempts to reconcile their differences (e.g., as has happened in certain sectors of the ecumenical movement), or they have continually separated themselves from other Christians who are deemed heretical or lapsed (e.g., as in North American evangelical Protestantism). These twin failures of North American Christianity betray a common inability to deal constructively with diversity in interpretation. Of course diversity in interpretation can be a sign of error, but might there not also be in some cases a plurality of right interpretations? Might it not be possible to speak the truth of Scripture in love, while recognizing that others may do so with different accents, perspectives, and concerns? Might not such a perspective be part of what it means to speak the truth *in love?* Hence this chapter seeks to address the problem of diversity in interpretation both critically and constructively.

But the problem of diversity in interpretation is not the only challenge we face as we seek to speak the truth of Scripture in love. At a deeper level, the challenge of postmodernism is brought on by our increasing loss of a universal frame of reference. We find it harder to keep our bearings and to connect with each other. The postmodern emphasis on the contingent, the particular, and the subjective makes it increasingly difficult to find bases for dialogue, common ground where diverse groups may gather and fruitfully interact with each other. Even within the church, it is becoming increasingly evident to us that there is no fixed point, free from presuppositions and biases, from which any of us may interpret the Bible. We all begin from some sort of model, some integrated framework of understanding about the nature of religion, the character of our social and cultural context, the status of the text, and so forth. Bultmann referred to such models as our "preunderstanding" *(Vorverständnis).* Gadamer and Thiselton refer to a "horizon of expectation." David Kelsey uses the notion of a *discrimen* to refer to such a model. Our differing horizons sometimes make it difficult for us to understand the way others read Scripture and even to talk with others about our diverse understandings of the biblical texts. Whatever the particular terminology we may use, we need to learn to identify what our hermeneutical models are and how they should work for us in our context.

Thus any biblical hermeneutic is not merely pretheological, laying out the ground rules for reading Scripture before theological reflection begins. Rather, a biblical hermeneutic that is honest and self-critical must necessarily be *theological* in character. The very image of "horizon" implies a cosmos, a world that is in view. That world, in turn, implies a cosmology, a comprehensive and synthetic perspective that makes understanding possible at all and that enables meaning to take shape. If we are to speak meaningfully to our complex situation, and if we are to understand the diversities that characterize Christian witness itself, we need to discuss the meaning and function of our "horizons." We must lay out our preunderstanding of the nature and character of God, of God's relationship with the world, and of our essential humanness. That horizon of expectation is always subject to revision, movement, and widening, based on the data of the text itself. Yet we must acknowledge and subject to critical examination our assumptions and presuppositions in interpretation. Otherwise we will be able neither to understand the points at which we differ from others in our interpretation of the Bible nor to speak meaningfully to our world.

A Hermeneutic of Diversity

In this section, I begin to sketch out a model for interpretation that takes seriously both the data of the biblical text and the nature of our contemporary context. I want to develop a model that faces honestly the realities, the opportunities, and the challenges of pluralism in our modern and postmodern world. I believe that at many points we read the Bible differently from one another, not because one person is wrong and another right, but because we come from different contexts. This raises the basic question: How can we approach biblical interpretation so as to allow for a plurality of readings of the text, while at the same time allowing the text to exercise its controlling and shaping influence on each particular reading? How can we acknowledge our own particularity — and the limits that that particularity entails — and yet seek to speak the truth, not just for ourselves, but for the world as well?

A Missional Hermeneutic: Some Presuppositions

I call the model I am developing a *missional* hermeneutic because it springs from a basic observation about the New Testament: namely, the early Christian movement that produced and canonized the New Testament was a movement with a specifically *missionary* character. One of the most obvious phenomena of early Christianity is the way in which the movement crossed cultural boundaries and planted itself in new places. More than half of the New Testament was in fact written by people engaged in and celebrating this sort of missionary enterprise in the early church. This tendency of early Christianity to cross cultural boundaries is a fertile starting point for developing a model of biblical interpretation. It is fertile, especially for our purposes, because it places the question of the relationship between Christianity and diverse cultures at the very top of the interpretative agenda. This focus may be of great help to us in grappling with plurality in interpretation today.

Before we attempt to substantiate such a missional hermeneutic biblically, we must first consider how it grows out of and addresses our own cultural setting described earlier in this chapter. The missional hermeneutic I am advocating begins by affirming the reality and inevitability of plurality in interpretation. Because every reading of the Bible is shaped by the individuality and the historical and cultural particularity of the interpreter, there will always be multiple interpretations of the Bible. Therefore our model suggests that plurality in interpretation is not necessarily a sign of interpretative failure but often of interpretative effectiveness, reflecting a distinctive convergence of the text with the particular context of the reader.

At the same time, a missional hermeneutic must be committed to dialogue with other readers of the biblical text. Every time we read a commentary or hear someone else talk about a passage, we discover new perspectives that we had not seen before. Dialogue in interpretation often results in the correction of idiosyncratic or distorted readings of Scripture within any given context. Therefore there is also a sense in which plurality in interpretation is not always a sign of interpretative effectiveness, but sometimes a result of defective or inadequate readings, which may be corrected or qualified through dialogue with other interpreters.

How can plurality in interpretation be at one point a sign of interpretative success and at another point a sign of deficiency? The answer lies in the multifaceted nature of interpretation itself. Every interpretative reading is an attempt to project a symbolic world in which the world of the text and the world of the reader are brought together in such a way that each mutually informs the other. Where there is a diversity of readers, there will always be a plurality of interpretations; each reader brings his or her own distinctive "world" into a conversation with the text. But these worlds in which text and context are brought together are not totally dissimilar. Every interpretation must do justice to the same text. Moreover, every interpretation must connect, in some way, with our basic humanity. To be meaningful, every interpretation must address in some way the common "stuff" of all our lives: the wider forms of rationality that we share, as well as our shared experiences of birth, death, hope, fear, joy, sorrow, grief, anxiety, love, loss, bliss, and the like. Diversity in interpretation is healthy when it emerges from our human diversity; it is deficient when it distorts our common text or fails to connect with our common humanity.

Our discussion of "common humanity" raises the need for an important caveat, however. The meaning of our common humanity and its relationship to our individual and cultural particularity is not established prior to the act of interpretation. Rather, it is discovered in the process of dialogic interpretation with others. Our understanding of what "our common humanity" means is not an a priori given but is itself a cultural construct that arises from the interaction of different cultural perspectives. A missional hermeneutic calls diverse interpreters to read a common text with a commitment to be faithful both to the world of the text and to their own shared and distinctive worlds. When such a reading takes place, the contours and characteristics of both the unity and the diversity of human life are more clearly disclosed.

Biblical Grounding of a Missional Hermeneutic

This dialectic between our common humanity and our cultural particularity — a dialectic that lies at the heart of a missional hermeneutic — is itself grounded in the narratives of Scripture. Already in the story of the call of Abraham, the divine call and blessing come to a particular person in a specific cultural context. Yet from the beginning, the texts set the story within a universal context: "I will make of you a great nation, and I will bless you, and make your name great, so that you will be a blessing. I will bless those who bless you, and the one who curses you I will curse; and in you all the families of the earth shall be blessed" (Gen. 12:2-3). In Abraham, the particularity of God's blessing also moves out to "all the families of the earth."

Later in the monarchical and second temple period, this convergence of a particular calling and a universal context gave rise to dreams of the hegemony of a beneficent Israelite sovereignty: Isaiah 2:2-4 puts the vision in these words:

> In days to come the mountain of the LORD's house shall be established as the highest of the mountains, and shall be raised above the hills; all the nations shall stream to it. Many peoples shall come and say, "Come, let us go up to the mountain of the LORD, to the house of the God of Jacob; that he may teach us his ways and that we may walk in his paths." For out of Zion shall go forth instruction, and the word of the LORD from Jerusalem. He shall judge between the nations, and shall arbitrate for many peoples; they shall beat their swords into plowshares, and their spears into pruning hooks; nation shall not lift up sword against nation, neither shall they learn war any more.

Again, the particularity of Israel's call moves out toward a universal salvific purpose.

We find the same dialectic in the Gospels. On the one hand, Jesus is consistently portrayed in all four gospels as one who enacts a highly focused and culturally particularistic vocation: "I was sent only to the lost sheep of the house of Israel" (Matt. 15:24). On the other hand, the Gospels portray Jesus in such a way that this particularity is always "stretched" and placed in a larger context. Jesus reaches out to the outcasts and the unclean. He uses a Samaritan as the hero of a parable. Most of all, he announces the coming reign of God, with overwhelming implications not only for Israel but for the whole world. Judgment and salvation are coming to the house of Israel, but that is only the beginning. The whole earth will be summoned to stand before the judgment seat.

A decisive turn takes place, however, in the story of the emergence of the church as recorded in the Acts of the Apostles and the Epistles. When Gentiles are incorporated into the people of God *as Gentiles*, the interaction between particularity and universality is completely recast. No longer is God's universal saving purpose spoken of as the beneficent hegemony of Israelite culture and power; rather, God's universal saving purpose is disclosed in the sanctifying of many different political and cultural contexts, both Jewish and Gentile. Gentiles need not become Jews, and Jews need not become Gentiles. All in their own contexts and cultures glorify the one God who is Lord of all. Revelation 5:9 celebrates the work of the Lamb who ransomed for God "saints from every tribe and language and people and nation." Every ethnicity, every language, every political context, and every different social grouping become a potential sources of doxology and praise to God. The particularity of each setting is placed in a universal context, not by dreams of hegemony, but by the apprehension of a single saving story that discloses a God who seeks to be glorified by a diversity of languages, ethnicities, and peoples. In the New Testament, the flow of blessing is reversed. No longer do the nations stream to Jerusalem; now the word of the Lord goes out to the ends of the earth. All of humanity is called to glorify God, not by suppressing diversity and particularity, but by sanctifying it. The universal bond of humanity appears, not so much in its set of common responses to its Creator and Sustainer, but rather by humanity's diverse responses to the singular vision of God disclosed in the story of the life, death, and resurrection of Jesus Christ.

Theological Grounding of a Missional Hermeneutic

When the overall message of Scripture is interpreted in this manner, the result is a distinctive rendering of the identity of God. In his book *The Uses of Scripture in Recent Theology,* David Kelsey has observed that the way we bring Scripture to bear in the making of theological proposals is directly connected to our understanding of "the mode in which God is present among the faithful." Kelsey argues that at the center of every theological proposal is a *discrimen,* "an imaginative construal of the mode of God's presence *pro nobis* that tries to catch up all its complexity and utter singularity in a single metaphorical judgment."[4] This *discrimen* is not so much a norm that governs each theological proposal as it is a criterion that enables various theological utterances to find their place with respect to the theological structure as a whole. It captures in relatively brief compass a characteristic vision and understanding of the way in which God's presence and saving activity manifest themselves.

Our attempt to ground a missional hermeneutic in this particular reading of the Bible implies a certain *discrimen* that characterizes our approach. To put it simply, a missional hermeneutic begins with the assumption that the mode in which God is present among the faithful is irreducibly multicultural. The reality of God's presence is at least potentially available through the symbolic world projected by any specific culture. Though each culture is called to repentance, its specific contours are not obliterated.

4. David Kelsey, *The Uses of Scripture in Recent Theology* (Philadelphia: Fortress, 1975), 160–61.

Hence in the New Testament, the sacred books were translated into Greek; church organization followed the patterns of other clubs and civic groups; the categories of Hellenistic philosophy were used to articulate the meaning of the gospel in that context. And yet at the same time, a missional hermeneutic includes the awareness that the reality of God is not exhausted by any particular culture's ways of naming and worshiping God.[5]

It is this awareness, I would argue, that explains the dynamism of the early church in its mission. There appears to be a powerful drive, throughout much of the New Testament, to move the Christian gospel across cultural lines and into new contexts. On the one hand, this drive emerges from a perception of God's mercy and grace that extends to all. In this sense, the gospel is an expression of the universal salvific purpose of God. On the other hand, however, the urge to bring the Christian gospel across diverse cultural boundaries has a doxological origin as well. In Romans 15:9, Paul says that the whole reason for the mission to the Gentiles was "that the Gentiles might glorify God for his mercy." God is more greatly glorified when praise comes from diverse peoples and diverse cultures.

The *discrimen* discussed above entails two further assumptions: that each culture's apprehension of God in Scripture may be accurate but is always provisional, and that God is most fully known and glorified through a diversity of cultures and cultural perspectives. These two assumptions provide the theological context for grappling with the whole question of the creativity and particularity of the reader. A missional hermeneutic presupposes one God, one Scripture, and one sacred story. At the same time, however, this sacred story does not serve to promote or sanction a monocultural religious perspective, but rather a multicultural one. God's presence is irreducibly multicultural. This affirmation serves to sanction the distinctive and particular dimensions of each reading of Scripture. At the same time, it challenges these particular readings to enter into a creative dialogue with other readings of the text. The goal is not to suppress the distinctive characteristics of each reading. Rather, the purpose is to enrich and to deepen the disclosure of God's glory through an awareness of the diverse ways in which God is moving through the world in mercy, eliciting doxology in many cultures. Diverse readings of the Bible find a point of coherence, not in some "standard" or universally accepted way of reading

5. For a more detailed discussion, see Lamin Sanneh, *Translating the Message: The Missionary Impact on Culture* (Maryknoll, NY: Orbis Books, 1989).

the text, but in the awareness that the God whose presence calls forth a distinctive form of doxology in their culture is the same God whose mercy calls forth grateful praise as well from other cultures, in other forms.

A missional hermeneutic therefore underscores a specific understanding of the experience of salvation. Its assumption is that God's saving power comes to each culture in both affirmation and critique. Paul in Acts 17 quotes Greek philosophers, and he also calls his hearers to repentance. The experience of salvation is always in some sense the experience of "coming home," of fulfilling one's destiny, of finding one's rightful place in one's culture, one's society, as well as the cosmos as a whole. The New Testament makes it clear, however, that the meaning of salvation takes diverse forms within the lives of specific Christian communities. Those diverse forms are directly related to the different cultural and social settings in which the gospel takes root. Hence Paul can write in 1 Corinthians 7:20, "Let each of you remain in the condition in which you were called." Each culture itself is also called to repentance, but a missional hermeneutic understands this call to repentance not as the obliteration of each culture but rather as the sanctification of each cultural setting so that it may offer a fuller and more perfect praise to God.

The Christian experience of salvation, however, is not only a matter of experiencing the purification and sanctification of one's own cultural and social setting. It also involves a heightened sense of connectedness to other diverse cultural settings where praise is also given to God. The Christian experience of salvation not only purifies and enriches one's distinctive cultural identity but also deepens the awareness that one participates with all of humanity in a multicultural worship of God that transcends any particular context. Hence the Christian experience of salvation creates a dual identity: on the one hand, I am a member of a particular community that offers its own distinctive praise to God; on the other hand, I am a member of a diverse human community that offers a much more powerful — indeed, astonishing — array of voices, singing a form of doxology that radically transcends my own distinctive voice. That is why Paul in his letters is able to offer very focused and specific pastoral advice tailored to each setting, and at the same time is able to affirm that "our citizenship is in heaven" (Phil. 3:20).

The great delight of a missional hermeneutic is found precisely in the interplay between these two sources of Christian identity. It entails a vision of a gracious God who enters deeply into the everyday particularity of each cultural setting, each society, each family, each meal, each social interaction. At the same time, this God invites us to widen our vision to a vast human community of which we are a small part. We are invited to sing our particular melody line in a vast polyphony that so dramatically transcends our own voice that we may wonder if it is ever heard. Yet this vision of God insists that each voice is always heard, that each voice has infinite value, and that there is no song unless each voice sings in its own distinctive way.

A Hermeneutic of Coherence

This grounding of a missional hermeneutic is only a starting point, however. I have affirmed a plurality of readings as not only necessary but also an expression of fundamental claims made by the Bible regarding the identity and purpose of God. Our discussion up to this point has focused primarily on what it means to speak the truth *in love,* aware of and respectful of diverse voices, longing for the emergence of a full humanity, rich in diversity. Once we have affirmed plurality, however, we need also to grapple with how the Bible may provide a center, an orienting point in the midst of such diversity. What does it mean to speak *the truth* in love?

The previous discussion has argued for a hermeneutical posture that affirms plurality in interpretation. By itself, however, such a posture could easily dissolve into an infinite number of diverse and conflicting readings of the Bible. In order for a model for interpretation to be healthy, the centrifugal tendencies toward diversity and particularity must be balanced by centripetal forces that also move toward consensus and coherence. There are two reasons why this centripetal tendency must also be recognized. First, all biblical interpreters are wrestling with the same texts. There already is a commonality to which all biblical interpreters commit themselves in one way or another. Because we are reading the same Bible, we cannot ignore the ways that others read it. Second, all interpreters share a common humanity. Although our experiences may be very diverse, we recognize common experiences that bind us to other human beings as well. Insofar as we are attempting to make the Bible meaningful to us today, we also are attempting to make it meaningful to others who share our common humanity.

These two realities — our common text and our common humanity

— require not only that we affirm diversity in interpretation but also that we seek coherence and commonality in the ways that we interpret Scripture. When we turn to the New Testament, however, our quest for coherence and for commonality encounters a difficult challenge: not only are specific New Testament passages interpreted differently by different people, but within the New Testament as a whole there appears to be a great deal of diversity. New Testament scholars have long recognized that there is a diversity of theological perspectives, contexts, and concerns expressed by the various New Testament books. The trend of most New Testament scholarship in the last two hundred years has been to highlight these contrasts in perspective.

This awareness of the diversity within the New Testament canon is both helpful and problematic. It is helpful because it underscores the thesis we have already advanced, that plurality in religious experience and perspective is to be regarded as normal within the context of early Christianity. It is problematic, however, because the diversity in the New Testament books calls into question whether the New Testament is capable of functioning as a truly common text. If there is no center to the New Testament, but only a set of competing religious perspectives that do not cohere, then the quest toward coherence in contemporary biblical interpretation is a vain one. There can be no coherence in interpretation if the texts themselves do not cohere.

The present discussion attempts to address the problem of the coherence or center of the New Testament. I wish to begin by looking, not at the individual New Testament documents, but at the New Testament as a whole. The very fact that twenty-seven early Christian documents are gathered into a single book called the New Testament entails a particular set of assumptions, of which the interpreter must become aware. At the very least, the collection of these various documents into the New Testament canon involves the ascription of some sort of wholeness or coherence to the collection of books. Correspondingly, if one wishes to identify oneself as an interpreter of the New Testament, one of the tasks involved is the attempt to grasp and to articulate the way in which reading the New Testament *as a whole* can convey meaning.

One may certainly engage in the interpretation of particular New Testament documents without recognizing or attributing any "wholeness" to the New Testament canon in its entirety. However, it is usually the case that people who identify themselves as religious interpreters of the New

Testament are engaged in the pursuit of meaning, not only in particular fragments or books of the New Testament, but in the New Testament as a whole, and it is precisely this kind of pursuit that this section seeks to examine. Perhaps even more important, our ability to move toward convergence and consensus with other interpreters on the meaning of Christian faith as a whole will be directly related to the extent to which we are able to articulate a sense of the coherence of the New Testament as a whole.

In my judgment, one of the most helpful ways to grapple with the question of the coherence of the New Testament is to raise the question, What is "the gospel"? In all three Synoptic Gospels, Jesus is portrayed as one who proclaims the gospel (e.g., Matt. 4:23; 9:35; Mark 1:14; Luke 4:18, 43). Paul identifies himself as one "set apart for the gospel of God" (Rom. 1:1) and regards the gospel as "the power of God for salvation to everyone who believes" (Rom. 1:16). A quick glance at a concordance shows that these examples could be multiplied many times. Clearly the term "gospel" is a kind of code word for many New Testament writers that summarizes something very basic about what early Christians thought Christian faith to be all about.

Yet it is not at all easy to press further and to specify exactly what the gospel is. The problem is twofold. First, there is an exegetical problem. Although the use of the term "gospel" in the New Testament suggests some coherent center from which New Testament faith springs, we have already noted how the last two centuries of New Testament scholarship have brought to light the wide-ranging diversity that exists within the New Testament canon. From a purely exegetical point of view, the various theological expressions in the New Testament threaten to become so diverse and disparate that no overarching unity may be found. We have grown accustomed to recognizing the contrasts between the theology of Luke and Paul, between Mark and Hebrews. On the whole, however, scholars in the last two centuries have found it easier to note the contrasts than to find the points of convergence.[6]

The second problem in defining the gospel arises in the hermeneutical arena. New Testament scholars who try to explore the center or heart of Christian faith have proposed a wide variety of models for conceptualizing and articulating that sought-for center, using terms and categories that are viable and meaningful to people today. These different models are often

6. For a helpful survey of different formulations of "the gospel" in the New Testament, see James D. G. Dunn, *Unity and Diversity in the New Testament* (Philadelphia: Westminster Press, 1977).

based on very different presuppositions about what New Testament theology or Christian faith is in the first place. Is Christian faith primarily a set of theological axioms? A moral posture? A way of understanding and defining one's own self? A response to God's "mighty acts"? A way of building and maintaining human communities? The way we answer such questions will determine the models we use to construe the "center" of the New Testament, and consequently the way we think about the meaning and function of the term "gospel." Even if one attempts to arrive at an understanding of Christian faith that embraces many of these categories in some overarching system, there will inevitably be characteristic emphases that emerge that will differ from person to person and from place to place. Indeed, the very attempt to define "gospel" in such a systematic fashion is itself laden with presuppositions about the nature of the term.

In essence, then, any attempt to articulate the essence or coherence of the gospel encounters problems arising from two different kinds of pluralism: (1) the diverse expressions of Christian life and faith within the New Testament, and (2) the diverse models for understanding Christian faith and life that are presupposed by various contemporary interpreters.

How is one to find a center in the midst of such diversity? From an exegetical point of view, one must look through the New Testament documents for recurring motifs and themes, common structures, patterns of narrative, lines of development, "trajectories," and the like. Such strategies may assist in finding commonality amid the pluralities of the New Testament. Yet this *exegetical* quest for the coherence of the New Testament must be accompanied by a *hermeneutical* self-criticism in which interpreters evaluate their way of conceptualizing Christian faith and life in light of the whole range of exegetical data, and in light of the plurality of articulations of Christian faith that have existed in the past and that are found in the world today. The overall models we use to understand and articulate the essence of New Testament faith must be established and confirmed by exegetical exploration and broadened by exposure to other interpretative approaches and assumptions.

In this dialectic between exegesis and hermeneutics, there are two natural tendencies to be guarded against. The discipline of exegesis naturally tends toward atomism in laying out the data in all its particularity and diversity; hermeneutical considerations are naturally inclined to be reductionistic, as the desire for coherence and meaning suppresses data that do not fit one's own mold. Such tensions can be neither escaped nor fully resolved. Each approach must simply restrain the excesses of the other. The quality of one's interpretative work will depend upon the degree to which these tensions are made explicitly the object of reflection and criticism. Hence it is important to acknowledge the preliminary interpretative assumptions that both launch and guide our investigation. My purpose in so doing is not to grant these assumptions a privileged or a priori status; quite the opposite. It is to present these assumptions as an initial hypothesis, to be attested or corrected by ensuing exegetical and hermeneutical exploration.

First, I attempt to articulate the coherence of Christian faith as it finds expression within the bounds of the New Testament canon. By restricting itself to these documents, this study attempts to make more explicit the nature of the Christian church's claim that the New Testament canon bears witness to "one holy, catholic, and apostolic faith." In a sense, this discussion is an attempt to determine the exegetical and hermeneutical basis for the church's use of the canon of the New Testament as the "rule of faith." Is there a coherence or center to be discovered in the New Testament, in the midst of the many theological and situational pluralities found there?

Second, this discussion seeks to avoid two hermeneutical extremes. On the one hand, we must avoid a hermeneutical imperialism that insists on only one possible interpretation of biblical texts and their center. On the other hand, we must also be wary of a deconstructionist nihilism that regards the biblical text as infinitely elastic and subject to an innumerable variety of conflicting interpretations, all of which have an equal claim to legitimacy. We shall seek a genuine coherence in the New Testament that allows for and invites a plurality of interpretations, but that also recognizes certain constraints, implicit in the text, that may set limits on the range of possible interpretations of the gospel.

In this effort to generate a constructive proposal, it may be useful to identify some basic questions that prompt the search for "the gospel" and that should guide the way in which it is articulated:

1. What is the unity amid the diversity of the New Testament by which the canon was formed, and by which the early Christian movement can be termed a coherent entity?

2. Early Christianity represents a religious movement that struck out in some surprisingly new directions, when compared with its Jewish origins. This raises the question: What are the criteria by which early Christians exercised such astonishing freedom with respect to their earlier Jewish tradition, but also preserved so much of that tradition?

3. Similarly, the early Christian movement that produced the New

Testament was itself a dynamic and developing phenomenon. How and why did it develop in the way that it did? What criteria did New Testament writers use when they selected and adapted the Christian tradition that they received? For example, by what hermeneutical logic do Matthew and Luke at some points draw on and repeat Mark, and yet at other points exercise a surprising freedom in rewriting the tradition as it is expressed in Mark? The problem appears with even greater sharpness when the fourth gospel is compared with the Synoptic tradition, although in this case the lines of dependency are more difficult to ascertain.

4. Our study has already shown how early Christianity manifested itself as a religious perspective that is extraordinarily adaptable to a variety of specific situations. At some points, this adaptability appears to be so pervasive that the points of divergence among different New Testament expressions of Christian faith almost seem more extensive than their points of convergence. What is the key to this adaptability, by what logic or pattern does it operate, and what are its limits?

It should be noted that in each of these questions, the diversity and dynamic character of the New Testament are affirmed; the challenge is to discover the implicit logic and assumptions that both drive and constrain that dynamism and diversity. If we can identify and render explicit that logic and those assumptions, we may be able to articulate a vision for the coherence of the New Testament that invites a variety of creative readings within a dynamic but coherent framework. In other words, if we can discover how the New Testament unites its creative and divergent expressions of faith, we, too, may discover how to engage in a genuinely dialogic act of interpretation that neither merely echoes the words of the New Testament nor imposes an alien perspective on the New Testament documents.

It will be useful to begin our quest for this paradigm in which to construe the gospel by talking about the New Testament itself. Any paradigm that seeks to provide an integrated understanding of these documents must grapple with the characteristic features that unite them, as well as the elements that distinguish them from each other or from other first-century religious texts. Perhaps the most obvious way to begin is to note that the New Testament texts have characteristic literary features that both distinguish them from and link them with other documents from the same period. The various New Testament books are written in different genres, using different forms and making use of the rhetorical and stylistic conventions that were widespread in the time of their writing. They also develop some of their own characteristic forms, styles, and rhetorical flourishes in hymns, salutations, parables, and the like; at points they even develop distinctive genres, such as that of the Gospels. Any responsible attempt to interpret the New Testament must take these various genres and literary styles into consideration.

In order to interpret effectively, however, we must examine the New Testament texts in ways that lead us beyond a mere consideration of their literary character. It has also become commonplace in biblical studies to speak of the specific historical situation from which New Testament documents emerged and to which they were directed. The specific situation, culture, and worldview of each writer and original reader/hearer affected to a significant degree the way the biblical writers expressed themselves. Although Paul uses the same letter genre in both Galatians and Romans, for example, he writes very differently in the two documents because these two congregations have very different relationships with Paul and are facing different issues in different historical and cultural settings. The consideration of historical context includes not only the attempt to make judgments regarding the historicity of particular events but, more important, the attempt to reconstruct the cultural, religious, political, socioeconomic, and environmental context in which these documents originated. In the last two hundred years, the consideration of the historical context of New Testament texts has made enormous strides, and scholars now have a wealth of data at their disposal that can help to illuminate the particular shape, form, and focus of the various New Testament documents, in light of their historical context.

However, even a consideration of literary and historical elements is not sufficient in itself to provide a comprehensive paradigm for the interpretation of the New Testament as a whole. The reason is that the biblical texts are more than mere ad hoc literary or rhetorical responses to specific historical situations and contexts. In some way or other, these documents seek to bring a religious tradition to bear upon their situations. That religious tradition has two basic components: the Hebrew Bible or Septuagint (and other Jewish literature) on the one hand, and stories about Jesus, Christian hymns, and other Christian traditional material on the other. In essence, the New Testament might be understood as the literary attempt of certain writers to address their specific situations in light of these Jewish and Christian traditions. Hence the various New Testament documents must be evaluated at the *literary level* (e.g., in style, form, rhetoric, and genre), but they must also be examined at the *level of tradition* (because they draw different elements from the same tradition or from different traditions) and at the *level of historical context* (because they appropriate those various literary and traditional elements in different contexts).

These are the basic elements that generally come under examination in the practice of historical-critical exegesis as that discipline has developed in the last two hundred years. Taken by themselves, however, they do not provide a sufficient framework for interpreting the New Testament. The reason is that much of the New Testament is polemical or at least hortatory in tone. That is, many New Testament writings are trying to correct or to modify other people's understanding of the true nature of the Jewish and Christian tradition and its applicability to specific situations. For example, both Paul and his Galatian opponents are attempting to apply the story of Jesus and the Hebrew Bible to their specific situation. Unfortunately, they are coming to diametrically opposing conclusions. Thus it is not enough to speak of a traditional and a literary/historical context. Another hermeneutical component must be added in order to understand the distinctive character of the New Testament writings. That component might be called an *interpretative matrix* — a set of interpretative rules or assumptions by which a New Testament writer discriminates between what he regards as legitimate and illegitimate uses of Jewish and Christian traditions in any specific situational or literary context.

This hermeneutical component does not, however, necessarily bring us to a coherent center for the New Testament as a whole. It may well be that different New Testament writers operate with different sets of interpretative rules. Certainly Matthew has an interpretative approach that he applies to the Hebrew Bible that is quite different from that found in Hebrews, for example. Thus at one level, each New Testament text can be described as emerging from its own tradition, its own historical and literary context, and its own hermeneutical or interpretative framework.

However, once we recognize that an understanding of the hermeneutical framework of a text is vital to its exegetical description and interpretation, another path is opened for finding new points of contact and convergence across New Testament documents. We are invited to search for points of contact and coherence among the New Testament documents, not only at the level of historical situations, literary milieus, and shared traditions, but also at the level of shared hermeneutical frameworks and structures. That is, in our search for a dynamic approach to the coherence of the New Testament, we may be helped by exploring the implicit forms of logic and shared assumptions that both energize and regulate the phenomenon of early Christianity.

In fact, the New Testament canon invites just this sort of inquiry across the whole range of New Testament documents. These documents together represent a body of literature that is distinct, both from the contemporary Jewish literature, and from other texts we find in the Hellenistic world, despite many points of contact between the New Testament and these other bodies of literature. This distinctiveness is not adequately described by appeal only to historical situation (first-century religious texts) or to a distinctive tradition (Jewish texts interested in Jesus) or to a common literary milieu (which does not exist, even within the canon). There is something more here. What makes the New Testament, at least in some basic sense, not only a distinctive body of literature but a distinctive mode of religious discourse? If this is at all a meaningful question, we may be justified in seeking, across the range of New Testament documents, a larger and more general interpretative matrix that these writers share together, which gives the New Testament as a whole its characteristic tone, emphasis, and dynamism. Although the seeking does not guarantee that we will find such a general interpretative matrix, the quest seems invited, both by the New Testament documents themselves, and by their collection into a canon of Scripture.

I would like to suggest that when we begin to inquire into this interpretative matrix, we are inquiring into the basic character of the gospel itself. We find consistently in the New Testament that the writers operate with an awareness of a central message that shapes and directs their discourse as a whole and their appropriation and adaptation of tradition in particular. This is clearest when we look at the way New Testament writers interpret the Old Testament. One can conceivably use stories from the Hebrew Bible to speak of many different kinds of religious consciousness. However, the New Testament writers are explicit in their insistence that the Hebrew Bible be read "in light of Christ." For the New Testament writers, the gospel of Christ provides a hermeneutical vantage point from which the Hebrew Bible can be "properly" understood — that is, from which it can be understood from a distinctively *Christian* perspective.

However, it is not only the Hebrew Bible that, according to the New Testament, must be interpreted in light of the gospel. Stories about Jesus, Christian hymns, and Christian confessional materials must also be interpreted within this matrix. This is precisely what the four gospels in the New Testament try to do. They create a new literary genre by placing the stories about Jesus in an interpretative context that will illumine what the writer believes to be their true significance and meaning. Mark, for example, insists that we do not know what it means to acclaim Jesus as "Son of God" or "Messiah" unless we put these titles in the context of the suffering and crucifixion of Jesus. Likewise Paul insists that the Galatians' approach to Jesus as the Messiah threatens, ironically enough, to violate "the truth of the gospel" (Gal. 2:5, 14). One can tell stories about Jesus, sing hymns, and confess faith, all with the aim of calling people to believe, and yet be in complete contradiction to the gospel, at least as Paul sees it.

Therefore, if we are to find an interpretative matrix that effectively renders the distinctive character of the New Testament documents, we must consider the possibility that what the New Testament calls "the gospel" may be the key to identifying that matrix. This way of conceptualizing the nature of the gospel poses the question of the coherence and distinctive character of the New Testament more sharply. As we have said, each New Testament document may be regarded as the interaction of three constitutive elements: the literary context, the tradition (both Jewish and Christian), and the specific situation of the writer. These three elements must also, however, be envisioned within an interpretative matrix — the gospel. Specifically, it is a particular writer's understanding of the gospel that provides the discriminating rules by which tradition, genre, rhetoric, and situation can be meaningfully and "Christianly" brought together. This approach can be diagrammed as in Figure 1.

The historical, literary, and traditional dimensions of each New Testa-

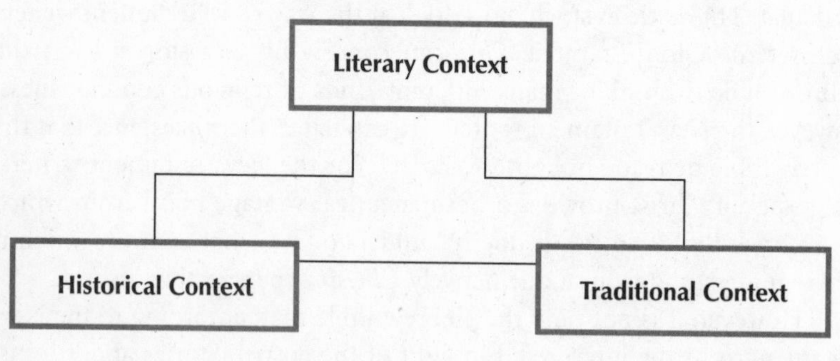

FIGURE 1. A Model for Interpreting the New Testament

ment document exist in a dynamic interaction with each other. That interaction as a whole is shaped and regulated by an overall interpretative matrix, a comprehensive and synthetic vision for what Christian faith entails at its core.

This way of looking at the New Testament carries within itself the possibility for a contemporary hermeneutic that itself grows from Scripture. If it is possible to uncover and render explicit the interpretative matrix by which the New Testament writers sifted, articulated, and appropriated the ongoing flood of Jewish and Christian traditions in new situations, it may well be that an analogous interpretative matrix can provide at least some clues for how we are to do the same today. In other words, I am proposing an approach to interpreting the New Testament that is concerned not only with describing and interpreting the content of the various New Testament documents. I am suggesting that our interpretation must make explicit the religious logic and implicit assumptions that govern the selection of traditional elements, the literary forms that are used, and the ways in which the historical context is being addressed. As we recover that logic and those assumptions, we may be guided in how we are to make use of the traditions recorded in Scripture, as they are now brought to bear in new ways in new historical contexts.

In what follows, I offer at least a preliminary attempt at defining further this interpretative matrix that governs and shapes the interaction of literary, traditional, and historical elements. It must be noted before beginning, however, that this probe must necessarily have a tentative and preliminary status with respect to its integrative range. The overall interpretative matrix that I will articulate here is not fully reflected in all the New Testament writings. Significant aspects of the matrix are not developed or made explicit in some New Testament documents. I have already observed that the various New Testament documents do not operate with identical hermeneutical structures or assumptions. Nevertheless, I hope to delineate a clustering of shared hermeneutical structures and assumptions, centered on the New Testament category "gospel," which operate across a wide range of New Testament documents. Obviously, the case for the gospel as hermeneutic needs to be established by a careful exegesis of the whole range of New Testament writings, a task that extends far beyond the scope of this study. But I offer at least a kind of suggestive model that may serve as a starting point for further investigation and a catalyst for a creative and pluralist dialogic encounter with the New Testament.

How does one describe something like a hermeneutical structure? And how might one determine the hermeneutical structure of a given biblical text or collection of texts? I suggest that we take our cue from the New Testament writers, who adopted the term "gospel" to express their basic hermeneutical assumptions. The New Testament's use of this term invites three avenues of exploration. First, we need to understand why the New Testament writers chose this particular term as a way to articulate the heart of their faith. This line of inquiry leads us to explore the semantic range and linguistic function of the word "gospel" in first-century Mediterranean culture generally. Such exploration may help us in identifying some of the assumptions and presuppositions implicit in the use of the term "gospel." Second, we must identify as clearly as possible the basic content of the gospel as the New Testament articulates it. What are the common themes, images, or motifs that characterize the New Testament's understanding of the gospel? Finally, we need to determine how the notion of gospel functions hermeneutically. That is to say, how can the New Testament's understanding of the gospel provide us with insight into the implicit logic and assumptions that energize and regulate the expressions of faith we find recorded in the New Testament?

The Term "Gospel"

The very choice of the term "gospel" (εὐαγγέλιον) already gives us some insight into the nature and character of the faith that gave birth to the New Testament. Perhaps the most striking thing about the term is that it seems to evoke an association with what we as moderns call "news." Usually it refers more specifically to "good news," but even when the news is not good, in its usage outside the New Testament the term almost always refers to some message that comes as news or announcement to those who hear it. It can refer to the news of victory in war or to someone's accession to kingship or even to more mundane announcements like the birth of a son or news of an approaching wedding.

The choice of this term to articulate something central about Christian faith becomes more significant when one contemplates the alternatives that were being used in this period to express the essence of religious faith and experience. In articulating the essential character of its faith, early Christianity could have adopted one of the terms commonly used in the

Hellenistic religious world such as "illumination" (φωτισμός) or "knowledge" (γνῶσις) or "mystery" (μυστήριον). Each of these terms appears at some points in the New Testament as a designation for Christian faith. However, none of these terms acquires the widespread and generic status of the term "gospel." One might observe that, in contrast to these other categories, the term "gospel" has a distinctly public character; it identifies Christian faith as news that has significance for all people, indeed for the whole world, not merely as esoteric understanding or insight, even though New Testament faith at times may have esoteric dimensions.

Early Christianity might also have continued the legacy of its Jewish heritage, referring to its newly emerging faith as "law" or "Torah" (νόμος), "instruction" (διδαχή), or "wisdom" (σοφία). As with the other Hellenistic terms we noted above, we also find the New Testament using this Jewish terminology to articulate its faith, but these terms also lack the widespread, generic character of "gospel" in the New Testament. The dimension of meaning that the term "gospel" adds to these other Jewish formulations is the event-oriented element of "news." The use of the term "gospel" in Koine Greek generally does not suggest at its core the transmission of universal truths, principles, values, or wisdom (though these are not excluded); rather, it focuses attention on the reporting of an event or happening of special significance: a victory in battle, an accession to kingship, or a political accomplishment.

The Content of the Gospel

Pressing further in order to delineate the specific content of the gospel in the New Testament, we encounter some difficulty. Different New Testament writers articulate the central message of Christian faith in different ways. For Paul, the gospel means that Gentiles are not required to undergo circumcision. Therefore Paul insists in Galatians that for Gentiles to receive circumcision is an abandonment of the gospel. In the Synoptic Gospels, by contrast, Jesus is depicted as proclaiming the gospel, but the message focuses on the coming reign of God. In the book of Acts, the proclamation of the gospel seems very closely related to the promise of forgiveness of sins. Even the most cursory review of the New Testament suggests that the gospel could be articulated in many different ways.

Yet even in the midst of that diversity, one detects common concerns and emphases as well. James D. G. Dunn identifies three motifs that are present throughout early Christian preaching: the proclamation of the risen, exalted Jesus; the call for faith; and a promise (grace, mercy, forgiveness, salvation, etc.) held out to faith.[7] I would add to Dunn's list the observation that almost all expressions of the gospel touch in some way upon the identity of Jesus, and upon his death as well. Hence in the midst of substantial diversity in articulating the gospel, it seems clear that for New Testament writers, the gospel is inextricably tied up with the identity, death, and resurrection of Jesus of Nazareth, a story that is announced as an act of God that offers a hopeful promise for the whole world. The New Testament finds its point of departure in the conviction that the person of Jesus, including his death and resurrection, is "news" of public significance that needs to be told.

This emphasis on the centrality and public significance of the person of Jesus and his death and resurrection in the New Testament can be found even where the term "gospel" does not occur. In the Gospel of John, for example, even though the words for "proclaim the gospel" (εὐαγγελίζομαι) and "gospel" (εὐαγγέλιον) are not found apart from the title of the work, the universal and public significance of the person of Jesus and his death and resurrection are clearly presupposed in the entire presentation of the story.

Furthermore, it is quite clear that the significance attached to Jesus' identity, death, and resurrection throughout the New Testament lies in the belief that this news has *saving* significance. The religion of the New Testament is preeminently a religion of "salvation" (σωτηρία). It promises good news for the poor, forgiveness for the sinner, wholeness for the body, freedom, joy, hope, and eternal life. This soteriological dimension is in keeping with the prevailing use of the "gospel" word group (εὐαγγέλιον, εὐαγγελίζομαι) in Koine Greek. These words are commonly associated with "salvation" (σωτηρία) and "good fortune" (εὐτυχία, εὐτύχημα).[8] The various New Testament writers differ at points on exactly what "salvation" means in concrete terms, but they share the assumption that their religion is a religion of salvation. The "salvation" word group (σωτηρία, σῴζω, σωτήρ) occupies an important place in every New Testament writer's vocabulary.

7. Ibid., 30.

8. See G. Friedrich, "εὐαγγελίζομαι," in *Theological Dictionary of the New Testament*, ed. G. Kittel (Grand Rapids: Eerdmans, 1965), 2:711.

To summarize the discussion to this point, we have observed that the New Testament's designation of its faith as "gospel" suggests that New Testament faith centers on the public announcement of the story of Jesus' identity, death, and resurrection as a story of salvation. To put it a bit differently, at the center of New Testament faith is the conviction that in the life, death, and resurrection of Jesus, God has revealed the completion of a saving purpose for the world, to be received by faith. Or we might use Paul's words in 2 Corinthians 5:19: "God was in Christ reconciling the world to God's self."[9]

Not every New Testament writer's work is equally derived from this kind of core formulation. However, the generic character of the term "gospel" invites us to consider this formulation as a kind of working model for the coherence of the New Testament, a model that we may further refine or qualify once the basic conceptual groundwork has been laid.

Gospel as Hermeneutical Framework

In such a bare-bones formulation there is a large amount of room for widely divergent interpretations and applications. This high level of generality is indeed necessary if our model is to be able to function across a wide range of New Testament writings. But this level of generality does not render such summaries useless. Such a summary of "the gospel," while not intended to be a basic set of propositions from which the rest of Christian faith is deduced, instead provides the hermeneutical perspective or matrix through which the Christian tradition and specific historical contexts are interpreted.

How can this gospel summary function as a hermeneutical matrix or structure? I would argue that almost every allusion to the gospel exhibits or implies a number of basic structural features.

First, the gospel always manifests itself as that which makes a claim, which summons to allegiance and decision. In its insistence that the identity and career of Jesus is of central soteriological significance, the gospel challenges people to accept the truth of that assertion and to modify their lives accordingly. The gospel is always that which is preached, the kerygma.

9. Numerous other summary statements could be cited, including John 16:33b; Rom. 1:16; 1 Cor. 15:1-5; Phil. 2:5-11; 1 Tim. 2:5-6; Titus 3:4-7; Heb. 1:1-4; 1 Pet. 1:3; 1 John 3:8b; 5:1; Rev. 5:9-10.

Hence we may also say that the gospel is intimately associated with the experience of transformed perception and action.

Second, the gospel presupposes a "public" horizon of interpretation — a horizon that is seen most clearly in apocalyptic literature, where the question of the relationship between the divine and the whole world is of central importance. When we are dealing with interpretations governed by the gospel, it is always finally the world as a whole, the public world, with which God is dealing. This universal scope prevents the divine claim discussed in the preceding point from becoming individualistic in orientation. The gospel envisions nothing less than God's claim over the entire cosmos. In a sense, one might say that this cosmic horizon of interpretation is simply entailed in the notion of monotheism. If there is only one God, then language about such a God must necessarily encompass a universal frame of reference.

Third, the gospel always presents this call to allegiance and universal scope in the context of the religious realities disclosed by the death and resurrection of Christ, which is regarded as paradigmatic for understanding the relationship between God and the world. One might say that this assumption assumes that the Christ-event is revelatory in an ultimate or basic way. This is not to say that one can speak the gospel only when one is talking about Jesus. Rather, the Christ-event provides the interpretative matrix by which the entire tradition takes form and meaning.

What, then, is the gospel? In simplest terms, it is the proclamation of God's soteriological purpose and claim on this world, a purpose and claim extended paradigmatically through the crucified and risen Christ. Yet in the final analysis this is not so much *what* is preached but rather the structure that delineates *how* the entire tradition is to be preached and interpreted.

Each of these basic structural elements of the gospel can and must be elaborated further. In particular, we must explore how a hermeneutical approach to the gospel such as the one we are advocating gives rise to theological and religious discourse. We must first remember that the gospel is fundamentally kerygmatic in nature. To use the categories of speech-act theory developed by J. L. Austin, the gospel is not only a "locutionary" act, conveying information, but an "illocutionary" act, calling forth some specific response from the hearer/reader. The gospel is language that not only conveys information but seeks to bring about a new state of affairs. Just as the words "I do" in the wedding service do more than simply describe the psychological state of the bride and groom at that particular time, so the acceptance of the gospel entails a reorientation of life in trust and obedience.

Now if the gospel is paradigmatic — if it is to provide a hermeneutical perspective from which to approach tradition and situation — it suggests that the Christian tradition must articulate the gospel in such a way that it makes a claim on the hearer. Central to the gospel is the notion that God is not detached and inert but is in search of human beings — in fact, given the apocalyptic coordinates of the gospel, in search of the world as a whole. The gospel in some basic sense represents the call of God, to which the world in general, and humans in particular, are called to respond. Moreover, this call is a radical claim on life in its totality. Hence the response of faith is to confess that Jesus is Lord — to affirm that God's universal claim over this world in Christ is valid and accepted.

This universal claim over the world manifests itself paradigmatically in the Christ-event, God's reign, which discloses a dialectical interaction between death and resurrection, mercy and judgment, radical renunciation and pity for the weak. Because God extends a claim over the world, God can be known to love the world, to desire that it be all that it should be. The same is true of individuals and societies. And yet, the very fact that God extends God's claim in Christ suggests that this claim is not universally acknowledged, that there is resistance to God's claim. Hence the Christian tradition is interpreted and applied Christianly when God's claim on life is presented dialectically, both in judgment and mercy, in affirmation and critique, in embrace and in a call to repentance.

Finally, the Christian tradition is interpreted and applied in accordance with the gospel when the present need for a restoration to a right relationship with God's sovereign claim is juxtaposed with an affirmation of God's action to bring this about. The gospel insists that the Christian tradition be interpreted in such a way as to affirm that God is in the process of "making good" on the divine claim to the world, and that this process has come to its climax in the Christ-event. Hence there is a characteristic dimension of hope and trust that is an ineluctable component of a distinctively Christian rendering of the tradition — a hope and trust that are specifically attached to, and that grow from, the stories about Jesus. One tells the stories about Jesus Christianly when one tells them in such a way that they elicit the response of hope and trust in the God who is revealed in them.

But who is the God who is revealed in the tradition and in the stories about Jesus? Our simple structural approach to the gospel does not, and cannot, tell us much. God is that which makes a claim on the world, a claim that manifests itself dialectically in judgment and mercy, a claim that does not deny present suffering but that also generates hope. Yet this is only a very abstract picture.

It is here that a narrative approach to the biblical texts must find a place in one's overall construal of the distinctive character of the biblical message. The naked structure of the gospel can never exist in isolation; its general symbolic structure must always be given specific content by the richness of the narrative texture of the tradition. The content we pour into the words "God" and "Jesus" spoken of in our interpretative matrix are the identities that are rendered by the cumulative impact of the many narratives about God and Jesus within Scripture. The interpretative matrix cannot survive apart from the traditions that it interprets.

However, the interpretative matrix of the gospel does provide some parameters that delineate a context by which even the specific narratives of Scripture may be read and understood. Thus, for example, the public dimensions of the gospel in its basic structural shape preclude the narrowly sectarian reading of the biblical narrative we find in the theology of apartheid.

In other words, the gospel functions to bring about a transformation of a very fundamental sort in the way people in a specific situation interpret the Christian tradition, in how they understand themselves, and in how they situate themselves in their world as a whole. An old mode of self-understanding and self-orientation must die, and a new one must come to birth. In a sense, the gospel is intended to function for the totality of perception and self-understanding in the same way that a specific metaphor functions within a limited range of perception and self-understanding. Just as a metaphor juxtaposes two disparate images in order to disclose a deeper way of perceiving and understanding in a specific domain of awareness, so, too, the root images implicit in the gospel, when juxtaposed both against the Christian tradition and against a specific situation, disclose a new and all-encompassing mode of self-understanding and orientation.

Obviously much more could be said, but this is at least a probing beginning. If this approach is to be borne out and established by exegesis, however, it means that we must always be asking four basic questions in our reading of the New Testament:

1. What is the specific situation that prompts this writing, to which it is addressed?
2. How are the Jewish and Christian traditions being brought to bear in this specific situation?
3. What are the literary dynamics and contexts that lend shape to this coalescence of tradition and situation?
4. What are the hermeneutical assumptions that guide this bringing together of tradition and situation in literary form, and how are these assumptions related to basic Christian affirmations about the center of the gospel?

The more these questions dominate our reading of Scripture, the more our reading of the Bible will bring us back, again and again, to the center of the New Testament and of Christian faith.

The Gospel and Plurality in Interpretation

This understanding of the New Testament documents helps to shed light on the act of interpretation itself. Every act of interpreting the Bible is, in essence, a repetition of the kind of activity that the biblical writers did themselves when they sat down to write. As interpreters, we find ourselves in a specific context, and we struggle to find meaning within that context. We, too, wrestle with the traditions that give us our identity. Those traditions include the New Testament documents, but also many other traditions: our confessions, hymnody, rituals, forms of worship, and the like. Like the New Testament documents, we also seek to express an interpretation through the use of language, requiring us to make use of various literary forms as well.

However, if we are to interpret the New Testament properly, there must also be another factor in our interpretation, namely, an awareness of the dynamics and structure of the gospel. The more clearly we are aware of how the gospel functions hermeneutically within the New Testament documents, the more clearly we will be able to embody that same framework within our own interpretations of the Bible.

An understanding of the hermeneutical function of the gospel is critical to a healthy approach to plurality and coherence in biblical interpretation. Interpretation will always emerge out of different contexts. There will always be different traditions brought to bear by various interpreters. There will always be differing literary forms in which interpretation expresses itself. In the midst of all this diversity, however, the gospel functions as a framework that lends a sense of coherence and commonality. Such a framework does not suppress our diversity but enables us to discover our common humanity, and our shared religious perspectives, in the midst of our diversity.

A Hermeneutic for the Missionary Encounter of the Gospel and Our Culture: Speaking the Truth in Love

In conclusion, we return to the questions with which we began: What does it mean to be called to speak of the gospel as truth in a world that declares that religious speech can never be true, but only "true-for-you"? How can we speak the truth from a posture of loving servanthood in a world that interprets truth claims as political strategies masking inevitable self-interests? And finally, what is the role of Scripture in leading us to the truth and in teaching us how to speak it?

With respect to the question of truth, a missional hermeneutic does not deny that in an important sense, the gospel is always "true-for-you." There is always a concrete, particular, local sense in which the gospel addresses us. A missional hermeneutic recognizes and affirms the postmodern emphasis on the contingent, local, and particular. However, the truth of the gospel can never be simply relegated to the sphere of the private, local, and particular. The gospel's claim to offer good news of cosmic significance is a constant prod to Christians to reach beyond their own enclaves to address and challenge their culture and world with the gracious and hopeful claim that Jesus is Lord.

At the same time, that truth of the gospel is always spoken in love. It is never spoken for the purpose of political advancement or domination, but in the hope that each person and community might discover its true voice and its own distinctive experience of full humanity as the gospel takes root in fresh and diverse ways. *How* we speak is as important to our missional vocation as *what* we speak. In this sense, Newbigin is quite right to speak of the local congregation as the hermeneutic of the gospel.[10] It is ultimately through our lives, in all of their contingency and local particularity, that the universal claims of the gospel will find a credible voice in the midst of our fragmented and suspicious world. It is only when the announcement "Jesus is Lord" is spoken by someone who takes the posture of a servant that it can ever be heard as the gospel. It is only through the convergence of word and deed that the fragmented suspicion of our postmodern world will be able to discover a new Way that is also Truth and Life.

10. Newbigin, *Gospel in a Pluralist Society,* 222ff.

Vernacular Theology

WILLIAM A. DYRNESS

Many working theologians have come to share a common dis-ease, namely, that academic theology is in a period of crisis and needs to be reinvigorated with a closer interaction with lay theological reflection. In an interesting way our role as theologians is in the process of being reversed. Rather than being the teachers, we must become learners again, or perhaps in a new way. Whether that will be possible in any deep and sustained way remains to be seen.

As a way into our discussion, I want to reflect on the feelings I had when I finished my book *Learning about Theology from the Third World.*[1] Here was an attempt to see what we might have to learn by listening to conversations going on in different settings. But I had the strange feeling that I was hearing only a very selective group of voices, and those that I "heard" often, I suspected, resonated with things I already knew. This is because they mostly came in languages I already understood. I knew I was not learning as much as I needed to learn, though I was not at all sure what I could do about it.

Part of this had to do with my limitations as a scholar and the vast amount of material one would need to master to really hear all that was there. But the real problem, I suspected, lay not with personal limitations, painful as these are, so much as with the tradition of theological reflection I was trained in. To take but one example: My understanding of theology

1. *Learning about Theology from the Third World* (Grand Rapids: Zondervan, 1990).

was limited almost entirely to reading and explicating published texts, and to helping my students write commentaries on these texts (i.e., produce more texts). What about the vast majority of Christian communities for whom texts are marginal and whose reflection is largely informal — what kind of "theological reflection" do people like this do?

About this time my daughter, who is an architectural student, introduced me to the concept of vernacular architecture, which is a technical term for buildings that are designed (and often built) by the people who will use the space. This has led to a vigorous movement called advocacy planning. According to Roger Hart, "Advocacy planning means speaking for those who will actually use the buildings, instead of doing research about them for those who hold the power. . . . It means helping people in a community do their own planning."[2] The implications of this notion for ministry in the body of Christ are profound and potentially revolutionary. Obviously one does not need a theological education to see the parallels; indeed, it is more accurate to say that theological education as it is currently carried on seems designed to hide rather than uncover these analogies.

Here it occurred to me that the participant-observer methods of the anthropologist are the most important skills that theologians who wish to do "advocacy theology" need to develop. In other words, they need to become ethnologists. As I began to collect texts of people's conversion experiences or narratives of their Christian lives, I began to notice the subtle and implicit ways that their faith made its impact on their lived world. The five studies that I have published I see as the merest beginning of reflection on this process, a study that is very much like the excellent work of Dwight Hopkins and George Cummings in *Cut Loose Your Stammering Tongue.*[3] I think they are among the few that understand the significance of this kind of work for the future study of theology. They show the need not only of focusing attention on peoples previously ignored but also of using methods not previously allowed in the theological academy.

In order to take this discussion further, I would like to make some general historical comments and then develop the implications of these for

2. As quoted by Daniel Goleman, "Architects Rediscover the Best City Planners: Citizens," *The New York Times,* June 2, 1992, B5 and B9.

3. William A. Dyrness, *Invitation to Cross Cultural Theology: Case Studies in Vernacular Theologies* (Grand Rapids: Zondervan, 1992); Dwight Hopkins and George Cummings, eds., *Cut Loose Your Stammering Tongue: Black Theology in the Slave Narratives* (Maryknoll, NY: Orbis Books, 1991).

our theological methodology. For I believe it is in new methods that we have the most potential for advance as well as for confusion. I say "general" historical comments because we are too immersed in what is happening to have any clear historical perspective on it. The best we can do is to see how we have come to the views taking shape around us. I have two reasons for taking this tack. One is that we need some sense of the context of what we are doing if this is going to make any sense to our students and colleagues. But the other, some would say more important, reason is that in case we decide we are lost, we need to know how to get back to the main road and start over again.

In making these observations, I would like to focus on two discoveries that have suggested the need for new ways of conceiving theology. The first is the growing realization of the role that the community plays in theological reflection. We might call this an *encounter with the people.* In many ways the Reformation and its notion of the priesthood of all believers gave this idea its initial importance. But in theological education older hierarchical and clerical structures were slow in dying out. The missionaries of the colonial period certainly did not encourage the people to take any active role in what we call today "doing theology." Even in the early part of our century when Social Gospel theologians like Walter Rauschenbusch began to shape their theology in the context of the teeming urban environment, they were still doing theology for the people rather than encouraging any serious indigenous theologizing.

It was really not until the 1960s that the people began to play a larger role in theological reflection. Partly this had to do with Vatican II and its emphasis on the church as the pilgrim people of God. Whether the Catholic leadership really wanted to take lay thinking seriously at that point may be debated. But theologians in Latin America soon followed up this suggestion. They sought to encourage the vast multitudes on the continent who had been victims of a violent and oppressive history to take an active role in reading and interpreting the Scriptures. Small groups of people gathered throughout Latin America and read and talked about the Bible, spawning a major movement of renewal that we associate with CEBs, or base communities. There they were said to be conscienticized, a word that was first associated with the important work of Paulo Freire in *The Pedagogy of the Oppressed.*[4] Behind these developments lies the Marxist model of class conflict.

4. Paulo Freire, *The Pedagogy of the Oppressed* (New York: Herder, 1970).

But this notion of conscientization appeared problematic to some observers. There was some suspicion that the people were not given complete freedom to "speak their mind." To the level of whose conscience were the people to be awakened? Is the purpose to empower people to think their own thoughts or to stimulate them to play a part in the revolutionary drama that Marx believes is the essence of all history?

The "powers that be" had their own reasons to feel it was dangerous to allow people to think for themselves. Indeed, in many cases people did have the courage to confront injustice in the name of their faith — doing the truth rather than simply talking about it. But theologians in some ways began having their own second thoughts. For however strong our views on the importance of broad participation in the work of theological reflection, people in fact do not always do the kind of theology that we think they should. In fact, they often stubbornly refuse to rise to our best wisdom of what they ought to be saying. Anyone who spends any time really listening to the people harbors no illusions about the clarity and creativity of the theology that often emerges. But neither can one escape surprise and even astonishment with what one does see. What is clear is that a theology *for* the people and a theology *by* the people are very different animals. Liberation theologians themselves have come to recognize this difference, suggesting that the movement in the 1980s entered a mature period, one Juan Luis Segundo has called the pastoral phase. This has arguably brought liberation theology to its most creative period. People like Pablo Richard have refined the method of genuinely listening to the people to see what their concerns are and making these the object of theological reflection.

Meanwhile an implicit critique of liberation theology has been registered by the phenomenal growth of the Pentecostal churches throughout Latin America. If ever there was a movement of and by the people, this is it. Often exceeding the ability even of its own leaders to fathom or control, these groups exhibit the vitality and enthusiasm of a genuinely indigenous movement, even as they eschew the political commitments dear to the heart of liberation theologians. Though we cannot be sure what this all means for theology in Latin America, we can safely say that the role the people will play in all this will be hard to predict and certainly impossible to control. What then does it mean to take them seriously?

Such considerations lead quite naturally to my second historical comment. Along with an encounter with the people, contemporary theology has had to reckon with the *growing importance of practice in theology.* Robert

Wuthnow has studied how the developing ideas relate to their social context in his book *Communities of Discourse*. He points out that classic sociological theory has been dominated by two streams of thought. On the one hand, some argue that change takes place by development and cooperation; on the other hand, some see change occurring through the shifting conflict of class relations. His book is a sustained argument that both are inadequate insofar as they emphasize the more subjective factors of culture — beliefs and attitudes. If discussions remain at this level, that is, at the level of ordinary theological discourse, "the processes by which cultural change actually becomes institutionalized remain unilluminated." Rather, Wuthnow insists, ideology must be explained at the level of cultural artifacts and actual discourse. For the activity of actual people in "specific historic conjuncture . . . makes cultural innovation possible."[5]

Wuthnow's observations are consistent with what appears to be a major trend in anthropological theory since the early 1980s. During this period the emphasis on symbolic or structural fields was replaced by attention to the practice of actors in particular contexts. Sherry Ortner, for example, has commented that Pierre Bourdieu was important in all this, but so were Herbert Blumer and Raymond Williams.[6] Previously the emphasis has been on systems and patterns, often existing as ideal frameworks in the minds of the people. Now, by contrast, the focus is on the actors who develop and understand the patterns.

The shift from an emphasis on patterns and structures to the agents who inhabit these worlds is very important for our purposes. Previously, under the influence of Marxist conceptions of ideology, social scientists often used terms like "mystification" or "alienation" to describe the ideas that people carried around in their heads. Such terms implied that the observer "knew better" than the people what the Real World was like. This is now seen to be wrong, or at least unhelpful. Observers are increasingly

5. Robert Wuthnow, *Communities of Discourse: Ideology and Social Structure in the Reformation, the Enlightenment, and European Socialism* (Cambridge: Harvard University Press, 1989), 532, 535.

6. Sherry B. Ortner, "Theory in Anthropology since the Sixties," *Comparative Studies in Society and History* 26 (1984): 144–45; see Pierre Bourdieu, *Outline of a Theory of Practice* (Cambridge: Cambridge University Press, 1977); Herbert Blumer, *Symbolic Interactionism: Perspective and Method* (Berkeley: University of California Press, 1969); Raymond Williams, *Culture and Society: 1780-1950* (Harmondsworth, Middlesex: Penguin, 1969).

impressed by the way the people "make do" with the bits and pieces of their world (cf. French *bricoler,* "to putter; do odds and ends"). Clifford Geertz has, for example, modified his own emphasis on symbolic systems by proposing more recently a "strain theory" of culture change. This suggests that people act so as to remove the strains that their experience manifests.

The idea of "making do" is elaborated in a most interesting book by Michel de Certeau, *The Practice of Everyday Life.*[7] Rather than lamenting the passive pleasures of the people seated in front of the TV, he notes, we should learn what they are making of their consumption. Nor is this necessarily apolitical, for, as he notes, this "use" can prove subversive; people are often able to develop tactics that make something of their oppression. The key is to discover what they are making of their world, what they intend to do, in the tinkering they do with the bits and pieces that they find lying around. Such descriptions, Ortner notes, often highlight what she calls "social asymmetry."

It is easy to see that these developments in sociology are correlated with those we looked at earlier. A focus on the people naturally suggests that we learn from all they do and believe, not simply from what they say about things. While theologians, especially those we like to hang out with, have demonstrated a distinct preference for the conflict model of society, if what we are saying is true, this needs to be complemented by other models of social change. Indeed, Wuthnow suggests that both streams are deficient in the same way — both are reductionist in that they attend too exclusively to the level of attitudes and beliefs. This needs to be supplemented by closer attention to the environmental resources (population, wages, capital) and what people make of these resources in the free spaces they are able to discover in their public world.

While the precise meaning of all this remains uncertain, its general contour seems to be clear enough to make some suggestions on the implications for doing theology. Some believe that the entire theological enterprise needs to be reconstructed from the ground up. While I am not one who would argue along these lines (certainly not within hearing of my faculty), I have no doubt that the impact of these developments will be great on all of theology; indeed, it is not hard to show that this has already happened. But what this encounter with the people suggests is that we intentionally articulate a new dimension of theology, one that we might

7. Michel de Certeau, *The Practice of Everyday Life,* trans. Steven F. Rendall (Berkeley: University of California Press, 1984).

call vernacular or descriptive theology. Here I briefly describe three aspects to this possible area of investigation.

The first and most obvious characteristic is that vernacular theology, as we have learned from Robert Schreiter, is a communal rather than an individual project.[8] The theology that will be the focus of this approach will be that of a people group who identify themselves as a distinct group with a special history and culture. This is not to say that individuals will not think or develop their ideas, even perhaps in writing. But the "texts" that we will be interested in will not be those that articulate new and original thoughts so much as those that give powerful expression to the deeply held beliefs of the community. When I was a missionary in the Philippines, I led small-group Bible studies in which I sought to encourage the people to study the Bible "inductively," as we used to say. Invariably someone in the group emerged as the spokesperson. From time to time this person would say something like, "So the Bible seems to say this, but that strikes us as unusual because in our culture. . . ." When she or he had finished, the others in the group would nod their heads, agreeing that that was so. The striking autobiography of Nobel laureate Rigoberta Menchu in one way is an excruciatingly personal account of a single Indian in Guatemala.[9] But it is at the same time a penetrating portrait of the life of her people. I believe in fact that intensely personal statements like this of Christians, recorded and handed down (as oral stories have been for generations), could function as "theological texts" in ways that would facilitate response and interaction on many levels.

Second, the communal nature of vernacular theology implies that what is transmitted or disseminated will not necessarily be limited to theological statements in the narrow sense but will include the practices and rituals that embody the underlying faith. The theological framework will be thought of as embodied and expressed in beliefs and attitudes, as well as practices, as all of these grow out of the specific social and cultural situation. Another way of putting this point is to say that theology emerges in the field created by beliefs, practices, and context. Narratives of faith naturally include all three of these dimensions. And creativity in

8. Robert J. Scheiter, *Constructing Local Theologies* (Maryknoll, NY: Orbis, 1985), especially "Community as Theologian," 16.

9. Rigoberta Menchu, *I, Rigoberta Menchu: An Indian Woman in Guatemala* (New York: Verso, 1985).

theological reflection would develop within the dynamic set up by this field.[10]

From the missionary literature some of us have learned to speak in terms of the worldview of a people; others of us, having sat longer with the social scientists, prefer to speak of the underlying ideology or interests that a people's faith expresses. In both cases we have been encouraged to see theology in its relations to the larger social and intellectual world. In the 1970s Clifford Geertz's notion of religion as a symbolic system showed that this reality was more complex than we had imagined. He defined religion as "a system of symbols that establish powerful, pervasive and long-lasting moods and motivations in people by formulating conceptions of a general order of existence and clothing those conceptions with such an aura of factuality that the moods and motivations seem uniquely realistic" (i.e., constitutive of our social order).[11] Incidentally, his description of the way this system could be a *model of* society as well as a *model for* is potentially helpful in showing how these realities come to function normatively in the community's life. That is, descriptive theology notes how a growing framework *reflects* values of the community around, but theological reflection will sooner or later note how the gospel becomes a dynamic that *shapes* the setting into which it comes.

Robert Wuthnow has now taken these ideas of ideology and symbolic systems further in his important study of what he calls communities of discourse.[12] There he asks how it is that ideology is allowed to develop within a social and historical setting. What are the social spaces in which various frameworks develop? This is an extremely important move because the Marxist heritage in the social sciences has taught us to be suspicious of unifying mythologies. According to Gregory Baum, "The secular left has been so suspicious of myth and symbols that its social theories offer only critiques of ideology and hardly ever spell out a set of symbols and values that ought to pervade the imagination of those who struggle."[13] Vernacular

10. See comments by Howard Gardner on aesthetics in his *To Open Minds: Chinese Clues to the Dilemma of Contemporary Education* (New York: Basic Books, 1989), 116.

11. Clifford Geertz, *The Interpretation of Cultures* (New York: Basic Books, 1973), 90.

12. Wuthnow, *Communities of Discourse.*

13. Gregory Baum, "Community and Identity," *Expanding the View,* ed. M. Ellis and O. Marduro (Maryknoll, NY: Orbis Books, 1990), 105.

theology allows us to redefine a people's collective identity with stories that bind them together in a common life.

Third, all we are saying implies that this way of elaborating a theological framework will work to see things from the point of view of the community. The vernacular character of this theology indicates that we want to know what the "consumer" of this framework means by it. This attitude will help us discover ways in which Scripture or parts of the tradition are used in ways suited to the people's needs. One of the advances that has been made in the study of comparative religions is what is sometimes called the phenomenological approach. That is, rather than seeing, say, popular Catholicism in Guatemala as a mixture of Christianity and pre-Christian tradition (a characterization that leads to the barren and futile attempt to separate out lines of influence), we should understand the resulting reality as a religious system in its own right and with its own integrity. A faith framework, after all, is seen as a whole by the people who live in it. Similarly in various settings in which Christianity has emerged, there are widely different attitudes and practices that spring from a common tradition and Scripture. In addition to any normative judgment that might be appropriate, and certainly well before any such judgment, it is required that we give each expression of faith its own voice and allow it to appear as a unique local theology.

Since I feel so strongly about these issues, I am in a poor position to judge the value of the project. But as a conclusion, and perhaps as a stimulus to discussion, I would like to make two comments. First, I have argued elsewhere that all that Christians do as they seek to follow the Christ they have come to know and love is a kind of hermeneutical exercise.[14] In other words, while they may not give any thought to how various texts of Scripture (and sundry writings of major theologians) are to be interpreted, many of them would gladly give their lives for their understanding of Christ's presence in their lives. As theologians of the church, our first responsibility is to encourage and develop this understanding. We are called, in other words, not to judge their attempt to think and live Christianly, but to encourage it and, often surprisingly, to learn from it. For if we are honest, this will usually not differ very much from our own stammering attempts to say (and do) what we believe. A way in which this might enliven academic

14. Dyrness, *Invitation to Cross Cultural Theology*, chap. 7 ("Cross Cultural Dialogue as Theological Conversation").

research might be mentioned briefly. Jonathan Z. Smith, after an illuminating discussion of various notions of God, concluded by noting that what we most need at this point is a study of what he calls comparative exegesis.[15] That is, we need to study not so much the conclusions of the traditions but the "strategies through which the exegete seeks to interpret and translate his received tradition to his contemporaries." Seeing these communities of faith in terms of the strategies of exegesis they employ might provide an important tool for advancing our common hermeneutical task.

My second comment is stimulated by a recent exciting discovery in educational theory. This is the development of the theory of multiple intelligences by Howard Gardner and his colleagues at Harvard. In his wonderfully autobiographical account of these discoveries, he argues that our educational system is structured to appeal to only two of the seven intelligences that have been isolated: the linguistic and the mathematical/scientific. Those gifted in other areas — music, spatial, kinesthetic-bodily, interpersonal, and intrapersonal — are often thought to have learning disabilities and are treated accordingly. The truth is that often they may well be highly skilled in one of these unexplored areas of intelligence. At one point he asks, What would it be like if we treated children not as little scientists but as artists-in-training or as connoisseurs-in-training?[16] Theological education, so it seems to me, suffers from a similar atrophied sense of what is important. A parallel question suggests itself: What if we treated Christians not as repositories of Christian truths but as little Christs-in-training?

15. Jonathan Z. Smith, *Imagining Religion: From Babylon to Jonestown* (Chicago: University of Chicago Press, 1982), 52.

16. Gardner, *To Open Minds*, 68.

"Translatability" in the Missional Approach of Lamin Sanneh

PAUL RUSS SATARI

Two major themes of Lamin Sanneh's *Translating the Message* lie at the heart of his work.[1] These are the translatability of Christianity (which deals primarily with the interaction of gospel and culture) and the relationship between mission and colonialism. These intertwining themes together converge to deal with the creative use of the notion of translatability in Christian mission. Translatability establishes a model that promises wide-ranging implications that will no doubt shed light on the efforts of doing theology. This is particularly so in a context like my own — Singapore — which bears a certain degree of parallelism with the African experience. It is also important for pluralist North America.

The Concept of Translatability: Gospel and Culture

For our discussion of Sanneh's notion of translatability, we should first observe that Sanneh appears to use the terms "translation," "mission translation," "mission by translation," "mission as translation," and "translatability" interchangeably. On closer examination, however, these words reveal a cluster of terms revolving around one concept, that is, the idea of translation.

1. Lamin Sanneh, *Translating the Message: The Missionary Impact on Culture* (Maryknoll, NY: Orbis Books, 1989). Page numbers in the text refer to this work.

"Translation" generally refers to the act of textual or biblical translation from one language to another (e.g., pp. 31, 36, 37, 42), whereas "mission as translation," "mission by translation," and "mission translation" speak of the process of mission whereby the receptor culture is made the true and final locus of the proclamation of the gospel (e.g., pp. 29, 30, 31, 82, 157). In this respect, "translation" is a general term that refers to an act of translating or communicating a message; thus it is more general and basic than "mission as translation," "mission by translation," or "mission translation." "Translatability," which is the term used most frequently by Sanneh (at least thirty-eight times in *Translating the Message;* e.g., on pp. 3, 4, 50, 69), refers to a process in which the Christian message expresses "its universal ethos, its capacity to enter into each cultural idiom fully and seriously enough to commence a challenging and enduring dialogue" (64). That is to say, the notion of translatability as a religious theme describes the mutual interaction of the gospel and culture. To refer to the actual action of translatability in Christian mission, Sanneh often uses the terms "mission as translation," "mission by translation," or "mission translation" (29, 30).

By the term "translatability" Sanneh indicates a process by which the intimate and intricate contact between the message and the message-receptor culture is so great that faith and culture may become closely identified (64). This interaction involves wide-ranging implications for both parties (196).[2] Thus, such a specific process of translation is neither simply nor naively a matter of substituting words from one language for words from another. It is not a translation of mere words but rather the translation of concepts and meanings in such a way that the message takes up residence in a new or different meaning structure. Translatability, as Sanneh describes it, is "the genius of the religion, the ability [of the Christian religion] to adopt each culture as its natural destination and as a necessity of its life" (69).

The dynamic translation of language (through translatability) therefore implies that the message is now being understood afresh in a new cultural structure. Thus translatability is other than "the deceptive power of seeking to translate in a straightforward manner, and then finding that more (or less) is being said by the translator than was intended" (5). As an authentic form of translation, translatability "provides meaningful access for self-realization and cultural fulfillment" (64). It renders Christianity compatible with all cultures.

2. See also Lamin Sanneh, "Christian Missions and the Western Guilt Complex," *Christian Century,* April 8, 1987, pp. 330–34.

Unlike mission by diffusion, a process by which a missionary culture is made to be "the inseparable carrier of the message," mission by translation focuses on the recipient culture (29, 31). It is receptor oriented. This means that when Christianity "arrives" in a new cultural setting, it does so "without the presumption of cultural rejection" (29). Translatability thus reveals that the Christian message or the gospel is not anticulture; it does not seek to destroy culture. By being receptor oriented, translatability also shows that the message may take different cultural forms as it leaves the previous culture and interacts with and enters into another living culture. This is possible because translatability implies a commitment to a contextual engagement and thus represents a radical shift from mission by diffusion.

Another important aspect of translatability, one theological in nature, is that it assumes and confirms divine preparation that precedes the missionary's arrival (158–59).[3] The divine preparation for the gospel in all cultures is a theological necessity for translating it into those cultures; from thence the Holy Spirit will work through the translation, reenacting the experience of Pentecost with the empowering of all peoples to understand God's message in their own respective languages. While this speaks of translation as the cutting edge of mission, it may nevertheless suggest that translatability introduces the aspect of "Christian vulnerability to secular influences and to the potential threat of polytheism" (37), or foreign religious influence. It is a "threat," since it could lead to the absorption of, or to being absorbed into, prevailing intellectual and cultural elements that may not be consistent with the gospel (47). Possibly, like the primitive Christians, present-day counterparts find themselves at risk of embracing wholeheartedly and uncritically the dominant culture of their age.

In spite of its vulnerability to this threat, translatability as a cutting edge of mission essentially promotes a critical attitude toward all forms of human arrangements. This attitude is best described, in Sanneh's own phrase, as the "critical function of mission" (32–33); basically, that means a critical interaction or an enduring dialogue between gospel and culture. That is why Sanneh, rather than retreating to cultural diffusion, is quick to lay his theological foundation for mission across diverse cultures, thus averting the so-called threat.

3. See also Lamin Sanneh, *West African Christianity: The Religious Impact* (Maryknoll, NY: Orbis Books, 1983), 166.

> If, as early Christians believed, God is the universal source of life and truth, then they were obliged to pursue that conviction across cultures. This conviction also implies that no culture would be fundamentally alien to the source of life and truth, and therefore mission was an assurance of the continuity with that source. But mission also represented the challenge and promise of a new beginning in faith and obedience. (P. 37)

Since no culture is essentially foreign to God, it becomes imperative for Christian mission through the translatability of Christianity to realize the bridge of mutual interaction between the gospel and culture. It is this enduring dialogue between the gospel and culture that has the capacity to link the relationship of the source of life and truth with all human cultures, thus leading to a contextual understanding and experience of faith in God. In posing both "challenge and promise," mission by translation allows and promotes the possibility of cultural change; as Sanneh puts it, "mission is also a catalyst for change" (32).

The "challenge and promise" may be clarified through the "critical function of mission," which takes place whenever there is translation and interpretation. It is worth repeating the idea that the "critical function of mission" speaks of the critical or "inherent tension" (32) between the gospel and culture. The following extract succinctly gives the tenor of Sanneh's argument:

> When we have rightly and properly distinguished between the desire to do mission in other cultures and the designs of cultural imperialism, we are still left with a substantial body of material in the Gospels that justifies adopting a profoundly critical stance toward culture by putting interests of God above those of the culture. . . . Paul tells a section of his audience that through Christ they are more than conquerors (Rom. 8:37). Yet, almost in the same breath, he catalogues the ceaseless contention that he as a Christian must continually experience in his relations with worldly authorities (1 Cor. 4:9-13; 2 Cor. 4:7-12). Christians are in the world, but not of it (1 Cor. 7:29-31). The claims of God, however successfully mediated and embodied in earthly structures, must ultimately be seen to be in radical tension with them, for obedience to God overthrows other rival sovereignties that make their home in culture. . . . Any absolutizing force is an offense to the gospel, and a cultural tradition that arrogates to itself a deifying prerogative can expect nothing but implacable opposition from Christians. (Pp. 32–33)

The notion that translatability calls for the critical interaction between the gospel and culture is also implied in the notion of "reform and prophetic witness" (40).[4] The following extract helps clarify the idea of what exactly is involved in the critical dialogue between the gospel and culture, that is, when a genuine translation takes place:

> Reform in itself does not reject the world, nor does it reject human instrumentality in setting the world aright. It distinguishes between the earthly kingdom and its heavenly counterpart and carries this distinction further into a matter of human means and the divine end for which they might be employed but not exchanged. . . . [The apostle Paul] challenges the church to say what distinguishes it from the world. In bringing the prophetic word to bear on the church, the apostle has also diagnosed the ills of the world, suggesting that Christian faithfulness is a prescription for the health of the wider society. . . . Prophetic action in history is the active participation of believers in the sign and promise of God rather than surrender to the world as the ultimate destiny. (Pp. 40–41)

The qualities identified are caution, openness, participation, versatility, adaptability, positive critical attitude, affirmation, and hope in God without rejecting the world and its human structures. Fundamentally, the "reform and prophetic witness" theme suggests a view of culture that is both serious and critical.

The process of translatability thus does not seek to annihilate culture. However, its intrinsic commitment to contextual engagement requires a critical attitude toward culture as suggested by Sanneh's reference to "the challenge and promise," "the enduring dialogue between the gospel and culture," "the critical function of mission," and "the reform and prophetic witness." Elsewhere, Sanneh explicitly states that "the gospel seems to find its natural congruence within the cultural stream while at the same time encountering there its most serious obstacles." From the perspective of translatability, Sanneh thus views culture as "both a natural ally as well as a natural foe of the gospel" (4–5). It is in this sense, too, that culture is given a penultimate status (16).

4. Sanneh speaks of three basic models of religious organization, each reflecting a different attitude toward mission: quarantine, syncretist, and reform and prophetic witness. Of the three models, according to Sanneh, the third one is in the end a "permanent feature of the Christian enterprise" (39–40).

Throughout his *Translating the Message,* Sanneh maintains the central notion that "translatability became the characteristic mode of Christian expansion through history" (214). Unlike Islam, Christianity has no single revealed language, a feature that may be traced to the Pentecost experience, when the believers testified to God in their mother tongues (Acts 2:6-11). But there were also times when mission by translation was ignored and neglected. After the translation into Greek, Sanneh argues, Christians of the second and third centuries adopted the norms of Hellenistic culture so much that they turned their backs on the principle that justified "the Gentile breakthrough" — the historical event that establishes the principle of translatability. Consequently, "the timeless *logos* of the Greeks was substituted for the historical Jesus" (214–15).

What is indicated here is that translatability as a genuine translation requires an ongoing critical interaction between the gospel and culture. In a more explicit call for an ongoing process of genuine translation, Sanneh argues that "since the gospel comes alive from translation, the slowing down of this process involves a certain fossilization of the message, although in brief moments of prophetic wakefulness the reform impulse might nudge an inured church forward" (36). If there is even a little slowing down of authentic translation, mission will tend to exist as cultural diffusion. It is clear that translatability requires a continuous critical engagement of the gospel and culture.

The Effects of Translatability: Relativization and Revitalization

The two most significant effects of the notion of mission translation are the relativization and revitalization of human cultures. These two forces combine to justify cultural pluralism, and together they form Sanneh's central thesis.

> Christianity, from its origins, identified itself with the need to translate out of the Aramaic and Hebrew, and from that position came to exert a dual force in its historical development. One was the resolve to relativize its Judaistic root, with the consequence that it promoted significant aspects of those roots. The other was to destigmatize the Gentile culture and adopt that culture as a natural extension of the life of the new religion. This action to destigmatize complemented the other action to

relativize. Thus it was that the two subjects, Judaic and Gentile, became closely intertwined in the Christian dispensation, both crucial to the formative image of the new religion. (P. 1)

Elsewhere, Sanneh underscores a similar thesis.[5] Unquestionably, at the core of the translatability of Christianity lie complex but important issues relating to the interaction of the gospel and culture. It is important to reiterate the point that translatability distinguishes itself as an authentic translation and not "the deceptive power of seeking to translate in a straightforward manner" (5). On the one hand, translatability denies that any culture is profane by asserting the legitimacy of instrumentalizing the gospel in the vernacular, that is, in ordinary, everyday life and speech. On the other, it relativizes culture by rejecting the notion that there is only one normative expression of the Christian message. Translatability, historically speaking, was profoundly expressed in the original tension between the cultural absolutization in the Jerusalem church and the Gentile breakthrough at Antioch. This tension serves as a powerful deterrent to the tendency of absolutizing any particular culture or form of Christianity. To Sanneh this tension has continued to characterize the church throughout the centuries.

Affirming the complementary forces of relativization and revitalization leads to cultural pluralism. Cultural pluralism is implied in the recognition that all human languages and cultures have an equal role to play in the expression of the gospel, a fact that emerges decisively out of the Jewish-Gentile tension, which to Sanneh indicates the "incipient radical pluralism of Pauline thought" (47). The idea that all human cultures are equal also suggests that all cultures, no matter how acclaimed, are open to the need for change. As Sanneh argues, "A divinized culture precludes the possibility of change."[6] Putting it differently, the possibility of cultural change is not eliminated through mission by translation. On the contrary, mission by translation promotes and enhances cultural change, since essential to this kind of mission is the notion that no culture is to be divinized or absolutized. In other words, human culture is to be relativized and revitalized, resulting in cultural pluralism.

5. See esp. his "Christian Missions and the Western Guilt Complex," 330–34; "Pluralism and Christian Commitment," *Theology Today* 45, no. 1 (1988): 21–33; and "Gospel and Culture: Ramifying Effects of Scriptural Translation," in *Bible Translation and the Spread of the Church*, ed. Philip C. Stine (Leiden: E. J. Brill, 1990), 1–23.

6. Sanneh, "Christian Missions and the Western Guilt Complex," 332.

In many traditional societies, the understanding of religious language has had the tendency to be confined, if not exclusively reserved, to just a small elite of professional religionists, as in the case of Arabic in Islam (211–13) and Pali in Buddhism. The Christian approach to translatability, however, contends that the greatest and most profound religious truths are compatible with the everyday and ordinary language of the people. This approach finds any absolutizing force of human culture an offense to the gospel and introduces the groundwork for the cultivation of vernacular literature and literacy. It results in the relativization and revitalization of culture, which to Sanneh is the radical form of pluralism (9).

Sanneh traces the development of pluralism from the disciples' understanding of the life and work of Jesus, the one who brought them fresh perspectives about God's impartial dealing with all human cultures (4–48).[7] The epochal and decisive departure for this new understanding was the Pentecost experience (Acts 2:6-11), which was reinforced by the Gentile breakthrough (Acts 10:34-35; cf. Acts 9:15; Gal. 1:16).

The Pentecost experience of "many tongues" manifests "God's acceptance of all cultures within the scheme of salvation, reinforcing the position that Jews and Gentiles were equal before God" (46). This experience powerfully echoes the blessing of cultural diversity portrayed in Genesis 10.[8] Since Pentecost, translatability has shown itself to be characteristic of Christian expansion through history. That is why Sanneh asserts throughout *Translating the Message*, both directly and by implication, that translatability is both an essential and an inevitable characteristic of Christianity. Though it had initial difficulties and struggles, the early church came to recognize and affirm the obligation of spreading its faith. And a "revolutionary" way of spreading it is through the translatability of the religion across cultural frontiers (214). As was pointed out earlier, the fact that Christianity acknowledges no single language to be a revealed one, unlike Islam's unique

7. See also Sanneh, "Pluralism and Christian Commitment," 24–27; idem, "Gospel and Culture," 13–16.

8. It is outside the scope of our study to deal with the various interpretations of Gen. 10 ("The Table of Nations"). This chapter is considered the most significant text in the Bible for understanding a theology of cultural plurality. For a discussion of the various interpretations of this text, see George R. Hunsberger, "The Missionary Significance of the Biblical Doctrine of Election as a Foundation for a Theology of Cultural Plurality in the Missiology of J. E. Lesslie Newbigin" (Ph.D. diss., Princeton Theological Seminary, 1987), 437–57.

recognition of Arabic, augments the testimony to its pluralistic nature (214–15).

This radical shift toward cultural pluralism is further exemplified in the Gentile breakthrough, which declares that God's act of redemption breaks powerfully into the Gentile world (25).

> The pluralism was rooted for Paul in the Gentile breakthrough, which in turn justified cultural pluralism. Paul's view is that God does not absolutize any culture, and he believed that all cultures have cast upon them the breath of God's favour, thus cleansing them all of all stigma of inferiority and untouchability. These two ideas constitute what we may regard as the incipient radical pluralism of Pauline thought. (P. 26)

Led by the apostle Paul, the Gentile breakthrough was to become a paradigm and a justification for the church's missionary expansion across cultural frontiers (46) and the formulation of a radical pluralism in that God does not absolutize any human culture but rather invigorates and relativizes them all. The invigoration or revitalization of cultures is realized when they become instruments of the sacred message. To the apostle, the effect of the gospel is to destigmatize every culture and the people associated with it; Jews, Gentiles, barbarians, and provincials all now stand on an equal footing under God's salvific plan (14). Thus Paul is far from attempting either to absolutize or to obliterate any culture. What he desires is rather the retention of cultural distinction or particularity of "Jew as Jew and Gentile as Gentile, though challenging both Jews and Gentiles to find in Jesus Christ their true affirmation" (47; see Gal. 3:28-29 and 1 Cor. 9:19-23). And so, contrary to the popular notion of Christianity being a notorious cultural iconoclast, Sanneh points to the apostle's mission to illustrate that Christianity is in essence a pluralistic religion. In this sense the gospel insists on a plural cultural frontier for its spread and looks alarmingly at the idea of an imperviously closed culture as the exclusive conveyance for God's truth (30).

The Modern Context of Translatability: Mission and Colonialism

In the modern era, the gospel's insistence on a plural cultural frontier for its expansion eventually collided with the claims of cultural absolutism and cultural imperialism, causing the dissipation of Western colonialism, on the one hand, and the upsurge of national aspirations, on the other (120).[9] This took place in the nineteenth and early twentieth century, when colonialism was confronted with growing nationalism. But it was mission by translation that provided nationalism with the resources for victory (106, 120). Christianity therefore stood in opposition to colonialism (105).

This point is exemplified by Sanneh's reassessment of the life and contributions of David Livingstone.

> First, Livingstone identified the vernacular Bible as the real engine of mission; numerical gains are now subordinate to the main task of missions. Second, missionaries are the real indigenizers, and the worth of their labors is to be assessed in the light of their capacity to preserve the older African heritage. Third, educated Africans are singularly unsuited to this indigenizing task, for which they would have to be specifically fitted through a fundamental appreciation of their own culture. Fourth, "civilization" is not a necessary qualification for salvation though it might be a remedy of sin. Fifth, primitive Africa as Livingstone saw it was at no special disadvantage vis-à-vis the West with regard to God's "plan of salvation"; on the contrary, those parts of Africa untouched by Europe constituted, in his view, a more auspicious bridge for the gospel than the Europeanized parts. Sixth, time was against the perpetuation of European dependencies in Africa, whether political or ecclesiastical. (P. 114)

Clearly, it is such a mission that shows itself as a cutting edge for societal change. It is a powerful force that has the capacity to confront the powers that be in the rising nationalism as well, restricting it from any divinization or cultural absolutism. The consequence is not cultural exclusiveness but indigenous revitalization and cultural relativization.[10]

9. See also Lamin Sanneh, "Christian Mission in the Pluralistic Milieu: The African Experience," *International Review of Mission* 74 (1985): 199–211.

10. "Most of the great missionary pioneers of the nineteenth and twentieth centuries became uncompromising advocates of the cross-cultural acclimatization of Christianity, a step that required them to concede the centrality of indigenous sources and materials. Men and women who were never distinguished as explicit champions of their own culture found the attractions of another irresistible, and as a consequence became promoters of the love and wisdom of other people. Examples abound in our age of missionaries who by dint of sheer application acquired the necessary equipment for penetrating and exploring the veins of truth and beauty to be found in other cultures. Whatever their motives, such missionaries were laying the foundations of indigenous revitalization to which the cause would be tied" (25).

Many scholars are agreed that the intertwining of mission and colonialism was not without complicity and complexity fraught with baffling ramifications.[11] So intricate was the entanglement of the two movements that not a few historians, including Christian writers, are inclined to hold the view that Christian mission has been the epitome of Western imperialism (see pp. 4, 88, 112).[12] Sanneh is aware of the arrogance of some missionaries and notes the charges that mission sought to penetrate indigenous cultures as a preparation for colonial collaborators, which was deemed a necessary measure to suppress native resistance.[13] In response, he argues against the hypothesis that "mission was the surrogate of Western colonialism and . . . together the two movements combined to destroy indigenous cultures" (4).

To unravel the knotty interlocking histories of mission and colonialism, Sanneh points out the fundamental differences between the two (112). First, with respect to their diverging goals, "mission aimed at the establishment of the national churches and envisaged a future without itself, whereas colonialism saw only the perpetuation of dependency" (116). This goal was particularly true of the mid-nineteenth-century mission. For example, Henry Venn, secretary of the Church Missionary Society, spoke as early as 1854 of the local church being "self-governing, self-supporting and self-propagating" (the so-called three-self movement) and of the "euthanasia of mission."[14] This was also the time when many mission boards were independent of ecclesiastical structures and their missionaries often envisaged the growth of local churches independent of the sending church. At any rate, it was here that mission set itself apart from the "dependency posture" that colonialism astutely sought to achieve from the indigenous.

11. David Bosch presents an outline history of the intricate intermingling of mission and colonialism. So complex was the issue that mission and colonialism had come to be known, though erroneously, as comprising the "three C's" of colonialism — namely, Christianity, commerce, and civilization (*Transforming Mission: Paradigm Shifts in Theology of Mission* [Maryknoll, NY: Orbis Books, 1991], 226–30, 302–10).

12. See also Sanneh, "Gospel and Culture," 4–5.

13. Lamin Sanneh, "Mission and the Modern Imperative — Retrospect and Prospect: Charting a Course," in *Earthen Vessels*, ed. J. A. Carpenter and W. Shenk (Grand Rapids: Eerdmans, 1990), 303.

14. See Bosch, *Transforming Mission*, 307; Aylward Shorter, *Toward a Theology of Inculturation* (Maryknoll, NY: Orbis Books, 1992), 173.

Second, unlike colonialism, mission as translation demonstrates its authentic commitment to the context in which the translation process takes place (192). Sanneh writes,

> Historically translatability has brought the church into line with vernacular aspirations. There is little doubt about vernacular sentiments stiffening the anticolonial resolve while at the same time deepening the roots of the church. . . . The African church movement of the nineteenth century [for example] was the result of the vernacular forces mobilized by the juggernaut of translation. (P. 120)

This perspective drives a wedge between mission and colonialism. Here, too, Sanneh finds support for his thesis that the ultimate effect of vernacular adoption is the adoption of the indigenous cultural criteria for the message. Furthermore, he asserts that the "seeds of the divergence between mission and colonialism were sown with the translation enterprise" (111–12). To Sanneh, history has shown that vernacularization has laid the foundation for cultural and linguistic pluralism, negating the colonial assumption about the intrinsic inadequacy of local cultures[15] or the "civilizing theory"[16] of Western expansionism (111; cf. p. 108).

The encounter between the missionary and the culture that is the receptor of the message made possible the prolific use of various vernaculars

15. Sanneh, "Mission and the Modern Imperative," 301–16.

16. The theory asserts the justification or legitimation of colonial rule on the assumptions of European supremacy and superiority vis-à-vis non-European indigenous inadequacy and inferiority. It also serves as a safe but pseudo-ventilation for the modern Western guilt complex over the victimization of peoples outside the Euro-American world (Sanneh, "Christian Missions and the Western Guilt Complex," 330–34; cf. Bosch, *Transforming Mission,* 3). David Bosch describes this theory as the "benevolent colonialism of the West," where it was widely accepted, even by those colonized, as a proof of God's providential act in history; Apartheid in South Africa and the Nationalistic Socialism in Germany *(Deutsche Wende)* were for many decades acclaimed wholeheartedly by many Christians as signs of God's intervention and favor (ibid., 429). Bernard Lonergan would argue that such bigotry is caused by the "classicist notion" of culture, which insists there is really only one culture, and it is both universal and permanent (*Method in Theology* [Toronto: University of Toronto Press, 1990], xi, 123–24). This classicist attitude or normative view of culture, according to Aylward Shorter, has for the most part inhabited the church's missionary activity and was easily transposed into a form of Christendom's political domination (*Toward a Theology of Inculturation* [Maryknoll, NY: Orbis Books, 1992], 20).

in missionary communication, the translation of sacred texts, and the production of grammars, dictionaries, and countless other types of literature (167). All these combined to weaken the foundation of colonialism while simultaneously strengthening local indigeneity (216). Describing it as a "vernacular paradigm" (4), Sanneh shows translatability as the underpinning for the development of ethnic and national consciousness, a sense of self-dignity, a relativity of cultures, and eventually the spawning of successful worldwide movements of nationalism that consequently brought about massive decolonization — an implicit but powerful affirmation of cultural pluralism. Most important, a people's mother tongue has been reckoned to be a worthy cultural medium for the transmission of the gospel.

> Mission translation was instrumental in the emergence of indigenous resistance to colonialism. Local Christians acquired from the vernacular translations confidence in the indigenous cause. While the colonial system represented a worldwide economic and military order, mission represented vindication for the vernacular. Local Christians apprehended the significance of world events, and as such the purposes of God, through [the] familiar medium of mother tongues, with the subject peoples able to respond to colonial events in light of vernacular self-understanding. (P. 123)

Vernacularization pushes Western culture to the periphery, at least from the perspective of the new context (161–62).[17] With the vernacularization (based on the translatability of the Christian message into the cultural criteria of the indigenous context) comes the decoupling of mission from Westernization. Thus, translatability is an instrument to consolidate and perpetuate the vernaculars in a way that it is able to dislodge the gospel message from the Western cultural assumptions. Consequently, it both negates all forms of cultural imperialism while at the same time enhancing cultural pluralism.

Summary

Sanneh distinguishes between mission and colonialism in terms of their objectives and their effects on indigenous cultures. Insofar as these two

17. See also Sanneh, *West African Christianity,* 166.

terms are concerned, we concur that what was activated in and by Christian mission was not colonial interest but rather the gospel's recognition of the particularity of the multiplicity of vernacular entities — a recognition that colonialism often found threatening and intimidating.

The vernacularization of the Christian message presents the necessary groundwork for dislodging the Christian religion from the persistence of Western cultural assumptions. Through genuine translation of the Christian message, missionaries came to view both the receptor culture and their own in a fresh perspective — in the same way that the Jewish-Gentile encounter revealed to Paul the basis of radical pluralism in which the terms of a people's self-understanding of God are not to become the absolute or exclusive norms for others.

There are two major consequences when the Christian message expresses its capacity to enter into an indigenous cultural idiom fully and seriously. First, that particular culture is de-absolutized (or relativized) altogether. It is also ennobled because the tendency to idolize itself has been stripped off. Second, that particular culture is destigmatized (or revitalized), as its people now stand under God's plan of salvation. It is invigorated in such a way that it becomes an instrument for the expression of the sacred message. It is only when the action to de-absolutize (relativize) is complemented with the action to destigmatize (revitalize) that translatability may be said to be taking place actively.

The relativization-revitalization effects upon cultures guide our attention back to Sanneh's description of translatability as a genuine translation with its intrinsic dialogic interaction between the gospel and culture. As a vital "force" in Christian mission,[18] translatability (and all it represents and implies) activates the dynamic relationship of the gospel and culture, producing the reenactment of the Jewish-Gentile encounter — a radical pluralism, at the core of which is the principle that no culture is the exclusive norm of truth and that, likewise, no culture is inherently unclean in the sight of God.

18. Sanneh, "Gospel and Culture," 8; cf. idem, *Translating the Message,* 216.

PART IV

DEFINING THE CHURCH

The church has a dual nature. On the one hand, it is an institution created by God that represents the presence and authority of God's reign on earth. On the other hand, it is an organization constructed by humans for the purpose of living out a corporate life and mission. This dual nature of the church always means that the visible church lives in tension within any particular historical period and cultural context. The location of its existence is "in" the world, while the distinctiveness of its life is to be not "of" the world. This dual aspect to the church's life means that it is to exhibit the reality of God's redemption in anticipation of the final consummation of history and formation of the new heavens and new earth.

For the church, the reality of heaven has already begun through the outpouring and indwelling of the Holy Spirit. Jesus' proclamation of the presence of the kingdom of God, the dynamic and redemptive reign of God within human history, means that the church must define itself in terms of the kingdom. The life and mission of the church are to be defined by participation in the mission of the triune God in all of creation. The church, then, while existing within a cultural context, also has a responsibility toward that context. It is responsible to live out the reality of the redeemed life within its culture. It is also responsible to bring the power of this redemption to bear on its culture as it seeks to welcome into the life of God those who live currently apart from such faith and allegiance.

This missiological challenge to participate in the mission of the triune God requires the church to critique carefully its cultural context, as discussed in Part II of this book. This challenge also means that the church, as noted in Part III, must test its life with standards called forth by the gospel. This last section of the book provides perspective on how the church is to understand its life and witness in light of these challenges.

George Hunsberger's essay "Acquiring the Posture of a Missionary Church" points out the importance of framing our understanding of the church and its mission within the context of "our" particular culture. This is done by seeing the purpose of the church in terms of its responsibility to experience the missionary encounter of the gospel with its own particular culture and to experience it right within its own life. This is a difficult thing for many churches in North America to do, since we have become accustomed to assume that our symbiotic relationship with this culture expresses biblical commitments. It will require the church to be engaged in a continuous inner dialogue between the culture that shapes its perspectives and preferences and the gospel that calls for a fundamental repatterning to those things. That will be the necessary prerequisite for carrying on an outer dialogue of witness among others outside the church who are also shaped by that culture.

Insight into how congregations can acquire such a missionary posture is provided by John R. "Pete" Hendrick in his essay "Congregations with Missions vs. Missionary Congregations." He provides a helpful review of some of the formative thinking that has led to our fresh understanding of congregations in terms of their essential missionary nature. He explains the difference between being "missionary congregations" and being merely "congregations that have missions." He develops six features that characterize genuinely missionary congregations.

It is clear that the churches of North America are passing through a fundamental period of transition. E. Dixon Junkin, in his essay "Up from the Grassroots: The Church in Transition," explores ways in which congregations will need to engage this new mission context. He notes the bankruptcy of the historic pattern of strategies devised and commended "from above," a pattern employed by most denominations in their effort to revitalize and reinvent congregations. In contrast to this, he proposes a model "from below" as a more effective approach for the rebirthing of the church in the new situation. He describes six intentional disciplines for the kind of "communities of prayer, discernment, and action" that he says will be necessary as the ground from which the future forms of the church will arise.

If we are to see the emergence of missionary congregations, it will require new kinds of missionary pastors who will lead them in that direction. This is the topic addressed by Alan J. Roxburgh in his essay "Pastoral Role in the Missionary Congregation." He provides a helpful summary of the concept of the pastoral role and some of the recent movements that have shaped it, such as therapeutic approaches, technical rationality, and privatization. All of these are rooted within modernity's assumptions of individualism, instrumental rationality, and self-interest groups. Drawing on Victor Turner's notion of liminality as characterizing the shift we are presently experiencing, Roxburgh offers an alternative conception of the role of the missionary pastor. Such a pastor must shape his or her work around the three roles of apostle, poet, and prophet.

George Hunsberger follows a line of analysis similar to Roxburgh's in his critique of the church's response to the culture of modernity in "Sizing Up the Shape of the Church." He notes that the church needs to shift its sense of its social function if it is going to participate in the mission of God in the world. In Reformation thinking, the church came to be viewed primarily as "a place where certain things happen." In the culture of modernity, the church has grown accustomed to functioning as "a vendor of religious services and goods." If, however, we are going to rethink the church in terms of its missionary nature, the church must come to see itself as "a body of people sent on a mission." Hunsberger offers suggestions for making the transition from vendor-shaped churches to mission-shaped churches.

The matter of rethinking our understanding of the church is further explored by Inagrace T. Dietterich in her essay "A Particular People: Toward a Faithful and Effective Ecclesiology." Her concern is to find a balance between being a faithful body of God's people who are sent on a mission and maintaining perspective on what it means to be effective in this work. Along with Roxburgh and Hunsberger, she notes the impact that Enlightenment assumptions have had on our thinking about the church. What is needed is the development of God's people as a particular people who live within what she labels an ecclesial paradigm. This paradigm roots our thinking about the church in theological understandings that identify that God's particular people are to be a people of praise who live with a kingdom understanding of the work of God in the world.

These essays combine to provide the reader with a helpful introduction to the challenge of rethinking the church. If the churches of North America are to engage in a missionary encounter with our culture, it will require that they understand their identity and purpose in light of the mission of the triune God in the world. This will lead them into expressing their missionary nature as a distinct people sent on a mission to bear witness to Christ among the people of our cultural context.

Acquiring the Posture of a Missionary Church

GEORGE R. HUNSBERGER

It strikes me as a curious, even bothersome, way of putting things to speak of the church's "mission to Western culture." The preposition "to" is the sticking point. If we are really talking here about culture (i.e. a commonly shared web of understandings of the way things are and a shared map for how life should be lived), then what would it mean to speak of a mission "to" a culture, whether our own or any other? Mission certainly reaches in the direction of the people of a society, those who together share a particular culture and both shape it and are shaped by it. And it has to do with addressing the powers that operate in the social arrangements and institutions of a particular people. But it does not so much direct itself "to" the shared culture of those people and powers as it happens always "within" that cultural framework. It addresses people and powers in such a way that it calls forth in them an encounter between the cultural understandings and values by which they live and the challenging impact of the gospel's announcements about the reign of God.

Once we understand this, we are warned against conceiving the "gospel and culture" encounter as one that is merely a matter of audience analysis, as though it has only to do with sizing up the thoughts, feelings, and values of the target population to make our communication of the gospel sharper. Nor is it adequate to conceive of the encounter as merely our effort to bring about changes in the personal and collective ethical choices of the society so that they more closely approximate the ideals we see to be those of the gospel. These responses, taken alone, too easily miss the more fundamental encounter that must engage the church if it is to be missionary, an encounter of the gospel with the inner, assumed logic by which the society orders its perceptions and actions. These responses represent the persistence of an "us to them" mission mentality too easily operating out of a conquering spirit or an urge to control, vestiges of a former Christendom that no longer lives anywhere but in the impulses of our minds. We were used to being a (or, the) key force for shaping the social order. But whatever limited role we may earlier have had to influence and inspire the American social order has fast evaporated. With the shift in the church's social location in recent decades and the radical change in core values going on in the culture itself, we are faced with a crisis of mission identity and direction.

These factors have stimulated the emergence of the Gospel and Our Culture Network (GOCN) in North America. The GOCN is a collaborative effort that focuses on three things: (1) a cultural and social analysis of our North American setting; (2) theological reflection on the question, What is the gospel that addresses us in our setting? and (3) the renewal of the church and its missional identity in our setting. Several hundred people from a wide spectrum of denominations and ministry vocations are working together in this network because of a commonly held belief that there is an integral relationship between these three — cultural analysis, theological reflection, and congregational mission — and that responses to the current pressures felt at any one point cannot be adequately engaged apart from the others. Those in the network do not pretend that they are the only ones addressing these issues. In fact, they are keenly aware that the ferment in each of the three areas is considerable and rapidly expanding. What makes this movement significant is the fact that it is drawn together by the central conviction that the current challenge and ferment is by its nature missiological and must be addressed as such.

What exactly does it mean to say that this set of issues is missiological in its essence? At the outset, a preliminary clue may be found in one particular critique of the Gospel and Our Culture movement as it has manifested itself not only in North America but in other Western societies. A major program of study involving missiologists from a wide range of Western nations is being headed by Wilbert Shenk under the title "A Missiology for Western Culture." In reaction to that phrase there has come the challenge that it is inappropriate to call the Gospel and Western Culture project "missionary" precisely because it is focused on our own Western culture. This is because it is said to lack the one quality considered to be essential for defining what it means to be missiological: that it must be cross-cultural. For this critic, mission takes place in the crossing of cultural frontiers. Therefore, unless we are talking about moving across ethnic boundaries, mission in our inner cities, or something of the sort, we ought not to call the Gospel and Western Culture project missiological.

Undoubtedly, there is some fear here that, in the words of Stephen Neill's famous dictum, "If everything is mission, then nothing is mission." Or it may be feared that mission, the church's "sentness," will be lost in the church's self-absorbed attention to its own circumstances and the introspective retooling of its inner mechanisms. Such fears are healthy and warranted. But the required quality of being cross-cultural is precisely why our whole culture-theology-church agenda *is* missiological. By treating the full range of the current ferment as missiological, we are attempting to reinvest the North American church's identity and character with this cross-cultural quality, a dynamic that becomes emphatically present when we are engaged in the "missionary encounter of the Gospel with our own Western culture" (as Lesslie Newbigin is in the habit of putting it).[1]

In other words, in this approach we are simply treating mission in our own cultural circumstances in the same way we treat the encounter in other places. There we enter as cross-cultural missionaries, and we naturally see the situation as a missional engagement. We also invite the fledgling churches that form in such places to encounter their own culture and to embody the gospel within it in such a way that its challenging relevance is felt. This we take to be their proper missional response. Surely, we assume, it is immediately their mission to do this!

We are only saying that now, for us who are in the place from which so many cross-cultural missionaries emanate, our most fundamental missional calling is to live the same way in our own culture that we counsel others to live in theirs. This we cannot do unless we are seriously attentive to the character of our culture, receptive to the shaping force of the gospel, and willing to bear our missional identity as a gospel-shaped community.

1. Lesslie Newbigin, *Foolishness to the Greeks: The Gospel and Western Culture* (Grand Rapids: Eerdmans, 1986). See also two other books by Newbigin: *The Gospel in a Pluralist Society* (Grand Rapids: Eerdmans, 1989) and *Truth to Tell: The Gospel as Public Truth* (Grand Rapids: Eerdmans, 1991).

To state this point even more directly, being missionary and being a "sent" community — a "body of people sent on a mission"[2] — is not first about the church's outward-moving actions, whether actions to attempt to convert or actions to try to make a difference, whether actions close at hand or actions at a distance. It is first about how the church goes about those actions and the character of its own life in the process. This character develops not when a church — or its representative — leaves its geographic location. Rather, it happens when a church takes leave of cultural loyalties alien to the gospel. This step can and must lead to movement outward. But it must be the prior disposition if geographic leaving is to be genuinely missionary.

In other words, being missionary is about conversion as a way of life for the church, a way of life that shapes its movement to convert and its actions to make a difference. Our current movements to convert and make a difference generally do not arise from such a way of life. They are too much marked by a failure to recognize as intrinsic to our faith a fundamental departure (over against comfortable accommodations to the culture) and a sacrificial immersion (over against sectarian withdrawals from the society). As Donald Posterski has put it, we have ironically done what is seemingly impossible. We have inverted the dictum of Jesus: we are *of* the world but not *in* it. We have become "both captured and intimidated by the culture."[3] In our minds and hearts we have not sufficiently departed to the loyalties of the gospel, and with our hands and feet we have not become deeply enough immersed on behalf of the gospel.

The fundamental question before us in the churches of North America is this: Where is the church in the gospel and culture encounter? This question lies implicit in the phrase by which the movement mentioned earlier labels itself, a phrase borrowed from its companion British movement: "The Gospel and Our Culture." The power of the slogan lies in the little word "our" tucked in so innocently. At first blush it seems merely to designate which culture is being considered. That is, "it is not an Asian culture or an African one that is in view. This time around, it is the one we Americans and Europeans inhabit." But the word is much more significant

2. This phrase was used by David J. Bosch in lectures given at Western Theological Seminary in April 1991. The notion is fully developed as part of the "emerging ecumenical missionary paradigm" in his *Transforming Mission: Paradigm Shifts in Theology of Mission* (Maryknoll, NY: Orbis Books, 1991), 368–89.

3. Donald C. Posterski, *Reinventing Evangelism: New Strategies for Presenting Christ in Today's World* (Downers Grove, IL: InterVarsity Press, 1989), 28.

than that. Its presence alters the mental furniture by expanding what we all too easily take to be a two-poled conversation (between the gospel and the culture) and forcing us to reckon with a third pole (the church). By doing that, the word brings to light and challenges a host of assumptions that ride with the two-poled version.

In the rich literature of missionary anthropology, we have grown accustomed to bipolar ways of putting the issue, and these undoubtedly push us to a shorthand way of talking about the current challenge as simply a "gospel and culture" agenda. H. Richard Niebuhr's watershed volume *Christ and Culture* set the pace for this. Sam Moffett, following Kenneth Scott Latourette, has tended to put it, "Christianity and Culture." Marvin Mayers follows suit in the title of his book *Christianity Confronts Culture.* Moffett and Mayers signal more explicitly what we and Niebuhr were really thinking all along. We somewhat automatically identified ourselves, those who are part of the Christian movement, as the "Christ" pole in the encounter. "Christ and culture" is taken to be about how we have related ourselves to the culture. More directly, the title of Louis Luzbetak's standard work, now revised, put the issue in terms of *The Church and Cultures.* In this title we have it more pointed still: the issue, as we tend to see it, is how the church relates to any and all cultures.[4]

Even in formulations that point in a slightly different direction, a similar identification of the church with the gospel pole tends to remain. The Willowbank Report shaped at the Lausanne movement's landmark Willowbank Consultation in the late 1970s used the rubric "Gospel and Culture."[5] The significance of that formulation was not directly articulated. It seems to

4. H. Richard Niebuhr, *Christ and Culture* (New York: Harper & Row, 1951); Sam Moffett, "Christianity and Culture" (a course taught at Princeton Theological Seminary during the 1980s); Marvin K. Mayers, *Christianity Confronts Culture: A Strategy for Cross-Cultural Evangelism* (Grand Rapids: Zondervan, 1974); Louis J. Luzbetak, SVD, *The Church and Cultures: New Perspectives in Missionary Anthropology* (Maryknoll, NY: Orbis Books, 1988). One of Luzbetak's important contributions is his underscoring the point that not only do we have multiple possible forms of relationship to culture, but we actually relate to multiple cultures. The world of cultural plurality beyond Western civilization remained outside Niebuhr's purview.

5. The Willowbank Report, along with papers presented at the consultation, appears in John R. W. Stott and Robert Coote, eds., *Down to Earth: Studies in Christianity and Culture* (Grand Rapids: Eerdmans, 1980). It is interesting to note the way the ambiguity and identification of the church and the gospel is represented in the easy shift from the name of the consultation ("Gospel and Culture") to the subtitle of the compendium ("Christianity and Culture").

help us move the discussion beyond church-centered assumptions to focus on the message from God. This is more emphatic still in Charles Kraft's reformulation of Niebuhr's categories. He compares various notions of the relationship between "God and Culture."[6] This is a more deliberate attempt to clarify the point that the issue lies beyond ourselves in the way that God, or God's message of good news, interacts with cultures.

But it is not so easy, even in such a formulation, to distance ourselves from identifying with that side of the equation (as may be evidenced even in the title of the book, in which Kraft poses his alternative, *Christianity in Culture*). Our role as the messengers, the missionaries, will immediately draw us back into the picture as the ones who sit comfortably on the gospel/God side of things over against culture.

Increasingly, the bipolar way of speaking has given way to a sense that there are really three interacting poles: the gospel of God, the culture of a human society, and the community of Christian believers within that society. This triangular perspective is the model used by Robert Schreiter in his *Constructing Local Theologies* and Lesslie Newbigin in *The Open Secret.* Peter Schineller reflects a similar perspective in his book *A Handbook of Inculturation.* He describes the pastoral circle (a hermeneutical circle) as incorporating three poles: the situation, the Christian message, and the pastoral agent or minister. While it describes the dynamics involving a person facilitating inculturation, his model could as well describe the church's missiological role. Similar also is the way Carlos Mesters, in *Defenseless Flower,* describes the way the Base Ecclesial Communities read the Scriptures. He offers a three-cornered hermeneutical model of pretext (the life situation of the community), text (its historical-literary meaning), and context (the church's faith, what they "come with" to the text).[7]

The presence of the word "our" in the "Gospel and Our Culture" slogan indicates the same sort of tripolar conception, doing so in a way that underscores two important reasons why we cannot simply assume that we ourselves represent the gospel pole. First, our way of understanding God

6. Charles H. Kraft, *Christianity in Culture: A Study in Dynamic Biblical Theologizing in Cross-Cultural Perspective* (Maryknoll, NY: Orbis Books, 1979), 103–15.

7. Robert J. Schreiter, *Constructing Local Theologies* (Maryknoll, NY: Orbis Books, 1985); Lesslie Newbigin, *The Open Secret: Sketches for a Missionary Theology* (Grand Rapids: Eerdmans, 1978); Peter Schineller, SJ, *A Handbook of Inculturation* (New York: Paulist Press, 1990), 61–73; Carlos Mesters, *Defenseless Flower: A New Reading of the Bible* (Maryknoll, NY: Orbis Books, 1989), 106–11.

and putting the gospel can never be equated with the God who engages us and the message God addresses to us and the whole of the world. Our grasp and experience are necessarily partial; they are historically and culturally framed. We dare not treat this "gospel and culture" thing as though we fit easily on the gospel side of it. Second, we dare not assume that we sit at some comfortable critical distance from the culture part of the equation, that we somehow are placed over against it. We are never that distinct from our culture. We are participants in it. We are shaped by it, and it pervades our entire framework of meanings and motivations. It shapes in a particular way our capacities to hear and grasp and decide about the gospel that is coming to us from God, and it colors the form of all our responses to it. It is "our" culture we are speaking about, as much as it is "our" God who encounters us within it.

We are forced by these circumstances to admit that we are not here dealing with a single dialogue (between the gospel of God and a human culture). Rather, such a gospel-culture encounter always unfolds for the Christian community as a twofold dialogue: the dialogue the gospel of God has with us within our culture, and the dialogue we then have representing the gospel among the others who share our culture.

We are the community that has been grasped by the claim of the gospel, a gospel that has inaugurated us into a process of conversion by which the assumptions and dispositions we share with our culture are being challenged and repatterned along the lines of new loyalties, visions, and commitments. But we are aware that we are neither so fully and finally shaped by that gospel nor so unique and distinct from the culture as we may have wanted to think. We have observed this truth more vividly of late as we sense the malaise in our churches born of the loss of our former identity as the moral support and spiritual caregiver to the social order. We notice in our loss how little identity remains, how little we have been shaped by the force of the gospel. And we see how accommodated we have become to the contours of our culture. We have assumed too quickly that our initial conversions were enough. What we have failed to recognize is that the gospel's first-order encounter with the culture we inhabit will be with us, not with any "them" out there. The encounter is first of all an inner dialogue before it is an outer one; it is what Newbigin calls the internal dialogue, which must be antecedent to the external one that lies at the center of a missionary's proper concern. This is what is missing in George Hunter's admirable depiction of the "secular people" he is trying to help us know how to reach. The description he gives portrays our characteristics in the churches as well as it does those of our companions in the culture. The "reaching" must take place inside of us as much as out there beyond us.[8]

If, on the one hand, this inner dialogue with the gospel engages us, so the nature of our dialogue with those of the culture is reformed on the other hand. We do not approach the dialogue as though we are somehow outside the culture with its commitments and ways of seeing things. We join the dialogue as companions in it. But we recognize that the gospel has captured us for God in ways that have brought about fundamental shifts in our culture-given assumptions. And we know that this capturing has launched us on a lifelong path of being encountered by that gospel repeatedly regarding shifts still in progress. We expect the hardness and delight of encountering these shifts along the way. Our place, then, in the outer dialogue, born as it is out of this inner dialogue, is to be the God-given "hermeneutic of the gospel" (to use another of Newbigin's phrases).[9] We are present with them to provide the lens, the language by which they may grasp and be grasped by the same gospel. As a community, we display in numerous ways the announcement that God's reign has come through Jesus Christ. In particular, we make visible the way such an alternate view of things as is indicated by that announcement becomes a lived transformation within our culture's terms. We show that life can indeed be lived out this way in our culture's context. This dialogue with others in the culture, as the gospel's hermeneutic, moves us beyond truncated missiologies for "reaching" the culture. Mission cannot mean merely espousing a message or commending a belief. Nor can it mean merely claiming a divergent view. Rather, it must come to form as a lived, daily-life experience that demonstrates the healing the gospel produces.

These two dialogues are interlinked. Without the gospel's inner dialogue with the culture inside of us, there will not be an adequate hermeneutic for the broader society. Apart from the hermeneutical character of our dialogue with that society, we abstract the gospel and block its incarnation in us before watchful eyes. The church — the "us" of the "our culture" phrase — stands at the same time at both places in the gospel-culture encounter: we stand on the culture side, encountered there by the

8. See Newbigin, *Gospel in a Pluralist Society,* 56; George G. Hunter, III, *How to Reach Secular People* (Nashville: Abingdon Press, 1992), 41–54.

9. Newbigin, *Gospel in a Pluralist Society,* 222–33.

gospel that engages the culture first as an inner dialogue with us; and we stand on the gospel side, called to be the visible hermeneutic of the gospel in and for its encounter with the culture. To put it another way, in the gospel's encounter with our culture, the gospel meets the culture first here in us, in an inner dialogue; similarly, the culture meets the gospel first here in us who are the hermeneutical lens through which it may be perceived.

In this posture — standing on both the culture side and gospel side — we must seek our identity. The crisis of the moment pushes us to it. The missionary essence of the church assumes it of us. The Spirit of Christ leads us there.

Congregations with Missions vs. Missionary Congregations

JOHN R. "PETE" HENDRICK

At the heart of our vision for the Presbyterian Church (U.S.A.) are its congregations scattered from rural Alabama to Sitka, Alaska; from suburban Pittsburgh to south-central Los Angeles; from the bustling city of San Juan, Puerto Rico, to the small towns of the upper peninsula of Michigan; congregations with a handful of members, and those where thousands gather.

We envision our congregations, singly and together, being so aroused and nurtured by the gospel of Jesus Christ that ministries are vibrant and inviting. We imagine our congregations, individually and in league with governing bodies and ecumenical partners, equipping us to share our gifts, to bear the burdens of others, and to be nurtured in return. Such congregations will be drawn irresistibly into ministries reflecting the love and justice of Jesus, with immediate neighborhoods and the whole of the world as arenas in which the gospel is to be proclaimed and lived.

Report of the General Assembly Council
to the 205th General Assembly, 1993

This new set of Presbyterian affirmations is heady and hopeful language. But how can such rhetoric be turned into reality? How can congregations (Presbyterian or otherwise), "aroused and nurtured by the Gospel of Jesus Christ," proclaim, live, and reflect "the love and justice of Jesus," locally and globally? In this essay I suggest that there are two ways we might try to fulfill this call to mission. The first is derived from the congregational critiques and studies of the last several decades. The second approach, less well understood, is suggested by the writings of Lesslie Newbigin and the thinking of the Gospel and Our Culture Network here in the United States. It is the latter that we must further explore and develop in our present circumstances.

Congregations with Missions

The years after the Second World War and well into the 1950s were often viewed as halcyon days by the mainline denominations in the United States. Mission was understood as ingathering, church extension, and, to a lesser degree, similar work overseas. For those who had eyes to see, however — and more and more did — there was urban blight and rural poverty, religious and racial discrimination, the proliferation of nuclear weapons, and paranoia in regard to Communism. For the most part, however, the energies of Protestant congregations were absorbed in maintaining their new buildings, their new members, and their new denominational programs.

Toward the end of the 1950s, mainline thinking in North America moved from a period of virtually uncritical self-congratulation, except for prophetic voices here and there, into a decade or longer of critical self-flagellation. Protestant church leaders began to ask, Is the local church obsolete? Discussions were launched around such titles as *The Missionary Structure of the Congregation, The Comfortable Pew, The Suburban Captivity of the Churches,* and *The Noise of Solemn Assemblies.* The criticism was that congregations were insular, world-neglecting enclaves of religious comfort and compatibility, guilty of shutting their eyes and hearts to the great social, racial, and urban crises of the day. Sources of discontent with regard to congregations were both sociological and theological. Sociologically, congregations were seen to be isolated and estranged from the centers of work and leisure and from the centers of power where major decisions were being made on crucial ethical issues that shaped public life. Theologically, congregations were charged with forgetting God's mission, with ignoring the fact that God was at work in the world and that God loved the world, not just the church.

Others, influenced by the consistent displeasure being expressed in regard to congregations, nonetheless believed it possible to reshape them in order to make them more faithful for authentic mission in the world. Thus in 1969 Loren Mead organized Project Test Pattern, the forerunner of the Alban Institute. In the early 1970s McCormick Theological Seminary developed its geographically far-flung doctor of ministry program, utilizing organizational development for the purpose of congregational revitalization.

Another major effort to enable congregations to restructure themselves for mission was the church growth movement. This approach, which came to be associated with Fuller Seminary, was built around the leadership of Donald McGavran. Insights from anthropology, sociology, business management, marketing, as well as international missionary experience were utilized to assist congregations in the fulfillment of their evangelistic calling in their own sphere of ministry.

By the early 1980s, what we now refer to as congregational studies was beginning, underwritten by Lilly Endowment, Inc. Results of this research have been published in *Building Effective Ministry, Varieties of Religious Presence: Mission in Public Life,* and *Handbook for Congregational Studies,* among other volumes. Most recently, Carl Dudley, an active participant in the congregational studies enterprise, wrote *Basic Steps toward Community Ministry,* which summarizes much of what has been learned regarding congregations and mission. It is a report of research done with forty or more congregations that were given both consultation and funds to discover and carry out social ministry in their communities. Dudley provides a step-by-step approach to discovering congregational identity, a step-by-step approach to understanding social context in order to discover openings for mission, and a discussion of how to organize and mobilize to take advantage of opportunities for social ministry.

The outcome of these criticisms and fresh approaches to mission has been significant. Mainline congregations all over the United States have had what can only be described as an awakening of good works. In every community one finds congregations that tangibly love their neighborhoods. They provide social services, support the marginalized, and advocate change for the public good. At the same time, many evangelical congregations have become much more sensitive in regard to persons without the gospel. They have introduced vigorous programs of outreach, both local and global, designed not only to get people to make a decision for Christ but also to lead them to active discipleship within a particular expression of the body of Christ.

Perhaps the best description of what has happened in regard to mission in the lives of North American congregations is to be found in the typology developed by Roozen, McKinney, and Carroll in *Varieties of Religious Presence: Mission in Public Life.*[1] The four types are evangelistic, civic, activist, and sanctuary. The evangelistic orientation stresses personal witness to others, sharing one's faith with those outside the church. These congregations have a strong openness to the Holy Spirit and seek the conversion of persons to their understanding of the Christian faith. Congregations with a sanctuary orientation view themselves as a refuge from the world and as conservators of tradition and doctrine. Both the evangelistic and sanctuary orientations are generally accepting of existing social arrangements and are reluctant in regard to congregational involvement in social affairs.

Congregations with the civic orientation emphasize the importance of individual members making their own decisions on moral and social issues. They stress the importance of Christian citizenship and emphasize compassionate ministries of a social service type. Congregations with the activist orientation take a critical posture toward existing social structures. They encourage the involvement of members, ministers, and the congregation as a whole in social action and are open to confrontation, conflict, and sometimes civil disobedience. Civic and activist orientations share a concern for the welfare of all people. They believe in the education and involvement of members in public life and cooperate ecumenically with others in addressing human need and social concern. In summary, it may be said that the criticisms of the 1960s and the studies of the 1970s and 1980s have challenged many congregations that previously had a sanctuary orientation. As a consequence, we see increasing numbers of previously insular churches developing attitudes and actions that make it possible to categorize them now as either evangelistic, civic, or activist or some blend of these. What has developed over these past decades and what deserves praise and gratitude are the many congregations that intentionally develop

1. David A. Roozen, William McKinney, and Jackson Carroll, *Varieties of Religious Presence: Mission in Public Life* (New York: Pilgrim Press, 1984).

mission projects and programs to reach out into the world on behalf of the world.

Missionary Congregations

Today as we move toward the twenty-first century, however, a fresh way for congregations to think about mission is being suggested and explored. It is rooted in a perception of our Western context and scrutinizes not only surface realities (e.g., demographic data and intergroup relations) but also the cultural assumptions, values, and norms that underlie our common life. Such analyses go back more than half a century. According to Hendrik Kraemer, who wrote in the 1950s,

> It is only about twenty years ago that in Europe and Great Britain some leading people, mainly from the background of the Student Christian Movement and of missions, began to raise their voices about the "missionary situation" of the Church in Europe. They appealed to their fellow Christians to see realistically the fact that the Church in the so-called Christian countries finds itself practically living in a de-christianized, pagan, nihilistic world and to draw the consequences. (It is my conviction that this applies as well to the United States of America. . . .)[2]

The seismic shifts of the intervening decades have amplified for many the serious misgivings about our culture noted by Kraemer.

Missionary bishop and ecumenical statesman Lesslie Newbigin, who incidentally may have been related to the members of the Student Christian Movement referred to by Kraemer, has argued more convincingly than anyone else that Europe and America are now in a missionary situation. In *Foolishness to the Greeks: The Gospel and Western Culture* and his other writings, Newbigin calls for "a missionary encounter of the gospel with our own Western culture." He has written

> [Ours is not,] as we once imagined, a secular society. It is a pagan society, and its paganism, having been born out of the rejection of Christianity, is far more resistant to the gospel than the pre-Christian paganism with

2. Hendrik Kraemer, *The Communication of the Christian Faith* (Philadelphia: Westminster Press, 1956), 100–101.

> which cross-cultural missions have been familiar. Here, surely, is the most challenging missionary frontier of our time.[3]
>
> What kind of churchmanship will enable us so to preach the gospel that men and women are called to be disciples in the fullest sense. . . ? How, in particular, are we to do this, we who are sent not to one of the ancient world religions but to a society nourished in its deepest roots by a Christian tradition but governed in its explicit assumptions by a pagan ideology? And how can we be missionaries to this modern world, we who are ourselves part of this modern world?[4]

In response to Newbigin's challenge and in recognition of the fact that Western culture manifests itself in the United States and Canada in ways that differ from Europe, a North American Gospel and Our Culture Network has been established, coordinated by George Hunsberger. The network's purpose is:

1. To discern how the church in North America is called anew to receive and participate in the mission of the triune God, within a variety of cultural and social settings.
2. To clarify the nature of the interaction between gospel, culture, and church, which both shapes that mission and is shaped by it.
3. To discover models of the church in North America capable of sustaining an effective and faithful witness to the gospel, appropriate to various and current emerging contexts.

From the writings of Newbigin, Hunsberger, and other members of the Gospel and Our Culture Network and also from my own reflection, some implications for congregational life begin to emerge. Here for discussion and debate are some thoughts on the characteristics of missionary congregations.

1. *A missionary congregation will understand that it exists in a cross-cultural situation.* When North American missionaries live and work in India, it is clear to all that they are in a cross-cultural situation. A fundamental premise of Newbigin and the Gospel and Our Culture Network is that North American Christians well grounded in the biblical way of think-

3. Lesslie Newbigin, *Foolishness to the Greeks: The Gospel and Western Culture* (Grand Rapids: Eerdmans, 1986), 20.

4. *Ibid.*, 133.

ing and living will recognize the distinction and distance between themselves and the generally accepted assumptions, values, and norms of North American culture. Recently at a dinner I attended, a Presbyterian minister, engaged in conversation about the future of the church, made this point most graphically. He said, "Culture was once our ally. Church and culture were aligned. Now our culture has decided to live godlessly and is collectively secular. At best, the future church will represent little enclaves of Christian faith in a pagan environment." The beginning point for developing a missionary congregation will be that it understand itself to be living in a cultural situation that in many, if not most, ways is antithetical to the life, teachings, and gospel of Jesus.

2. *A missionary congregation will enter into dialogue with its context and culture.* God loves the world. The world, close at hand for every congregation, is its immediate social context and the web of culture by which it is knit together. In earlier times, missionaries from Western nations have been known to depreciate or snub the cherished ways of their host countries. Members of a missionary congregation, however, remembering God's care for all peoples and their ways, will approach their own context and culture with an open and teachable spirit. They will learn its "language," befriend its people, endeavor to understand its mores and traditions, and, where possible, make common cause on matters related to the good of all. This will be done despite the suspicion that they may be theologically worlds apart. The immediate area of the congregation will be studied to understand demographic trends, ethnic group relations, unjust systems and power arrangements, the situation of marginalized persons, and so forth. But a missionary congregation will go beyond the examination of these surface features of context and endeavor to understand the deep underlying features of the culture in which they and their neighbors are enmeshed; this, in fact, is one of the characteristics that distinguishes a "missionary congregation" from a "congregation with missions." Such serious and respectful attention to both context and culture provides the ground on which authentic mission can be built.

3. *A missionary congregation will provide opportunities for its members to reflect on culture from a biblical view.* The Bible will be made once again the normative guide for the faith and life of a missionary congregation. George Hunsberger, in an article entitled "The Changing Face of Ministry: Christian Leadership for the Twenty-First Century," goes into considerable detail about the way in which leaders of missionary congregations, given

our new understanding of the alienating effect of our culture, will have to become quite intentional about setting forth alternative world-and-life views compatible with Scripture.[5] John DeWit of Birmingham, England, has developed a study book in which he identifies and then leads his congregants in discussion of nine widely held cultural assumptions, including the following: only scientific knowledge is factual; the good life is characterized by possessions; there is no such thing as sin; and belief in God is no longer necessary. He provides a Christian reply to each of these assumptions. Another approach might be to give a specific cultural assumption to an adult group and then ask them to dig for their own biblical and theological resources in order to reach their own, thoughtful conclusions. An assumption is that members of missionary congregations will increasingly feel it necessary to give reasons grounded in Scripture for their decisions in regard to culture.

4. *A missionary congregation will pray for and seek its own transformation.* A missionary to India from the United States might quickly see the way in which caste thinking has intruded into church life. We for our part, however, find it difficult to understand the degree to which, for example, individualism and materialism shape the way business is done in North American congregations or the degree to which tolerance has crossed the line to become religious indifference. Immersion in our own culture virtually blinds us to the ways in which our congregations are shaped and pervaded by it. The gospel call to follow Jesus certainly means that we will make the decision to depart from at least some of our social and cultural loyalties. A missionary congregation understanding that it, too, partakes of the values, assumptions, and norms of culture will constantly seek to understand how it has accommodated uncritically to its surroundings, seek forgiveness where appropriate, and pray for freedom from cultural ways that enervate faithfulness.

5. George R. Hunsberger, "The Changing Face of Ministry: Christian Leadership for the Twenty-First Century," *Reformed Review* 44, no. 3 (1991): 224–45. The following articles by Hunsberger develop similar themes: "The Newbigin Gauntlet: Developing a Domestic Missiology for North America," *Missiology* 19, no. 4 (October 1991): 391–408, reprinted as the first chapter above; "Cutting the Christendom Knot," in *Christian Ethics in Ecumenical Context: Theology, Culture, and Politics in Dialogue,* eds. Shin Chiba, George R. Hunsberger, and Lester Edwin J. Ruiz (Grand Rapids: Eerdmans, 1995), 53-71; and "Acquiring the Posture of a Missionary Church," *Insights* (Fall 1993), reprinted on 289–97 above.

5. *A missionary congregation will accept the marginal position in which it finds itself.* The "most favored organization" status formerly given to mainline congregations is over or rapidly coming to an end in most communities. Polls tell us that clergy are not admired as previously, that churches are not as influential as before, and, perhaps worst of all, that a large majority of Americans anticipate making up their minds about what they will believe without benefit of a congregation. Missionary congregations overseas have long understood what it means to be peripheral to the mainstream of their national culture, but now congregations in North America may also expect to be treated by the public at large as just another religious sect. However, missionary congregations will not respond in a sectarian manner. In terms of our relations to other churches or the world about us, a missionary congregation will be ecumenical and constructive.

6. *A missionary congregation will bear witness in its social and cultural situation.* Missionaries in other cultures have not hesitated to call persons to be followers of Jesus, to challenge forms of behavior deemed detrimental to human well-being, or to teach values, assumptions, and norms in line with a Christian worldview. Today in North America, missionary congregations without special privilege or protection are called to bear similar witness. A main point of the Newbigin/Hunsberger agenda stresses that congregations will be the primary lens through which persons in the world will see and hear the gospel of the Lord Jesus Christ. At the same time, they are to demonstrate in their common life a new social order.

Social ministry for the public good and evangelism for personal transformation will continue to be carried out. Public ministry will go forward not as an effort to prove the usefulness of Christians but for the purpose of doing good without thought of praise. Sharing the faith will go forward not for the sake of recruitment but for the purpose of offering new life possibilities to people whom God already loves. All of this and more a missionary congregation will endeavor to carry out in Jesus Christ's way. By this means missionary congregations will become a sign pointing beyond themselves to God's reign. The goal is not to cure all ills or change all people but to model now the truth and the final purpose of God, even if imperfectly.

The characteristics of missionary congregations set forth above in no way exhaust the thinking about congregations that appears in the writings of

Newbigin, Hunsberger, and the Gospel and Our Culture Network. Even when taken altogether, the picture of a missionary congregation that emerges is more like an architect's sketch — suggestive but not definitive. The full reality of what we are calling missionary congregations will begin to appear only when ministers and members break ground, pour foundations, erect scaffolding, and start building. The next step in this project is to learn from such pastors and peoples just what a missionary congregation in the North American context will really be like. Models are urgently needed.

Up from the Grassroots: The Church in Transition

E. DIXON JUNKIN

Our task is to work for a Church of the people, in which people are no longer the object of patronizing treatment but the subject of their own history before God.

Hans Küng, *Reforming the Church Today*

The church in the United States stands on the verge of even more significant change than that experienced in recent decades. In arguing this case, some persons will put the emphasis on our changing context, others will stress the institutional crisis through which we are passing, while others will point to a more personal crisis — that of faith itself.

There is much talk these days about our "postmodern situation." Peter Hodgson describes it as follows:

> What is our situation, as mostly white, middle-class North American Christians? It is not that of the "underside" of history, like the position of Third World and minority theologies. Rather, it is a situation of the "passage" of history — the passing of Western bourgeois culture, with its ideals of individuality, private rights, technical rationality, historical progress, the capitalist economy, the absoluteness of Christianity, and so on. It feels as though we are reaching the end of a historical era, since

> we find ourselves in the midst of cognitive, historical, political, socio-economic, and religious changes of vast importance, comparable perhaps to those of the great Enlightenment that inaugurated the modern age.[1]

This whole new situation, the argument runs, requires a rethinking of the church. As we move into the new period of history that is upon us, ecclesiologies and forms of church life that served an earlier era well seem to have outlived their usefulness.

Other persons put the emphasis not so much on what is happening in the world around us as on what is happening to the church as an institution. The so-called mainline denominations in the United States seem to have lost their sense of self and to be in decline. Many of the disciplines and practices that more or less successfully nourished and formed previous generations of Christians have been abandoned, and we are acutely aware that much of a generation has been lost, if not to faith itself, at least to the churches. There is no theological consensus among us, nor is there any agreement about the way the church should understand itself in relation to the world in which we live. We remain divided by race and class. People at the grassroots level do not have the confidence in their denominational leadership that they used to have, and the churches' financial picture is increasingly bleak.

Still more evidence, however, makes those of us in the mainline churches aware that something is happening or needs to happen among us, and that is the state of our hearts. Many persons are recognizing that it is not just the world and not just the church but also faith itself that is a problem. Perhaps they find it hard to forgive themselves for living well in a world where most people live poorly, hard to hope in a world where they feel like pawns in the hands of gigantic historical forces. Certainly not everyone has such problems with faith. But while some persons are doing well, others have restless, lonely, hungry hearts.[2] Try as they might, they find believing difficult, and they long for a "second naïveté" that would allow them to trust God again as they used to before life became so complicated.

1. Peter C. Hodgson, *Revisioning the Church: Ecclesial Freedom in the New Paradigm* (Philadelphia: Fortress Press, 1988), 11.

2. The document *Hungry Hearts, Hungry Minds: The Quest for a Reformed Discipleship and Spirituality* (Louisville: Theology and Worship Ministry Unit, 1991), adopted by the General Assembly of the Presbyterian Church (U.S.A.), articulates these concerns.

The world itself, our churches as institutions, and our hearts: none are what they used to be, none are what they could be, and none are what they need to be. In truth, the three concerns are inextricably interrelated. All of them point to the fact that where the church is concerned, we are on our way — or need to be on our way — to something new.

Coping in a Time of Transition

It will not be a matter of simply tinkering a bit with the form of the church that we have on our hands. What is called for under the present circumstances is much more thoroughgoing than that. It is "re-" work that we need to do: "revisioning" or "reinventing" the church.[3] It is to that subject that we now turn our attention.

The challenge is not so much to suggest what the reinvented church should look like as to suggest how the reinvention itself might take place. If the situation is as we have described it, deciding what the new thing will be is precisely what cannot yet happen. The shape of the new world is not clear enough, nor is there in the churches sufficient theological consensus with which to work. Our "re-" work therefore consists mainly in learning how to read the changing times and in seeking to create the conditions out of which a new consensus may emerge.

As we begin such work, it is probably important to realize that reinventing the church is not the only option that might occur to people who are aware of their religious plight. For instance, persons who are especially in touch with their crisis of faith might seek to reinvent or reawaken faith itself. Over the past few years many Christians have shown a renewed interest in personal religious experience and disciplines. This interest is itself a piece of "re-" work — "re-ligion," a *re-ligare*, or a "retying," of persons to God. Such work is important, even indispensable. But if we were to cultivate only the personal religious disciplines, we would inevitably see an exacerbation of the present fragmentation of the church; as people continued to emphasize their individual faith journeys and insights, the ultimate result would bear little resemblance to biblical faith, which is so thoroughly communal. The recovery of the latter would seem to presuppose

3. See Hodgson, *Revisioning the Church;* Leonardo Boff, *Ecclesiogenesis: The Base Communities Reinvent the Church* (Maryknoll, NY: Orbis Books, 1986).

the reinvention of the church, a recovery of that kind of re-ligion that is a retying of ourselves not only to God but also to one another.

For some decades now, as the consensus in the mainline churches has slowly evaporated, there have been efforts to recover the unity that existed at an earlier time. Within Presbyterianism, for instance, there have been attempts to make a case for a single mission focus (e.g., "evangelism" or "social justice" or both things at once), or to articulate a new theological center by such means as the writing of new confessions of faith. Such efforts have foundered, however, on the soft sands of our diversity; they have been more a matter of wishful thinking about what the denomination should believe and do than an expression of what the denomination in fact believes and wishes to do.

Such attempts to create consensus would appear to be a form of what Hans Küng calls "church from above," an effort by "leaders" to persuade church members to adopt the leaders' viewpoints and desires.[4] But if telling people of faith what to believe and do was ever a successful strategy, its time has passed. Most of us simply no longer give our religious institutions that kind of authority over us.

As some persons in leadership positions have recognized the difficulties the church faces, they have decided that it is better to ask than to tell; they have sought ways to be in touch with the "grassroots," inviting the opinions of church members on a variety of subjects. Yet under present circumstances, such an asking is as doomed to failure as the telling previously mentioned, at least if the asking is intended to discover some underlying unity. The grassroots do not speak with a common voice, and canvassing the opinions of church members reveals little more than their enormous diversity and disunity. There is an even greater problem, however, which is that many church members have so lost touch with the gospel, Scripture, the tradition, and one another that they no longer know how to make considered judgments about their faith and life, judgments that have the ring of truth because they are coherent with the experience of those who make them.

To the extent that people at the grassroots are aware of this perplexing situation, they are likely to want their leaders to "do something," and to the extent that the leaders themselves are aware of it, they will surely want to

4. Hans Küng, *Reforming the Church Today: Keeping Hope Alive* (New York: Crossroad, 1990), esp. 52–63.

try to make things better. But it may be that, when all is said and done, this very mind-set, shared by grassroots and leadership, is our greatest problem. For what we need most of all is a church membership that is determined to be church in the fullest sense of the word, and resolved to be church whether its leaders lead or not. And what we need is a leadership that has resolved to place its energies and talents at the service of that determination and resolve. Our goal should not be that a few make decisions on behalf of all, even if the decisions are good ones, but rather that all might become reacquainted with the gospel, with Scripture, with the tradition, and with one another. Becoming "church from below" is our calling in this world in transition.[5]

Instead of continuing to expend such energy trying to make outworn patterns of institutional life serve us, it seems appropriate to devote more attention to the task of creating new forms of common life that may, over time, allow a new consensus to emerge. And it seems probable that the relearning of the meaning of Christian faith and life is most likely to occur in communities that are small enough to permit all their members to participate fully in the process of reflection, decision, and action.

One could probably describe such communities in many ways, but for the purposes of this chapter, let us imagine thousands of communities whose members in an intentional, disciplined fashion do the following six things:

1. Pray together.
2. Share their joys and struggles.
3. Study the context in which they find themselves.
4. Listen for God's voice speaking through Scripture.
5. Seek to discern the obedience to which they are being called.
6. Engage in common ministry.[6]

5. Ibid.

6. This is essentially the proposal of the Theology and Worship Ministry Unit of the General Assembly Council, Presbyterian Church (U.S.A.), for which the author works, although the unit bears no responsibility for the way the proposal is interpreted in this article. See *Hungry Hearts, Hungry Minds.* See also the study document of the Presbyterian Church (U.S.A.) entitled *Growing in the Life of Christian Faith* (Louisville: Theology and Worship Ministry Unit, 1989), as well as two works by Walter Brueggemann: *Disciplines of Readiness* (Louisville: Theology and Worship Ministry Unit, 1989) and "Rethinking Church Models through Scripture," *Theology Today* 48 (1991): 128–38.

The suggestion sounds both simple and obvious. Surely, we say, that is what the church is supposed to be. Yet as simple and obvious as the suggestion seems, the sad truth is that relatively few of us are presently participating in a community characterized by such intention and discipline.

Indeed, the model that is suggested stands in considerable contrast with the reality of life in our congregations. The proposal intends that in such small communities the participants might become the subjects of their own religious experience. However, all too often the members of our churches are primarily the objects of ministries of others. Others pray over them. Others tell them what Scripture says. Others tell them to what obedience they are called. And others engage in ministry on their behalf. But this means that many of our church members never learn how to pray, never become skilled in using their gifts in the interpretation of Scripture or of their own experience. They remain children in faith, dependent upon others,[7] and such dependency breeds voicelessness, powerlessness, apathy, or even anger. The suggestion of this chapter is that within the church, we should multiply communities that are small enough to permit full participation by all, a participation that will enable persons to become mature in faith, able to think, discern, and act for themselves.

The proposal furthermore intends that in such communities the participants might learn in a new way how the gospel addresses the pain of their lives. The truth is that all too often congregational life as we experience it fosters a kind of pretense. We are afraid to bring to the community much of that which most deeply concerns us, lest we experience condemnation or rejection. Our fear alienates us not only from one another but also from ourselves and from God. We learn to be ashamed of our pain, learn to think of ourselves as alone in our life struggles, learn to think that the gospel has little if anything to do with our suffering. The point is not that the communities in question should be therapy groups, for that is not their purpose. But we need places where we can learn at least enough about one another to be able to rejoice with those who rejoice and weep with those who weep, for in so doing we will also learn how the gospel addresses the deepest pain of our own lives and what promise it has for the world around us.

7. Virginia Hoffman, in an interesting book "from below" in the Roman Catholic Church, uses the concept of codependence to discuss the problems we face when members are dependent upon their leaders (*Birthing a Living Church* [New York: Crossroad, 1988], esp. 76–85).

The proposal also intends that in such communities the participants might learn in a new way the coherence of their lives before God. All too often congregational life as we experience it encourages a kind of compartmentalization. Our study of Scripture in a church school class is likely to be separated from any disciplined reflection on the world around us, from any analysis of our own experience, or from any serious efforts to discern the path of faithfulness. Our congregational life also tends to keep us separate from those who are different in race or class or life experience. The hope is that in the kinds of communities suggested in this chapter people of faith with all their differences might learn how to live together as well as how to bring the disparate parts of their lives into a whole under the gospel.

It is my contention that as we live our way into a new period of history, we are called to do all we can to promote within the church such a life in community. We furthermore contend that new initiatives are not only desirable but possible, for the widespread interest in spirituality that we are experiencing would seem to indicate that many people are eager to try new ways of being church.

The most natural thing, perhaps, will be for hungry persons to find one another, forming groups whose lives will be shaped by some such discipline as that suggested above. One can imagine that congregations might choose to organize themselves as a community of such smaller communities.

It is also worth noting that if there is anything that we are not lacking in our present church life, it is small groups. Church members already find themselves in families, church school classes, women's circles, men's groups, youth groups, sessions, boards of deacons, committees of all sorts, church staffs, support groups, and so forth. The difficulty is that, at present, many decision-making groups within the church appear to discipline their lives according to secular models, rarely if ever attempting to practice significant discernment, while groups that exist for such purposes as mutual support, education, mission, or fellowship often go about their task in ways that finally serve to further the compartmentalization of their members' lives. Therefore we should certainly encourage people of faith, in addition to forming new communities, to reshape existing communities along the lines of some such integrating discipline as that suggested above.

We may as well acknowledge the fear and suspicion that would be engendered by the dynamism of such communities. One has only to imagine 100,000 of them spread across one of the mainline churches in the

United States, all of them praying and sharing their lives and analyzing their contexts and listening to Scripture and seeking God's will and then trying to do it, in order to realize the threat that would be perceived by persons whose primary interest is in maintaining order or control. As Howard Snyder has written:

> From the institutional perspective, any kind of renewal movement immediately provokes suspicion, if not actual hostility. A new structure dedicated to church renewal is intuitively, and correctly, perceived by the keepers of the institution as calling into question (at least potentially) the validity of the institutional church itself, at least in its given form. Thus tension is inevitable, and the results are predictable.[8]

Any honest analysis of the present situation, however, will surely reveal that the confusion and disorder that we fear either already exist or are avoided only at the cost of our failure to confront the most important issues that face us. The question is whether we are willing to risk a new, more open, and more honest kind of disorder in the hope that through it the Spirit might eventually lead us into a new unity of faith and life.

If we in the mainline denominations in the United States were to choose to run such a risk, we would not be alone. There are already Christian communities in many parts of the world that are seeking to live in the intentional and disciplined fashion envisaged in this article. They range from the Base Christian Communities of Latin America to the "church from below" in Europe; from the "small Christian communities" of Africa to the "house churches" of Australia and other lands.[9]

It is not that we should imitate or copy that which is happening in other places. The point of suggesting that careful analysis of context should be one of the disciplines that shape the communities' lives is precisely to ensure that the forms of life that develop among us will be appropriate for our time and place.

8. Howard A. Snyder, *Signs of the Spirit: How God Reshapes the Church* (Grand Rapids: Zondervan, Academie Books, 1989), 271.

9. For a discussion of such communities in other countries, see Bernard J. Lee and Michael A. Cowan, *Dangerous Memories: House Churches and Our American Story* (Kansas City: Sheed & Ward, 1986), esp. chap. 2; David Prior, *Parish Renewal at the Grassroots* (Grand Rapids: Zondervan, Francis Asbury Press, 1983); and Jeanne Hinton, *Walking in the Same Direction: A New Way of Being Church* (Geneva: WCC Publications, 1995).

Richard Schaull has suggested that frequently in the past "a new form of church has emerged in response to the needs and aspirations of a new social class."[10] In our time as well it seems inevitable that our reflections about a new form of church will not be unrelated to what is happening in our culture, economy, and political life. The fact that most of us in the mainline churches are part of a shrinking and increasingly fearful middle class will of necessity condition the way we hear and respond to the gospel. But as we listen carefully for the gospel as the unique persons we are, we can be encouraged by the knowledge that there are many throughout the world who are engaged in a similar effort.

The movement toward communities of greater intentionality and discipline is not only one that extends throughout the world but one that extends throughout time. Our commitment of ourselves to such disciplines as those suggested above is in fact a recommitment to practices that have constituted and reconstituted the church throughout the ages.

Howard Snyder, in his study of various renewal movements in the history of the church, notes that two characteristics of such movements seem to have been of particular importance in their ability to serve a renewing function: "The emphasis on and practice of some form of 'more intimate fellowship' for prayer, Bible study, and personal sharing, and the practical expression (not always articulated) of the priesthood of believers through ecclesiastically unordained or 'lay' leadership."[11] We have every right to hope and trust that the formation of such "more intimate fellowships" in our own congregations will once again serve to further church renewal, allowing new ways of being the church to grow up within our older structures.

All too often we have honored the tradition by trying to learn what Christians before us have thought in order to think it after them. This chapter suggests that the most important honoring consists in living the way the tradition at its best has lived. No one can teach us what we need to learn about being the church in this place and time. We will learn it only by doing it, by carrying out those practices that are "means of grace" and have always marked the church's life.

10. Richard Schaull, "The Christian Base Communities and the *Ecclesia Reformata Semper Reformanda*," *Princeton Seminary Bulletin*, n.s., 12 (1991): 202.

11. Snyder, *Signs of the Spirit*, 33; see also 276 and 285.

Christian Communities and Their Leadership

This living into the future is in no way a matter of rules and formulas, six steps to be followed rigidly whenever the community gathers. What is recommended is a style of living together that will be worked out in an infinite variety of ways.

It is one thing to describe what we would like to see, and it is quite another to imagine it happening. The disciplines that are to characterize the life of the communities may sound quite simple, but the reality is something else again. The communities will need help. Finally, therefore, we turn our attention very briefly to the matter of the leadership that will be required as the church lives its way through the present transition.

Our mainline churches have to a great extent been living not "from below" but "from above," to use the phrases of Hans Küng. True, we Protestants have not had to deal with the same issues of authority with which Küng is concerned, but we have had our own version of them. The practice has all too often been for a few to study the Bible and then to tell others what it says, for a few to voice prayers that others are supposed to make their own, for a few to exercise discernment on behalf of others, for a few to exercise a "mission" and a "ministry," from which most seem to be excluded.

As a result, we now find ourselves without the skills to live the life in community to which we are called. We have forgotten how to pray together and how to engage in an appropriate sharing of the joy and pain of our lives. We lack skills in analyzing what is happening in the world around us.[12] We do not know how to enable a community to become the interpreter of Scripture. And we lack practice in uniting our knowledge of ourselves and of one another, our insights into the world around us, and our knowledge of the Word of God, in an effort to discern what it means to live lives characterized by wholeness and integrity.

There is therefore enough theological, pedagogical, and organizational work to be done to demand the full attention of our present genera-

12. This is not simply a matter of our inability to do good social analysis but also a theological issue. Lewis S. Mudge writes in his recent book *The Sense of a People: Toward a Church for the Human Future* (Philadelphia: Trinity Press International, 1992): "Perhaps one may generalize about the entire post–World War II generation of theologians, Protestant and Roman Catholic alike. They have failed adequately to clarify the relation between faith and history, between doctrine and lived experience" (p. 77).

tion of leaders. But the efforts of our leaders will be helpful only if those efforts themselves have their origins in communities of prayer, discernment, and action. If it is not in such communities that pastors, professional theologians, and church executives discern what it is that they should be doing, they will almost inevitably end up serving the interests of "church from above." With respect to the issues we are presently discussing, all of us are "grassroots"!

Finally, however, if the experience of the church in other parts of the world and at other times is any guide, it is likely that the grassroots communities of which we are speaking will come into existence and function successfully only with the help of a new, "lay" leadership. The formation of such leaders is something for which the church is not presently equipped, and it is something that we will have to learn to do. But we can be sure that, when the time comes, there will be no lack of persons who will be ready to invest their gifts on behalf of the communities. They will have one of the most exciting tasks imaginable, that of helping all of us practice, and in the practicing learn, what it means to be the people of God in an uncharted world.

Pastoral Role in the Missionary Congregation

ALAN J. ROXBURGH

In his paper "The Changing Face of Ministry: Christian Leadership for the Twenty-First Century," George Hunsberger characterizes the crisis facing the churches as that of the loss of their social function.[1] This crisis, he suggests, has two parts; first, the caretaker days of the churches are over; second, the broad culture in which the churches find themselves is itself in a period of major transformation. Both elements challenge not only congregations but particularly pastors. Hunsberger suggests there are at least four responsive tasks for pastoral leadership in this crisis:

1. Forming a communal world.
2. Casting a wider rationality.
3. Healing our fragmentary "worlds."
4. Igniting a subversive witness.

The question is, What shape ought the pastoral role to take in the light of these challenges? In order to address this matter, we first need to offer some description of the context in which pastors lead today.

1. George R. Hunsberger, "The Changing Face of Ministry: Christian Leadership for the Twenty-First Century," *Reformed Review* 44, no. 3 (Spring 1991): 224–45. See also the Introduction to this volume.

The Pastoral Context

I speak from a Canadian perspective. From that point of view several things are obvious. First, these are extremely anxious, confusing, and tenuous days for pastors and congregations. Second, major congregational decline continues and will only get worse in the decade ahead.[2] The process of marginalization of the churches in Canada is far more obvious and advanced than in the United States. For example, in one medium-sized Canadian city of 100,000 people, no more than 4 percent of the population attend church on a given Sunday. And congregations are blaming the malaise on their pastors. They are described as incompetent, not entrepreneurial enough, too intent on change, or failing to meet the expectations of renewing the congregation. Pastors in turn feel vulnerable, defensive, and confused. In my own denomination an increasing number of congregations are firing their pastors. Denominational executives are functioning as firemen dealing with one crisis after another. What this means is that few pastors are asking questions about their role in missionary congregations. For too many, ministry has changed so dramatically that they are simply trying to hold on and survive. Congregations that had 300 members a decade ago have dwindled to 100. The precariousness of these realities makes it difficult for pastors to discuss questions of missionary encounter models. Furthermore, the culture itself has become so confusing and threatening that pastors in many ways retreat into their congregations for security.

There has been no shortage of criticism of congregations and pastors over the past thirty years, nor has there been a shortage of answers as to what needs to be done. An increasing number of books are written about the church in the twenty-first century and the shape of leadership for the new millennium. One is cautious, therefore, about adding to the criticism and offering more solutions. Our confidence is in what God may yet do in the Spirit, through both congregations and their leaders.

Nature of the Pastoral Function Today

I comment first on the nature of the pastoral function today. The symbol "pastor" has become a generic container for all the functions of ordained,

2. See Reginald Bibby, *The Unknown Gods* (Toronto: Stoddart, 1993).

recognized leadership in the church. But certain overriding images have shaped our comprehension of the pastoral role in modernity. The pastor, to use Harvie Conn's critique, is seen in terms of pedagogue and professional.[3] As pedagogue, the pastor is primarily the teacher, unfolding the concepts of God's Word to those who come faithfully to the church. The pedagogue role is based upon the cultural assumption of a church in the center of a society in which people present themselves and their public lives for spiritual instruction. As a professional, the pastor owns the expertise necessary to dispense religious care and functions to the people on behalf of God. Congregations are consumers of professional services. Seminaries are classified as professional schools like those of law, business, and medicine. The pastor is indeed a professional. Despite a half-century of discussion about the lay apostolate, clericalization remains entrenched in the churches.

Precisely these roles, however, have ceased to be meaningful in my country. And yet, because we have functioned over a number of generations in this paradigm, practically the only model presented to each new generation of potential leaders is pastor as professional and teacher; the caretaker and chaplain of dwindling, aging congregations. As a result, pastors are unable to function outside the paradigm. Equally tragic, the most creative young leaders, with the passion and skills desperately needed in our churches, take one look at this model of pastoral leadership and turn elsewhere for vocational fulfillment. Seminaries are, by and large, empty of the most creative people and filled with weak pastoral candidates. The schools must heed Newbigin's call and train missionary leaders for our congregations.

As the culture marginalized the church, pastoral identity became problematic. For much of the latter half of this century, we have witnessed a searching around for ways to reconfigure pastoral identity in the light of this marginalization. The way that has taken shape is germane to our discussion. We can identify three types of responses to this struggle for identity.

3. Harvie M. Conn, *Eternal Word and Changing Worlds: Theology, Anthropology, and Mission in Trialogue* (Grand Rapids: Zondervan, 1984), 263–89.

Therapeutic Approaches to Pastoral Leadership

First, there has been an increase in counseling and clinical/pastoral models of ministry. In seminaries, if the elective choices are between evangelism or domestic missiology and counseling, there is no doubt about which course will be filled. In this approach pastors respond to people's needs and receive identity by becoming caregivers and clinicians. Soul care becomes self-discovery with a loss of a larger horizon. A paradigmatic model of pastoral leadership, especially through programs like Clinical Pastoral Education, becomes self-awareness and self-discovery. Pastors then pass on to the congregation the model they have learned. Lurking behind all of this is expressive individualism.

Technical Rationality as Pastoral Leadership

Second, anxiety over decline translates into a high interest in entrepreneurial models of leadership. Church growth, church marketing, and leadership models drawn from the latest innovations of business or consultants on how to lead in the corporate world shape the image of pastoral leadership. Numerical growth is the talisman that all is well with our ecclesiological souls. The cultural values of instrumental rationality, expressed in the motto "If it works and is successful, then it's true," guide pastoral strategy. Technique is the primary method for reestablishing the church's place in the culture. In all of this God is but a footnote to ecclesiology. Pastors' workshops are filled with eager acolytes of success receiving their initiation, from yuppified gurus, into up-to-date techniques for how to achieve all manner of things. Business, pop psychology, and psychographics become paradigms for identity and success. The Harvard School of Business, Faith Popcorn, George Barna, Ann Wilson-Shaef, and John Bradshaw are the contemporary saints, revealing how much we mirror the heart of modernity in our leadership.

The Private World as the Realm of Pastoral Leadership

Borrowing language from de Tocqueville, congregations have become enclosed within their own hearts, with little sense of a public life. Pastors lead congregations that have little sense of a vocation as a people called to lives larger than themselves. So much preaching simply reflects this cultural captivity, calling parishioners to discover a personalized Jesus who acts as a guarantor of inner, personal happiness in a hazardous and dark world. The perilous fragmentation in the larger culture is kept at bay by creating a group of one's own kind that is baptized with the name "community."

These three responses focus pastoral leadership inwardly on the congregation, on its needs and its survival. But even more significantly, what each one reveals is that pastoral leadership is expressed in terms of the immanent values of modernity: personal need, technique, and privatized community. Pastors are servants of the culture rather than followers of Jesus. While desiring to serve God's people, they become technicians, servicing the needs of expressive individualism and the hunger for success through technique. In anxiety over identity and the pressure of survival, these options shape the followers of Jesus.

It is interesting to note that Charles Taylor, in his book *The Malaise of Modernity,* identified three characteristics of modernity.[4] Compare Taylor's characteristics with the primary themes of pastoral ministry just mentioned.

Themes Shaping Modernity	Themes Shaping Ministry
1. Individualism	Therapeutic approaches
2. Instrumental rationality	Technical rationality
3. Fragmentation into groups of self-interest	Private communal world

In each case the functional paradigm of pastoral leadership is shaped by modernity. Once we have understood this situation, then we need to examine how we might appropriate leadership images for this reality.

A Model for Engagement

The marginalization arguments that are used to account for the church's changed social position have affinities to the model of liminality of anthro-

4. Charles Taylor, *The Malaise of Modernity* (Toronto: House of Anansi, 1991), 2–10.

pologist Victor Turner.[5] This model can help us to identify not just the nature of the issues facing pastors today but also directions for the future. For Turner, any group experiencing the loss of social position goes through three distinct phases:

1. Separation (from the larger culture in which it was embedded and received its identity)
2. Margin (or limen; marginalization/disestablishment)
3. Reaggregation

The separation phase occurs as an individual or group is detached from its accepted role in society. Christianity, in the modern world, has moved through this phase for the past several hundred years. During periods of separation the symbols that once gave the group its place and identity in the culture weaken and lose their power. This can be observed, for example, in architecture. Cathedrals and churches of the medieval period functioned as places of refuge, as places of commerce, and as centers of worship. They symbolized both the immanence and transcendence of God through their interior space. Vaulted ceilings drew the eye upward to a destination beyond the roof; the cruciform design symbolized the centrality of Christ. This interior architecture carried the symbolic meaning for the religious experience of the people. It exemplified a society in harmony with its inner/outer, public/private life. The world outside the church was not separate from the world inside the building in the sense that people understood intuitively where God could be found. God's social location lay, architecturally, *inside* the culture. But in the nineteenth century another symbol was added to many of these buildings: the steeple. Note the location of this symbol on the outside of the building, where the public world could see and identify the place where God was to be found. The shift is subtle, but the message is clear: as the two worlds begin to separate, the steeple, as an external symbol, connects the secular with the religious. As yet the role identity of the religious, the pastor, remained intact; but the symbols were starting to indicate separation.

The second, liminal, phase is of primary interest to the discussion of pastoral identity. In this phase the group is aware of its marginality. It is

5. Victor Turner, *The Ritual Process* (Ithaca: Cornell University Press, 1969); idem, *Dramas, Fields, and Metaphors* (Ithaca: Cornell University Press, 1977).

clear that the former symbols of identity do not work. Throw up a thousand spires higher than the Sears Tower, but they no longer have the power to attract. Spend $100,000 repairing the organ, but still they will not come. This phase of liminality is the end point of separation; the group now is outside the mainstream.

Liminality, according to Turner, is a threshold experience; a paradoxical state of both death and renewal, confusion and opportunity. Groups and pastors, for example, find themselves betwixt and between; their roles no longer fit the classifications of society. What pastors? What do they do? Where do they fit? What kind of social function do they have? The further one moves into liminality, the greater the cognitive confusion about the designation of the role "pastor."

At this stage the temptation is to find a symbolic crutch to support one's identity. And so, what we observe is pastors seeking to discover new role "fits" to deal with the loss of identity. Most of these role fits are borrowed, suggesting the level of role confusion for the pastor in liminality. For example, the pastor is clinician (therapeutic metaphor), chaplain (institutional metaphor), coach (sports metaphor), entrepreneur, marketer, and strategist (business metaphor). Beside the Bible, the pastor *must* read John Bradshaw, know the Twelve Step process, discuss codependency, and memorize the business strategies of Attila the Hun. In a parallel manner, denominational judicatories reemphasize identity through credentials and certification. There is a stress on professional accreditation and the gathering of new degrees after the pastor's name. These are borrowed symbols of credibility and identity in a society that has declassified the pastoral identity. Much of this borrowing is an attempt to deny or bypass the experience of liminality rather than recognizing and embracing its reality. No wonder it is so difficult to be a pastor today.

But not all the news is bad. According to Turner, liminality is also a phase of opportunity for creativity and transformation. It is an occasion to recognize inappropriate metaphors and rediscover more fitting images of leadership. The biblical tradition contains images waiting to be reappropriated in the unsettling land of liminality. This is not the locale for technicians, for mechanics of the latest method offering two hundred surefire ways of making your congregation the most alive, fastest-growing, seeker-sensitive, liturgical, charismatic church in North America. Nor is it a place for those wanting to be king of the castle. Liminality requires leaders who listen to the voices from the edge. This is where the *apostle,* the *poet,* and the *prophet* are found. These are the metaphors for congregational leadership today. The pastor's ears must be attuned not to the popular trend or expert but to those who recognize that marginality is the church's reality. By the waters of Babylon there is no way back to the old Jerusalem. Liminality requires a different kind of leader if congregations are to be encountered by, and in turn encounter, our culture with the gospel.

The remaining section outlines elements of what we mean when we call upon pastors to be apostles, poets, and prophets.

Pastor/Apostle

In liminality, pastors must lead congregations as witnesses to the gospel in lands where old maps no longer work. This requires an apostolic role. Küng and others have rightly argued that the congregation is foundationally apostolic. But does it actually assume this role, given its captivity to modernity? In response it is frequently suggested that congregations will become apostolic when pastors become equippers and disciplers, with Ephesians 4:11-12 being cited as the axiomatic text. This is fair enough, but it begs the question of how, in a time when congregations are confused and ghettoized and have few, if any, models of what it means to be a missionary people, pastors actually equip and disciple. Equipping and discipling must be more than small-group Bible studies on the gospel and culture. This is not to demean the place of Scripture, but we must realize that ours is a culture that believes that if it has been studied, then it has been done. Discipling and equipping require a leadership that demonstrates, in action, the encounter with the culture. This is the role of pastor as apostle. In the days ahead, the gown of the scholar must be replaced with the shoes of the apostle. This is not to diminish the importance of intellectual engagement but, rather, to call for a shift of paradigm toward contextual engagement with the culture. Pastor, as apostle, is foundational to all other functions.

In a broad sense of the term, the apostle is commissioned by Christ for missionary proclamation and strategy in the world. This is not just a matter of taking the gospel into the world and modeling for the congregation how to recruit members for the church. Rather, the apostle holds up the gospel in order that it may encounter the cultural context and challenge the congregation's need to be shaped by its calling to be apostolic. This approach stands in contradistinction to our instinctual images of pastor.

For example, at a meeting of local pastors that I attended recently, one pastor said, "Pastoral care is the business we're in; if we're not preparing worship, we're doing pastoral care." In such a view, pastors are supposed to be *in the church* rather than *in the world.* In a Christendom model this was the case. But such separations are not acceptable in a missionary situation. If we hear Newbigin's call for missionary leaders, then the apostolic function must come to the fore.

Discussions of pastoral leadership have tended to center on roles *within* the congregation. Models are offered that shift leadership images from hierarchical to servant, from top down to bottom up. The image often used is that of a triangle. Rather than a triangle with a wide base, as in the accompanying diagram, with the leader at the top and the people at the base of a hierarchy, renewalists call for an inverted triangle with the laity at the top and the pastor at the bottom as servant. Redefining pastoral leadership in terms of servanthood and lay empowerment is laudable, but the model is problematic. There is a saying in Canada about Quebecers: they are always last to catch the train, but once on it, they go way past the stop. This image reminds me of that saying. It swings the pendulum from one extreme to another, continuing the dichotomy between servant and directive leadership. (They are not opposites!) Of more critical importance, the servant/equipping model only rearranges the Christendom image of congregational leader as one whose role is entirely *within* the church for the well-being of the people. Here, "pastor" is a symbol of the ecclesiocentric nature of the church. This is what must change.

The image of apostle is a powerful one for our day precisely because it is related so closely to a kingdom understanding, rather than a church understanding, of God's activity in Christ. In the contemporary understanding of the pastoral role, pastoring implies someone who needs care. The pastor image is that of someone who works within the structures and order of the culture. By contrast, the image of apostle suggests something that needs to be addressed. Buried in the notion of apostle is the recognition that one is located at the margins. If that were not the case, there would be no need for the apostle in the first place. There is a clarity of location on the margins that is not present in that of pastor. Furthermore, the apostle is commissioned by Christ, and we need such strong images of leadership in order to move away from the current views of pastors as enculturated professionals hired by congregations to provide religious services.

Let us place the triangle on its side as an elongated wedge with a directional point. This diagrams a church called to function as a mission band, directed toward the world and moving toward a destination other than its own self-preservation or inner growth. The place of leadership is neither at the top of the triangle nor at the bottom but at the leading edge, modeling engagement with the culture in the name of the gospel. This is what is intended by the notion of apostolic leadership as primary and foundational for pastors today. Such a model shifts the pastoral role outward to the forefront of missional engagement.

There are structural implications to this change. Such leadership cannot function in a *sola pastora* model. Rather than the omnicompetent professional, running the congregation's inner life, there is a team, or multiple leadership, at the heart of the congregation. This does not imply professional staff. Indeed, it shouldn't. Pastoral care, worship, proclamation, and administration are part of the work of the whole people of God, not the designated territory of someone with a seminary degree and an ordination certificate. The guild of the ordained will have to be removed; this is one social function that will not move us through liminality. The pastor/apostle is one who forms congregations into mission groups shaped by encounters with the gospel in the culture, structuring the congregation's shape into forms that lead people outward into a missionary encounter. Discipleship emerges out of prayer, study, dialogue, and worship by a community learning to ask the questions of obedience *as they are engaged directly in mission.* In such a congregation, however, the pastor will be able to lead only as he or she models the encounter with the culture.

Pastor/Poet

The primacy of the apostolic role does not remove the need for continuing pastoral care. But this pastoral function must be interpreted through the missionary nature of the congregation. The pastoral role in the context of liminality is that of articulating the congregation's experience in modernity. In this sense, pastors must reinterpret their roles not primarily as caregivers but as poets. Poets are the articulators of experience. They image and symbolize the unarticulated experiences of the community, identifying and expressing the soul of the people (functioning as the dancer in worship who interprets the experience). The poet is a listener and an observer,

TRADITIONAL MODEL

RENEWALIST MODEL

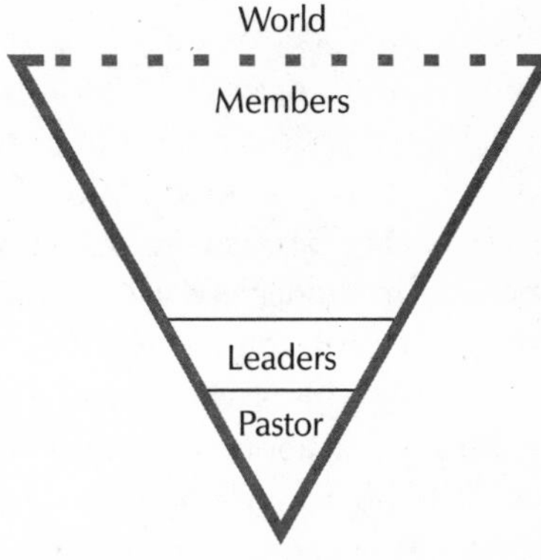

MISSION MODEL

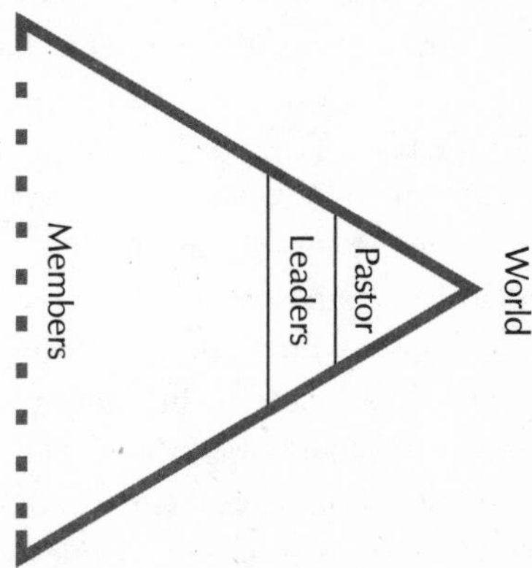

sensing the experience of the body and giving that experience a voice. As poet, the pastor needs all the skills of pastoral care, but these skills are the servant of a larger end rather than ends in themselves.

Many voices speak in the church today at a superficial level. They speak of how our personal needs may be met, of patching up the old ship so that it sails as it did before in the sea of the culture, of one more new method of renewal or evangelism. But the poet hears voices at a deeper level — the fragmentation and alienation of modernity, the loneliness of our individualism as experienced by those in our congregations. The poet knows that these are cries for something more than self-development or techniques of success; they are cries that long to be connected to a Word that calls them beyond themselves. The poet's vocation is to bring these voices to expression so that we may listen again to the voice of God speaking into our situation of marginality. There will be no vision of a missionary people without the poet/pastor living into the congregation's experience and giving voice to its desire for transformation and renewal.

The pastor/poet does not begin by teaching ideas so that the congregation understands modernity. Rational accounting is not the first step. Paradigmatic change begins with reflection of the people of God on their own immersion in modernity. This, too, is an important part of discipleship. In such discourse the poet/pastor brings to voice their story so that there occurs a "Yes! This is who we are! This is who we meet when we touch the fear and confusion about being God's people in this culture!" The pastor weaves together the people's voices so that the story of who they are and what they actually experience is articulated, called forth, and owned. In this process the tapestry of their lives is made visible. This is, in part, what Scripture means about speaking the truth in love. As we are brought to the truth about ourselves, we are opened to hear the gospel anew. Such poetry writing begins the process of calling out an alternative vision for God's people. But the pastor cannot be that poet without reflecting upon his or her own experience as a person of faith in modernity. This, in turn, requires intellectual reflection on the meaning and contours of this land in which the gospel lives as a stranger. The poet is of no pastoral use to the congregation if he or she can do no more than express personal feelings of anxiety and confusion. Such poetry is little more than therapy, the reconditioning of people to live in the ambiguity of their context. Rather, the poet writes so that the congregation hears their story as God's pilgrim people. This means writing with as much intellectual engagement with the culture as passion for the experience of the people. The tapestry must be woven of both elements before the possibility of transformation can emerge in the condition of liminality.

Pastor/Prophet

It is clear from the description of liminality that one of the most important roles of congregational leadership in this time is the recovery of the prophetic. Prophecy is the addressing of the Word of God directly into the specific, concrete historical experience of the people of God. Unless the gospel addresses God's people, we are lost. The prophetic imagination directs the poetic discourse of the people toward a vision of God's purposes for them in the world at this time. The recognition in the poetic role that "We are this people living at the edges of modernity" finds hope for transformation as the biblical witness is brought to bear upon the community's experience. Without this other Word, the community turns its pain into the ghetto experience of marginalization rather than the recognition that it exists for the life of the world. Without the prophetic, poetic leadership is little more than adaptation and consolation. The prophetic addresses the hard side of discipleship, where we must face the reality that in God's kingdom we are not at the center of the universe. Its intention is to identify and uproot from our selective reading of Scripture and culture those yet-to-be-voiced places in our lives where we rationalize ideologies of the culture as values of the kingdom.

In liminality what is needed is the Word from the outside that gives a new vision and fresh definition to being God's people. Here the prophet liberates hope for authentic missional engagement. The prophetic word cuts across the assumptions that we have been called to create the kingdom of God out of the kingdoms of this world. It re-presents the cosmic picture of Christ who came into the world to address the ideologies and structures that leave us dehumanized, as commodities to be manipulated, or as isolated individuals called to salvation by self-fulfillment. And this includes the ideologies within the churches that believe that congregational life and practice are to be shaped by the exigencies of the popular. Here the pastor, as prophet, calls forth a different story of God's people, a people who are out on a mission journey that calls them far beyond themselves, to a gospel that does not belong to any social order or ideology. The alternative community is not formed primarily through small-group ministries or seminars on how to be community for one another; it is formed as the prophetic word addresses the pained recognition of our liminality.

Conclusion

In the introduction to his book *Earthing the Gospel,* Gerald Arbuckle writes about the "sense of pastoral chaos the churches feel when confronted with a world in rapid cultural change." He argues that the chaos is so great today that the old ways do not work and we can no longer speak in terms of renewal of the church but its refounding. He says: "If re-founding is to occur, however, the church desperately needs people of imagination and creativity."[6] This is the pastoral leadership required for the challenge that is before us.

6. Gerald Arbuckle, *Earthing the Gospel* (Maryknoll, NY: Orbis Books, 1990), 2.

Sizing Up the Shape of the Church

GEORGE R. HUNSBERGER

A recent issue of *Reformed Review* contains a collection of articles whose aim it is to "size up" the Reformed Church in America (RCA), with a look at the fortunes of the whole as well as the experience of several of its parts. The articles include a look at the past and hints of dreams for the future. They pay attention to factors both within and without the church.

But there is an essential problematic that remains to be uncovered. It becomes evident when the myth-breaking study of Roger Nemeth and Donald Luidens takes a prescriptive turn. The advice that the RCA "needs to be more intentional in reaching out to groups that have not been well represented in the denomination if membership trends are to be reversed" comes on the heels of their dramatic news that during the last century, RCA membership has essentially grown, and now declined, as a consequence of the rate of having babies.[1] How does a centuries-long habit in which "membership trends were principally dependent upon 'natural' growth" shift toward a new spurt of intentionality in recruitment? What historic character or quality would that shift hope to draw upon? What would it take to recast dramatically the corporate culture of the churches, and where does the hope lie that the churches could or would, with a flash of recognition, decide to make such dramatic changes? What would motivate the change?

The suggestion to "be more intentional" — that is, beef up our evangelistic fortitude — too easily underwrites the now all-too-familiar habit

1. Roger J. Nemeth and Donald A. Luidens, "The Reformed Church in the Larger Picture: Facing Structural Realities," *Reformed Review* 47, no. 2 (Winter 1993–94): 94.

of thinking that the signs of crisis in the church are really not so dire, that with a bit a tweaking and tuning, a midcourse correction can turn the fortunes around, and that if we try harder, we can move out of the doldrums.

But the crisis *is* dire. Tuning the engine and trying harder will not change the growing malaise in the churches or their increasing experience of being finally and firmly "disestablished" from roles of importance we thought we had in the larger society. The fundamental crisis we are facing is the one Douglas John Hall calls a *crisis of thinking.*[2] In particular, it is a crisis of thinking about what the church is and how we fit into the scheme of things in the world. Or perhaps more accurately, the crisis is that we have *not* thought carefully, critically, or theologically about our assumptions regarding the church and have failed to notice how much they have been shaped by the character of modern American life.

Shape, Not Size

Our current *crisis of size* is only a symptom of deeper and broader changes in the form and place of religious life in North American society. The crisis of size should therefore be recognized as a signal that we are facing a more pressing crisis, a *crisis of shape.* The fact that we experience the current crisis primarily as one of size is itself one of the important clues to the crisis of shape: namely, we have come to regard the church as being in the religion business, and right now sales are down.

The crisis of shape about which I am speaking is by its nature a theological crisis, one of great magnitude and consequence. It is theological because it has to do with how we understand what was and is in God's mind regarding this social configuration called "church." But it is important to clarify that in calling attention to the theological nature of this crisis, I am not contradicting one of the most important points made by Nemeth and Luidens. They show that the factors involved in the decline of the denomination "are of long standing, and generally pre-date any of the ideological debates of 'left' and 'right' that are so audible and high-voltage." The changes, they say, "seem to be little impressed by this noisy polemic."

2. Douglas John Hall, *Thinking the Faith* (Minneapolis: Augsburg Press, 1989), 12.

They show that the winding down of the RCA's "market share" of American church adherents was well under way at the beginning of the century and that the shift of monies from denominational to local and congregational needs occurred well before the turbulent 1960s. Their point is well made that the normal scapegoats do not qualify when assessing the causes of decline. The intramural, ideological battles were not factors. Nor was the organizational restructuring or changes in denominational leadership. Nemeth and Luidens insist that "we must look to the social structural context within which the RCA and other denominations function in order to learn what happened to the membership trends."[3]

To find reasons for decline in the broader social context does not mean that there are not internal, theological ones. Luidens, in collaboration with several other scholars, demonstrates this point. In an article entitled "Mainline Churches: The Real Reason for Decline," Luidens and his companions report the findings of a study of the religious attitudes and practices of baby boomers who had been confirmed in mainline Protestant churches (in particular, the Presbyterian Church [U.S.A.]) during the 1960s. They found that "the single best predictor of church participation turned out to be *belief*— orthodox Christian belief, and especially the teaching that a person can be saved only through Jesus Christ." They concluded that mainline denominations "seem to be weak in the sense of being unable to generate and maintain high levels of commitment among a substantial portion of their adherents." This they attribute in part to the fact that denominational leaders did not, in response to the currents of modernity, "devise or promote compelling new versions of a distinctively Christian faith. They did not fashion or preach a vigorous apologetics." The advice is that "if the mainline churches want to regain their vitality, their first step must be to address theological issues head-on."[4]

Another study that has gained a lot of attention is the seven-volume series entitled *The Presbyterian Presence: The Twentieth-Century Experience.* In the concluding volume, the editors of the series (Milton J Coalter, John M. Mulder, and Louis B. Weeks) draw together the fruits of the massive study. There they write that "fragmentation of its life and witness . . .

3. Nemeth and Luidens, "Reformed Church," 85.

4. Benton Johnson, Dean R. Hoge, and Donald A. Luidens, "Mainline Churches: The Real Reason for Decline," *First Things,* no. 31 (March 1993): 13–18.

best explains the historical contours of twentieth-century American Presbyterianism." This interpretation has value, they say, because it suggests that "the problems of American mainstream Protestantism are not due simply to human mistakes or institutional missteps; rather, the difficulties are part of the broad process of modernization that has shaped so much of twentieth-century American culture."[5]

Having summarized the most important findings of the study, Coalter, Mulder, and Weeks conclude with a chapter entitled "An Agenda for Reform." The agenda in the end is a theological one. They suggest five crucial "theological questions posed by these epochal changes." The fourth is especially pertinent to the theological issue I am raising about the shape of the church:

> Why, after all, is there a church — an ordered community of Christians? Why is faith a communal experience, rather than a private one? Swirling beneath the sociological trends in American society is not only the institutional crisis of American Presbyterianism and mainstream Protestantism but the haunting query of individuals about the need for and purpose of the church. . . . The church's community must have a forthright and compellingly persuasive vision of what the church is and should be for Christian witness.[6]

While we need to understand the sociological trends that influence our churches, our calling to witness faithfully to Jesus Christ requires that we also give keen attention to the theological issues implicated in our analysis of the trends.

I am suggesting that beneath the ebb and flow of contextual factors lies a substructure of commonly accepted notions about the church and its public role that has gone largely undetected. There is need for theological analysis that goes beyond discussions about the changing context or the effect of ecclesiastical debates and gets at this substructure.

5. Milton J Coalter, John M. Mulder, and Louis B. Weeks, *The Re-Forming Tradition: Presbyterians and Mainstream Protestantism* (Louisville: Westminster/John Knox Press, 1992), 24.

6. Ibid., 283–84.

The Church as a Vendor of Religious Services

What is the present shape of the church? The question must be asked honestly. Simple references to biblical phrases or creedal definitions may mask what is really operating in our day-to-day notions, which have much more to do with our actions and choices. David Bosch addressed this issue in lectures on the eve of the publication of his major work *Transforming Mission.*[7] He noted that we Protestants have inherited a particular view of the church from the Reformers. Their emphases on the marks of the true church — the right preaching of the gospel, the right administration of the sacraments, and the exercise of church discipline — have bequeathed to us an understanding that the church is "a place where certain things happen." However, in this century this view has been changing. The fruits of the missionary movement and the emergence of a global church have led us to see that the church is essentially "a body of people sent on a mission."[8] This he identified as a crucial element in the "emerging ecumenical paradigm" of mission.

Bosch has surely put his finger on an important twentieth-century rediscovery of a biblical perspective. But is that the way that congregations conceive themselves and live? In North America, we live out of a very different model, even when we mouth formal statements like the one Bosch articulates. We are not very far from the notion that the church is "a place where certain things happen." Our common language betrays that. Church is something you "go to." We ask, "Where is your church?" The word may refer to a building, but even when it does not, it tends to refer to an institution as embodied by officers and staff or to a set of programs offered according to a certain schedule of days and times. When I was a child, we talked about "going to Sunday school and church," a statement in which the word "church" referred to the Sunday morning eleven o'clock worship service.

More specifically, though, our contemporary notion is a variation on the "place where" way of defining the church. In the North American setting, we have come to view the church as "a vendor of religious services

7. David J. Bosch, *Transforming Mission: Paradigm Shifts in Theology of Mission* (Maryknoll, NY: Orbis Books, 1991).

8. David J. Bosch, in lectures given at Western Theological Seminary, Holland, Michigan, April 1991.

and goods" (fig. 1). To this notion we attach the language of production, marketing, sales, and consumption. A congregation becomes a retail outlet or franchise of the denominational brand. Staff at all levels become sales and service representatives. The denomination is the corporate headquarters in charge of everything from research and development to mass media imaging.

Most of us value the use of many businesslike techniques and procedures in the life of the church but would be aghast at the suggestion that we fundamentally operate out of a model of the church as a business, a vendor of religious services. But consider the unconscious and unquestioned form of

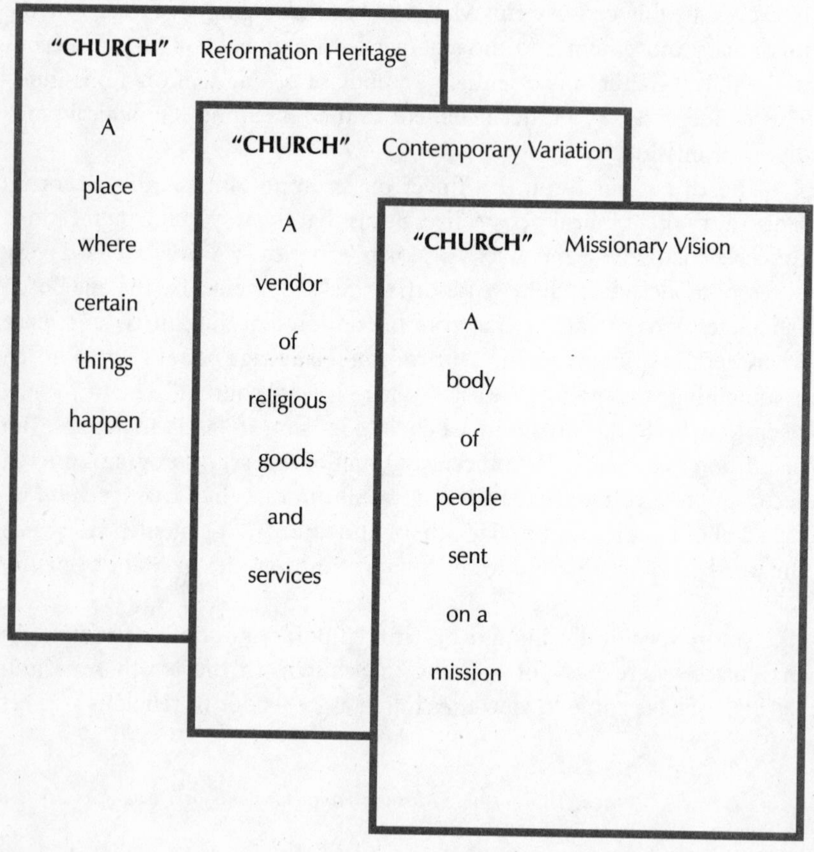

FIGURE 1

many of our carefully worded mission statements. It is amazing how many are cast something like this: "The mission of Anytown Community Church is to nurture its members in Christian faith and equip them for service and witness to Christ in the world." What follows tends to detail the educational, worship, witness, and justice commitments of the church. But notice how the text reads. The mission of this *church* is to nurture its *members.* In a statement like that, to what does the word "church" refer? It sits over against the members, for whom it has a mission to do certain things. Church here refers either to the official governing body that feels responsible to meet the needs of the congregational members or those outside it, or to the staff whom they charge with that responsibility. But the members are not conceived, in such a statement, as *being* the church and themselves *having* a mission on which they have been collectively sent. Instead, they are the customers, the regular consumers for whom the religious services and goods produced by the "church" are intended. On such a model, evangelism devolves into membership recruitment, which may more accurately be called "capturing market share." This kind of "church" is in the business of religion, and its livelihood is dependent on having a sufficient number of satisfied, committed customers.

In their study, Nemeth and Luidens give hints along this same line. They report the findings of Roger Finke and Rodney Stark that "a major change in organizational thinking hit Protestant circles in the late 1800s." Following developments in industry and business, churches incorporated models of efficiency and rationalization, implementing consolidation and specialization with a view toward an "economy of scale." They conclude: "Finke and Stark argue that this rationalizing and consolidating movement led directly to the demise of a sense of religious community among members of mainline congregations."[9]

Nemeth and Luidens go on to show how postwar "professionalization of the church and the decline of traditional volunteerism" (which may not be so unconnected as they imply) affected congregational spending patterns. They report that dominant concerns in that era included such things as raising the standards of services, upgrading programs and facilities, widening the scope of programs offered, and using paid experts to run programs, all of which were part of the congregations' answer to "the call to a heightened competition for new members."[10]

9. Nemeth and Luidens, "Reformed Church," 89.

10. Ibid., 92.

The difficulty comes when we fail to see that these developments are all theological. Nemeth and Luidens imply they are not, an implication that is heightened by their (rightful) emphasis on the influence of the context on membership trends. But many trends, particularly external ones that shape the church's self-understanding, are very theological and must be examined as such.

For example, the structural revolution in the churches at the beginning of the century is important because it is part of a much longer development that has shaped the American church's notion of itself and has structured its life. The pervasiveness of this shaping is underscored by the approach used in the study of Finke and Stark to which Nemeth and Luidens refer. The study assumes an economic understanding of religious life and practice that has been characteristic of the American setting. Finke and Stark defend the persistent use of "market" terminology by making the case "that where religious affiliation is a matter of choice, religious organizations must compete for members and that the 'invisible hand' of the marketplace is as unforgiving of ineffective religious firms as it is of their commercial counterparts." They use "economic concepts such as markets, firms, market penetration, and segmented markets to analyze the success and failure of religious bodies" and in the process evaluate clergy as sales representatives, religious doctrines as product, and evangelization techniques as marketing techniques.[11]

Finke and Stark do not defend this approach as a good theology of the church but regard it as the necessary historical and sociological tool for assessing its disestablishment, a situation that resulted in churches operating like business firms in a religious economy. They note that "religious economies are like commercial economies in that they consist of a market made up of a set of current and potential customers and a set of firms seeking to serve that market."[12] This form of analysis, they believe, best corresponds to the experience of the churches. But by making their case, they show how much the churches of North America have come to live out of a long-standing notion that a church is a vendor of religious services and goods.

11. Roger Finke and Rodney Stark, *The Churching of America, 1776–1990: Winners and Losers in Our Religious Economy* (New Brunswick, NJ: Rutgers University Press, 1992), 17.

12. Ibid.

A Body of People Sent on a Mission

It is frankly hard to conceive of the reaction Christians of the New Testament era would have had to the notion of the church as a religious vendor. It is thoroughly foreign to the New Testament portrayals of the nature and style of the church's presence in the communities of that time. The New Testament never envisioned a church that was defined in so economic a way. Churches were not business firms. They were living, pulsing communities grasped by the news that the light and salvation of the world had come in Jesus Christ. As a consequence, their relations to the world were changed. They represented to the world the news that had seized them. They did not look for religious customers; they gave the gospel away to the spiritually hungry and thirsty.[13]

The prevalence of the vendor notion in our understandings today, and the disjuncture between that notion and anything the New Testament suggests, indicates that we are face to face here with the most basic of theological questions. The question is crucial, especially in a day when we struggle so hard as denominations and congregations to ascertain our identity. Our identity crisis must achieve this level of theological engagement if we are to find our way again.

How, then, do we shift from the structure of church life that revolves around the vendor notion to one that forms itself around the notion that we are "a body of people sent on a mission"? If we do not recognize such a shift to be a tall order, we have not grasped the seriousness of the difference. And if we think that we can easily extricate ourselves from one operating assumption and implement another, we do not comprehend how

13. It may be worth noting that much church growth literature appears to contradict this understanding of the New Testament. In this literature, the concern for size and growth so characteristic of churches living out of a "religious economy" model is defended as theologically appropriate because the Great Commission leads us to expect growth as a dynamic of the church. But even when that growth criterion is redeemed, as it is in the hand of Charles Van Engen (who makes "yearning for growth," and not growth itself, the mark of the true church), what remains unexamined is the operative notion of "church" with which we are dealing and the way that has been so reshaped in our modern American experience that the biblical growth motifs become irrelevant to it. The biblical motifs are speaking in reference to a form of church other than a "vendor of religious services." See Charles E. Van Engen, *The Growth of the True Church* (Amsterdam: Rodopi, 1981).

historically rooted the church always is and must be. But our historical rooting can never be an excuse for avoiding change. We are always subject to the gospel's call to make fundamental departures from assumptions about ourselves that the surrounding society holds. It is that call which we need to allow.

Nothing close to a full answer to our question can be given here. But several aspects of the necessary re-forming of the church may begin to indicate something of the path we must take.

The Church Localized

First, we need to localize our sense of the church. This is the burden of the recent organizational ferment in the Presbyterian Church (U.S.A.). The study edited by Coalter, Mulder, and Weeks traced the rise of the "corporate denomination" beginning at the end of the nineteenth century. "The denomination as a corporation is a bureaucratic, hierarchical organization dependent on managers and capable of delivering goods and services to congregations as well as mobilizing and coordinating support of national and international mission causes." Some have suggested that this trend led ultimately to a two-church model: the national, corporate church and the local church of the congregations. The widening gap between the two brought about the unraveling of the corporate denomination, and the outcome is not entirely evident. What is evident, however, is that "the congregation is now the locus of power and mission in American Presbyterianism."[14] Recent restructuring in the PC(USA) intends to embed that understanding in the denominational structures.

This shift in the locus of mission makes denominational systems nervous. Frequently in Reformed and Presbyterian circles it leads to a knee-jerk charge of "creeping congregationalism." In reality the shift is a reversal of the "creeping denominationalism" of the last centuries and a reemergence of what I would prefer to call *congregationism.* "Congregationalism" refers to the system of church government that maintains the autonomy of the local congregation. In contrast, "congregationism" retains a sense of the mutuality and accountability of congregations with each

14. Coalter, Mulder, and Weeks, *The Re-Forming Tradition,* 101.

other but stresses that the mission and identity of the church takes form most essentially in the local congregation.[15]

This shift of locus provides a critique of the vendor model of the church, which became especially prominent in the corporate denomination. Another line of critique shows how the corporate denomination was designed around a "modern" style of business organization that is itself experiencing change in a postmodern situation. Nancy Ammerman has provided an analysis of the current struggles within the Southern Baptist Convention that suggests that we are seeing the emergence of new forms of denominational style. The contrast is between modern organizations (of which the corporate denomination is an example) and postmodern ones. What made sense as an economy of scale in the modern organization has now become subject to a pluralized and fragmented marketplace (religious or otherwise) in which one size does not fit all. Ammerman illustrates the forces at work in this transition by giving a series of comparisons. In regard to the activities of the organization, it means a shift from mass production to finding niches. In regard to technology, it is based on the shift from technological determinism to a range of technological choices. As regards organization, it entails a shift from highly specialized to highly generalized styles. Regarding relationships, it means a move from a large and centralized organization to a decentralized and flexible one.[16]

Two movements are going on here. On the one hand, the locus of the church's vitality and mission is being reassigned to the local congregation. On the other hand, there are revised patterns emerging in denominational structures. What must be observed is that these shifts, important as they are, do not get at the root of the problem. They do not question deeply enough the vendor notion of the church. The shift to a postmodern style may relieve the pressures building in the modern form of organization, but denominations may continue to function in a vendor manner. If the shift from a denominational locus of identity and mission to a congregational one in any way opens up a critique of the vendor model, then it simply begs the question at the congregational level. As Coalter, Mulder, and Weeks

15. Discussions on the theme of the unity and catholicity of the church at the New Delhi (1961) and Uppsala (1968) assemblies of the World Council of Churches give shape to such an understanding.

16. Nancy T. Ammerman, "SBC Moderates and the Making of a Postmodern Denomination," *Christian Century,* September 22–29, 1993, pp. 896–99.

observe, "The impulse toward incorporation permeated congregations, as well as national structures."[17] So a shift from modern to postmodern organization would be as important for the congregation as it is for the denomination. But even more fundamental is the question whether a vendor model is theologically faithful or adequate. In addition to localizing the church, therefore, we must test the way local congregations structure their life and must look for the revolutions that are needed there.

Practical Shifts

A number of practical shifts will be necessary if we are to move from treating the church as a vendor of religious services to being a body of people sent on a mission.

A shift from program to embodiment. It makes a difference whether a church is oriented toward producing programs and services for potential consumers, or whether it is committed to cultivating habits of life that help us be faithful to the gospel together. The latter focuses attention on how we embody the gospel and how we make it light, salt, seed, and aroma for the world around us. Our identity as a community of disciples must again be the center of our life together. Programs must be clearly subservient to that purpose. Programs are not for consumption but for growth.

A shift from committee to team. We are being committee-ed and council-ed to death in our churches. In many of them, the primary way that a member actively participates in the church beyond attending worship is serving on a committee. Most of our volunteer time is then spent in planning and policy-making functions that remain one step removed from actual involvement in ministry. In reflections entitled "The Changing Shape of the Church," Ed White of the Alban Institute notes the trend "from an emphasis on *program* to an emphasis on *ministry:* Instead of preplanned programs that get organized and carried out according to a set pattern, there will be more willingness to approach the world with open hands and to respond to what one finds."[18] As groups come together and discover

17. Milton J Coalter, John M. Mulder, and Louis B. Weeks, "Revolution and Survival," *Presbyterian Survey,* January/February 1992, p. 14.

18. Edward A. White, "The Changing Shape of the Church," *Presbyterian Outlook,* March 23, 1992, p. 6.

their context, calling, and gifts, a ministry team forms with an energy never achieved by a committee.

A shift from being clergy dominated to being laity oriented. Ed White adds this shift to his list of trends: "From an emphasis on *professional Christians* (clergy), who are center stage in the gathered church, to *Christian professionals* who are ministering in the world and in the workplace: It is the laity who will be the 'leaven in the lump' as agents of renewal in our failing institutions."[19] When the primary involvement of members is sitting on planning and policy committees, is it any wonder that they look to staff to implement programs and that staff have difficulty "giving ministry away," as Bruce Larsen is fond of putting it?

A shift from recruitment to mission. The two words move in opposite directions. Recruitment is the orientation inherent in the vendor church, which tries to attract people to be regular and committed consumers of its programs and services — that is, to be satisfied customers. Mission moves in an opposite direction. It moves outward. It is concerned about giving the gospel away, not getting people in.

A shift from entrepreneur to missionary. In recent years it has become fashionable to advocate a shift in pastoral style "from maintenance to mission." Among other things, leaders are challenged to move from being passive and responsive to being active and proactive. Based on a vendor model, this new "mission leader" becomes an entrepreneur instead of a mere manager. Yet if we are to move beyond the vendor model, we need to be clearer about what a missionary leader is. A true missionary leader is one who forms the kind of community that embodies and represents in its life, deeds, and words the reign of God that Jesus announced is here.

A New Sense of Viability

Finally, we will need to revise our notions of viability, especially as we apply them to the small church and to new church development. What do we think makes a church viable? By what standard do we determine what a *real* church is? Does viability assume certain levels of financial resources? Does it assume a certain set of programs? Does it assume paid, professional leadership? According to the vendor model of the church, the answer to

19. Ibid.

each question is yes, and this is where the greatest stress is felt in our churches. It is felt especially in our smaller churches, where a sense of inferiority sets in when they cannot support a full-time pastor or sustain a full array of services and programs. It is felt in new church developments where there is pressure to become a "*real* church" in terms of facilities, programs, staffing, and budget.

Consider the way we approach new church development in many of our mainline denominations. Operating with a vendor notion of the church, we ask the marketing question: Where will a church of our type (brand?) have a good chance of succeeding? What would happen if we asked instead the mission question: Where is there a need for the healing presence of a Christian community? The marketing question is asked in order to determine cost-effectiveness. The mission question invariably leads to something that is more costly than effective. But is this not the nature of our calling? Pondering the difference between these two questions, we may find new ways to think about small and new churches. Pondering the difference, we may even find innovations in small and new churches that will help us re-form all of our churches as missionary communities.

A Particular People: Toward a Faithful and Effective Ecclesiology

INAGRACE T. DIETTERICH

In considering how to relate theology and church management in an appropriate and productive fashion, I will let Robert Jenson's observations on the results of the separation of theology and polity within the Lutheran tradition set the context of my discussion.

> [It was assumed] that questions of polity are neutral with respect to the gospel, and may safely be left to those who enjoy organizing things. . . . We have generally supposed that questions of polity were not to be argued by theological considerations, but by considerations of "efficiency." The result has regularly been that Lutheran polity has merely imitated — usually about fifteen years behind — the sort of organization currently dominant in society. . . . We have thereby merely accepted that bondage to the world's example from which the gospel is supposed to free us.[1]

The challenge that theology faces in doing ecclesiology that embraces church management in a critical and constructive manner is not simply to engage in an interdisciplinary endeavor — to link theology with one more secular discipline (the social, and in particular the management, sciences) — but to develop a systemic and holistic ecclesial approach. If the day-to-

1. Eric W. Gritsch and Robert W. Jenson, *Lutheranism: The Theological Movement and Its Confessional Writings* (Philadelphia: Fortress Press, 1976), 204–5.

day life of the church is not grounded in and does not embody its theological commitments, and if the theological expressions do not arise from and relate to the church's concrete life and work, then both are inappropriate and deficient. As Jenson declares: "The people of God organize for one purpose only: to serve the gospel-mission."[2] In the actualization of that mission, church organizations are called to be *faithful:* to discern, interpret, and proclaim the gospel of Jesus Christ as the liberation and transformation of the world. And they are also called to be *effective:* to structure and manage themselves in such a way that they practice efficient stewardship of all available resources (i.e., human, financial, program, and facilities).

Faithfulness and effectiveness, however, do not have equal status. The way in which the church manages itself — makes and implements decisions regarding planning, organizing, staffing, coordinating, and evaluating — is to be determined by faith commitments concerning the nature and vocation of the church. Theological understandings of the church and its calling must serve as the criteria by which the discoveries of the human or social sciences are critically analyzed and utilized. Thus effectiveness must be in service to faithfulness and indeed, when considered in isolation, may lead to unfaithfulness. The interrelationship of faithfulness and effectiveness can be adequately confronted only within a comprehensive ecclesiology that includes both theological foundations and practical manifestations in a mutually critical and constructive relationship.

Unfortunately, the contemporary separation — and often mutual suspicion and hostility — of the theological academic establishment and the institutional church does not encourage the needed creative and collaborative discussion that appreciates and utilizes their diverse interests and expertise. Within the academy the practical issues of the church are considered too "soft" to be intellectually stimulating and worthy of disciplined attention. And not surprisingly, those concerned with the life and work of the church often consider the academic disciplines to be too "abstract" and theoretical and thus irrelevant for their concrete concerns. Associations and journals have emerged that cater to the various special-interest groups within both the academy and the church, but seldom is there any cross-fertilization. These groups read different books, listen to different experts, identify different problems, consider different issues, contribute to different journals, and congregate in different groupings as they pursue diverse and sometimes competing agendas.

2. Ibid., 204.

A major challenge for the development of an ecclesiology that is both faithful and effective is the conceptual framework that is uncritically assumed by the majority of those who are giving attention to the practical interests and issues of church life. This framework is grounded in and constituted by the mind-set or worldview of modernity: the hidden rules, the anonymous principles, and the unquestioned presuppositions that provide the perspective, categories, and images through which experience is interpreted and meaning discovered and expressed. "Secular reason" is alive and well in most of the resources and processes seeking to utilize the social sciences to understand and strengthen the practical life and work of the church.[3]

In this chapter, I will illustrate four aspects of secular reason that block a dynamic and rich ecclesiology as they are expressed in current approaches to the concrete experienced reality of congregational life: anti-institutionalism, individualization and privatization, the romanticization of the congregation, and the distinction between the social and the religious. These four "blocks" are not separate and distinct but are interrelated and mutually support and reinforce one another. Finally, I will briefly consider an ecclesial paradigm that attempts to confront and move beyond the blocks in the effort to express a constructive and creative framework within which to relate theology and polity.

Blocks to a Faithful and Effective Ecclesiology

Religious Anti-Institutionalism

Within Western culture formal and structured organizations — human institutions — are overwhelmingly viewed as impersonal, irrelevant, and often even oppressive bureaucracies. This perspective is grounded in modern secular social theory with its distinction between sacred and secular, between the private realm of religious experience and the public realm of social reality, between church and world. While there has always been a rather marked difference between the spiritual and the secular spheres of

3. Most of the current approaches to the relationship between theology and the social sciences reflect the situation brilliantly critiqued by John Milbank in *Theology and Social Theory: Beyond Secular Reason* (Oxford: Basil Blackwell, 1990).

life, this difference reflected "the eschatological awareness of the transitoriness of the order of the world," rather than the secular culture of modernity, which has "completely privatized, spiritualized and transcendentalized the sacred, and concurrently reimagined nature, human action and society as a sphere of autonomous, sheerly formal power."[4]

This approach leads to a religious anti-institutionalism that contrasts "personal religious charisma and substantive value on the one hand, and the various public processes of routinization and instrumental reason on the other."[5] Institutions are assumed to be human creations that function technically and instrumentally within the secular public sphere of human power, needs, desires, and achievement. The church — in its true form — is believed to be not a public institution but a voluntary collection of like-minded individuals who come together to support and encourage one another in the development of their private faith. It is the religious individual who provides the link between the private and public spheres — between church and world. Thus the church as institution has no validity except as it stimulates and supports the religious life of the individual out in the "real" world.

For example, although appropriately recognizing the need for a dynamic revisioning of the missional "outreach" of the church, some commentators lament the institutionalization of the church and create a false choice between church and world. Kennon L. Callahan, whose books advocating the development of "effective" churches and "effective" church leadership are very popular and widely used within local churches of diverse denominations, illustrates this tendency by contrasting a "theology of institutionalism" with a "theology of mission." He claims that while institutionalism may have been appropriate in the "churched culture" of the 1950s, in the "unchurched culture" of today, what is needed are "mission outposts."

> With the best of intentions, good people in the church — pastors and leaders — have worked from the assumption that they must first tend to the needs of the church before they can tend to the needs of the world. They must first tidy up their room before they can go outside. The problem comes when they seldom or never get outside.

4. Wolfhart Pannenberg, *Christianity in a Secularized World* (New York: Crossroad, 1989), 23; Milbank, *Theology and Social Theory,* 9.

5. Milbank, *Theology and Social Theory,* 76.

> The hook is this: God is in the world. Whenever the church is in the world, God is in the church. Whenever the church is not in the world, God is in the world. God sent his only Son to save the world, not the church. In John 3:16, the text clearly states, "For God so loved the *world*" — not "the church."[6]

Callahan assumes an artificial and almost spatial distinction between church and world. The church has been depoliticized and privatized. Social interactions and practices, and the norms and values that guide and critique them, are not the concern of the church. Thus he gives little attention to the internal management system of the church: the communal practices that inform, shape, motivate, and manifest the life and witness of the church. The import of the organized community of faith — the corporate realm of common understanding and action grounded in shared experience — is totally disregarded. A "new" direction and structure is proposed: mission outposts that serve "human hurts and hopes,"[7] without substantive ecclesiological grounding or theological reflection. Faithfulness has been defined in terms of effectiveness. The role of the church is to meet the needs of persons within modern society — those "outside" the church — as those needs are defined by society. Christianity is to be "applied" to the current "hurts and hopes" of the world.

Within this perspective, the church is not to engage in a theological critique of society — transforming society's self-understanding — but to be "pragmatic" by providing the services that secular society expects of, and allows to, the church. In this endeavor the insights of the marketing sciences are viewed as extremely helpful. The mission of the church is defined in terms of the demands of the "market," and to this end the church is to utilize market research (statistics, surveys, trend analyses) to determine the needs and desires of its desired "targets," that is, the currently much sought after "baby boomers" in the United States. And the effectiveness of the church's mission depends upon how well the church fulfills the unique and particular needs of various selected market populations. The church is not vision-led by God's eschatological reign but is market-driven by the needs

6. Kennon L. Callahan, *Effective Church Leadership: Building on the Twelve Keys* (San Francisco: Harper & Row, 1990), 30–31.

7. Kennon L. Callahan, *Twelve Keys to an Effective Church: The Leader's Guide* (San Francisco: Harper & Row, 1987), 123.

of the world. "To be market driven is to structure the church on the basis of 'supply-side' ecclesiology, which begins by asking what needs exist in the wider culture and how we can meet those needs."[8]

Callahan illustrates an unreflective anti-institutional ecclesiology that can lead to a functional consumer orientation — a "supply-side" ecclesiology. This perspective assumes that those who pay attention to the internal dynamics, practices, programs, and structures of the Christian community are neglecting the real work of the church: mission in the world. A congregational identity is opposed to a missional identity. Thus concern for the management of the life of the community is viewed at best as secondary and instrumental, and at worst as elitism and narcissism. The complex and important issues of the relationship between the gospel and human needs — the importance of continual critical and constructive communal analysis and study that engages but reframes human desires — is ignored in the rush to be relevant and thus effective and successful in "sharing help with the tough hurts and hopes present among our people."[9]

The Individualization and Privatization of Religion

Anti-institutionalism is intimately linked with the individualization and privatization of religion, the view that faith is an individual and purely private matter. The bureaucratization of church structures and the individualization of faith are two sides of the same coin that support and enable one another. This perspective is grounded within secular cultural presuppositions about the nature of public human institutions and the nature of private personal experience. "Americans often think of individuals pitted against institutions. It is hard for us to think of institutions as affording the necessary context within which we become individuals; of institutions as not just restraining but enabling us; of institutions not as an arena of hostility within which our character is tested but an indispensable source from which character is formed."[10]

8. D. Stephen Long, *Living the Discipline: United Methodist Theological Reflection on War, Civilization, and Holiness* (Grand Rapids: Eerdmans, 1992), 11.

9. Kennon L. Callahan, *Twelve Keys to an Effective Church* (San Francisco: Harper & Row, 1983), xxii.

10. Robert Bellah et al., *The Good Society* (New York: Alfred A. Knopf, 1991), 6.

Even though, with the publication of *Habits of the Heart,* there has been a widespread explicit rejection of "utilitarian" and "expressive" individualism,[11] the fundamental problem of the divorce between the interior and personal life of religion and the external and public world of social reality has not been adequately confronted. The predominant interpretation of religious experience — that which is assumed to provide the content for theological reflection and critique — is still not thought to be found in the communal dynamics and interactions of the community of believers, but in the solitary and interior life of the individual.

> The religious community is seen as a by-product — an external social objectification of the private needs or ideas of discrete individuals, set up and maintained by such persons to serve their ends. An organization or institution of this sort, however, can scarcely be regarded as a proper subject for *theological* discourse. It does not, after all, fall within that interior and personal realm that is the only sphere where talk about God makes sense. On the contrary, it belongs to the exterior object-world of secular reality. In this way, the Church becomes the name of something external to the life of faith.[12]

An example of this divorce of religious experience and social life that is firmly rooted in the modern perspective is C. Ellis Nelson's recent book *How Faith Matures.* The paradox is that Nelson intends to confront the secularization and individualism of Christianity in America and to stimulate thinking about practical theology and Christian education. Yet his basic presuppositions reflect an uncritical assumption of the very phenomena he is attempting to challenge. While he does place personal religious experience in the context of the community of faith, Nelson has not moved beyond the dualism of "spiritual" individuals and "secular" institutions. By assuming the sociological analysis of Max Weber, Nelson accepts the contrast between inward, private, irrational religious experience and outward, public, rational institutional religion. On the basis of this distinction he concludes that Christian communities, as they become

11. Robert Bellah et al., *Habits of the Heart: Individualism and Commitment in American Life* (Berkeley: University of California Press, 1985). See in particular the strong critique of individualism in chap. 6.

12. Richard A. Norris, "The People of Grace," in *Theology in Anglicanism,* ed. Arthur Vogel (Wilton, CT: Morehouse-Barlow, 1984), 90–91.

institutionalized, will inevitably "compromise, weaken, or modify the teaching or vision of the original religious leaders." According to Nelson, redirection of the life of the community occurs as "God's will is communicated to believers through individuals," modeled on the biblical experience of theophanies. As the instrument of the revelation of God's will, an individual within the congregation has an experience that is "so personal and so inward" that it can only be labeled as "nonrational or transrational." Yet through the use of critical reflection (theology), the "personal experience with God can be translated into directives for the community."[13]

If the dualism of internal/external, nonrational/rational, private/public, personal/institutional is uncritically presupposed, the biblical images of the corporate nature of the Christian faith — as the people of God, the body of Christ, or the koinonia of the Holy Spirit — and of its mission to proclaim and embody the new "society" of the kingdom of God will be profoundly undermined, distorted, and misrepresented. If attention is given to the organized expression of Christianity at all, it will be to critique the way in which the church has had to compromise its "original" vision and teaching, and thus to lament the "death-dealing rigidity of institutional order."[14] Within this dualistic context, the church as institution is not simply instrumental and functional, an "aid" to the religious experience of the individual, but actually distorts and threatens the purity of personal religion. This perspective is classically expressed by William James:

> A survey of history shows us that, as a rule, religious geniuses attract disciples, and produce groups of sympathizers. When these groups get strong enough to "organize" themselves, they become ecclesiastical institutions with corporate ambitions of their own. The spirit of politics and the lust of dogmatic rule are then apt to enter and to contaminate the originally innocent thing.[15]

13. C. Ellis Nelson, *How Faith Matures* (Louisville: Westminster/John Knox Press, 1989), 66, 63, 77.

14. Nicholas Lash, *Easter in Ordinary: Reflections on Human Experience and the Knowledge of God* (Notre Dame, IN: University of Notre Dame Press, 1988), 88. Lash here offers a good critique of this dualistic position.

15. William James, *The Varieties of Religious Experience* (New York: Mentor Books, 1958; orig. pub., 1902), 261–62.

The point is that when the public, institutional, organized character of religious experience is underestimated, because it is assumed that the core of religion is "the sublime of ineffable private experience, situated before and outside linguistic expression,"[16] then the corporate and public expression of the Christian faith — the church — has no intrinsic validity, no religious relevance, no theological content, no inherent purpose. The institutional church is not thought to be constitutive for Christian life; rather, it functions as a "place" to express, develop, and share one's individual Christian growth and development. Thus attention and intention are given only to developing the beliefs, morality, and piety of the individual believer. The organized expression and management of the institutional church — structure, policies, and procedures — are viewed as morally and religiously neutral, as being beyond the realm of theological input or critique. But this means that the institutional church then functions in an uncritical manner, reflecting particular cultural and political systems that are not expected to have any relationship to the Christian faith (except as they may be artificially clothed in religious language or symbols).

Unfortunately, there is sufficient evidence to support conclusions regarding the abuses and distortions arising from the organizational life of the church. Throughout history ecclesiastical institutions have exerted oppressive and negative influence as they have resisted creative and necessary innovation and change. And as indicated earlier by Robert Jenson, the polities (and the politics) of mainline Christianity tend to be determined more by the historical and cultural context of the particular tradition than by their theological convictions. An American bishop of the Episcopal Church, commenting on the recent national convention of his church, affirms this diagnosis: "I observed in Phoenix a political system of confrontation attempting to be a means of discernment and teaching. Both sides have put the Gospel in the service of a particular political agenda. The Gospel begins to sound like the Democratic or Republican platform. It no longer stands in judgment on all ideologies. It serves them."[17]

American denominations have tended to assume that the democratic process is identical with the Christian faith, as illustrated in the 1939 assertion of the Methodist Church: "Political liberty is indeed nothing less than

16. Milbank, *Theology and Social Theory,* 109.

17. Bishop Edward Salmon, in *Jubilate Deo: The Episcopal Diocese of South Carolina,* September 1991.

a necessary fruition of the gospel of Jesus Christ."[18] Thus using *Robert's Rules of Order,* determining church policy and doctrine by majority vote, accepting the power politics of special-interest groups, and making decisions at the highest level of the organization are assumed to be the normal way to carry out the "business" of the church. The institutional church is not expected to practice what it preaches, to challenge society's expectations of and norms for human institutions, nor is it held accountable by how well its organizational structures and management practices reflect or manifest its theological commitments. But this is to be expected if it is assumed that only the individual Christian can believe, only the individual Christian can have religious experiences, and only the individual Christian can authentically practice the Christian faith.

The Romanticization of the Congregation

The currently popular area of congregational studies is firmly entrenched within the perspective of modernity, yet it is oriented not to the "hurts and hopes" of the world or to the religious experience of the individual believer but to a recognition of and appreciation for the social reality of the congregation. Within American theological seminaries, many professors and students in the "practical" fields (education, ethics, administration, music, worship, field education) are exploring and engaging in studies of congregations.

The late James Hopewell, whose book *Congregations* was published posthumously, made a major contribution to the development of the field of congregational studies. Trained in comparative religion with a specialty in Islamics, Hopewell expressed a novel and creative approach to congregations through ethnographic description. The study of a congregation is to be carried out as the researcher assumes the role of a participant-observer who watches, participates, listens, interviews, and reads all that occurs in the life of the congregation. The participant-observer uses a symbolic approach that seeks to discover the expressive nature or unique identity of a congregation in the narrative, the story, or "web of significance" by which it gives order and meaning to its life.

18. *Book of Discipline of the Methodist Church* (Methodist Publishing House, 1939), quoted in Long, *Living the Discipline,* 55.

Hopewell views the congregation as "a microcosm of human culture" that "reflects the imaginative struggle of societies everywhere to congregate." Thus he emphasizes not the uniqueness of Christian community but the solidarity of Christian congregations with all other human groupings: "The congregation is a specific and available instance of human society expressed in symbolic activities that grasp society's plight and hope." Declaring that his goal is neither prescriptive nor simply descriptive, Hopewell asserts that while other approaches to the congregation may seek to explain, judge, or change a certain pattern of behavior, he wants to explore and bring to expression the symbolic or narrative pattern that shapes the culture of a particular congregation. In this endeavor only the symbolic approach is "sufficiently sensitive to amplify the unique accents of a congregation's idiom, sufficiently intricate to explain the congregation's constitutive power, and sufficiently comprehensive to link congregational events and meanings."[19]

The congregation's patterns of meaning — its ethos — are believed to participate in universal patterns that transcend time and place. In the formation of its identity, "a household of God draws its idiom from its complex heritage of Christian and non-Christian sources." Claiming that "in none of my studies has a biblical story seemed to me adequately to identify the ethos of a particular congregation," Hopewell turns to the great myths of the Western cultural tradition. "Myths are the fascinating, evocative, succinct metaphors by which societies throughout all time, including our own, catch sight of themselves." Since, by congregating, "the congregation participates in the narrative structures of the world's societies," within every congregation there is a latent mythic narrative that will correspond to one of those myths. Here, in these archetypal patterns of mythology, the congregation will discover its true "identity."[20]

Hopewell's approach is innovative and imaginative. His work has stimulated an appreciation for the complexity and significance of the local congregation. The emphasis upon narrative and the symbolic nature of the congregation open up possibilities for congregational analysis that go far beyond creedal checklists and numerical accounts. A major contribution of this approach is the recognition of the power and importance of the

19. James F. Hopewell, *Congregation: Stories and Structure,* ed. Barbara G. Wheeler (Philadelphia: Fortress Press, 1987), 10, 49, 12, 50.

20. Ibid., 8, 114, 106, 46.

corporate identity of the congregation, of "the narrative that the congregation historically enacts through its day-to-day behavior and by its particular views and values."[21] Thus Hopewell's "natural" ecclesiology, which sees the Christian congregation as an immediate microcosm of all society's attempts to associate, can make a creative contribution to the larger discussion of ecclesiology. Too many approaches to ecclesiology are not even interested in the lived experience of the congregation. Yet in the effort to offer a corrective, Hopewell approaches the identity or ethos of the congregation in an ahistorical and atemporal manner and thus relies too much on ethnographic methodology, uncritically adopts the presuppositions of a literary and symbolic approach, and overestimates the value of archetypal myths as an expression of the corporate experience and identity of Christian congregations.

The field of congregational studies reflects the strengths but also the limitations found in Hopewell's work. While appropriately recognizing that theology does not make much sense without a relation to the thought and experience of contemporary faith communities, there is a "subtle romanticization of the congregation" that naively assumes that questions, issues, and perspectives will be magically transformed by attention to the narrative or ethos of the congregation.[22] Congregational studies presupposes the primacy of the "lived experience" and the distinctive identity of the particular local congregation. Thus the purpose of the field, as developed by those working with and following Hopewell, is to enable the transformation of individuals and congregations by taking "seriously and appreciatively, through disciplined understanding, the present *being* of congregations — the good and precious qualities that are within them — as means of grace themselves that enable the transformation of congregations into what it is possible for them to *become*."[23]

Congregational studies arose, in part, in response to a narrow and negative view of the congregation. In the 1960s several very popular books put forth a strong critique of the local church: *The Noise of Solemn Assemblies, The Suburban Captivity of the Churches,* and *The Comfortable*

21. Ibid., 171.

22. Rebecca S. Chopp, "Practical Theology and Liberation," in *Formation and Reflection: The Promise of Practical Theology,* ed. Lewis S. Mudge and James N. Poling (Philadelphia: Fortress Press, 1987), 124.

23. Jackson W. Carroll, Carl S. Dudley, and William McKinney, eds., *Handbook for Congregational Studies* (Nashville: Abingdon Press, 1986), 7.

Pew.[24] These books contributed to the perspective that local churches were captive to the privatistic interests of middle-class families. While they may be necessary, congregations are self-centered and self-serving. Since at that time the mission of the church was predominantly defined by mainline denominational leaders in terms of social service and justice-oriented ministries, the congregation was not viewed as a worthy object of attention or investment.

In the endeavor to move beyond the negative perspective to an appreciation of the congregation, the development of the social sciences is viewed as critical.

> It simply never occurred to anyone to rigorously examine the local congregation in its concrete particularity until social scientific methods were applied to analyzing human and organizational behavior.[25]

> Congregations and other local organizations for ministry are social configurations, and thus one should use sociology to understand their relationships to their environments, organization theory to elucidate how they function as complex systems, psychology to grasp their dynamics, and anthropology and ethnographic research to display them as structures laden with value, symbol, and story.[26]

Congregational studies, using a multidisciplinary approach, seeks to describe the "richness of congregations in all their empirical facticity." The local congregation — its life and practice as a whole — has become an object of study. While providing interesting and illuminating data, this approach presents problems. In studying congregations, seminary professors and students frequently assume an "objectifying stance." Rather than engaging the congregation in a self-study and thus giving them the opportunity to interact with, contribute to, and learn from the study, the partic-

24. Peter L. Berger, *The Noise of Solemn Assemblies* (New York: Doubleday, 1961); Gibson Winter, *The Suburban Captivity of the Churches* (New York: Macmillan, 1961); Pierre Berton, *The Comfortable Pew* (Philadelphia: Lippincott, 1965).

25. Carl S. Dudley, Jackson W. Carroll, and James P. Wind, eds., *Carriers of Faith: Lessons from Congregational Studies* (Louisville: Westminster/John Knox Press, 1991), 187.

26. Joseph C. Hough, Jr., and Barbara B. Wheeler, eds., *Beyond Clericalism: The Congregation as a Focus for Theological Education* (Decatur, GA: Scholars Press, 1988), xvi.

ipant-observers too often function like Olympian, objective, and basically detached scholars who give the congregation little opportunity to confront and challenge the observers' preunderstandings, observations, or conclusions. Thus the congregation becomes an object to be observed, dissected, analyzed, critiqued, and used to further academic goals. This orientation fits well within the subject/object split of modernity, where "the penetrating and objectifying gaze of the human scientist occupies that centralized space from which one can look without being seen."[27]

The Distinction between the Social and the Religious

An award-winning book by Carl S. Dudley and Earle Hilgert, which seeks to utilize "the best modern reflections and research on parish dynamics as a key to understanding the New Testament," illustrates the dangers of the multidisciplinary approach of congregational studies. Concerned with tensions that threaten the contemporary church's "effectiveness," the authors want to interpret as well as challenge the modern church by looking at "the biblical and other ancient material through the lenses of the social sciences to catch glimpses of the organizing decisions and social behavior of Christian gatherings in the first and early second centuries after Christ."[28]

While the book is intriguing in approaching Scripture from the perspective of congregational studies, the authors speak from within the realm of secular reason, uncritically assuming the distinction between the "religious" and the "social," and subsequently between the role of theology and the role of the social sciences. While acknowledging "the pitfall of reductionism," Dudley and Hilgert's solution is to avoid it by distinguishing between the empirical observation of the sociologist and the theologian's concern for the nonempirical transcendent: "each discipline should observe its limits and respect those of the other." Claiming that theologians can learn much from the social sciences, they assume that "human social groups tend to follow discernible patterns of development, action, and reaction,

27. Ibid., 116; Jürgen Habermas, *The Philosophical Discourses of Modernity* (Cambridge: MIT Press, 1991), 245.

28. Carl S. Dudley and Earle Hilgert, *New Testament Tensions and the Contemporary Church* (Philadelphia: Fortress Press, 1987), back cover promotional statement (by Loren B. Mead), 1.

given analogous circumstances."[29] Thus sociological studies of contemporary social and socioreligious groups are expected to throw light upon the patterns of action and reaction among religious groups of first-century Christianity.

Dudley and Hilgert conclude that since theology deals with "questions of ultimate causation and meaning" rather than with the concrete practical dynamics of church life, in the realm of the "social" theologians must rely upon the methodology and conclusions of the social sciences.[30] Ecclesiology is reduced to functional sociology, which seeks to move behind faith commitments and historical descriptions to a more profound and useful "explanation" of the early church. Here are encountered the methodology and intent of the secular "policing of the sublime," whose

> secret purpose is to ensure that religion is kept, conceptually, at the margins — both denied influence, and yet acclaimed for its transcendent purity. . . . What is refused here is the idea that religion might enter into the most basic level of the symbolic organization of society, and the most basic level of its operations of discipline and persuasion, such that one would be unable to abstract a "society" behind and beneath "religion."[31]

The work of Dudley and Hilgert is an example of the tendency within the field of congregational studies to characterize and then to contrast the "objective and value-free descriptions" of the social sciences with the "subjective and normative prescriptions" of the theological disciplines. As the pastoral-care disciplines became "almost irretrievably captive and embarrassingly indebted to reductionistic psychological and psychotherapeutic methods," so congregational studies runs the risk of adopting the "fundamental assumptions of positivism, reductionism, relativism, and determinism" that have frequently typified the human or social sciences.[32] In the search for ways to describe and understand the concrete and practical life of the congregation, the social sciences far too often have been appropriated without a critical sense of either how scientific they actually are or of how their normative presuppositions may be neither philosophically sound nor theologically defensible.

29. Ibid., 7, 5.

30. Ibid., 7.

31. Milbank, *Theology and Social Theory,* 109.

32. Thomas Oden, "Pastoral Care and the Unity of Theological Education," *Theology Today* 42 (1985): 35; Bellah et al., *The Good Society,* 162.

Because "theologians and churches have increasingly both used and envied the human sciences," a critical and sustained discussion about the relation of theology to these disciplines is greatly needed.[33] Central to this discussion must be a conversation with the philosophies of science that have challenged the presupposition that the human sciences occupy a privileged position of pure observation by emphasizing the societal and communal nature — the inevitable "cultural captivity" — of all scientific endeavors.

> Social science is not a disembodied cognitive enterprise. It is a tradition, or set of traditions, deeply rooted in the philosophical and humanistic (and, to more than a small extent, the religious) history of the West. Social science makes assumptions about the nature of persons, the nature of society, and the relation between persons and society. It also, whether it admits it or not, makes assumptions about the good person and a good society and considers how far these conceptions are embodied in our actual society. Becoming conscious of the cultural roots of these assumptions would remind the social scientist that these assumptions are contestable and the choice of assumptions involves controversies that lie deep in the history of Western thought.[34]

Thus within congregational studies with its "appreciation" for the lived experience of the local church, the congregation is predominantly viewed not as a theological but as a sociological and historical entity. This perspective relegates religious experience and expression to the "sublime" of the private, the subjective, and the normative, where it "is to be protected and treasured, although it causes no positively definable effects within the objective factual world."[35]

A Particular People: An Ecclesial Paradigm

Modern secular reason has positioned religion either at the margins of society as the private and internal religious experience of the individual or

33. Don S. Browning, *A Fundamental Practical Theology: Descriptive and Strategic Proposals* (Minneapolis: Fortress Press, 1991), 80.

34. Bellah et al., *Habits of the Heart,* 301.

35. Milbank, *Theology and Social Theory,* 106.

as an immanent civil religion that provides a diffuse moral and public solidarity for the whole of society. To the extent that civil religion functions primarily to secure "the sanctity of private freedom and private religious experience," both perspectives affirm the privatization and individualization of religion.[36] The social experience of religion within the historical and temporal ecclesial practice of a particular community is denied reality and thus relevance or validity. To move "beyond secular reason" and offer an alternative to the destructive tendencies of modern society requires the utilization of resources within the Christian tradition in the expression of an ecclesiology that reunites what secular social theory has torn asunder: church and world, individual and group, the religious and the social.

In the remaining space, I will briefly sketch out an ecclesial paradigm that begins not sociologically, not organizationally, but theologically. The approach starts with the assumption that worship is the one activity unique to the church. Worship is the celebration — the anticipation, remembrance, and enactment — of God's creative purpose, redemptive activity, and transformative presence for and with humanity. Through worship, individuals are shaped and formed into a particular people — a people of the kingdom — who are called and equipped to manifest life within the realm of God's gracious and liberating rule. "In the worship life of a community a vision is fostered of the universal order of peace and justice in relation to which diverse peoples become a people of God."[37]

Thus a faithful and effective ecclesiology must begin with the vocation and destiny of the church that is discovered and actualized in worship. While this approach may be new in that it challenges the current paradigm of Western ecclesiology, it is very old, in that it attempts to draw upon the rich resources of the Christian heritage that provide not ready-made answers but rays of illumination for contemporary endeavors.

A People of Praise

> We who first hoped in Christ have been destined and appointed to live for the praise of his glory. (Eph. 1:12 RSV)

36. Ibid., 130.

37. Paul D. Hanson, *The People Called: The Growth of Community in the Bible* (New York: Harper & Row, 1986), 527.

Encompassing but moving beyond specific ritual activity, worship designates the style and purpose, the nature and mission of the church, as the calling and forming of a people who offer praise to the glory of God. Worship is not separate from "normal" or "secular" life but symbolizes the redemption and fulfillment of all of life, the constitution of the wholeness of life as intended by God for all humanity. The challenge is to rediscover the true meaning and potential of worship — its power of judgment and transformation in a God-centered or theological realism. Not an exercise in introspective piety, private devotion, or superficial escape, the church worships so that all of life may become worship. Thus worship is not retreat from the world but "an exercise in vision, a practice in seeing," which enables Christians to see the world as it really is — the creation of a loving and forgiving God.[38]

Worship is not a "supernatural" cultic act but the "natural" and appropriate way of participating in the fullness of created life. Affirming God as the source of all abundance, the world is not perceived as an autonomous entity but as God's sacramental creation, "the sign and means of God's presence and wisdom, love and revelation."[39] All creation is a gracious and generous gift that enables communion with God, and all humanity is called to bless God — to participate in and celebrate God's manifold blessings through praise and thanksgiving.

> We know that we were created as *celebrants* of the sacrament of life, of its transformation into life in God, communion with God. We know that real life is "Eucharist," a movement of love and adoration toward God, the movement in which alone the meaning and the value of all that exists can be revealed and fulfilled. . . . It is the movement that Adam failed to perform, and that in Christ has become the very life of man: a movement of adoration and praise in which all joy and suffering, all beauty and all frustration, all hunger and all satisfaction are referred to their ultimate End and become finally *meaningful.*[40]

In its worship — the movement of adoration and praise — the church rejoices in God's good creation, acknowledges the fallenness and

38. Robert E. Webber and Rodney Clapp, *People of the Truth: The Power of the Worshipping Community in the Modern World* (New York: Harper & Row, 1988), 94.

39. Alexander Schmemann, *For the Life of the World: Sacraments and Orthodoxy* (Crestwood, NY: St. Vladimir's Seminary Press, 1973), 14.

40. Ibid., 34–35.

alienation of the world, celebrates the world's re-creation through the event of Jesus Christ, and in the joy and peace of the Holy Spirit experiences the "firstfruits" of the fulfillment of the destiny of the world in the eschaton. Thus the distinction between world and church, secular and sacred, natural and supernatural is transcended in the affirmation that "all that exists is God's gift to man, and it all exists to make God known to man, to make man's life communion with God." Within the worship of the church the world is liberated and restored to its rightful place as creation — as God's gift and means of grace. In its adoration, praise, and thanksgiving the church announces and experiences the "supreme ecstasy of inexhaustible knowledge and love in the enjoyment of God that is the true life of creation."[41] The worship of the church truly exists for the life of the world.

A Particular People

> . . . the people whom I formed for myself, so that they might declare my praise. (Isa. 43:21 NRSV)

A people of praise is a particular people, a people with a distinctive identity and vision. Not only is the view of the world recast by reconnecting the creation with its Creator, but the understanding of the very nature of personal human life is also reconceived. The isolation of autonomous individualism is transformed by the experience of the mutuality of communal personhood in ecclesial community. While incompletely and inadequately utilized, the Christian tradition contains a rich theology of communion that was formulated within the liturgical life and communal practice of the church. Breaking the Greek ontological monism and avoiding the gnostic gulf between God and the world, the patristic theologians Ignatius, Irenaeus, and Athanasius approached God through personal relationships and personal love. They thus developed a ontology of communion: "Being means life, and life means *communion*. . . . This ontology that came out of the eucharistic experience of the Church, guided the Fathers in working out their doctrine of the being of God. . . . In this way, communion becomes an ontological concept in patristic thought. Nothing in existence is conceivable in itself, as

41. Ibid., 14; Daniel W. Hardy and David F. Ford, *Praising and Knowing God* (Philadelphia: Westminster Press, 1985), 120.

an individual . . . since even God exists thanks to an event of communion."[42] The word "God" means nothing other than the life that is actively shared by Father, Son, and Holy Spirit. God *is* communion.

Just as the modern secular perspective presupposes and reinforces an individualistic and subjectivistic understanding of God (with God as Supreme Being or Absolute Subject), so a truly trinitarian doctrine of God can provide the framework for a social theory — a theological understanding of community — that reunites the individual with the group. When God is perceived as a dynamic community of relation and freedom united in a reciprocal communion of life and work, then trinitarian theology becomes a relational theology that explores the mysteries of love, relationship, personhood, and communal life. A model of community is offered that affirms the profound uniqueness of each person as distinct yet inseparable from others; their personal existence consists in their relationship with one another.

Within this perspective, participation in the community of faith symbolizes and actualizes participation within the communion of the triune God — human persons share in the life of God. And this participation redeems and transforms human life. The "sociological illusion" that makes society and individuals spatially external to one another is overcome.[43] Through praise and worship, Christians enter into communion with the triune God. They become children of God, freed from the bondage of individualism and united with their brothers and sisters in a dynamic community of love and service. Christians are a particular people, a people called and formed by a particular God — the interdependent and interrelated communion of Father, Son, and Holy Spirit.

A Kingdom People

> Blessed is the Kingdom of the Father, the Son, and the Holy Spirit, now and ever, and unto ages of ages.

This affirmation, which begins the Orthodox Eucharistic liturgy, declares that the church is to "bless" the kingdom of the triune God. The

42. John D. Zizioulas, *Being as Communion: Studies in Personhood and the Church* (Crestwood, NY: St. Vladimir's Seminary Press, 1973), 14, 17.

43. Milbank, *Theology and Social Theory*, 226.

church is a sacrament of the kingdom that symbolizes the communion of all human beings in God's society of perfect love, justice, and peace.

> There is no reason for the existence of the church except to symbolize the future of the divine kingdom that Jesus came to proclaim. This explains in what specific sense worship is in the center of life of the church: the worship of the Christian community anticipates and symbolically celebrates the praise of God's glory that will be consummated in the eschatological renewal of all creation in the new Jerusalem.[44]

To speak of the concrete lived experience of the local church in relation to the kingdom or reign of God seems presumptuous. Yet an examination of the New Testament indicates their integral relationship: "Jesus's mission is seen as inseparable from his preaching of the kingdom, and inauguration of a new sort of community, the Church." The reign of God does not fall from the clouds; it is mediated historically by the eschatological calling forth of God's particular people. "The rule of God presupposes a people, a people of God, in whom it can become established and from whom it can shine forth." As a kingdom people, the church is entrusted with the good news of the rule of God inaugurated in Jesus Christ, which is the salvation of the world. Its mission is to invite all humanity into the new social order found in relationship with Jesus Christ: "to participate in the blessings of the kingdom, to celebrate the hopes of the kingdom, and to engage in the tasks of the kingdom."[45]

It is the active rule and the eschatological mission of God — the kingdom of God — rather than institutional survival or efficiency or even societal service that provides the criteria for church management. Management activities have no validity in and of themselves, but only as they are oriented to the accomplishment of the desired theological "results" that actualize the church as a sacrament or symbol of the reign of God inaugurated in the ministry and destiny of Jesus Christ and present in the midst of God's particular people through the power and illumination of the Holy

44. Wolfhart Pannenberg, *Christian Spirituality* (Philadelphia: Westminster Press, 1983), 36.

45. Milbank, *Theology and Social Theory*, 387; Gerhard Lohfink, *Jesus and Community: The Social Dimension of Christian Faith* (Philadelphia: Fortress Press, 1982), 27; Mortimer Arias, *Announcing the Reign of God: Evangelization and the Subversive Memory of Jesus* (Philadelphia: Fortress Press, 1984), 105.

Spirit. These results symbolize the quality and purpose of life to be found when God's will is done, "on earth as in heaven," instituting a relational and communal life of "love, joy, peace, patience, kindness, generosity, faithfulness, gentleness, and self-control" (Gal. 5:22 NRSV).

The nature and quality of the social reality of Christian community can serve as a powerful witness. Through the "creation of a distinct community with its own deviate set of values and its coherent way of incarnating them," the church can offer the world an alternative to its patterns of social order. It can model an open and loving community of creative conflict, of innovative freedom, and of authentic reconciliation. Christianity is not an individual and deeply private experience but a very concrete and practical way of life that is learned, practiced, supported, and empowered in community. While not yet fully consummated, the reign of God is not solely a future or a transcendent reality but the irruption of a new order and a new people into human history. In the event of Jesus Christ the kingdom of God — God's creative, redemptive, and transforming relationship with God's people — became a liberating, healing, and invigorating actuality. The mission of Christian community is to be a sign, foretaste, and instrument of God's reign. As a particular people of praise — God's kingdom people — who celebrate the gracious miracle of the inbreaking rule of God, the church offers to the world an alternative or "contrast" society "in which the freedom and reconciliation opened in principle by Christ must be lived in social concreteness."[46]

Conclusion

> But you are a chosen race, a royal priesthood, a holy nation, God's own people, in order that you may proclaim the mighty acts of him who called you out of darkness into his marvelous light. (1 Pet. 2:9 NRSV)

What if Peter's description of the Christian community as a people called, redeemed, and empowered for an important mission was taken seriously as the organizational blueprint for the Christian congregation? What if the life and work of the institutional church truly attempted to

46. John Howard Yoder, *The Original Revolution: Essays on Christian Pacifism* (Scottdale, PA: Herald Press, 1977), 28; Lohfink, *Jesus and Community,* 145.

incarnate the distinctive social reality of the kingdom of God? What if, rather than accepting and reinforcing the values and beliefs of modern secular culture, the church offered its people an experience of "awestruck joy at the presence of God with us and among us"?[47] As the church seeks to confront secular reason in the realization of its mission of proclaiming and embodying the loving and reconciling society of God's reign in the face of the injustice, alienation, despair, and hatred of modern society, an alternation of consciousness is required, a new way of looking at things, a new way of organizing — a new paradigm — that retrieves and reinterprets a very old but revolutionary message.

> We cannot answer the world's problems by adopting toward them an attitude either of surrender or of escape. We can answer the world's problems only by changing these problems, by understanding them in a different perspective. What is required is a return on our part to that source of energy, in the deepest sense of the word. . . . What the Church brought into the world was not certain ideas applicable simply to human needs but first of all the truth, the righteousness, the joy of the Kingdom of God.[48]

In the development of a theological paradigm — a faithful and effective ecclesiology — that incorporates and expresses a valid and appropriate approach to church management, the "false humility" of modern theology that accepts the division between the secular and the sacred, and thereby gives the social sciences the right and responsibility to lay claim to the description and understanding of empirical reality, must be confronted and overcome. Theology must challenge its confinement by secular reason and move into the messy and confusing communal reality of church life and work in the development of a "theological sociology" or "social theology" that seeks to relate all of life to the creative, redemptive, and transforming activity of the triune God.[49] Theology and polity must be reunited in an imaginative and dynamic relationship in order that God's people may become both more faithful and more effective in their ministry and mission so that God's creative intent for all reality will be fulfilled.

47. A. M. Allchin, *Participation in God: A Forgotten Strand in Anglican Tradition* (Wilton, CT: Morehouse-Barlow, 1988), 4.

48. Alexander Schmemann, "Liturgy and Eschatology," *Sobornost* 7 (1985): 13, quoted in Allchin, ibid., p. 5.

49. Milbank, *Theology and Social Theory*, 1, 225.

St. Teresa of Avila
Catholic Community
Parish Library